AN ACCOUNT OF AN EMBASSY TO THE COURT OF THE TESHOO LAMA IN TIBET

CONTAINING A NARRATIVE OF A JOURNEY THROUGH BOOTAN, AND PART OF TIBET

AN

ACCOUNT OF AN EMBASSY

TO THE

COURT OF THE TESHOO LAMA IN TIBET

CONTAINING

A NARRATIVE OF A JOURNEY

THROUGH BOOTAN, AND PART OF TIBET

SAMUEL TURNER

TO WHICH ARE ADDED, VIEWS TAKEN ON THE SPOT
BY LIEUTENANT SAMUEL DAVIS
AND
OBSERVATIONS BOTANICAL, MINERALOGICAL, AND MEDICAL

BY ROBERT SAUNDERS

GYAN

Published by

Gyan Publishing House
5, Ansari Road
Daryaganj, New Delhi-110002
Phone: 011-47034999, 9811692060
E-mail: books@gyanbooks.com

Distribution Network
gyanbooks.com
India, USA, Canada, UK, Australia, France

ISBN : 978-81-212-3009-4 (PB)
First Published, London, 1800

2nd Impression 2020

Printed at: Gyan Press, Delhi.

An
Account of an Embassy to the Court of the Teshoo Lama in Tibet
Author: Samuel Turner

TO THE

CHAIRMAN,

DEPUTY CHAIRMAN,

AND

DIRECTORS

OF THE

HONOURABLE EAST INDIA COMPANY,

THIS ACCOUNT OF AN

EMBASSY

TO THE COURT OF THE TESHOO LAMA,

IN TIBET,

IS RESPECTFULLY INSCRIBED,

BY THEIR MOST OBEDIENT, AND

MOST HUMBLE SERVANT,

St. James's Place,
May 1, 1800.

SAMUEL TURNER.

INTRODUCTION.

It is not known that any direct communication existed between Bengal and Tibet[a] before the year 1774. A physical reason might be assigned for this, in the enormous height, and vast extent, of the mountains which are interposed between the two countries, did not an almost equal degree of strangeness, prevailing between Bengal and Bootan, which lie adjacent to each other, necessarily imply a different, or at least some concurrent cause. The most probable one, which the history of little more than a century can afford us, is to be found in that spirit of conquest which forms the common character of all Mahometan states, and in that hostility which their religion enjoins against all who are not its professors. The Booteeas, who, though a strong and hardy race of people, are little versed in the arts of war, and thinly scattered over a mountainous region, derive from their local situation the only means of defence against invaders; an advantage which they would inevitably lose, if they were to allow a free passage through their territories. It is certain, however, that,

[a] This name in Bengal, as well as Tibet, is pronounced with a duplication of the letter b; but out of respect to long established orthography, I have written it according to the more usual mode of spelling it in Europe.

at this time, a strong jealousy of all intercourse with the inhabitants of Hindostan, prevails universally amongst the natives, on its northern frontier. From Bootan, indeed, a caravan now annually visits the district of Rungpore, in Bengal, bringing with it oranges, walnuts, and the coarse woollen manufactures of that country, with the horses that carry them, for sale; and it returns, after a month's stay, with the cotton cloths, salt, and other articles, of the produce of Bengal. But the same privilege has never been allowed by the government of Bootan to the inhabitants of Bengal. Perhaps a people more enterprizing than the latter, might have contrived to overcome this difficulty, since some individuals of the religious orders occasionally find their way both into Bootan and Tibet. One of these, named Poorungheer, accompanied the first deputation from Tibet to Bengal, in the year 1773, and afterwards attended the Lama on his visit to Pekin. Something, therefore, co-operating with the political cause above assigned, to produce the same effect, may have arisen from the difference of manners, and of atmosphere, of the two countries. It is not possible to conceive a greater dissimilarity between the most remote inhabitants of the globe, than that which distinguishes the feeble bodied and meek spirited natives of Bengal, and their active and Herculean neighbours, the mountaineers of Bootan. Their religion, which might be supposed to have a powerful influence on their manners, has totally failed of producing similar effects on the two nations, though it is evidently drawn from the same source. The province of Bootan is, from its elevation, so cold, that few of its southern neighbours could endure its severity; while its natives, clad in woollens, and little accustomed to the purifications which prevail so universally among the former, suffer nearly as much from the sultry and humid atmosphere of Bengal. Nor do the two countries differ less in salubrity. To the same cause, therefore, may be ascribed the difference in the bodily construction of the two people, and in their moral character, which is, in a great degree, the result of that construction.

The mountains of Bootan form a part of the great chain, which geographers call by the general appellation of Mons Imaus, and of which frequent mention is made, in the mythological histories of the Brahmens, by the term of Himâloya. At their feet, a wide and extensive plain, covered with woods, and sunk in morasses, forms a natural division between Bengal and Bootan, being nearly unfit for the support of human life, and almost entirely destitute of inhabitants. Yet in the year 1772, the Raja of Bootan, with what plea, or from what provocation, I have not been able to learn, laid claim to the district of Cooch Bahar, which adjoins to it on the side of Bengal; and, meeting with little resistance from the natives, rapidly gained possession of it. This appears to have been the first instance of hostility between the two countries; and it had proceeded to its last extremity, before the government of Bengal, which had hitherto derived no benefit from the contested territory, was well apprized of what had befallen it. The example, however, was dangerous, and a detachment of native infantry, gradually augmented from a few companies to two battalions, was sent to dispossess the invaders, and drive them back to their own frontier.

The military weapons of the Booteeas are the bow and arrow, a short strait sword, and a faulchion, reflected like a pruning knife. These, though wielded by strong hands, and directed by much individual courage, were of little avail against the discipline, artillery, and musquetry of their antagonists; who experienced a much more destructive foe, in the pestiferous region through which they continued their pursuit, after having driven the Booteeas from the scene of contention into their own confines. There the Raja, weary of the conflict, and alarmed for the safety of his own dominions, applied to Teshoo Lama, and obtained his mediation for a peace.

Teshoo Lama was at that time the Regent of Tibet, and the guardian of Dalai Lama, his superior in religious rank, who was yet in his minority. He was about forty years of age, greatly venerated on account of his sacred office, and not less beloved for the benevolence of his character, and the courtesy of his manners. All who approached him were his worshippers; so that he united, in his own person, both the political authority, and the spiritual hierarchy of the country. In his political character, indeed, he acknowledged the sovereignty of the Emperor of China, who had a delegate, with a small military force, I think about one thousand men, resident at Lassa[b], the capital of Dalai

[b] In the pronunciation of this word, both in Tibet and Bengal, a strong aspiration is placed upon the beginning, Lahàssa: but for the same reason that I have rejected a

Lama, but who had not yet much interposed in the interior government of either division of the province.

The Lama, moved by the prayers of the Raja, and interested for the safety of Bootan, which was a dependency of Tibet, sent a deputation to Calcutta, with a letter addressed to the Governor, which I am glad to insert, as an authentic and curious specimen of his good sense, humility, simplicity of heart, and, above all, of that delicacy of sentiment and expression, which could convey a threat in the terms of meekness and supplication.

Translation of a Letter from Teshoo Lama to Warren Hastings, Esq. President and Governor of Fort William in Bengal. Received the 29th of March, 1774.

" The affairs of this quarter in every respect flourish: I am night and day employed in prayers for the increase of your happiness and prosperity. Having been informed, by travellers from your country, of your exalted fame and reputation, my heart, like the blossoms of

double b in Tibet, I retain the established mode of spelling Lassa. It is rare, indeed, that our own mode of spelling the names of persons, or places, corresponds with their local pronunciation. I have endeavoured to express the sound of such names as will be found in the following pages, just as they caught my ear, in all cases where custom has not already appeared to sanction some particular mode of spelling. We need not travel beyond our own nation to discover how often, in this respect, custom and propriety are at variance.

spring, abounds with satisfaction, gladness, and joy. Praise be to God, that the star of your fortune is in its ascension! Praise be to him, that happiness and ease are the surrounding attendants of myself and family! Neither to molest, nor persecute, is my aim: it is even the characteristic of our sect, to deprive ourselves of the necessary refreshment of sleep, should an injury be done to a single individual; but, in justice and humanity, I am informed, you far surpass us. May you ever adorn the seat of justice and power, that mankind may, in the shadow of your bosom, enjoy the blessings of peace and affluence! By your favour, I am the Raja and Lama of this country, and rule over a number of subjects, a circumstance with which you have no doubt been made acquainted, by travellers from these parts. I have been repeatedly informed, that you have engaged in hostilities against the Dêh Terria, to which, it is said, the Dêh's own criminal conduct, in committing ravages and other outrages on your frontiers, gave rise. As he is of a rude and ignorant race, past times are not destitute of instances of the like faults, which his avarice has tempted him to commit. It is not unlikely that he has now renewed those instances; and the ravages and plunder which he may have committed on the skirts of the provinces of Bengal and Bahar, have given you provocation to send your avenging army against him. Nevertheless his party has been defeated, many of his people have been killed, three forts have been taken from him, and he has met with the punishment he deserved. It is as evident as the sun, that your army has been victorious; and that, if you had been desirous of it, you might, in the space of two days, have entirely extirpated him; for he had not power to resist your efforts. But I now take upon me to be his mediator; and to represent to you, that, as the said Dêh Terria is dependent upon the Dalai Lama, who rules in this country with unlimited sway, though, on account of his being yet in his minority, the charge and administration of the country, for the present, is committed to me; should you persist in offering further molestation to the Dêh Terria's country, it will irritate both the Lama and all his subjects against you. Therefore, from a regard to our religion and customs, I request you will cease from all hostilities against him; and in doing this, you will confer the greatest favour and friendship upon me. I have reprimanded the Dêh for his past conduct; and I have admonished him to desist from his evil practices in future, and to be submissive to you in all things. I am persuaded he will conform to the advice which I have given him; and it will be necessary that you treat him with compassion and clemency. As to my part, I am but a Fakeer; and it is the custom of my sect, with the rosary in our hands, to pray for the welfare of all mankind, and especially for the peace and happiness of the inhabitants of this country; and I do now, with my head uncovered, entreat that you will cease from all hostilities against the Dêh in future. It would be needless to add to the length of this letter, as the bearer of it, who is a Gosein, will represent to you all particulars; and it is hoped that you will comply therewith.

"In this country, the worship of the Almighty is the profession of all. We poor creatures are in nothing equal to you. Having, however, a few things in hand, I send them to you as tokens of remembrance, and hope for your acceptance of them."

This letter appears to have been laid before the Council on the same day that it was received: they yielded, without hesitation, to the intercession of the Lama, and consented to a peace with the Booteeas, upon the easy terms of replacing the dominion of each government, within its former boundaries. The Governor himself more readily embraced the opportunity, which he thought this occurrence afforded, of extending the British connexion to a quarter of the world, with which we had hitherto no intercourse, and of opening new sources of commerce, of which our provinces stood greatly in need, to replace the vast drains which were annually made of their wealth and manufactures, in supplying the wants of our other establishments, and the commercial investments of the Company. What specific articles of trade might be drawn from the northern countries, or what physical or political accommodations, or difficulties, might be found to promote or obstruct it, were even beyond conjecture; but under such circumstances, it seemed an object of much curiosity, well deserving the attention of government, to explore an unknown region, for the purpose of discovering, in the first instance, what was the nature of its productions; as it would afterwards be, when that knowledge was obtained, to inquire by what means it might be most effectually converted to advantage. The contiguity of Tibet to the western frontier of China (for though we knew not where they were joined, yet we knew that they did actually join), suggested, also, a possibility of establishing, by degrees, an immediate intercourse with that empire, through the intervention of a person so revered as the Lama, and by a route not obviously liable to the same suspicions, as those with which the Chinese policy had armed itself against all the consequences of a foreign access by sea.

Of the persons deputed on this occasion by the Lama, two only ventured to encounter the burning atmosphere of Bengal; one, a native of Tibet, named Paima; the other, a pilgrim from Hindostan, whose name I have already mentioned, Poorungheer Gosein. These were both men of acute understandings, and ready information; and from them much knowledge was collected both of the country from which they came, and of the way which led to it. Even the presents, which they brought from the Lama, added something of information, and even of interest, to the other means of intelligence, which the occasion furnished. Amongst these were sheets of gilt leather, stamped with the black eagle of the Russian armorial; talents of gold and silver, and bulses of gold dust; bags of genuine musk; narrow cloths of woollen, the manufacture of Tibet; and silks of China. The chests which contained these, were of no bad workmanship, and the parts, which composed them, were joined together by dovetails. All these circumstances were construed into indications of an extensive commerce, internal wealth, and an advanced knowledge of the arts of common life.

These considerations induced the Governor to lay before the Council, on the fourth of May following, a proposition, to which they cheerfully and unanimously assented, for deputing an English gentleman to Tibet, on the justifiable plea of paying a proper tribute of respect, in return for the advances which had been made by the Lama. Mr. George Bogle, a man eminently qualified for this mission, by a discerning capacity, and uncommon gentleness of manners, was nominated, on the recommendation of the Governor, to carry back an answer to the Lama, and to offer him suitable presents. He was furnished besides with a great variety of articles, consisting chiefly of British manufactures, to be produced as specimens of the trade in which the subjects of the Lama might be invited to participate. Mr. Hamilton, a Surgeon of considerable reputation in his profession, was appointed to accompany him.

Mr. Bogle received his instructions on the 6th of May, 1774. He was detained for some time at Tassisudon, the capital of Bootan, waiting for passports; nor was it, I believe, without some reluctance, on the part of the Lama himself, that he at last obtained them. On the 12th of October, he arrived at Desheripgay, then the residence of the Lama, by whom he was received with great hospitality and kindness. Here, and at Teshoo Loomboo, he remained with him until the 8th of April following, when he took his leave, to return to Bengal. During this interval, by employing his whole time and talents, in cultivating the good will of the Lama, and gratifying his insatiable thirst for foreign knowledge, Mr. Bogle so ingratiated himself into his confidence, as to be intrusted, some time after, with a considerable remittance in money, for the purpose of building a temple and a dwelling house, for the accommodation of his votaries to Bengal, on the banks of the Ganges. A piece of ground, on the opposite side of the river to Calcutta, was purchased, and granted to the Lama, on his application to the Governor for this purpose.

In the letter which the Lama wrote to the Governor upon this occasion, he stated, as a motive for making the request which it contained, that although in the different periods of his reviviscence he had chosen many regions for the places of his birth, yet Bengal was the only country in which he had been born twice; for which reason he had a predilection for it beyond any other, and was desirous of making it a place of his abode, apparently esteeming the sanctity of the Ganges, as a consideration of inferior importance. At length, in the year 1779, when the Lama, yielding to the repeated solicitations of the Emperor of China, visited Pekin; he, with the same spirit of personal kindness, and in the desire of improving his connexion with the government of Bengal, desired Mr. Bogle to go round by sea to Canton, promising to obtain the Emperor's pass for him to proceed, and join him at the capital. The Emperor's promise was also obtained, to permit the first openings of an intercourse between that country and Bengal, by receiving any letters which might be written to him by the Governor General, through the channel of the Lama. Unfortunately, however, the death of the Lama, and that of Mr. Bogle, which happened at nearly the same time, clouded this fair prospect, and completely frustrated every expectation which had been formed. I am sorry to add too, that events, of a much more recent date, have concurred to throw almost insuperable difficulties in the way of re-establishing our intercourse with Tibet, at least for some considerable time to come. It is well known, that, within a few days after his arrival at Pekin, the Lama was seized with a disorder, supposed to be the small pox, of which he died[a]; and his body was soon after carried back, with great pomp, and interred at the place of his former residence. Upon this occasion, the Emperor of China wrote a letter to Dalai Lama, at Lassa, then the chief of all the Lama hierarchy in Tibet, a copy of which will be found in the Appendix, No. I. The original of this letter was some time in the hands of P. Amiot, a missionary at Pekin, by whom, it appears, a transcript of it was then made, which, in 1783, found a place in *Memoires concernant le Chinois*, Tom. IX. Paris. A translation of this is inserted in that valuable compilation, Mr. Dalrymple's Oriental Repertory, Vol. II. p. 275.

[a] The detailed particulars of the Lama's journey to Pekin, and of his death, were related by Poorungheer Gosein, already mentioned, who was one of his chosen retinue, and are recorded by Mr. Dalrymple, in his Oriental Repertory, Vol. II. p. 145. But as a curious and interesting performance, it is inserted in the Appendix, No. IV.

These events were communicated to the Governor General, by the Regent Chanjoo Cooshoo, brother of the deceased Lama, and by Soopoon Choomboo, his favourite and cup-bearer. Faithful translations of their letters, as curious specimens of Tibetian manners and habits of thinking, are given in the Appendix, No. II. and III.

Soon after the receipt of these letters, intelligence arrived from Tibet of the re-appearance of the Lama amongst them. The soul of the late Lama, according to the doctrines of their faith, having passed into, and animated the body of an infant, who, on the discovery of his identity, by such testimonies as their religion prescribes, was acknowledged and proclaimed by the same title and appellation as his predecessor.

Mr. Hastings, upon the receipt of these accounts, proposed to the Board, to send a second deputation to Tibet. He did me the honour to recommend me for this service, to which I was accordingly nominated on the 9th of January, 1783.

On my return, I delivered to Mr. Hastings, whom I met at Patna, a Report on the result of my mission, which was transmitted by him to the Board, and also a hasty Narrative of my interview with the young Lama; which latter was, by their order, sent to the Asiatic Society, to be inserted in their Researches.

This, I, at that time, considered as the final result of my mission, and the only part of it which appeared to merit any public, or official notice. Nevertheless, as I had carefully committed to writing, upon the spot, every thing remarkable, which occurred to me in the course of my employment on this extraordinary service, I have, since my return to England, been induced to flatter myself, that my Journal might not be deemed altogether unworthy of the public curiosity. The trite plea of the importunity of friends, would naturally suggest to me the ridicule which has so often and so justly been cast upon it, if I had not, in the lateness of the publication, an evidence to acquit me, at least of too great forwardness to obtrude myself on the public notice. I have exceeded the rule laid down by Horace, of *nonum prematur in annum*, if it may be construed to extend to compositions of this nature. I may, also, without presumption, venture to hope, that, however incompetent I may be to embellish my narrative with the dress best fitted for it to appear in, yet the novelty and curiosity of the subject will, in some degree, compensate for my own deficiencies, as an Author, of which I cannot possibly be unconscious.

CONTENTS.

PART I.

CHAPTER I.

PAGE

Leave Calcutta—proceed through Plassey to Moorshedabad—cross the Ganges near Bauleah—arrive at Rungpore—Calamatty.—Tuffoon, or tremendous Hurricane.—Mungulhaut, respectable for its Manufactory.—Zeenkaubs.—First View of the Mountains of Bootan.—Cooch Bahar.—Bungalo—singular Custom in this District—extensive Woods—Practice of felling Timber—wild Elephants—Pine-apples, present Abundance of—first Introduction into India.—Inroad of the Moguls into Assam—Fate of the Invaders. - - - - 3

CHAPTER II.

Chichacotta—Frontier of Bootan.—Approach to Buxadewar—noxious Quality of the Atmosphere beneath this Range of Mountains—its Effects on the Inhabitants—fatal to Captain Jones, and great Part of the Troops that served under him—Colonel Sir John Cuming another Instance of its injurious Consequence.—Tangun Horse, a Species peculiar to these Mountains.—Ascent and Entry into Buxadewar.—Chong, and Arra, the Spirit prepared from it.—Character of the People.—Visit the Soobah—Impediment to our Advance—Curiosity, and Urbanity of the Soobah—invited to accompany him during the Performance of a religious Ceremony—Description of the Ceremony—its Design.—Beautiful Scenery in the Vicinity of Buxadewar.—Skilful Archers.—Commencement of the rainy Season.—Dispatches from the Daeb Raja.—Prepare to proceed.—Poorungheer.—Short Stricture on the Manner and Character of the Soobah.—View of Buxadewar—Etymology of its Title.—Mode of travelling in Bootan. - 18

CHAPTER III.

Leave Buxadewar.—Ascend Peachukom Mountain—its prodigious Altitude.—Caution of the Booteeas.—Gigantic Creepers.—Bamboos, a peculiar Species.—

PAGE

Sheenshilla.—Pheadinchim.—Fatal Accident.—Gygoogoo.—Post of Communication.—Tehintchieu, Hatchieu, Patchieu Rivers.—Snow upon the Summits of the Mountains.—Tangun Horses, their surprising Energy.—Pipes conducting Water for the Accommodation of Travellers.—Bridge and Cataract.—Sheenshilla.—Approach to Murichom—laborious Employment of the People, in which the female Sex bear a heavy Share—extensive Use of the Bamboo.—Village of Murichom—Advantage of Situation—Fertility of the adjacent Lands.—Teezpaut, a Species of Cinnamon.—Remarkable Instance of great Age.—Pestiferous Fly.—Tetim.—Terrible Disaster.—Baboosoo and Merifaka Mountains.—Peanjoo.—Minzapeezo, a most copious Waterfall.—Ingenious Method of constructing Roads along the Sides of Precipices.—Awful Scenery.—Dewta Tehuptehup.—Peculiar Way of passing deep Ravines.—Chain Bridge of Chuka—Castle of Chuka.—Change in the Face of the Country—Temperature of the Weather—natural Productions.—Punugga.—Hatchieu.—Kepta.—Lomeela Mountain.—Selo-cha-zum.—Durbee Castle.—Mudwallahs for the Defence of Hill Fortresses.—Pauga.—Tehintchieu, Patchieu.—Noomnoo.—Poës.—Wangoka.—Symtoka.—Bridge over the Tehintchieu.—Valley of Tassisudon. - 43

CHAPTER IV.

Tassisudon—my Arrival notified at the Palace—the Raja or Lama occupied in religious Ceremonies—strict Observance of all Duties appertaining to their Religion.—Message from the Daeb Raja—Interview—Zoompoon, Zoondonier, Zempi—Citadel—Audience Chamber—Ceremony of Introduction—Particulars of the Interview—Tea—local Observance—extensive Fashion—peculiar Mode of preparing it.—Polite Attention of the Raja—Dress, of the religious Order—Manner of our Reception.—Second Interview.—Silk Scarfs—their Use on all Occasions of Ceremony or Compliment.—Comparative View of Manners.—Natural Productions.—Peculiar Sentiments of the Rajah—Variety of Expression—Art of Drawing—Mr. Davis's superior Skill.—Visit to the chief Officers under Government—Tasse-Zompoon, Zoondonier, Zempi—Outline of their Rank and Authority.—I undertook to mediate the Peace of the Zeenkaubs, who are pardoned, and re-admitted into favour—Instance of implicit Obedience to the Will of their Chief.—General Design of the present Work.—A Bootan Repast.—Boora Soobah, or Toonso Pilo.—Bees.—Benevolent and humane Sentiment.—Order of Gylongs—regulated Periods for religious Service—some Rules of the Society—Ablutions—Temperance—Cleanliness—general Appearance—endemial Disorder termed Gheig, or Aubi. - - - - - - 64

CHAPTER V.

PAGE

The Valley of Tassisudon.—Palace of the Chief—its extensive Accommodation, containing all the Officers of State, a very numerous establishment of Gylongs, and a Temple of Worship.—Coldness of the Season—Buildings ill calculated to obviate its Effects.—The Rajah's Stud.—Ancient Site of Tassisudon—Palace of Lam' Ghassatoo.—Mode of supplying the Valley with Water from the surrounding Hills.—The sacred Sentence enclosed in Temples, inscribed on Tablets, on Flags, and on Rocks.—Brahmennee, or sacred Bull.—Artisans—Paper Manufactory.—Season of the Rains moderate—general Salubrity of our Situation.—Poshtee.—An Excursion.—Wandeechy.—Settlements of the Religious.—A Recluse.—Caution of the Daeb.—Mr. Saunders taken ill—Incantations for his Recovery. - - - - - - - 89

CHAPTER VI.

Commotions—excited by Wandipora Zoompoon and a degraded Chief.—Punukka Zoompoon arrives at the Capital to pay the customary Duty of Allegiance.—Popular Administration of the present Daeb Raja.—Ascribed Cause of the Rebellion—prudent Precautions—Subjects called upon for their Allegiance—weak Condition of the Capital—extreme Vigilance—general Alarm—Letter from the Rebel Leader—Insurgents gather Strength—Skirmishes between the contending Parties—some Loyalists badly wounded with Arrows—their Dread of Poison—strong Position of the Rebels.—Invited to visit the Rajah—his compassionate Concern for the deluded Mob, and confident Expectation the Tumults would soon be quelled.—Miserable Artillery—humane Motive for desiring to employ it—cautious Conduct of the Combatants—general Trait of these Warriors—the Rebels, after an obstinate Contest, totally defeated.—Military Character of the Booteeas—not deficient in Courage—feeble Attack—want of Discipline—Accoutrements and Arms—Use of Poison.—Raja Mocum Narrain—his Vakeel.—Wandipore invested by Zoondonier and Punukka Zoompoon.—General Thanksgivings.—Reduction of the Castle.—Flight of the Rebels.—Plunder and Spoils.—The Raja meditates a Visit to Wandipore, to settle Affairs in the disturbed Districts—announces his Design—invites me to meet him. - 106

CHAPTER VII.

The Raja proceeds to Wandipore—sends a Messenger—we prepare to follow—pass Symtoka—dreariness of the Way—meet a Party of the Daeb Raja's.—

PAGE

Improving Appearance of the Country.—A Procession.—Faculty of prolonging the Sound of wind Instruments—instanced also in Bengal.—Matchieu-Patchieu—Tahantchieu Rivers.—Bijnee—Berhampooter—Wandipore.—Liberal Supply of Refreshments from the Raja.—Miserable Quarters.—Lines of the Besiegers—Advantages of Position.—Castle of Wandipore—Tradition regarding it.—Bridge—Lightness and Beauty of its Structure.—Mineral Springs.—General Ignorance of the Contents of these Mountains.—Curious Effect of a strong Current of Wind.—Turbulent Situation of Wandipore.—Process of making Butter.—Departure from Wandipore.—Tame Elephant.—View of the Mountain of Ghassa—Snow—hot Bath.—Palace of Punukka.—Matchieu-Patchieu Valley—Banks of the River—sheltered Situation.—Expensive Decoration of the Palace.—Gardens—Variety of Fruits—advantageous Site for Horticulture.—Laborious Services imposed upon the Female Sex.—Zemrigatche.—Nymphæa Nilotica—its religious Estimation in Bootan as well as in Egypt.—Propitiatory Offerings to the Dewtas.—Narrainee, particular Account of.—Leave Punukka.—Telagong.—Stupendous Mountains.—Hunnoowunt.—Muttura.—Madejee Sindia.—Jumna.—Ultimate Defeat of the Rebels. - - - - 124

CHAPTER VIII.

Return of the Raja to Tassisudon—our Visit to him—anxiety to hear our opinion of his favourite Seat—displeased that we were refused admittance—recital of what appeared peculiarly striking.—His marked approbation of Mr. Davis.—Buxa Soobah.—A Buffoon.—Electrical Machine.—Mechanic turn of the Raja—medical Genius.—Ipecacuanha.—Wandeechy.—Fatal accident to our Camp Equipage.—Tibet Dogs.—Entertainment at the Villa.—Marvellous Stories of the Raja—of a Gigantic race of Men—of People with Tails—of Unicorns.—The Rajah's Pilgrimage to the sacred Shrine of Pootalah.—Temple of Wandeechy.—Repast—Bull Fight.—Return of the Rajah to the Palace.—Messengers from Tibet.—Durga Pooja.—The great Autumnal Festival of the Hindoos.—Dussera.—Dewali. - - - - - - 149

PART II.

CHAPTER I.

PAGE

Take leave of the Daeb Raja, and the principal Officers of his Durbar.—Depart from Tassisudon.—Ascend the lofty Mountain of Pomæla—pass Phajudee, famed for the Birth of the present Lam' Rimbochay.—Extensive Monastery.—Religious Associations, their obvious Tendency on Population.—Cross the Summit of Pomæla—descend to Paimaitong.—Tibetian Custom of taking Tea—Appendages of Dress—gross Superstitions of these Mountaineers.—Paibesa.--Picturesque View from Dalai-jeung—hospitable Entertainment of its Keeper—Review of the Way.—Paro.—Patchieu.—Paro Pilo, his Extent of Jurisdiction.—Seccum Raja.—Castle of Paro, Parogong, or Rinjipo.—The Valley—its Extent.—Mookhy—temporary Edifices—Exercise of Archery—Market—Manufactures—Mechanics—Thrashing.—Market-place of Paro.—Zeenkaub, Attention of his Friends.—Brood of Tangun Horses.—Fortress of Dukka-jeung.—Snow—Harvest—romantic Scenery.—Sana—last Post in Bootan—Guard-house—Patchieu Bridge.—The Yak of Tartary, particular Description of.—Gloomy Wilds.—Rude Region of the Frontier.—Of Bridges in Bootan.—Vast Difference between the muscular Form of the Booteea and Tibetian.—Social Groupes of Mountaineers.—Ghassa.—Lama of Phari.—Dhy, Kummuz of the Tartars.—Tartar Herdsmen.—Dukba.—Elevation and bleak Site of Soomoonang. - - 167

CHAPTER II.

Small Banners, the Boundaries between Bootan and Tibet.—Plain of Phari—low Mount dedicated to funeral Rites.—Fortress.—Chassa Goombah, Station of the Lama of Phari—his Jurisdiction.—Là, or Musk Deer.—Ghouz—Severity of the Cold—Range of snowy Mountains.—Chumularee.—Hindoo Superstitions—Tongla—Tartar Tents.—Goorkhaw.—Homage to Chumularee.—Superior Elevation of this Part of Tibet—deduced from the Sources of Rivers, the cold Temperature of the Air, and the Mountains clothed perpetually with Snow.—Teuna—feeble Vegetation—numerous Herds—dreary Aspect.—Tempestuous Character of the Frontier.—Mineral Springs—fossil Alkali—Natron.—Dochai.—Lake Ramtchieu—vast Resort of Water-fowl.—Encampment.—Sedjy mutti.—Sublime Scenery—a Tibet Village.—Farther Traits of Superstition.—Dogs of Tibet—their Ferocity.—Comparison between Bootan and Tibet. - 197

CHAPTER III.

PAGE

Deserted Villages—fatal Effects of the Small-pox—Ignorance of its Treatment—a serious Calamity—Occasion of the Removal of the Seat of Government and Monastery from Teshoo Loomboo to Chamnamning.—Gangamaar—hot Bath—Surface of the Ground adjacent—Labourers in the Fields—rude Expression of Surprise.—Place of Fragments—huge Idol—Mahamoonie—a religious Rite.—Shoohoo.--Nainee--improving Appearance of the Country.--Tehukku.--Jhansu-jeung.—Valley of Jhansu.—Woollen Manufactory—Economy in Dress.—Monastery of Jhansu.—Beggars.—Dukque.—Corricle.—Castle of Painom—Bridge—Town.—Keesoo.—Tsondue.—Distant View of Teshoo Loomboo—Enter the Monastery. - - - - - - 218

CHAPTER IV.

Messages of Compliment and Congratulation from the Regent and Soopoon Choomboo—Custom of presenting a white Scarf—favourable Tokens of a friendly Disposition.—Preparations for out Reception—Hall of Audience—Lama's Throne—Introduction to the Regent—The Regent's Assurance of the Identity of the Lama—his Friendship for the Governor General in his pre-existent State—Attention and Respect paid him at the Court of China—his Regeneration acknowledged by the Emperor—Satisfaction derived from the Receipt of the Governor General's Dispatches.—Projected Removal of the Lama to Terpaling—the Monastery prepared for his Reception—Tea—Dismission.—Sketch of the Person—Manner—Dress of the Regent.—Bells, a Summons to Devotion.—Visit to Soopoon Choomboo.--Emperor of China--his Influence—a Votary of the Tibet Faith.—Umbas.-Jasoos--Gesub Rimbochay—Dalai Lama—Soopoon Choomboo, Sadeek—honoured by the distinguished Attention and Favour of the late Lama—promoted by the Emperor—his Character held in high Estimation—important Period in the Annals of Tibet.—First public Tribute of Acknowledgment and Allegiance to the regenerated Lama—Preparations for his Removal from Kylee to Terpaling—Offer to attend the Ceremony.—Party proceeds to escort the Lama—Homage paid by his Votaries on the Way—Entry into Terpaling—Return of the Regent—Cavalcade—Bonfires—Chinese.—Correspondence with Dalai Lama.—Hostile Disposition of Gesub Rimbochay. - - 231

CHAPTER V.

PAGE

Permission from the Regent to view the Interior of the Monastery.—Gorgeous Temples.—Solemn and mysterious Ceremonies.—Numerous Assembly of the Gylongs.—Periods for Devotion.—Loud Vociferation.—Clamorous Noise attending the Performance of their religious Rites.—Serious Attention to the Duties of their Faith.—Profound Respect for their sovereign Lama.—Visit the Mausoleum dedicated to the Memory of the late Teshoo Lama.—Cursory View of this highly venerated Structure. - - - - - - 255

CHAPTER VI.

The Regent.—Soopoon Choomboo.—Countries contiguous to Tibet—Bengal endeared to the Tibetians by religious Prejudices.—Gunga Sagur—the Confluence of the Ganges with the Sea.—Jagarnaut.—Performance of Pilgrimage by Proxy.—A Devotee—Geography—Astronomy.—Pranpooree—his extraordinary Course of Mortifications.—Russia—the Czarina.—Taranaut Lama.—Kharka.—Intercourse between Russia and China.—Pilgrims from Khumbak.—Gallery of Idols—Means by which the Cabinet is occasionally augmented.—Teshoo Loomboo famed for the Manufacture of Images.—Lama of Luddauk.—War between England—America and France.—Commerce—of the English Nation.—Spirit of Inquiry and Research.—Siberia—Baikal.—Wandering Tartars.—No Tradition extant of an ancient People inhabiting towards the North.—General Belief of the Origin of Learning.—Inference drawn from the Similarity of the Sanscrit and Tibet Alphabet.—Character in which their sacred Writings are preserved and printed—that of Correspondence and Business.—Regent notifies his Design of leaving the Monastery—commends me to the Care of Soopoon Choomboo in his Absence.—Visits my Apartments, accompanied by Soopoon Choomboo and the Lama of Luddauk.—Science of Palmistry.—Attar, Pawn. - - - - - - 266

CHAPTER VII.

Departure of the Regent—his Desire to travel unobserved.—Egypt—Eunani—Singhi.—Use of the Symbol of the Lion in Tibet and Egypt—superstitious Regard for celestial Phænomena—Skill in Science—Bigotry—Court of China—Spectacles for the Entertainment of the Lama—Soomeroo.—Coincidence with the Hindoos in scientific Knowledge.—Benares esteemed the sacred Seat of all human Learning.—Teshoo Loomboo—Geographic Site—particular Description of.—Plain of Teshoo Loomboo—Shigatzee-jeung—Luddauk—Cashmeer—Nipal—China—Russia—Siberia.—Abruptness of the Hills—local Effect.—Vortexes of

PAGE

Wind.—Rock behind Teshoo Loomboo—View from hence.—Berhampooter—Megna—Pudda—Sundrabunds—Pirates—Maunserore—Rise—Course of the Ganges and Berhampooter.—Seasons in Tibet.—Meat preserved by the Action of intense Cold.—Use of undressed Meat.—Sheep, their Value for Food, Raiment, and Use.—Dryness of the Atmosphere in Tibet—Precautions used against it. 287

CHAPTER VIII.

Local Appellation of Tibet—Stricture on the Religion—Use of musical Instruments in their sacred Services—Comparison with the Hindoos—Assemble in Temples for the Performance of religious Duties—Lama, the sacred Superior—Gradations in the sacerdotal Class—Gylong—Tohba—Tuppa—Establishment of the Monastery—Interdictions of the religious Order—Noise and Pomp of their religious Ceremonies—Kugopea—Habit of the Priests—Yellow, the distinguishing Colour, worn by the Sect Gyllookpa—of which the Superiors are Dalai Lama—Teshoo Lama—Tarranaut Lama—Red, by the Shamar.—Lam' Rimbochay—Lam' Sobroo Nawangnamghi—Lam' Ghassatoo—their Contentions—Prevalence of the former.—Humane Trait in the Character of the Tibetian.—Tribute of respect paid to the Dead—Festival in Honour of the Dead—superstitious Practices—sanctioned and performed by the Class devoted to Religion.—Omens.—Calendar of Time—Cycle of twelve Years.—Art of Printing. - 305

CHAPTER IX.

Return of the Regent—Time appointed for my Departure—rapid Advance of Winter—Audience of Leave—Soopoon Choomboo—farewell Visits from numerous Friends—prepare to leave Teshoo Loomboo—previous Observance of some superstitious Ceremonies.—Beggars—Mohammedans—Hindoos.—Benevolence displayed at Teshoo Loomboo.—Tsondue.—Skating.—Terpaling.—Interview with Teshoo Lama—Manner and Conduct of the Lama—his Age—Parents—Gyeung—her splendid Dress—Gyap—Invitation to an Entertainment—Officers of the Lama's Household—Impression of profound Respect.—Veneration entertained for the Memory of the late Lama—his humane, intelligent, conciliating Character.—Amiable Manners of Mr. Bogle.—Parents of the Lama—Pavilion—Entertainment.—Gyap—his Delight in manly Sports—his superior Skill—polite Offer to instruct me in the Arts he practised.—Repast—raw Meat—Gyeung, particularly abstemious.—Music—Vocal—Instrumental.—Conclusion of the Entertainment.—Wait upon the Lama—Votaries of the Lama—Calmuc Tartars—liberal Offerings.—Last Visit to the Teshoo Lama, and his Parents. 326

CHAPTER X.

PAGE

Quit the Monastery of Terpaling, on my Return towards Bengal—Annee Goomba —Annees, Nuns—Gylongs, Monks.—Cursory View of the interdicted Orders. —Polyandry—Influence on the Manners of the People—Tendency to check the too great Increase of Population—and prevent the inhuman Practice known to prevail in China.—Marriage Ceremonies.—Bleak and dreary Aspect of the Country—Rigour of the Winter—extreme Purity of the Atmosphere.—Precautions to secure the Surface of the Soil, and at the same Time enrich the Lands. —Course of the Seasons.—Dukque.—Lake Ramtchieu.—Skating—Solidity of the Ice—intense Severity of the Frost.—Shawl Goats.—Soomoonang—Punukka —Buxadewar—Rungpore. - - - - 347

PART III.

Report delivered to the Hon. Warren Hastings, Esq. Governor General of Bengal, upon the Result of my Mission to the Court of Teshoo Loomboo. - 361

A List of the Usual Articles of Commerce between Tibet and the surrounding Countries. - - - - - - - 381

PART IV.

Some Account of the Vegetable and Mineral Productions of Bootan and Tibet. 387

PART V.

Letter addressed to the Hon. John Macpherson, Esq. Governor General of Bengal, containing some Particulars relating to the Journey of Poorungheer to Teshoo Loomboo; the Inauguration of Teshoo Lama; and the State of Tibet from 1783 to 1785. - - - - - - 419

PART VI.

Some Account of the Situation of Affairs in Tibet, from 1785 to 1793. - 437

APPENDIX.

PAGE

No. I. Translation of a Letter from Kienlong, Emperor of China, to Dalai Lama, the Grand Lama of Tibet. - - - - - - 443

No. II. Translation of a Letter from Changoo Cooshoo Punjun Irtinnee Neimoheim, Regent of Teshoo Loomboo, to Warren Hastings, Esq. Governor General, &c. &c. Received the 12th of February, 1782. - - 449

No. III. Translation of a Letter from Soopoon Choomboo, Mirkin Chassa Lama, Minister to the late Teshoo Lama, to Warren Hastings, Esq. Governor General, &c. &c. Received the 12th February, 1782. - - - 454

No. IV. Narrative of the Particulars of the Journey of Teshoo Lama, and his Suite, from Tibet to China, from the verbal Report of Poorungheer Gosein. 457

TABLE OF PLATES.

Survey of the Road from Buxadewar to Tassisudon, in Bootan; and from Tassisudon to Teshoo Loomboo, in Tibet, to be placed with a guard, fronting - - page 1

Views taken upon the Spot by Lieutenant Samuel Davis, and engraved by Basire, from the original Drawings in the possession of Warren Hastings, Esq.

Plate I. Buxadewar, - - - - - - - page 39

II. The Cascade of Minzapeezo - - - - - 53

III. Plan, Section, and Elevation of the Bridge of Chains at Chuka - 55

IV. Chuka - - - - - - - 55

V. The Valley near Tassisudon, with a Procession of the Religious to their Ablutions 86

VI. The Palace of Tassisudon - - - - - 90

VII. The Residence of Lam' Ghassatoo - - - - - 96

VIII. The Castle of Wandipore - - - - - - - 132

IX. The Palace of Punukka - - - - - 138

X. The Yak of Tartary, from a Picture, painted by Stubbs, in the possession of Warren Hastings, Esq. - - - - - 186

XI. The Mausoleum of Teshoo Lama - - - - 265

XII. The Dwelling of Tessaling Lama, with the religious Edifice, stiled Kugopea 314

XIII. Specimens of the Umin, and of the Uchen characters, in the language of Tibet, to be placed with a guard - - - - - 324

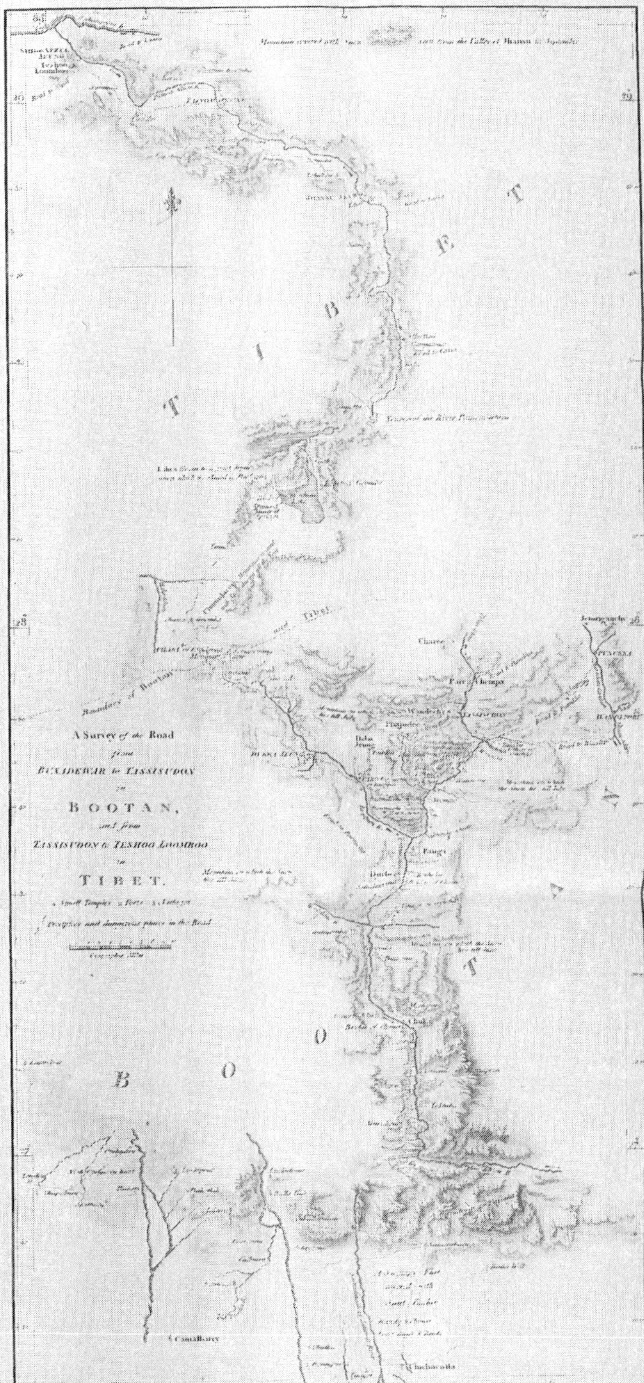
A Survey of the Road
from
BUXADEWAR to TASSISUDON
in
BOOTAN,
and from
TASSISUDON to TESHOO LOOMBOO
in
TIBET.
T I B E T
B O O T A N
Boundary of Bootan and Tibet
Tassisudon
Wandechy
Punukka
Chuka
Paro
Chalamarchy
Dukka Jeung

PART I.

NARRATIVE OF A JOURNEY

FROM

BENGAL TO TASSISUDON, &c.

NARRATIVE, &c.

BENGAL.

CHAPTER I

Leave Calcutta—proceed through Plassey to Moorshedabad—cross the Ganges near Bauleah—arrive at Rungpore—Calamatty.—Tuffoon, or tremendous Hurricane.—Mungulhaut, respectable for its Manufactory.—Zeenkaubs.—First View of the Mountains of Bootan.—Cooch Bahar.—Bungalo—singular Custom in this District—extensive Woods—Practice of felling Timber—wild Elephants—Pine-apples, present Abundance of—first Introduction into India.—Inroad of the Moguls into Assam—Fate of the Invaders.—Chichacotta.—Frontier of Bootan.

THE beginning of the year 1783, I received my final orders and instructions, and left Calcutta, to execute the service which was intrusted to my care. Lieutenant Samuel Davis, and Mr. Robert Saunders, were included in the commission with which I was honoured, and appointed to accompany me, the former as Draftsman and Surveyor, the latter in the capacity of Surgeon. I had every reason to congratulate myself on the choice which had been made of these gentlemen as my associates; and in their kind and friendly attention, I had the satisfaction to find a constant source of comfort, amidst all the toils and difficulties of a long and tedious journey.

Notice of the Governor General's intention to send a Deputation to the Court of Teshoo Loomboo, had been previously given to the Daeb Raja, the independent chieftain of the intermediate mountains, which separate Bengal from Tibet. This measure was indispensably necessary, since, without his permission and assistance, it was impossible to accomplish the object of my mission.

In the first part of my journey, as far as the Company's most northern station, nothing occurred which deserves particular notice. I ascended my palanquin at Ghyretty, on the opposite side of the river Bhagirathy, the name of the principal branch of the Ganges, which at this place bears the descriptive appellation of the Hoogly river; an appellation given to it by the first European inhabitants of Bengal, and since retained in the common modes of speech and writing. Hoogly was anciently the principal port and mart of this province. I forded the Bhagirathy at Aughadeep; thence travelling over the island of Cossimbazar, across the plains of Plassey, rendered ever memorable by the brilliant and decisive victory of Lord Clive, and passing near the suburbs of Moorshedabad, I arrived on the banks of the Ganges, almost opposite to Bauleah. After ferrying across the river, I traversed as wide a space of flat and fertile country as that which I had already passed; and at the expiration of four days from the commencement of my journey, was set down at Rungpore, which is distant two hundred and sixty miles from Calcutta.

Upon my arrival at Rungpore, I found my progress impeded for the present, in consequence of the indispensable necessity of obtaining previous license for our admission into Bootan from the Daeb Raja, without whose special authority no person is permitted to enter the passes of the frontier mountains. Having therefore waited for an answer to the letters which I had dispatched to acquaint the Daeb Raja with our intended departure for his dominions, and received his passports, I proceeded on my journey from Rungpore, accompanied by Mr. Davis and Mr. Saunders.

We travelled in our palanquins; the road lay through an open level country, inferior to no part of Bengal in cultivation and fertility. The chief produce was rice, of which it yields two harvests in the year, and sometimes an intermediate crop of mustard seed : a great quantity of good tobacco grows also in this district, and some indigo. We came at noon to Calamatty, a plain of wide extent, sixteen miles from Rungpore, and having pitched our tents near the centre of it, with a small village upon our right, and a fordable brook in front, we halted for the remainder of the day. At night there came on an excessively high wind and heavy fall of rain, attended with thunder and lightning, which was succeeded at break of day, on Wednesday the 7th, by another storm equally violent and awful.

It may be observed, that this sort of tremendous hurricane, which is not unfrequent at this season of the year, is distinguished by the name of *Tuffoon* in Asia, and is known among the English in Bengal by the familiar appellation of *North-wester*. It is a storm of extreme violence, but of short duration; rarely coming on in the open day, or twice during the absence of the sun, but usually commencing about the time of the evening twilight.

These storms rage with greatest force between the passage of the sun from the vernal equinox to the summer solstice. His vertical power then loads the atmosphere with humidity; and his action diminishing as he goes down, a dense cloud advances from the edge of the horizon, which is seen to come on with slow and solemn motion, till it has attained a certain altitude, when a most tremendous gust of wind bursts forth at once with sudden fury, frequently tearing up trees by the roots, and carrying away before it every light substance it can take up; filling the whole surrounding atmosphere with obscurity. A burst of loud thunder, with flashes of vivid lightning, next succeeds, which seems to clear a passage for a torrent of the heaviest rain, that descends with wonderful impetuosity. After this commotion of the elements, which seldom exceeds half an hour in duration, has subsided, a tranquil, temperate season ensues; all oppression is removed, and the air refreshed and cooled: a most grateful close, in this torrid region, to an intensely hot day.

We were detained on Wednesday the 7th of May, by waiting for a part of our baggage, which had not yet come up from Rungpore; and in addition to this impediment, many of the coolies, or porters, had left us in the course of the night, so that we were unable to go on until Thursday.

At about ten o'clock in the forenoon of the following day, having received a reinforcement to our numbers from Rungpore, we left Calamatty plain, and half an hour after passed Saftabarry, crossing a wide nullah, or creek, over which was thrown an elevated bamboo bridge, constructed upon forked props. Bamboos resting in the fork, and covered with split bamboos woven into mats, composed the platform. It was strong enough for foot passengers, but unsafe, as I should suppose, for carriages, or cattle. On the opposite side of the river was an extended high bank, which had the appearance of having been intended for a line of defence. It was situated about two hundred paces from the edge of the nullah. Its sides formed a square, and at the extremities of the embankment, on the side facing the plain, there seemed to be the vestiges of two bastions. We continued our way, passing at noon by Ootney nullah, and afterwards came to Mungulhaut, a large manufacturing town, twelve miles from Calamatty, situated on the south side of the river Durlah, which divides the district of Cooch Bahar from that of Rungpore. The inhabitants of Mungulhaut seem to pay more attention to the comforts and commodiousness of living, than those of any other town I have seen in India. Their houses, composed of mats inserted between frames of bamboo, were neatly thatched, and each had a portion of land encircled with a bamboo palisade. The streets were spacious, and the principal one conducted us to the river side, whence we ferried across, and encamped at Ghiddildow, upon the northern bank. We saw many boats of large burthen upon the river, which, added to the striking neatness and regularity of the town, gave it an air of industry and traffic. Coarse cotton cloths I understand to be the staple commodity; and that they furnish the most considerable part of the large returning cargo, which is carried by the Booteea caravan annually from Rungpore.

We found the Zeenkaubs[a] and their party, who had been lately deputed by the Daeb Raja to the Governor General, waiting at Mungulhaut. Their departure from Calcutta had been accelerated, that they might conduct me to the capital of their master. They came to me in the afternoon; and, as they were encumbered with much baggage, and many attendants, to avoid the inconvenience of travelling with so large a party, I persuaded them to go on before us. They accepted my advice; and we parted, not to meet again, as I expected, until we reached Chichacotta.

Departing from Ghiddildow, we continued to pursue the course of the river Durlah for some distance, until it turned short to the left. We then proceeded through a very highly improved and fertile country, where the luxuriant growth of the trees, among which the most conspicuous were the soopareе[b], semmel[c], and bannian[d], intermixed with clusters of the bamboo[e], and the rich verdure of the fields, covered with rice almost ready to shoot into ear, presented on every side a most pleasing prospect. We came late to the ground on which we intended to encamp, and it was much later when our provisions and baggage arrived. The tents were pitched upon an open eminence, overlooking the villages of Pahargunge on the left, and Balladinga

[a] Zeenkaubs are officers of government under the immediate command of the Daeb Raja, a large party of whom are always personally attendant on him, and ready to be employed, either in a civil or military capacity, as he directs.

[b] Areca cathecu. *Linn.* [c] Bombax pentandrium. *Linn.*

[d] Ficus indica. *Linn.* Bhur, *Ind.* [e] Arundo bambos. *Linn.*

on the right, ten miles from Ghiddildow; immediately in the front was a large jeel, or marshy lake, in the form of a crescent. The ground on the opposite side, rising as it receded, was covered with a variety of shrubs, and exquisitely adorned with a wild but lively verdure.

The country through which we advanced on the following day, had less cultivation than that we had just left. We ferried over the river Maunsi, about half a mile above the point where it meets with the Toorsha; after their confluence, they assume the name of Neelcoomar, and shaping their course through Baharbund, fall with their united streams into the Berhampooter[f]. As the day dawned, we obtained a transient view of the summits of the mountains of Bootan, which resembled a deep shadow on the distant horizon; but the sun soon raised up an impenetrable veil of thick vapour from the marshes at their base, and they were no longer visible. The vastness and obscurity of this enormous boundary, remote and indistinct as it appeared, when it first burst upon the sight in ill-defined and fantastic shapes, could not but excite very powerful emotions in the mind; and I looked upon the formidable barrier I had to pass, with mingled awe and admiration.

On our approach to Bahar we were met, at a short distance from the banks of the Toorsha, by the Aumils, or principal officers of the revenue, who conducted us to a spot of ground that bore the ruinous remains of a large bungalo[g], fourteen miles from the camp near Balladinga. Their preference of this spot arose not from its superior plea

[f] Properly Brahmá pootra, offspring of Brahma.

[g] This is an appellation given to any single building covered with thatch. It has its name from the province of Bengal, where they are most in use, and whence other countries have borrowed the mode of constructing them.

santness, but because it had been inhabited by the first English gentlemen who resided here, before these districts were reduced under entire subjection to the Company. A lofty artificial bank of earth, which still surrounded it, shewed that its original proprietor chose rather to rely for his security on the strength of his fortifications, than on the fidelity of the people. The ground around it was extremely low, and the situation acknowledged to be singularly unhealthy; but as we intended only a short stay, we set up our tents, and in the course of the day a messenger arrived, with offers of assistance, from Nazir Deo[h]. We also received visits from the Dewan[i], the Buckshee[k], and other officers belonging to the household of the Raja, who offered me every service in their power: indeed we stood much in need of their assistance, to supply the deficiency of carriage, which, at every stage, occasioned us much perplexity and trouble.

The Raja of Bahar, an infirm old man, was absent at a place called Bahrisser, about ten miles off, performing his devotions. I was strongly pressed by his officers to wait his return; but I excused myself in consideration of the advanced season, and resolutely withstood the solicitations, both of his servants and of my own, who were equally urgent for my stay.

In the district of Cooch Bahar an usage of a very singular kind has prevailed from remote antiquity, and I was assured by many of the inhabitants of its actual existence at this day. If a Reiat, or peasant, owes a sum of money, and has not the ability to satisfy his creditor, he is compelled to give up his wife as a pledge, and possession of her

[h] Superindant. [i] Treasurer. [k] Paymaster.

is kept until the debt is discharged. It sometimes happens, as they affirm, that the wife of a debtor is not redeemed for the space of one, two, or three years; and then if, during her residence and connection with the creditor, a family should have been the consequence, half of it is considered as the property of the person with whom she lived, and half that of her real husband[l].

The country has a most wretched appearance, and its inhabitants are a miserable and puny race. The lower ranks without scruple dispose of their children for slaves, to any purchaser, and that too for a very trifling consideration; nor yet, though in a traffic so unnatural, is the agency of a third person ever employed. Nothing is more common than to see a mother dress up her child, and bring it to market, with no other hope, no other view, than to enhance the price she may procure for it. Indeed the extreme poverty and wretchedness of these people will forcibly appear, when we recollect how little is necessary for the subsistence of a peasant in these regions. The value of this can seldom amount to more than one penny per day, even allowing him to make his meal of two pounds of boiled rice, with a due proportion of salt, oil, vegetables, fish, and chili[m].

[l] It is not possible for a traveller, passing rapidly through a strange country, to catch the manners, or judge of the influence which custom, or a sense of honour, may have on the natural propensities of the people. We may conclude that this bias must be very strong in a community where such a law continues to exist; since in any other, which should adopt it as a novel institution, the creditor would have a very insecure hold on the probity of his debtor, not less, perhaps, from the reluctance of the latter to recover his wife, than to part with his money. The law would not subsist, if it was not known to be effective of its purpose.

[m] A kind of red pepper, in universal use, made from the *capsicum annuum* of Linnæus.

The situation of this district exhibits a melancholy proof of different facts too frequently united; the great facility of obtaining food, and, at the same time, the wretched indigence of the lower order of inhabitants.

At six o'clock on the morning of the 11th of May, we departed from Cooch Bahar, and travelled near the banks of the river Toorsha, for upwards of three miles. The land was low and marshy, interspersed with thick woods, and with many nullahs, or rivulets, having not more than three feet depth of water. The whole face of the country was dreary and unpleasant, being thinly inhabited, and sparingly cultivated. No animals appeared to enliven and cheer the scene, except here and there a solitary hargheela[n], or maunukjoor[o]. The vegetation was coarse; the ground being almost every where clothed with rank grass, reeds, and fern. We crossed some creeks, whose water was chin deep; a rainy day would have rendered them absolutely unfordable. We now entered the dreary region which divides the district of Cooch Bahar, the present frontier of Bengal, from the country of Bootan, and which, from its inaptitude to supply the wants, or facilitate the functions, of human life, may be considered as appertaining properly to neither. Its extent, from the foot of the chain of mountains, with which the district or principality of Bootan commences, is little less than twenty-five miles.

We passed through a wood called the Pistajar-wood, in which many

[n] A bird, the largest species of the crane kind, which feeds only on putrid flesh, snakes, and frogs. It is commonly called by the English in Bengal, Adjutant.

[o] A water fowl of the crane species.

of the largest trees had been lately felled, not by means of the axe, but by fire; and their charred stumps were seen on every side peeping through the thick brushwood with which this forest abounds. The only method of felling timber in practice here, I was informed, is by fire. In the trees marked out for this purpose, vegetation is destroyed by burning their trunks half through: being left in that state to dry, in the ensuing year the fire is again applied, and they are burnt till they fall. The road through this forest was narrow and confined; many hollows were even filled with water, and we found the passage both difficult and dangerous.

Our followers came up late, having been dreadfully frightened, in passing through the woods, by the sight of several wild elephants. The mohut, or elephant driver, was not less alarmed than his companions; and the noise and vehemence of his utterance and action, whilst he related the story of his adventures, plainly proved, that, though he had escaped the danger, he had not yet shaken off the fears it had excited[p].

Near a small village, which we passed in our route to-day, I saw some clusters of wild pine-apples. That they grew wild, their condition, and the situation in which they were found, left me no room to doubt. It is a well known fact, that the pine-apple is not among the indigenous fruits of India, though at this time they are so abundant in Bengal, as to be sent to market like turnips on a cart, and, in the

[p] The principal cause of apprehension is, the probability that the wild elephant will attack the tame one, and, if not destroy him, be the means, at least, of effecting his release during the conflict.

most plentiful part of the season, no less than twenty may be bought for a rupee, about the value of half a crown.

The first plants of this fruit that grew in Hindostan, were brought into India, in the reign of the Emperor Akbar, by the priests of the Portugueze mission, who at that period eagerly pursued every method they could devise to ingratiate themselves with the court; indeed they had so far succeeded, that they began to flatter themselves with having gained a complete ascendency over the inquisitive and liberal mind of their patron, and that he was even about to become a convert to their faith; be this as it may, of all their services, perhaps, this delicious gift may deservedly be deemed not the least valuable; the fruits of which have spread so far, and proved so extensive in their utility, as well as so permanent in their duration. A part of the original stock, that is, some plants derived from it in direct descent, was pointed out to me in the garden of Moorteza Zemani, at Delhi, where they first grew. The Ayeen Akbari mentions both the time and manner of their introduction; and I consider it as an additional evidence of their having been derived from one original stock, that they are called, in every part of India which I have visited, by the same common name of ananas. To account for their appearance in an obscure village on the borders of Cooch Bahar, we must have recourse to an event in the reign of the Emperor Aurungzebe, when the General Moüzzum Khawn commanded an army employed in the reduction of these districts, which had not before submitted to the Mogul dominion. In the prosecution of his designs he was detained a considerable time in this neighbourhood, during which, among the other choice fruits which he received from the far greater distance of Cabool and Cashmeer, pine-apples made a part of his supply; and hence, in all probability, they are indebted for the introduction of pine-apples into the province of Bahar. That they are not common, may be assumed as another proof of this supposition; for no person in the least acquainted with the character of the Bengâlees, who look upon these creatures as a race infinitely inferior to themselves, could for a moment entertain the idea of their torpid apathy being roused to transplant, from ever so short a distance, even this elegant luxury. I doubt, indeed, whether the inhabitants of Cooch Bahar know its use, or that it is even growing under their feet.

From this neighbourhood Moüzzum Khawn advanced with his army to attempt the conquest of Assam. Against artillery, and the formidable array with which this expedition was equipped, the wretched and feeble Assamees could make no resistance. Their towns and their strongholds fell after each other, in rapid succession, into the hands of the victorious army, whose progress was obstructed by no other impediments than those which arose from the nature of the country, and the rivers in their way, until they arrived at Ghergong, the seat of government, and capital of Assam. Here then they considered the expedition as entirely accomplished, and their success complete. Accordingly, while they sat down to make their various arrangements, and were occupied in the distribution of offices, the standard of the prophet was displayed in holy triumph, and proclamations were read, taking formal possession of the kingdom in the name, and by the authority, of the Great Mogul. In these proclamations, the high attributes of the sovereign were announced with all the pomp of oriental imagery and diction; and they were enriched by a splendid recital of the blessings which it had pleased a gracious Providence to shower down upon this favoured land. But mark the sequel. The cunning of the Assamees, a quality, which no less frequently than eminently distinguishes the feeblest of all creatures, impelled them to seek refuge at first in inaccessible mountains and wilds, till the season of the rains began; they then poured down in multitudes from their haunts, hovered around the imperial army, circumscribed their range, and soon reduced them to extreme distress both for forage and provisions: thus harassed and fatigued, as well by perpetual alarms, as by the inclemency of the weather, the effect of noxious exhalations from a low and humid soil was soon added to complete their ills. The robust Mogul, accustomed to a climate in all respects so opposite, now felt the poison creep irresistibly through his palsied frame; sickness made alarming strides, and every day reduced the strongest to a level with the weak. The necessity of a retreat became too obvious to admit of hesitation. Already the flower of the Afghans, the Persians, and Moguls, were cut off; the rest, entangled in gloomy forests, and hemmed in by impracticable morasses, had no way to escape but by a perilous passage over long and narrow causeways. In a hasty flight, bewildered and pressed on all sides, numbers fell into the snare that had been so long preparing; few indeed reached the banks of the Berhampooter; and still fewer lived to cross its wide and rapid stream, and relate the miserable fate of their fellow soldiers.

Thus ended an expedition which has seldom been paralleled in the pompous and expensive style of its preparations, or the injustice of its object. If it be the aim of conquest to disturb and plunder a remote and inoffensive people, content with a region hardly suited to human habitation, but which indeed a beneficent Creator has planted with inhabitants adapted to its nature, such is the fate it justly deserves. Yet the fanatical zeal of the Mussulman historian, who can acknowledge no virtue, when opposed to the followers of the faith, unmercifully loads these poor persecuted beings, on account of their providential escape from the chains that had been forged for them, with the epithets of Kaufir, Booht, Shitan; *Infidels*, *Hobgoblins*, and *Devils*.

BOOTAN.

CHAPTER II.

Chichacotta—Frontier of Bootan.—Approach to Buxadewar—noxious Quality of the Atmosphere beneath this Range of Mountains—its Effects on the Inhabitants—fatal to Captain Jones and great Part of the Troops that served under him—Colonel Sir John Cuming another Instance of its injurious Consequence.—Tangun Horse, a Species peculiar to these Mountains.—Ascent and Entry into Buxadewar.—Chong, and Arra, the Spirit prepared from it.—Character of the People.—Visit the Soobah—Impediment to our Advance—Curiosity, and Urbanity of the Soobah—invited to accompany him during the Performance of a religious Ceremony—Description of the Ceremony—its Design.—Beautiful Scenery in the Vicinity of Buxadewar.—Skilful Archers.—Commencement of the rainy Season.—Dispatches from the Daeb Raja.—Prepare to proceed.—Poorungheer.—Short Stricture on the Manner and Character of the Soobah.—View of Buxadewar—Etymology of its Title.—Mode of travelling in Bootan.

AT three in the afternoon we came to Chichacotta, and met with the Zeenkaubs, who conducted us to a habitation situated in the centre of a large square, formed by a strong embankment, with a double row of bamboos; and this they termed a fort. The house was totally of a different construction from any in Bengal. The first apartment, to which the ascent was by a wooden ladder, was elevated about eight feet from the ground, and supported on forked props. Bamboos, resting on the forks, served as beams: the floor of one room was formed by mats of split bamboo, that of the other by pieces of plank from three to six feet long, and one, or one and a half broad, hewn by the axe, and laid on beams of fir. A prop rose from the centre of the ground floor, to the roof, which was of thatch; and the sides of the room were encompassed by split bamboos, interwoven lattice-wise, so as to leave interstices for the admission of light and air: the apartments were divided by reeds placed upright, confined at top between two flat pieces of bamboo, and resting at bottom in a groove. There was no iron whatever in the whole fabric: the thatch was very low, and it projected considerably beyond the walls, so that the rooms were equally defended from the rain and sun.

Chichacotta is famous, as having been an object of contest between the first detachment of our troops, and the people of Bootan, in the war carried on upon their frontier in the year 1772. As a fortification, it was then, what it is at this day, a large oblong square, encompassed by a high bank, and thick stockade. The Booteeas defended it with obstinacy, and a battle was fought in its vicinity, in which they displayed much personal courage, though it was impossible they could long contend against the superior advantage of firelocks and cannon, over matchlocks, the sabre, and the bow. But though compelled to give way, they made Chichacotta, for a considerable time after, a post of danger and alarm, which we were alternately obliged to possess and relinquish, till they were finally driven back, and pursued beyond Buxadewar. It was restored at the close of the war, and now constitutes the Bootan frontier.

We were conducted by the Zeenkaubs from Chichacotta. The first part of the road was bad, until we came upon a raised causeway, having on either side, high grass, which abounded with tigers and wild buffaloes. Continuing our course through this dreary country, for more than eight miles, we entered a wood of large and lofty trees, in which, we were told, there were elephants, rhinoceroses, and bears without number, though we saw none of these animals.

The country was still flat, until we reached the foot of the Buxadewar hill. Here we found the ascent at first easy, and conveniently accessible to a palanquin half way up the hill, as far as Santarabarry, a place equally famed for its extensive orange groves, and the excellence of their fruit. Here the road became more steep, narrow, and rugged, being perpetually intersected by large masses of coarse marble. The prospects, between abrupt and lofty prominences, were inconceivably grand: hills, clothed to their very summits with trees, dark and deep glens, and the tops of the highest mountains, lost in the clouds, constituted altogether a scene of extraordinary magnificence, and sublimity. As the road winds round the hills, it sometimes becomes a narrow ledge, hanging over depths which no eye can reach; and were not the horror of the scene, in some degree softened by the trees, and climbing plants, which line the precipices, the passenger would find it impossible to advance. Proceeding, however, with hesitation and difficulty, over this tremendous path, we arrived at a small hut, inhabited by a poor but hospitable cripple, who refreshed us, as well as he could, with tea, and with a kind of *whisky;* a treat which we afterwards frequently experienced. In the mean time, a messenger sent by the Soobah arrived, with orders to the officer in charge of the pass, to give admittance to our party. I looked about for this important personage, and was surprised to find him at my elbow; a creature that hardly bore the resemblance of humanity; of disgusting features, meagre limbs, and diminutive stature, with a dirty cloth thrown over his shoulders. He was of a mixed race, between the Booteea and the Bengalee; and it was wonderful to observe how greatly the influence of a pestilential climate, had caused him to degenerate from both. At the foot of the Bootan mountains, a plain extends for about thirty miles in breadth, choked, rather than clothed, with the most luxuriant vegetation. The exhalations necessarily arising from the multitude of springs, which the vicinity of the mountains produces, are collected and confined by these almost impervious woods, and generate an atmosphere, through which no traveller ever passed with impunity. Its effects were fatal to Captain Jones, and to a great part of the troops that served under him, in 1772; and Colonel Sir John Cuming[a], one of the few that escaped with life, still feels its injurious consequences. Yet even this spot is not without inhabitants, although its influence hath wholly debased in them, the form, the size, and the strength of human creatures.

The Soobah's messenger was soon followed by a led Tangun horse, which came neighing and prancing with such impetuosity, that I ex-

[a] Colonel Sir John Cuming is since dead.

pected he would have engaged the Zeenkaub's more pacific animal, as he was patiently labouring up the hill, and by his discomfiture, put us all completely to the rout. This species, which is indigenous to Bootan, has its title from the region in which they are bred; being called Tangun, vulgarly Tannian, from Tangustân, the general appellation of that assemblage of mountains, which constitutes the territory of Bootan. The breed is altogether confined within these limits, being found in none of the neighbouring countries; neither in Assam, Nipal, Tibet, nor Bengal. I am inclined to consider it as an original and distinct species: they are distinguished in colour by a general tendency to piebald; those of one colour are rare, and not so valuable in the opinion of the Booteea, but they are more esteemed by the English, and bear a higher price than the party-coloured, which are composed of the various shades of black, bay, and sorrel, upon a ground of the purest white. They are usually about thirteen hands in height, and are remarkable for their symmetry and just proportions; uniting, in an eminent degree, both strength and beauty. They are short bodied, clean limbed, and, though deep in the chest, yet extremely active. From this conformation they derive such a superiority in strength of muscle, when condensed by the repeated effort of struggling against acclivities, as can never be attained by a horse of a thin and light shoulder. It is surprising to observe the energy and vigour apparent in the movements of a Tangun. Accustomed to struggle against opposition, they seem to inherit this spirit as a principle of their nature; and hence they have acquired a character, among Europeans, of being headstrong and ungovernable; though, in reality, it proceeds from an excess of eagerness to perform their task.

Indeed, some of those that come into our hands aged, have acquired habits of resistance, which it is rather difficult to modify or reform. These are chiefly to be attributed to the strong hand with which they are governed: I have seen a Tangun horse tremble in every joint, when the groom has seized both reins of a severe bit, and compressed his jaws, as it were, in a vice. Under the strongest impression of fear, they execute their labour with an energy unsubdued even by fatigue; and their willingness to work, added to their comparatively small value, has drawn upon them a heavy share of the hardest services in Bengal, equal with that of the tallest and most powerful horses in India, both for the road and draught; yet, in the heaviest carriages, they are never seen to flinch, but often betray an impatience, and start forward with a spring, that sometimes surprises their driver. If they happen to have been unskilfully treated, they will not unfrequently bear against the bit with a force which seems to increase with every effort to restrain them. Sometimes, with less apparent cause on their side, they lean against each other, as though it were a struggle, which of them should push his companion down; at other times, they lean with so great an inclination from the pole, that a person unacquainted with them, would apprehend every instant, that they must either fall, or the traces break. These are habits, indeed, which it requires the greatest patience to endure, and a long course of mild and good usage to subdue. By such means it is practicable to govern them; but to a person not endued with a very even temper, I would by no means recommend the contest; for, after all, strong and hardy as Tanguns are, they are less able to bear the heat of an Indian sun than any other breed, and they often fall victims to it, when hard driven in very hot weather.

We were now within half a mile of Buxadewar. Here, at the foot of the last ascent, we were met by a herald who preceded our party, sounding a trumpet; and when we came near the summit, we were joined by five mountain nymphs, with jetty flowing tresses, who escorted us with strains of gratulation, as I conceived, into Buxadewar, twenty miles from Chichacotta.

The day was far spent; it was past three o'clock, and we remained under the shade of a tree, until a house was made ready for our reception. After waiting some time in the open air, we were conducted into a wretched habitation, which impressed us with very unfavourable ideas of the attention of our new hosts, either to cleanliness or convenience. All the Zeenkaubs, and officers in public stations, came to see us, each presenting a white pelong handkerchief, and offering copious draughts of tea, and a spirit extracted from rice, or wheat, by them called *Chong*, but to which, as a more familiar appellation, we gave the name of whisky.

Chong is a slightly acid and spirituous liquor, extemperaneously prepared by the infusion of a mass of grain in a state of fermentation. Wheat, rice, barley, and other kinds of grain, are indiscriminately made use of for the purpose. The process employed in the preparation, as well as I could learn, is as follows: to a given quantity of grain is added rather more water than will completely cover it, and the mixture is placed over a slow fire till it begins to boil; it is then taken up, and the water drained from the grain, which is spread abroad upon mats, or coarse cloths, to cool. When it is cold, a ball of the composition, here termed Bakka, (which is the blossom of the Cacalia Saracenica Linnæi, collected and rolled together in small balls), is crumbled, and strewed over the grain, and both are well mixed together. The usual proportion is a ball, the size of a nutmeg, to two pounds of grain. The grain thus prepared is put into baskets lined with leaves, and pressed down with the hand slightly, to draw off the superfluous moisture. It is then covered with leaves and cloths, to defend it from the external air, and put in a place of moderate warmth, where it is suffered to stand three days. It is afterwards deposited in dry earthen jars; a little cold water is sprinkled upon the top, in the proportion of about a tea-cup full to a gallon of grain; the vessel is then covered close, and the cap fortified with some strong compost, or stiff clay. It remains thus at least ten days, before it is fit for use; and, if it be suffered to continue longer, it always improves from age.

To make the Chong, when required, they put a quantity of the fermented mass into some capacious vessel, pouring boiling water upon it, sufficient completely to cover it, and stirring the whole well together. A short time is sufficient for it to digest; a small wicker basket is then thrust down in the centre, and the infusion, called Chong, immediately drains through, and occupies the vacant space. This liquor is with equal expedition distributed to the expecting guests, the segment of a gourd, fastened upon a staff, serving the purpose of a ladle. Each person holds a shallow wooden cup upon the points of his fingers, for its reception, and is seldom satisfied with one supply.

A short experience proved to me that this was a most grateful beverage, being slightly acid, and possessing no powerful spirit. It was the custom, in these regions, to drink this liquor warm; a practice at the same time safe and agreeable, and which might be recommended to universal imitation, wherever fatigue and heat induce intemperate thirst.

From Chong an ardent spirit is obtained by distillation, here termed Arra, which is fiery, and powerfully inebriating.

APPARATUS used for the distillation of ARRA, from the liquor termed CHONG.

A. An earthen vessel, in which the prepared Chong is placed immediately over the fire.

B. Another without a bottom.

C. A smaller earthen vessel, which is the recipient.

D. An iron bason filled with cold water, renewed occasionally as it grows warm, may be termed the condenser.

eee Three cross staves of wood on which the recipient is placed.

The junction of the three vessels A, B, and D, being secured with cotton bandages and clay lute; a fire is lighted under A, which contains the Chong. The spirit arises through B, is condensed upon the convex bottom of the bason D, and the spirit Arra is received into the smaller vessel C.

f The fire-place. *gggg* Openings over the fire for the reception of a similar apparatus.

In the afternoon our tent came up, a party of Booteeas having been sent to bring it over the steep and difficult part of the way. The elephant followed soon after, much to our astonishment, for the road seemed in some places too narrow even for the safe passage of a horse. Our tents were at length pitched, but with great difficulty; for there was scarcely soil enough upon the rock to admit the pins. They afforded a subject of admiration to the crowds of Booteeas that were continually assembling to gaze at us.

A strong similarity of feature runs through the whole race. They are much fairer and more robust than their neighbours, the Bengalees, with broader faces and higher cheek-bones. So wide a difference indeed is evident between these individuals of the human species, that were a stranger to both, desired to give an opinion of them, when placed together, he would not hesitate to pronounce them natives of regions the remotest from each other, and could never suppose that they belonged to a contiguous soil.

In the evening we made a visit to the Soobah[b] of Buxadewar, who advanced to the entrance of his apartment to receive us; when, in conformity to the custom of Bootan, I presented a white pelong handkerchief: he gave me one in return, and shook hands as the exchange was made. We advanced, and took our seats: his was placed in the corner of the room, close under a window: here he sat opposite to us, on a scarlet cloth, having a square piece of tiger's skin in the centre, spread upon a stage of wood, which was elevated about a foot from the floor. On his right hand was a silver vessel, containing a fire of

[b] Provincial Governor.

aromatic woods; and on another vessel were burning, three long tapers, of some perfumed composition, about the size of a reed. The room was decorated with pictures of their deities; and in a recess, in the further part of the room, were placed some idols, with lamps of oil burning before them, the bone of a human skull lying immediately in front, and flowers, fruit, and grain, scattered between. Our visit being merely ceremonious, it will be uninteresting to repeat what passed, as it consisted of little more than compliments and enquiries concerning the health of our respective masters. Our stay was short; we walked away without ceremony, and descended by a ladder to the ground. This habitation is erected on props, like that at Chichacotta: it exhibited no greater efforts of art, though something more of labour had been bestowed upon it. The lower part was enclosed on all sides, and served as a magazine for merchandize and lumber. I am at a loss to account for the use, or convenience, of this method of building in so hilly a country. In a low and marshy soil, the advantages of artificial elevation are obvious; but where there is little danger from noxious reptiles, or sudden torrents, I can suggest no reasonable motive for such a singularity.

I received notice on Tuesday the 13th of May, that the Soobah intended me a visit in the evening, to settle the plan for forwarding our journey, and transporting our baggage; but I was told, that he thought it necessary to wait for answers to the letters written to the Daeb Raja, notifying our arrival at Buxadewar, before we could be permitted to proceed. He came after dinner, with his attendants, to my tent. The Zeenkaub sent by the Daeb Raja to escort us, was with him, as well as those two who had accompanied me from Rungpore. We had much conversation respecting our journey to the capital: great objections were started, on account of the thin population of the frontier, and the consequent difficulty of carriage, as every thing must be conveyed on men's backs; the steepness of the mountains, and badness of the roads, not admitting the use of beasts of burden. The Soobah professed himself desirous of affording every supply in his power, but seemed to hint, that it would be necessary to procure assistance from the capital, for the conveyance of our baggage.

These impediments vexed me much, and I could not help expressing my disappointment at finding that no preparations had been made for my journey, after I had already passed so much time at Rungpore; especially as I had conveyed intimation of my approach to the Daeb, and received his answer to my letters, with information that every thing should be ready. Much violent altercation then followed between the Zeenkaubs and the Soobah. I did not exactly know the purport of it, but I suspected the latter to be in some measure to blame. It ended, however, in a declaration to me, that, as they were servants of the Daeb, they were equally servants of the English, and would exert all their powers to serve us. It was at length agreed that they should send to the adjacent villages, and assemble together all the people that could be found. The Soobah assured me, that if he could not send all my things with me, he would forward, after my departure, and with the utmost dispatch, such as should be left behind.

About noon on the following day the Soobah came down to our tents. I had given him a telescope, and I shewed him how to adjust the focus; an operation which he quickly comprehended, and readily lengthened or shortened the tube until it suited his sight. He looked through his glass, at a frontispiece to one of the numbers of Bell's British Theatre, Miss Young in the character of Artemisia, and exclaimed with amazement, " How small about the waist, and what a vast circumference below!" The impression was natural; and in general, the observations that he made indicated a shrewdness of apprehension, and much sound judgment. Mr. Davis had taken a view of Buxadewar, which was laying on the table: the Soobah was instantly struck with it, and recognized all the different parts of his habitation; the beams, the stairs, the people looking out at the windows, and even the packages that lay beneath. He staid with us till the servants came to prepare for dinner.

I invited him to dine, to which he readily agreed. At table he ate and drank as we did, without scruple; yet I suspect his urbanity might incline him to suppress expressions of dislike, and to do some violence to his taste; for beer and claret could hardly be agreeable to a palate, unaccustomed to such liquors; he drank of them, however, as well as of Madeira, and said he liked them much: he admired our bread, and ate of it heartily. After dinner, in the way of conversation, I mentioned that we were desirous of going to the top of an adjacent hill, towards which I pointed, and asked him if there was any road. He observed to me, that it was a consecrated place, and that he would choose by all means to accompany us. My guns were standing in a corner of the tent, and he expressed some curiosity to look at them: they were charged, and I fired one at a kite. Presently, as we walked out to a bamboo stage erected on the side of the hill, and hanging over a declivity, Mr. Davis shot a crow. Though not sanguinary in their dispositions, these were murders they could easily pardon, for both these marauders are considered as mortal enemies to the strings of raw meat, which it is their common custom to pull into shreds, and hang in the sun to dry; an effect which does not completely take place, before the meat has acquired an odour, extremely attractive to kites and crows. The Soobah proposed firing at a mark, and one was placed in the valley, at three hundred yards distance. We each shot twice, but without success; but in justice to the Soobah it must be owned, that, when he took my fowling piece, he shot more truly than either of us. When the sun was nearly down, I turned about to walk; the Soobah followed, and we went to the tent. I told him, that as I understood him to have been lately ill, I was apprehensive the walk we proposed to take, would fatigue him too much, and begged, therefore, he would not trouble himself to accompany us. His answer was equally polite and attentive; nor could we dissuade him from escorting us, and he accordingly went home to make some preparations.

I was told, that it was a custom with the Soobah to ascend this hill every month, when he sets up a white flag, and performs some religious ceremonies to conciliate the favour of a Dewta, or invisible being, the genius of the place, who is said to hover about the summit, dispensing at his will, good and evil to every thing around him. I was advised to set up a flag also; and I did not think it prudent to give offence by refusing to comply with their customs, however absurd or ridiculous. In half an hour the sound of the nowbut[c] and the trumpet

[c] A kind of kettle-drum, used only as an appendage of state by persons in authority.

announced the Soobah's return. He came surrounded with a numerous crowd, clad in various coloured habits, and we walked together to the bottom of the stone slope, opposite to his house, where we mounted our horses. When the party was arranged in regular order, the cavalcade was by no means contemptible. In front were carried, on bamboo poles, five white flags; two staves immediately followed, on which were fastened shreds of silk of various colours, blue, red, yellow, and white, in alternate rows from the top to a foot and a half downward: the bearers kept constantly twirling these in their hands. Seven young girls with loose hair went next, chanting, in a sort of religious tone, as we advanced: they were led with a slow and solemn pace by the Lama, or chief priest, in a deep crowned cap of clotted wool, and a scarlet vest, riding on a Tangun horse. Two Zeenkaubs followed, and immediately after came the Soobah, dressed in a vest of blue satin, with gold embroidery, and a garnet-coloured shawl, one end of which passing under his right arm, was thrown negligently with the other over the left shoulder. The crown of his hat was shaped after the European fashion, and the brims were three or four inches broad. The top of the hat was decorated with a crest of yellow metal, which in shape bore some resemblance to a leaf. After him rode two priests, with caps similar to those of the Lama: I followed next, with Mr. Saunders, and a number of attendants: Mr. Davis was lame, and could not go.

The road was very steep and narrow, and our horses were frequently obliged to halt to recover their wind, as well as to relax the tone of their muscles; for it was with the greatest exertion that they scrambled up. When we gained the summit, the girls, who had preceded us, were drawn up in a row, and sung to us after their manner, as we passed them, marking the time by a slow movement of the hands and feet, which I considered as a solemn dance, in strict unison with the monotony of their music. The whole variety of their motions consisted in alternately resting on each foot, as they advanced one before the other; their hands being raised about as high as the shoulder, and placed a little before them, were perpetually turned with a circular kind of motion that reversed their backs and palms. On the top of the hill, we found a small level spot, which situation seems to be always preferred for the scene of their devotions. Here, against a large tree, was placed a kind of altar, elevated about three feet from the ground: the back and two narrow sides were covered with yellow silk, and on the back hung four handkerchiefs, red, blue, yellow, and white; a white handkerchief, fastened on one side, was suspended in front, and falling in an easy festoon near the top, was sustained by another on the opposite side. There were three lamps burning upon the altar, with flowers and fruits in plates. Before the altar were six persons, arranged in a row, and in the following order: on the left of the whole stood the Lama; next a priest, who beat on a large tabor, with a long curved iron instead of a stick; a priest with cymbals; a priest with a tabor; and a priest blowing an instrument made of the shin bone of a man: on the right hand side stood two trumpeters.

We were presented with a lighted rod of the perfumed composition, which we held in our hands. A cup full of rice was brought to us, with one of the lighted rods stuck upright in it: we touched the rice, as did the Soobah also, and it was then placed upon the altar. The Soobah stood on the left side of the altar; we were opposite to him, on a rising ground. The ceremony began with the chanting of the priests; the tabors, trumpets, and cymbals, all sounding: this was continued with short intermissions, and but little variation, for ten minutes, when the instruments ceased, and some prayers were repeated in a deep and hollow tone: a short silence afterwards ensued. The Soobah tied a white cloth before his face, covering his mouth and nostrils, and a vessel of water was brought to him, in which he washed his hands. A white pelong handkerchief was then presented, one end of which we held as we approached the altar, a priest holding the other: we released it, and it was waved over the smoke of the lighted rods. The prayers continued; some rice was scattered about by the priests, and the pelong handkerchief was then fastened on a staff. The Soobah had now come over to the side on which we stood: some cowry shells[d] intermixed with rice were brought; the flags were all fixed, and the consecrated rice and fruits, that stood upon the altar, were thrown down, and eagerly gathered up by the poorer spectators. The Soobah had a quantity of the rice and shells, some of which was given to us; and we, following his example, every now and then scattered it about, while the performers were chanting and sounding their instruments. When the whole was distributed, the priest stopped and drank tea: a plate of Jack[e] fruit was brought to the Soobah, which he touched and tasted; we did the same, and then the whole was divided among the priests and performers: the girls

[d] Porcellana, *Linnæi*, found among the Nicobar Islands in the Bay of Bengal, and current in Hindostan and Bengal as money.

[e] Jack fruit, Artocarpus integrifolia. *Linn.* Kuttul, *Ind.*

now advanced, dancing, and the ceremony was ended with loud acclamations.

We turned and descended the hill on foot (as the declivity was too steep for us to ride), in the midst of loud shrieks and shouts. We found, on our return, a large mat spread before the Soobah's house, with a bench placed in the middle of it; and we went and stood upon the mat, while the priests chanted some prayers. A paper, containing shells and rice, was put into the Soobah's hand, some of which he gave me, and we scattered them about: the cowries were quickly collected by the girls. A large vessel of liquor was before us: a ladle full of it was brought to the Soobah: he touched it; I did the same; and it was afterwards distributed among the people. We then adjourned to the Soobah's apartment, drank tea and liquors, and were presented with fruits and provisions.

The Soobah told me, that this religious ceremony had been performed because we were just arrived in Bootan; and it was proper to invoke their deity to grant us protection, and a prosperous journey through their country, that we might return in safety to our own. This was a duty, he said, which they owed to the English Company, and the Daeb would be pleased to know that it had been performed. They were happy, he added, that we had joined in this act of devotion; and it was his wish that on our return we might revisit this abode, and again perform together the same ceremonies. We then took leave, and retired to our tents.

In the evening of the ensuing day the Soobah came to visit us, and I amused him by explaining the different games at which we played;

F

chess, cards, and backgammon. He introduced a paper divided into squares, and played upon it with one of his people at a game apparently not very intricate. He then produced another paper, with a number of variously coloured circles filled with writing; but the design of this, was not clear. Before he left us, I mentioned to him my great anxiety to proceed on my journey, and my disappointment at being subjected to so much delay; I urged also my apprehensions that we should experience much difficulty and inconvenience from the approaching rains. He said a great deal, to justify himself from the suspicion of wilfully detaining us: he said that the Daeb would be highly displeased with him, if he did not obey my commands, and do every thing in his power to accommodate us; that in the mountains near Buxadewar there were but few villages, and those utterly unable to furnish the number of people I required; he added, that the inhabitants in the valley on the Bengal side were unable to carry burdens, and travel up such steep ascents: in fine, he preached up patience to me; telling me he had written to the Raja on the subject, and expected his answer within four or five days.

I ascended a very steep hill on Friday the 16th of May, (for the country exhibits nothing else) the south side of which was cleared of trees for cultivation: there was a good deal of black mould upon it, sustained by the stumps of trees and projecting roots. We saw many spots of land cleared in the same manner, on the surrounding eminences; which, in general, seemed to produce thriving crops of barley and wheat, and a small grain of which they make a fermented liquor to drink. In the afternoon we penetrated into the thickest part of the woods in search of plants, and found none but such as were common in Bengal, except raspberry bushes, and a shrub in blossom with an orange-coloured flower, immediately under which grew a number of leaves perfectly white, but in form entirely similar to those on other parts of the bush, which were of a lively green. This mixture of colours produced a very singular and pleasing effect. I collected some plants, and sent them to Rungpore. Returning from our walk, I found the Soobah, with many of his attendants, and the principal inhabitants of Buxadewar, shooting with the bow and arrow at a mark, which, though small, was frequently pierced, at the distance, as I guessed, of one hundred and fifty yards: the arrows were always thrown in an horizontal direction.

The next and following day we had much rain, both in the morning and the evening; heavy showers, unattended by thunder or wind, and every appearance of the commencement of the rainy season. We paid a visit to the Soobah, who rose to receive us at the entrance of his chamber, and when we were seated, tried to entertain us by an account of the omnipotence of his gods, represented in pictures which were hanging near him: but his explanation was so blended with fable and mystery, that to me it was quite unintelligible. An enamelled snuff-box lay by him, which he gave me to look at, and, when I had it in my hand, he desired me to keep it; he presented me also with a purse, into which he put three rupees; for I found it the custom of the people here never to give away an empty purse. After some trivial conversation, we took with him one cup of tea, and another of spirit; and, on taking our leave, we were presented, as usual, with trays of fruit.

I received a letter on Monday the 19th of May, from the Daeb, to signify his having given particular injunctions to all his officers, at the different stations, that they should exert their utmost efforts to forward me with all possible convenience and dispatch; intimating at the same time that I must expect much difficulty and hardship from the badness of the road, which I might also learn from Poorungheer[f].

As the Daeb Raja had sent no people for our accommodation, the Soobah proposed the expedient of dispatching thirty men, with part of our baggage, the same day, to Murichom; upon their return, he promised to be able to provide for our immediate departure, and I very eagerly accepted his proposal.

The Soobah dined with us, and partook very heartily of our meal. He drank but little, although he seemed to relish our wine; but I understood that his countrymen considered him as particularly abstemious. His inclination seemed principally directed to trials of skill. After dinner he invited us to fire at a mark; and as both himself and his people seemed to have been much practised in this diversion, our

[f] A Hindoo Gosein, a kind of religious hermit, or pilgrim, who formerly accompanied Mr. Bogle to Tibet, and who now attended me on my journey.

Motives of religious duty, which, among the order of Goseins more especially, attaches peculiar respect to every kind and degree of penance, having occasionally led Poorungheer among the different tribes of Tartars, he had acquired, during his residence amongst them, a very competent knowledge of their manners, and of their language, which he spoke with apparent ease; and by the exemplary regularity of conduct he had uniformly preserved in his intercourse with the inhabitants of these regions, I found that he had strongly recommended himself to their notice, and obtained the favour of all their chiefs.

Pl. I

Lieut. S. Davis del. James Basire sc.

Buxadewar.

Published March 25th 1800, by G. & W. Nicol, Pall Mall.

acceptance of the challenge, turned out more to the credit of our politeness, than to our exhibition of any superior dexterity.

Great part both of the preceding and the present day was employed in receiving the visits of the inhabitants of Buxadewar, who came to take leave previously to my departure, which I had fixed for the next day.

Early on the morning of Thursday, the 22d of May, we went to pay our last visit to the Soobah. The interview was employed in apologies for our detention, on his part, and in acknowledgments for our polite and attentive reception, on mine. After several compliments, we took a cup of tea, and the usual spirituous liquors; and he conducted me to the bottom of the stairs, where he presented me with a white pelong handkerchief: we then shook hands, and parted.

The Soobah was about thirty years of age, of a middling stature, his person good, neither meagre nor corpulent; his complexion clear, and not quite of so deep a hue as that of most of his countrymen, though they are all much less swarthy than the natives of Bengal. His countenance was open and ingenuous; and if any opinion of the internal character may be formed, from the general outline and gesture of the person, I should judge him to possess an artless and benevolent mind. Easy in his manners, and graceful in his deportment, his orders were delivered in the mildest tone of voice, totally exempt from every dictatorial air of authority.

Buxadewar[g], called also Passaka, is a place of great natural strength; and, being a frontier station of these mountains, has been rendered

[g] Plate I.

still stronger by the aid of art, which has been most ingeniously employed to strike off the summit of the hill, and to level an extensive space, capable of affording accommodation to a body of men, sufficiently numerous for the defence of this difficult pass, against all assault. A range of temporary sheds, thrown back to some distance from the edge of the eminence, are designed to shelter a garrison that may be stationed to defend it. A deep ravine divides this from the opposite hill, which is steep, and has a narrow road formed on its side, not capable of admitting the passage of two persons abreast. It winds in a semicircular form, round the jutting eminence immediately opposed to it, which stands high above, and within reach of their common arms, the bow and arrow, for a great distance; till the road is at length connected with, and leads to, Buxadewar, by a very steep ascent. Such is the nature of this pass, which, however it may have been strengthened and improved by art, does real honour to the judgment of those who originally selected it as a post of defence.

The village (for it deserves no better name) consists of ten or twelve houses, invisible till the very moment of approach; it is placed upon a second table of levelled rock, which has little soil upon it, yet is covered with verdure, in consequence of its very sheltered situation, being surrounded on three sides by lofty mountains, and open only to the south, which affords a narrow prospect of Bengal. Buxadewar, as it is termed by the people in the low lands, derives its name from a very whimsical circumstance. It was formerly a custom with the Bootan horse-dealers, before they quitted this pass of the mountains, and descended with their caravan into the low lands, to cut off the tails of their Tangun horses almost close to the rump, which greatly disfigured their appearance, and depreciated their value. When the English established a fixed station at Rungpore (the mart of Bootan commerce), disgusted at this cruel treatment, they interested themselves with the dealers to obtain a discontinuance of the practice, offering *buckshish*, that is a liberal reward, if they would permit the poor animals, to keep their tails. They listened with extreme unwillingness to a proposal that militated against immemorial usage, for which, however, they had no better argument to advance, than the truly Asiatic plea, against all sorts of innovation; " it was the *dustoor*," or custom; but the love of money being superior to the force of prejudice, at the ensuing season, some of the horses made their appearance at the fair, unmutilated. These found so quick a sale, and gained so high a price, that the same dealers were induced the following year, to repeat the experiment, and with similar success. They who were anxious for a good market, soon found it their interest to follow the example; and thus at length that cruel custom was totally abolished, which deprived a noble animal of a member no less useful than ornamental; and ever since that time Tangun horses have been permitted to descend by this pass, without the loss of their tails. Hence it was stiled Buxa-dewar, *the bounteous pass*, and the commandant of the post, *Buxa Soobah;* but otherwise, in the Bootan language, it is named Passaka, and Passa Gçatong. Thus I take my leave of etymologies.

Our first care in the morning was to dispatch our camp equipage and palanquins to Rungpore, being obliged to become dependent for our future accommodation, upon such lodging as the villages might afford, and to make up our minds to the prosecution of our journey either on foot or horseback, as the nature of the rugged country before us should admit.

CHAPTER III.

Leave Buxadewar.—Ascend Peachukom Mountain—its prodigious Altitude.—Caution of the Booteeas.—Gigantic Creepers.—Bamboos, a peculiar Species.—Sheenshilla.—Pheadinchim.—Fatal Accident.—Gygoogoo.—Post of Communication.—Tehintchieu, Hatchieu, Patchieu Rivers.—Snow upon the Summits of the Mountains.—Tangun Horses, their surprising Energy.—Pipes conducting Water for the Accommodation of Travellers.—Bridge and Cataract.—Sheenshilla.—Approach to Murichom—laborious Employment of the People, in which the female Sex bear a heavy Share—extensive Use of the Bamboo.—Village of Murichom—Advantage of Situation—Fertility of the adjacent Lands.—Teezpaut, a Species of Cinnamon.—Remarkable Instance of great Age.—Pestiferous Fly.—Tetim.—Terrible Disaster.—Baboosoo and Merifaka Mountains.—Peanjoo.—Minzapeezo, a most copious Waterfall.—Ingenious Method of constructing Roads along the Sides of Precipices.—Awful Scenery.—Dewta Tehuptehup.—Peculiar Way of passing deep Ravines.—Chain Bridge of Chuka—Castle of Chuka.—Change in the Face of the Country—Temperature of the Weather—natural Productions.—Punugga.—Hatchieu.—Kepta.—Lomeela Mountain.—Selo-cha-zum.—Durbee Castle.—Mudwallahs for the Defence of Hill Fortresses.—Pauga.—

Tehintchieu Patchieu.—Noomnoo.—Poës.—Wangoka.—Symtoka.—Bridge over the Tehintchieu.—Valley of Tassisudon.

IT was seven o'clock when we left Buxadewar; our way led across the Peachukom mountain, and it was nine before we reached its summit, by a steep and rocky road, some parts of which consisted entirely of stairs of stone. We found here a small hut, which seemed intended as a resting place for travellers, and we availed ourselves of the convenience, to look back on the difficulties we had passed, in the hope of enjoying an uninterrupted prospect of the low country of Bengal. The sun shone, and the atmosphere was clear, but from the excessive height of the mountain we could see only a short distance beyond the woods, that extended from its base, for more than ten miles upon the low lands. The woods are intersected by the channels of many streams, which in the season of the rains, become considerable rivers, and greatly contribute to the magnitude of the Berhampooter.

Every object beyond the wood appeared indistinct, and the horizon was lost in haze. In a few minutes our prospect was entirely changed; clouds came gliding towards us, and every object was enveloped in a thick mist. The air became very chill; a thermometer, carried in the pocket, at the foot of the mountain stood at 80°, on the top at 74°, but in the shade it fell in ten minutes to 65°.

While resting on this elevated station, we were cautioned by the Booteeas to preserve the profoundest silence, and to beware of the danger of disturbing the elements, by any sound louder than a whisper.

We were seriously assured that the concussion of the air, occasioned by loud conversation, would inevitably bring down on us, torrents of rain. We escaped the danger: but we had not long left Peachukom, when the clouds, which we had seen collecting, broke in abundant showers. Thus we obtained credit for attention to the advice of our guides; nor were their precautions lost upon us, as they taught us to avoid wasting too much time on so commanding a spot, which, from its superior elevation, stands in the way, to intercept much of the vapour exhaled from the extensive waste, that lies spread far and wide beneath its base.

We next ascended the Oomkoo, a mountain higher than the former, covered to its summit with trees, all clothed with moss, and with creepers intertwined amongst them, of surprising length and thickness, and not less remarkable for their flexibility and strength; qualities which render them an excellent substitute for rope, the use of which indeed they entirely supersede[a]

The mountain is composed in some places of clay; but for the most part it consists of a flinty stone, striated with talc, and intermixed with marble. It produces a great quantity of bamboo, which is very hollow, and smaller than that of Bengal, having its knots at a greater

[a] In the forests of America are found a sort of ozier, or withs, called by the Spaniards, Bejucose; by the French, Lianes; by the Indians, Nibbees; which are usually employed as ropes in America. This plant twists about the trees it meets with, and rising above their highest branches, its tendrils descend perpendicularly, strike into the ground, take root, rise up around another, and thus mount and descend alternately. Other tendrils are carried obliquely by the wind, or some other accident, and form a confused and interwoven cordage, which resembles the rigging of a ship.—Bancroft's Nat. Hist. of Guiana, p. 99.

distance from each other, and growing to full maturity in one season. Its leaves are very large, and are gathered as food for their horses, instead of grass: clusters of plantain trees were not uncommon. Descending on the other side, we came to a sacred spot called Sheenshilla, dedicated to a deity of the same name. In compliance with the earnest advice of my guide, I threw down a rupee here, by way of purchasing a prosperous journey. After passing this spot, we travelled along the sides of Pheadinchim, a perpendicular rock, the road being only about two feet broad, formed entirely of large loose stones, and projecting over a deep precipice below, which is twice the height of the tallest trees; above, large masses of impending rock, frown horribly on the passenger, and threaten every moment to overwhelm him. It is an awful situation: and were the rock stript of the trees and vegetables with which it is covered, the boldest adventurer would be filled with terror and dismay. My head almost turned round. In this place was lost the fine Arabian horse sent by the Governor General as a present for the Daeb Raja. He started at the overhanging rock; and falling from the road, was dashed to pieces at the bottom of the precipice.

About two o'clock we came to our quarters at Gygoogoo, a village situated on the declivity of a hill, twelve miles from Buxadewar, consisting of five or six houses supported on bamboo props; the joists, the beams, the matted walls, the connecting bands, and every part of the fabric, being made of bamboo, except the covering of the roof, which was composed of plantain[b] leaves doubled. We were welcomed by the principal inhabitants, an old man, his daughter, and another

[b] Musa.

female, who each presented us with what their little stock afforded, vegetables, eggs, and poultry, and the usual offering of a pelong handkerchief, tea, and whisky. These people are stationed here by the Daeb Raja, for the purpose of preserving a quick and free communication with his possessions on the borders of Bengal, and of conveying with expedition, letters and parcels to and from the capital. They cultivate a small parcel of ground, which furnishes grain for their subsistence. Their herds of cows and swine, seek their own food in the spontaneous produce of the woods. Here we found two large peach trees, some lime and orange trees, and raspberry bushes.

We heard the loud and hoarse murmurs of the Tehintchieu, rolling in a deep channel at the foot of the mountain. This river runs by Tassisudon, and being swelled by the united streams of the Hatchieu, which passes near a place of the same name, and by the Patchieu, which takes its course near Paro, finds a passage between the mountains, from whence it is precipitated in tremendous cataracts, and rushing with rapidity between the high cliffs and vast stones that oppose its progress, descends at length into the valley, a few miles east of Buxadewar, and finally joins the Berhampooter. I ascended a lofty eminence to look for the river, but it was too deeply buried in the obscurity of the cliff.

The farthest visible mountains to the northward, which I conjecture to be at the distance of twenty miles, were covered with snow. We saw one also at half that distance, with some remains of snow upon it.

Quitting Gygoogoo at six o'clock on Friday the 23d of May, we proceeded on our journey to Murichom, reckoned to be distant about thirteen miles, by a rough and rocky road, the ascents and descents of which, in general, were too sudden to admit of a regular slope; but the Tangun horses are accustomed to stone steps, and scramble with wonderful facility over disjointed rocks, and up the steepest precipices. On these, as well as the preceding mountains, the traveller frequently finds water conducted to the road side, from distant springs through hollow bamboos, with which he will seldom fail to allay his thirst; but the Booteea generally adopts the precaution of previously straining the water, for fear of meeting with leeches, or with any other of the various kinds of insects that harbour among trees, or are generated by the putrescent vegetable matter, which covers the surface of the rock beneath their shade. Nor must I omit to mention the safer and more delicious fountain, to which the wary Booteea most commonly has recourse. This is a hollow buffalo's horn, adapted by straps to be slung across the shoulder, and of considerable capacity, which the prudent traveller takes daily care to fill with a new and fiery spirit, such as is here promiscuously extracted from any sort of grain, and called *arra*. I could never partake with them in their ardent draughts; but when I became accustomed to travelling among these mountains, I learnt to replenish my horn with *chong*, which, being slightly acid, was a grateful liquor; and when wearied with struggling against acclivities, and panting for breath, it not unfrequently gave gladness to the parched palate of many a thirsty passenger.

In the course of this day's march, we passed by a wooden bridge across a large stream, which came tumbling down, cataract over cataract, from the top of a lofty mountain. We stopped at the village of Sheenshilla to drink tea, and partake of the fruits which the inhabitants had brought out, and placed on benches by the road side, ready for our repast.

Near the bottom of this hill, water constantly drips from the overhanging rock; and in a deep recess at the foot of the mountain, a cascade, rushing from a thick wood, formed a large stream of water, over which was placed a bridge constructed of trees, whose ends rested on either side of the rock, with split pieces of timber laid across them. We sat down here awhile to rest; and the deep shade, the melody of the birds, and the murmuring of the waters, which imparted at the same time a grateful coolness to the air, inspired us with fresh spirits and vigour. All this indeed was necessary to enable us to climb up the Murichom mountain, where the road was extremely toilsome, and the ascent very steep. We attained the summit about noon, much wearied with the journey; a considerable portion of which, we had been compelled to perform on foot. These mountains are covered with very large and tall trees, similar to those which compose the forests of Bengal, with little underwood. Numbers of people were employed in bringing water from the springs below, for the use of the inhabitants of Murichom. The vessel made use of for the purpose, was a hollow bamboo, as large as could be conveniently grasped with both hands. This was filled, and carried like a club, resting against the shoulder: some took one on each; and laborious as it seemed to be, I could not but observe that girls and women were chiefly employed in this service.

I was obliged to halt on Saturday the 24th of May, from the want of carriage for our baggage, and our servants also began to require rest, after travelling over a country so difficult and rugged as that we had passed.

Murichom consists of about twenty houses, in their structure much superior to any I had yet seen in Bootan. They are built of stone, with clay as cement, of a square form, and the walls narrowing from the foundations to the top. The roof is supported clear of the walls, has a very low pitch, and is composed of fir boards placed lengthways on cross beams and joists of fir, and confined by large stones laid upon the top. The lower part of the house accommodates hogs, cows, and other animals. The family occupies the first story, to which they ascend by a ladder, composed of one half of a split fir tree; into the flat side of which, rude holes are cut at proper distances to serve as steps.

The floors are boarded and the doors double; they turn on pivots, and shut against an upright post in the middle of the doorway. The rooms are lofty, and there is commonly, on one or two sides, a projecting balcony for the admission of light and air, which affords also a pleasant place to sit in. The space between the ceiling of the upper apartment and the roof, is used for a granary or store-room, and serves for a repository of fire wood, and other lumber. The village is situated on the top of the mountain, crowned with an extensive space of level ground. This was covered with a rich verdure; and on its borders were many ancient spreading pepul[c] trees, peaches, and willows. From our windows we could behold much cultivated land, covered with different sorts of

[c] Ficus indica, *Linnæi.*

grain, rising with an easy ascent, and bounded by thick woods. Several cottages were interspersed over the corn fields. It is to be remarked, that the husbandmen here level the ground they cultivate on the sides of the hills, by cutting it in shelves, and forming beds of such a size as the slope will admit; and these beds being bordered with a low mound of earth, the water may be retained on them, or let off, at will. Having heard that there was cinnamon growing in this neighbourhood, I sent a native into the woods to search after the tree; he returned to me within half an hour, with a great quantity both of its roots and branches. Its value is well known in this country, and it is used both for culinary and medicinal purposes. Its leaves are much used in cookery in Bengal, and known by the denomination of Teezpaut. It appears to me, that the cinnamon in this species is the rind of the root only, the bark of the tree having little or no spicy flavour; but the plant being neither in blossom nor bearing fruit, it was impossible to pronounce, whether it were the true cinnamon, or that inferior kind termed cassia. The leaf, however, corresponded with the description given of the true cinnamon, by Linnæus.

We gathered strawberries and raspberries in the fields here, and found peach trees in great abundance, all laden with fruit.

I cannot quit Murichom, without taking notice of one remarkable antiquity; it was an old woman, who was almost deprived of all her strength and faculties, by age. I never beheld in a human being marks of age so strong: she sat in the sun, all day; the skin of her face was drawn into innumerable wrinkles; her arms were almost entirely devoid of flesh, the bones being covered with a skin, which by time had acquired a surprising thickness. I asked her how old she was: she told me, ninety; that this was the place of her birth, and that she had lived here, ever since.

The neighbourhood of Murichom is dreadfully infested by a small fly, differing much from the musquito, both in form and size; but it fixes itself in the same manner, and draws blood with a proboscis, whose puncture is not felt, till some time after the attack. When satiated, it flies off, leaving behind a small blister full of black contaminated blood, which enlarges, inflames, and becomes exceedingly irritating and troublesome. Most of the inhabitants are so marked by the wounds of this venomous fly, that the parts of their skins exposed to the air, are covered with scurf, and being sometimes attended with tumours, acquire a most diseased appearance: a severe tax this upon so delightful a place as Murichom, which by nature is one of the most beautiful I have seen. While we were there, though in the height of the hottest season in Bengal, we enjoyed a pleasant temperature of air.

We proceeded from Murichom, on Sunday the 25th of May, on our way to Chuka, and passed by Tetim, once a considerable village, situated on the left side of the road, upon the brow of a lofty mountain, but of which the greatest part was destroyed by a dreadful accident, not many years since. In one tempestuous night, a hurricane swept nine houses down the steep, with the people that were in them; and though much search was afterwards made, not a vestige of their inhabitants was ever seen. Three houses now remain, and their tenants, unawed by the dismal fate of their neighbours, still keep

Lieut. S Davis del. James Basire sc.

The Cascade of Minzapeezo.

Published March 18th 1800 by G&W. Nicol Pall Mall

their ground. In an hour and a half we came to the river Tehintchieu, running between the Baboosoo and Merifaka mountains; we next passed the bridge Dadookoo, which is thrown across a torrent that rushes from the thicket over an immense ridge of rock: after this we passed also the Padoochieu bridge. At nine o'clock we reached the village of Peanjoo, which is considered as half way from Murichom to Chuka, and is remarkable for nothing but that the ground about is overrun with rocks. We crossed the river Tuttee, which here joins the Tehintchieu, that rushes, foaming like the surges of a tempestuous sea, between the mountains Tuttepakoo on the right, and Taturee on the left. On the face of the opposite mountain is a water-fall, called Minzapeezo[d], which issues in a collected body, but descends from so great a perpendicular height, that before it is received in the thick shade below, it is nearly dissipated, and appears like the steam arising from boiling water.

We had now to climb on foot up a very high mountain; the road led along its side, in a serpentine and exceedingly steep direction, the ascent almost all the way being by stone steps, which in some places were sustained only by beams let into the rock, and secured with cramps of iron.

It was after much labour, and repeated halting, that we reached the summit. At every pause we beheld a different prospect, each of which, perhaps, might justly be reckoned amongst the grandest and most awful in nature. Cascades of water issuing from the bosoms of lofty mountains, clothed with noble trees, and hiding their heads in

[d] Plate II.

the clouds: abrupt precipices, deep dells, and the river dashing its waters with astonishing rapidity, over the huge stones and broken rocks below, composed the sublime and variegated picture.

Near the top of the mountain we passed through a chasm in the solid rock, of the depth of eighteen or twenty feet, just wide enough to admit a man on horseback. It was by this way, tradition tells, that the dewta Tehuptehup, in his flight from Bootan to the country of the Racusses, (whose ruler he put to death, and assumed the government himself,) took his course; and in scrambling over the rock, he left here a deep impression of his hands and feet upon the stone. My conductor, who firmly gave faith to the story, pointed out to me the vestiges.

A very curious and simple bridge, for the accommodation of single passengers, communicated between this and the opposite mountain. It consisted of two large ropes made of twisted creepers, stretched parallel to each other, and encircled with a hoop. The traveller, who wishes to cross over from hence, has only to place himself between the ropes, and sit down on the hoop, seizing one rope in each hand, by means of which he slides himself along, and crosses an abyss on which I could not look without shuddering. Custom, however, has rendered it familiar, and easy to those who are in the practice of thus passing from one mountain to the other, as it saves them, by this expedient, a laborious journey of several days.

We descended the mountain, and crossed the chain bridge called Chuka-cha-zum, stretched over the Tehintchieu river, a short distance above the castle of Chuka, which is reckoned eighteen miles from

Lieut. S. Davis del. James Basire sc.

Chuka.

Published March, 25th 1800, by G & W. Nicol, Pall Mall.

Plan Section and Elevation of the Bridge of Chains at Chuka.

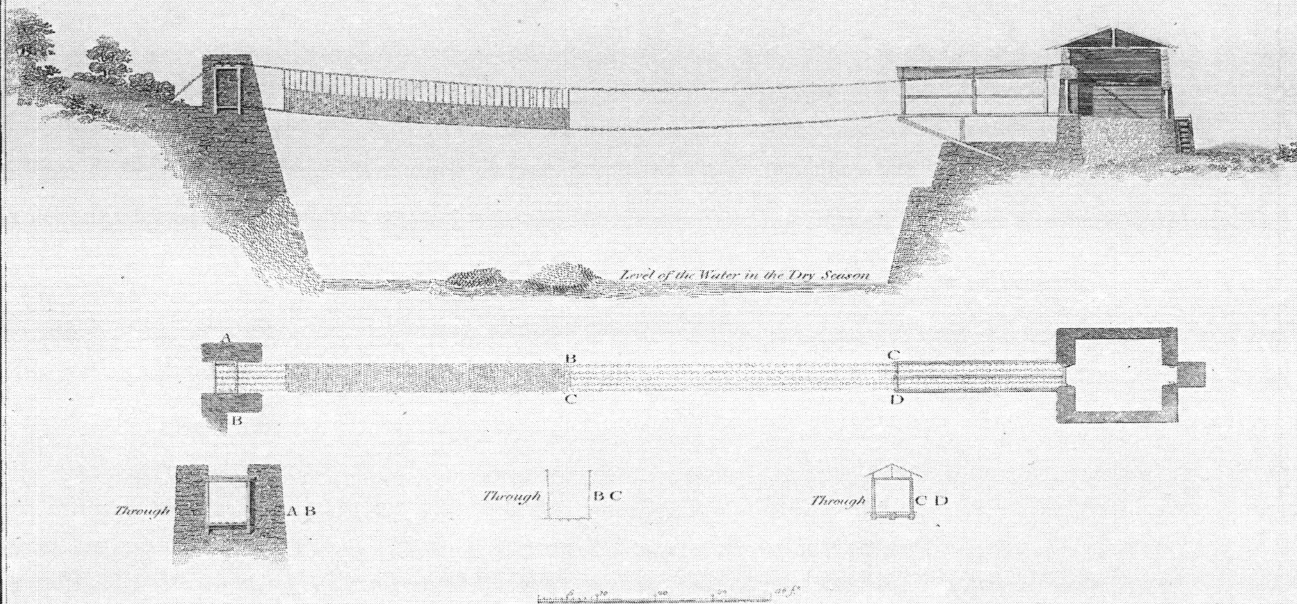

Published March, 20th 1800 by G & W Nicol, Pall Mall.

Murichom. For the best explanation of its construction, I refer to the annexed plan and sections, constructed from a measurement of the different parts. Plate III. A perspective view of it, and the adjacent scenery, is given in Plate IV.

Only one horse is admitted to go over it at a time: it swings as you tread upon it, reacting at the same time with a force that impels you, every step you take, to quicken your pace. It may be necessary to say, in explanation of the plan, that on the five chains that support the platform, are placed several layers of strong coarse mats of bamboo, loosely put down, so as to play with the swing of the bridge; and that a fence on each side, of the same materials, contributes to the security of the passenger. A similar bridge, over the river Tees, is described by Hutchinson, in his History and Antiquities of Durham. " About two miles above Middleton, where the river falls in repeated cascades, a bridge, suspended on iron chains, is stretched from rock to rock, over a chasm near sixty feet deep, for the passage of travellers, but particularly for miners: the bridge is seventy feet in length, and little more than two feet broad, with a hand rail on one side, and planked in such a manner that the traveller experiences all the tremulous motion of the chain, and sees himself suspended over a roaring gulph, on an agitated restless gangway, to which few travellers dare trust themselves."

The castle of Chuka makes a very respectable appearance. It is a large square building, placed on elevated ground: there is only one entrance into it, by a flight of steps, and through a spacious gateway, with large heavy doors; it is built of stone, and the walls are of a prodigious thickness. We were conducted hither, on our entrance, and lodged by the commandant in a large and lofty apartment, in which there were two or three loop holes towards the river, and on the other side, a projecting balcony: the floor was boarded with thick planks that were pretty well joined together.

In a nation where no records are kept to perpetuate the memory of the achievements of genius, and in which the minds of the people are remarkably prone to superstition, perhaps more than a century may not be necessary, to deify the author of a great work. Thus it is, that the bridge of Chuka is reckoned to be of more than mortal production. No less a being than the dewta Tehuptehup could possibly have contrived so curious a piece of mechanism. Neither the origin nor the history of this renowned Tehuptehup, can be traced with any degree of certainty; but the works they assign to him, the road up the mountain we lately passed, (many parts of which are held, it may be said, upon a precipice, by pins and cramps of iron uniting together the stones that form it,) and the bridge at Chuka, do credit to a genius, who deservedly ranks high upon the rolls of fame, and justly claims from the inhabitants, decided tokens of respect and gratitude.

At twelve o'clock, on Monday the 26th of May, we departed from Chuka. The mountains in our way to Punugga, for the distance of about ten miles, were in some parts not so completely covered with trees, as those we had passed, and we observed a material change in the face of them, as well as in the climate. The road side was covered with strawberries, which ripen, and decay, unnoticed by the plodding peasant of Bootan. I could not view them with the same apathy, but dismounted from my horse, and loitered away much time in culling the ripest from the banks. I was much pleased with the recognition of many well known English plants, such as docks, nettles, primroses, and dog-rose bushes, which were now in full bloom. The cuckoo's call, brought strongly to my imagination, the season and situations, in which I had formerly listened to that harbinger of spring; and the harmony of various other birds gave additional force to the impression. We now passed one of the numberless cascades, which, rolling over mossy stones, seek concealment in the groves below. The mountains here began to wear some marks of husbandry and fertility, and many large spaces of ground were dressed for cultivation, being sown with different kinds of grain.

Near Punugga there was a very fine crop of barley almost fit for reaping: here too were the first pine trees I had seen in Bootan, some ashes, and peach trees. The summits of the mountains in this day's journey were constantly concealed by the clouds. We travelled the greatest part of the way through these clouds, and felt the air extremely chilly. It was five o'clock when we came to Punugga, a village situated in a hollow, and surrounded with mountains for the most part covered with pines, along whose sides clouds were perpetually flitting. After the sun had withdrawn it became very cold, and we were all glad to have recourse to a lively fire, made of the turpentine fir. On the borders of this village, were many large heaps of fir leaves, collected, I was told, for the purpose of manuring the ground. They are heaped together as they fall from the trees, and left to ferment and rot, in which state they are esteemed excellent manure.

On Tuesday the 27th of May, after ascending from the deep hollow in which Punugga is situated, our road to Chupka lay winding along the sides of the mountains, which are richly clad with pines, the only native trees of these lofty eminences. After travelling about eight miles, we passed by the river Hatchieu, leaving it to the left, near the spot where it joins the Tehintchieu and the Patchieu, called by the Booteeas Jumtchieu, or the junction of three rivers. At the foot of the Chupka mountain, we crossed a bridge, styled Russoo Noomboo, and ascended by a very steep and rugged road to the castle. The castle of Chupka, or Kepta, is built about half way up the mountain, in a bleak, but beautifully romantic situation: the mountains in its neighbourhood, I judged to be the highest we had yet seen in Bootan. The light clouds in some parts swiftly glided past their sides; in others they had assembled, and sat with deep and heavy shade upon their brows: and as they were continually shifting their position, they varied and improved the views. On the summit of Lomeela mountain, bearing from hence to the east, and in direct distance about five miles, there lay a great deal of unmelted snow: we felt the cold even at noon.

The ensuing day we were detained at Chupka by rain; but luckily we were now beyond the region of leeches, and that pestiferous insect with which we were particularly assailed at Murichom.

We crossed Chupka mountain on Thursday the 29th of May, in our way to Pauga, distant about eleven miles, leaving Kelligym, a village situated upon the ridge of a high mountain, on our left, and Dokhottyghym on our right. Descending on the other side, we laboured over the sides of the mountains, on which there are nothing now but pines and firs. We had proceeded about five or six miles, when, at a small distance from the road, my eye was caught by a bridge for foot passengers, of an extraordinary construction. It was composed of two chains stretched parallel to each other across the river, distant four feet from each other, and on either side resting upon a pile of stones raised upon each bank about eight feet high: they were carried down with an easy slope and buried in the rock, where, being fastened round a large stone, they were confined by a quantity of broken rock heaped on them. A plank about eight inches broad, hung longitudinally, suspended across the river with roots and creepers, wound over the chains with a slackness sufficient to allow the centre to sink to the depth of four feet below the chains. This bridge, called Selochazum, measured from one side of the water to the other seventy feet. The creepers are changed annually: the planks are all loose; so that if the creepers give way in any part, they can be removed, and that particular part repaired without disturbing the whole. At a distance from hence we passed Durbee castle, built upon the crown of a very steep rock, which stands on the road to Paro, and within its district.

The foot of the rock is washed by the Tehintchieu-Patchieu, over which, is thrown a wooden bridge, constructed of long beams of fir, reaching from side to side, with deal planks placed crossways on them, and bound down with bands of bamboo. Although these bridges are strong, yet they are of a most simple structure; and there is this peculiar advantage in them over heavy masses of masonry, that in times of commotion, they can be very quickly removed on the slightest emergency. Half way up the rock stands a square stone tower, with a bastion to defend the approach to the castle, which is gained by an exceeding steep ascent. The rock supplies it abundantly with ammunition: those who have possession, require no other weapons to repel their assailants, while they have stones to roll down upon them.

This kind of natural artillery is common to all the fortresses of India, which are situated on hills: they are called *mudwallahs,* or drunkards, from their continually varying direction in their descent, occasioned by their irregularity of shape, and the protuberances they meet with in their way. In the assault of Chunarghur, in the year 1764, or 1765, our European grenadiers were twice repulsed by these formidable weapons.

The mountains we saw this day, were but thinly covered with pines. We met with maple and willow trees, the dog-rose bush in full bloom, and sweetbriar with, and without thorns. We rested for the night, at Pauga.

The road, on Friday the 30th of May, led by the river along the sides of the mountains, and there were few inequalities from hence to Nomnoo, an easy stage of about eight miles. We saw hermitages and villages spread over the sides and summits of the mountains, to each of which is allotted a spacious portion of cultivated ground: still much more appeared capable of improvement; for over the whole of these mountains, except where precipices or steep points project, there is a great deal of soil; yet vegetation is not so strong as in the neighbourhood of Bengal. The trees are no where so numerous or flourishing, nor do the pines grow with that luxuriance, which might be expected in a favourable soil. There are wooden bridges across the river at Choomboo, Sese, and other places that we passed. We saw the Patchieu, as it comes round the mountains to the north-west, forming a junction with the Tehintchieu, which runs on to receive the river Hatchieu, near Kepta. As we approached Nomnoo, the husbandmen were busied in the fields; the reapers were cutting down the corn with sickles, which others collected in handfuls, and bound up with a wisp of straw: we saw also oxen yoked in a plough, which was guided by a boy at the plough tail. We came early to Nomnoo, and were lodged in a large apartment in a spacious house, the walls of which were black from the smoke of a fire, which in the winter they commonly burn upon a large flat stone, in the middle of the room; the commodiousness of a chimney being here unknown.

I visited an orchard in the neighbourhood, and found it well stored with walnut, apple, peach, pear, apricot, and barberry trees.

Two Poës[e] had arrived on the preceding day at Pauga: they were sent by the commandant of the garrison of Tassisudon, to procure for us whatever we might want, as the chief of Nomnoo was absent from his station. The next morning they set off early, to advise their master of our approach.

From Nomnoo, on Saturday the 31st of May, we still travelled near the banks of the river, and left Jeemi Jumboo, a handsome village in the valley, on our left, as we advanced to Wangoka, distant from Nomnoo near ten miles.

[e] Inferior officers in the service of government, employed occasionally both in a civil and military capacity.

The country now began to open; the Tehintchieu ran with less rapidity, over a more even bed of ground, watering a most beautiful narrow valley, in which not a spot of land was unemployed. Their labour merited a more grateful soil, for I never saw lands cleaner, or better dressed. Heaps of manure in every field, at proper distances, lay ready to be scattered amongst the corn; yet with all their care the crops were thin, running much to straw. In addition to this, the bareness of the hills, and the diminutive size of the pines, were evident indications of an unkindly soil.

The road, however, improved; and we seemed to have conquered the enormous mountains and craggy steeps, which were now reduced to moderate hills, with gradual and easy slopes. Traces of winter yet remained; and upon some of those hills that were near to us, there was much unmelted snow.

Leaving Wangoka, we continued our course, on Sunday the 1st of June, through the same kind of verdant valley, intersected by the river, as we had travelled through the day before. Upon our right, on the summit of a lofty mountain, we saw an extensive monastery above Symtoka, and soon after, at the end of a valley, on our left, another mountain, whose top was covered with snow. We crossed a substantial and elevated wooden bridge over the Tehintchieu, six miles from Wangoka, where the bed was a rocky descent, and the stream, of course, extremely rapid. At the distance of two miles, Tassisudon now opened to our view, situated in a valley, which I compute to be about three miles in length, and one in breadth, lying north and south; the Tehintchieu running through it. We were conducted to a house lying to the northward of the palace, and at no great distance from it, situated on an eminence high above the river, which runs on the other side of a narrow road, that winds round the base of the hill.

Opposite, and not half a bowshot off, there is a very good covered bridge across the Tehintchieu, and from our apartment, we had an extensive view, both up and down the valley, which is in a high state of cultivation, bearing various kinds of grain, and diversified by clusters of houses. There is no regular town, nor any village, within a mile of the palace. Upon a low hill, about a mile distant from us towards the south, is seen the palace of Lam' Ghassatoo, and at somewhat more than the same distance westwards, highly elevated upon the ridge of a mountain, stands a handsome villa belonging to Lam' Rimbochay. The banks of the river are lined with willows, and the surrounding mountains have some timber trees, intermixed with the fir and pine, as well as a great variety of flowering shrubs; whilst a number of single houses, and some monasteries, having orchards and hanging fields of corn about them, ornament the finely romantic views, with which we were delighted from every part of this valley.

CHAPTER IV.

Tassisudon—my Arrival notified at the Palace—the Raja or Lama occupied in religious Ceremonies—strict Observance of all Duties appertaining to their Religion.—Message from the Daeb Raja—Interview—Zoompoon, Zoondonier, Zempi—Citadel—Audience Chamber—Ceremony of Introduction—Particulars of the Interview—Tea—local Observance—extensive Fashion—peculiar Mode of preparing it.—Polite Attention of the Raja—Dress, that of the religious Order—Manner of our Reception.—Second Interview.—Silk Scarfs—their Use on all Occasions of Ceremony or Compliment.—Comparative View of Manners.—Natural Productions.—Peculiar Sentiments of the Raja—Variety of Expression—Art of Drawing—Mr. Davis's superior Skill.—Visit to the chief Officers under Government—Tasse-Zompoon, Zoondonier, Zempi—Outline of their Rank and Authority.—I undertook to mediate the Peace of the Zeenkaubs, who are pardoned, and readmitted into favour—Instance of implicit Obedience to the Will of their Chief.—General Design of the present Work.—A Bootan Repast.—Boora Soobah, or Toonso Pilo.—Bees.—Benevolent and humane Sentiment.—Order of Gylongs—regulated Periods for religious Service—some Rules of the Society—Ablutions—Temperance—Cleanliness—general Appearance—endemial Disorder termed Gheig, or Aubi.

THE morning after my arrival at Tassisudon, I sent the Gosein Poorungheer, who accompanied me as interpreter, to the palace, to arrange the ceremony of our introduction, and fix a time for the delivery of the dispatches, with which I had been charged by the Governor General, to the Daeb Raja.

After a short absence, he returned with information, that the Raja, who is also a Lama, had for some days past devoted himself to Pooja (religious ceremonies), on account of the death of a Gylong, of high rank in the religious order, and greatly renowned for his sanctity and age. How much longer those rites might employ him, Poorungheer could not, with any degree of certainty, ascertain; but, he was told that, until their conclusion, the Raja would continue in private, his attention being wholly turned from the affairs of the world, and no person would be permitted to interrupt him. At the same time, it was intimated to me, that the principal officers about his court would, in the interval, be ready to receive our visits; but I chose to decline waiting upon them, until I had seen the Raja himself.

Having just arrived among a people, whose peculiar customs I had yet to learn, I confess that the mysteriousness which seemed to prevail, and this apparent difficulty of access, suggested to me, no very favourable opinion of my new friends. It occurred to me, that the delay probably originated, in a plan concerted to magnify the importance and piety of their chief: an opinion to which many of my attendants industriously endeavoured to give strength. This, however, was a rash and hasty inference; as I had the satisfaction to have afterwards effectually proved, by what occurred to my own observation, and this too in a way highly honourable to the religious zeal of this people, which, in the performance of any prescribed duty, will never admit of interruption.

Early on the morning of Tuesday the 3d of June, a messenger came to me, with notice that the Raja proposed receiving us in the course of that day. We accordingly made the necessary preparations, and at the appointed hour, with Mr. Davis, Mr. Saunders, and all our attendants, I proceeded to the palace, which we entered about noon, to the evident astonishment of multitudes, who had filled the balconies, crowded about the doors, and occupied the avenues, to gaze at their strange visitors. We were first conducted to a large apartment, on the west side of the great square of the palace, where the three principal officers, Zoompoon[a], Zoondonier[b], and Zempi[c], had assembled to receive us. Here we rested until Zoondonier, who went to announce our arrival, returned to usher us into the presence of the Daeb. We followed him, the other officers with many Zeenkaubs accompanying us, through several passages, and up a number of lofty ladders, which connect the different floors, till at length we arrived at the elevated station occupied by the Raja, near the summit of the citadel.

After a short pause upon the landing place, the door was thrown open, and we were ushered into a small, but well proportioned room, having on the west side an arched balcony with sliding curtains, being the only aperture for the admission of light, immediately opposite to

[a] Commandant or keeper of the castle of Tassisudon. [b] Treasurer.

[c] Cup-bearer to the Daeb Raja, and master of the ceremonies.

the door by which we entered, and before which a skreen projected nearly one-third of the breadth of the room. The remaining space on the wall, beyond the skreen, was decorated with the portraits, wrought in silk, of some champions of their faith, as stiff and formal as any heroes that ever appeared in tapestry. The walls of the room were coloured with blue, and the arches of the balcony, pillars, doors, &c. were painted with vermilion, and ornamented with gilding. The Raja was habited in a deep garnet-coloured cloth, and sat cross-legged upon a pile of cushions, in the remote corner of the room, with the balcony upon his right hand; upon his left side stood a cabinet of diminutive idols, and a variety of consecrated trinkets; close upon his right was placed an escrutoir, for the deposit of papers required to be at hand; and before him was a small painted bench, to place his tea cup on, and answering all the other purposes of a table. We each advanced, presenting, one after the other, a white silk scarf, or long narrow piece of pelong, fringed at both ends (as is the custom in these countries), to the Raja, who, keeping his seat all the time, took them in his hand, and passed them to his Zempi. I delivered also into his hand, the Governor General's dispatches, which he received with a smile upon his countenance, looking upon them, and nodding with a slow motion of the head several times, before he laid them upon the bench before him. On the other side of the room were placed, immediately opposite to the Raja, three separate piles of cushions; the Raja extending his arm, pointed to them, and at the same time with his hand directed us to be seated. It was some time before the last of our attendants had entered, and made the usual obeisance: they then ranged themselves behind us, on the same side of the room by which they entered; the three officers stood in front of the balcony, between us and the Raja, and the interpreters by them.

When the commotion of settling in our respective places had ceased, and silence ensued, the Raja addressed me with many earnest and particular enquiries respecting the Governor General; he congratulated us on our safe arrival at Tassisudon, and expressed his apprehensions for the fatigue and inconvenience, we might have endured in travelling through a country, abounding with so many natural difficulties, and so scantily furnished with the necessaries of life.

I was happy in the opportunity thus afforded me, of paying every acknowledgment due to the civilities and attention, we had experienced in the course of our progress; I expressed my thanks also for the ample supplies of provision provided for us, by the inhabitants and his officers, at every stage, as well as for the diligence and good care of the guide, who had conducted us from the frontier of his dominions.

The Raja was not wanting in attention to the superior members of our government, but asked respectively after the health of the gentlemen of the Supreme Council, and the Chief Justice; and in endeavouring to convey to me an adequate idea of the strength of his regard and friendship for the Governor, he used various modes of expression, which he concluded with the action of advancing his arms, and bending the forefingers of each hand, linking them one in the other, and pulling them at right angles, with a strong exertion, as if to give force to his sentiments. The letter I delivered, being written in the Persian language, could not be then read; for there were none among his servants, or all his subjects, who were conversant in it. The Bengalee language is the only one, differing from their own, in which any business or correspondence is carried on; and in this, their commercial intercourse with Bengal, as well as what relates to the territory situated on its borders, is always and exclusively transacted. This was intimated to me; and I was asked, whether the delivery of the letter I had borne from the Governor, was my only motive for coming to Tassisudon. So pointed and laconic a question was quite unexpected; but I answered it, by briefly stating the reasons that induced the Governor General, at this time in particular, to depute a person to the Lama's court; and added, that, when I learnt the road to Tibet lay through his dominions, and not very distant from his capital, knowing also his attachment to the Governor, as well as having heard the fame of his exalted name, it became an object of much anxiety with me, to have the honour of paying my respects to the friend of my patron, and to a prince of so great renown. With respect to any other reasons there might be, for my waiting upon him, the contents of the letter would amply explain them.

Three small benches, similar to that before the Raja, were brought and placed before us; and presently a servant came, bearing a large tea pot of white metal, embossed, and highly ornamented with some other metal, of a yellow colour. He approached the Raja, and then giving a circular turn to the tea-pot, so as to agitate and mix its contents, he poured a quantity into the palm of his hand, which he had contracted to form as deep a concave as possible, and hastily sipped it up. To account for a custom which has so little either of grace, or delicacy, in its observance, however recommended by extensive fashion, we are obliged to have recourse to the suspicions suggested in remoter times, by the frequent and treacherous use of poison. Hence originated a caution, in which the national character of this people readily disposed them to acquiesce; and the same jealousy and distrust, which gave birth to its adoption, has contributed inviolably to preserve it to the present day; so that however humble, or exalted the rank of the person, who introduces to his guests the refreshment of tea, the cup-bearer, which is an office of the first credit, never presumes to offer it, without previously drinking some of the liquor that he brings.

The Raja held out, upon the points of the fingers of his right hand, a shallow lacquered cup, of small circumference, which was filled with tea. Three cups had been sent, and were set down before us: the Raja directed his servant to fill them also; still holding the cup in his right hand, he repeated, in a low and hollow tone of voice, a long invocation; and afterwards dipping the point of his finger three times into the cup, he threw as many drops upon the floor, by way of oblation, and then began to sip his tea. Taking this as a signal, we followed the example, and partook of the dishes of parched rice, that were served up with it. We found this liquor extremely unlike what we had been used to drink, under the same name; it was a compound of water, flour, butter, salt, and bohea tea, with some other astringent ingredients, all boiled, beat up, and intimately blended together. I confess the mixture was by no means to my taste, and we had hitherto shunned, as much as possible, these unpalatable libations, yet we now deemed it necessary to submit to some constraint; and having at last, with a tolerable grace, swallowed the tea, we yet found ourselves very deficient in the conclusion of the ceremony. The Raja with surprising dexterity turned the cup, as he held it fast betwixt his fingers, and in an instant passed his tongue over every part of it; so that it was sufficiently cleansed to be wrapped in a piece of scarlet silk, which bore evident marks of having been not very recently devoted to this service. The officers, who had entered with us, were not permitted to partake of this repast, and, but for the honour of it, we would willingly have declined so flattering a distinction. They spoke several times during our visit, delivering themselves deliberately in a ready flow of language, by no means inharmonious, with confidence, but at the same time with profound respect.

The Raja descanted on the very limited produce of his mountains, and magnified greatly the scarcity of provisions, yet begged me to command every thing that the country could supply. Trays of fruit were placed before us, consisting of oranges, dried apples, walnuts, vegetables, and some preserved fruits of China and Cashmeer. He delivered to the Zempi, or master of the ceremonies, a silk scarf for each of us, which being thrown across our shoulders, he dismissed us, with many admonitions to be careful of our health, and wishes that it might suffer no injury from the change of climate.

We then took leave, and returned to our quarters, with no unfavourable impression of the Raja, from his manner and reception of us. His figure was much concealed, from the attitude in which he continued sitting all the time, cross-legged, and enveloped in a quantity of thick frieze-like woollen cloth; yet he exhibited enough of his person to shew that he was tall, and muscular in his make, but not inclined to corpulency. His garment was of the religious order; a close vest, leaving the arm bare to the shoulder, unless when drawn beneath the mantle, which serves occasionally to cover the head, and reaches almost to the feet.

His reception of us, was supported with dignity and good humour; he was grave, but animated; his behaviour collected and composed. He spoke rather in a low tone of voice, but very articulately; his delivery was accompanied with a moderate action; and the whole of his conduct, exhibited a degree of urbanity, that I confess surprised me, in one separated from intercourse with the world, by a mass of impervious mountains, and who was almost totally secluded from the sight of any other, than his own subjects.

The next day, receiving an invitation from the Raja, I made him a second visit, and offered to his acceptance, a few English manufactures, and other things, which I had brought from Bengal. I omit the repetition of the ceremonious part of our interviews, which, as established by universal custom, is invariably and indispensably the same.

An inferior, on approaching a superior, presents the white silk scarf; and, when dismissed, has one thrown over his neck, with the ends hanging down in front. Equals exchange scarfs on meeting, bending towards each other, with an inclination of the body. No intercourse whatever takes place without the intervention of a scarf; it always accompanies every letter, being enclosed in the same packet, however distant the place to which it is dispatched. Two colours are in use for this manufacture, which is of China, white and red: the latter is rather confined to the lower orders: the white is respectful in proportion to its purity and fineness: there are various degrees in both. I am yet ignorant of the origin of this custom, but shall endeavour, at some future time, to obtain an explanation of it.

A long conversation ensued with the Raja on the dress and customs of the English. He admired, and minutely examined, every part of our clothes; nor did the pockets least of all excite his wonder and surprise, by presenting such a number of comprehensive and concealed resources. He gave due credit to the convenience of our dress, its lightness, and the liberty it left to the limbs; but I could plainly perceive he judged its structure defective, as differing from his own, in shewing too plainly the general outline of the body. Thus it is, that the less enlightened Booteea, accustomed to observe the dignity of human character exist in factitious concealment, looks for importance in exterior ornament: divest his sacred superior of the robe of state, and his pontifical insignia, and he would, no doubt, conclude all authority and religion to be entirely at an end.

The Raja exercised his fancy in endeavouring to trace a resemblance between the natives of Bootan and Englishmen; but there was more of ingenuity, than truth in the picture. Woollen cloths for raiment, meat, spirits, and tea, it is true, are in equal use amongst us; and the Booteea, like ourselves, is an utter stranger to the subtle niceties and refined distinctions of the Hindoo, which constitute the infinitely absurd perplexity that results from Cast; yet nothing can be more different than our habits, and our manners. I had a pleasure in recognising a more striking similitude in the productions of his country and our own, as well as in the temperature of the climate. We had often met with strawberries and raspberries growing wild, in great abundance; and had seen apple, walnut, pear, peach, and apricot trees; the ash, the birch, the maple, yew, pine, and fir; but I looked for the oak in vain. The forests abounded with other handsome timber trees, to whose names and kinds I was equally a stranger.

The Raja expressed a wish that my servants should leave the room. He then began to lay aside something of his formality, and conversed with less reserve. He dwelt much upon his friendship for the Governor General, and ascribed a durability to their connexion, in strict unison with the doctrine of the metempsychosis. He told me that he understood the contents of the Governor's letter, in which I was mentioned in high expressions of confidence and regard; and assured me of the particular satisfaction he experienced, in seeing a person so intimately known to, and deputed by, his friend; enjoining me to esteem him in the same light. Then carrying on an allusion, which agreed perfectly with the tenets of their faith, he claimed with Mr. Hastings the nearest spiritual alliance; and, rejecting every degree of mortal relation, asserted theirs to be no other than emanations from the same soul; thus indicating a new species of affinity of unlimited extent and compass; embracing, in one comprehensive system, the immaterial spirit, or animating principle of all the good and great, unconfined to place, to nation, or religion, but indelibly distinguished by a more permanent and definite similitude, than the operation of nature ever accidentally stamps, upon the perishable materials of the human form.

The Raja produced many unbroken seals, carefully cut from letters, and observed how much he prized every thing he had received from the Governor's hand. I cannot pretend to follow him through the variety of expression, by which he strove to testify the strength and sincerity of his friendship; but it all tended to convince me, that he knew at least very well, what belonged to gratitude and affection. He asked me many questions about a view of the palace of Punukka, his winter residence, which he had sent to Mr. Hastings: I had seen it in Calcutta, and assured him that it was received. He expressed his wishes for a picture of the Governor's habitation; and a question arose, if either of us could draw. My interpreter (with that false policy which is inseparable from a suspicious mind), eagerly grasping at an evasion, began to answer, that an Englishman was master of every art and science; astronomy, geography, mathematics, mechanics. I stopped him; for no vanity could allow such indiscriminate and preposterous praise; and I told the Raja in plainer terms, that drawing constituted in England a branch of education; and that as we made unequal progress in the art, I could boast but little skill in it, but that my friend Mr. Davis had attained a great degree of perfection. Mr. Davis happened to have with him, a view of Calcutta, which he had taken from Fort William, comprehending the line of buildings that skirt the esplanade, and the shipping on the river: it had sustained some damage from the carriage; but he promised, as soon as it could be repaired, to present it to the Raja. The employment of an interpreter was no less troublesome, than protractive of our conferences: the hour of two had passed; tea was introduced, of which we drank with the Raja. We received presents of fruits and vegetables, and retired to our house.

It was expected, and seemed necessary, that we should pay the superior officers under government, the compliment of a visit; I dispatched therefore a messenger to each of them; and, a convenient time being appointed, we proceeded the following day, to perform the ceremony. They were all three accommodated in the palace; and, though invested with offices of different duty, were looked upon as nearly of equal rank. Their titles, and, as well as I could understand, the nature of their employments were as follow: first, the Tasse-Zoompoon, who is commandant of the castle of Tassisudon, keeper of warlike stores, and governor of all that tract of country over which we had travelled, between the capital, and the Company's dominions. Second, the Zoondonier, who is treasurer, as well as captain-general of all the forces, which in times of emergency he heads in person. Third, the Zempi, who is master of ceremonies, cup-bearer, and keeper of the wardrobe; he is constantly attendant upon the Raja, and conducts the plan of all his operations: his office, being rather of a private nature, is of less ostensible consequence than the other two; but, as he is always near the person of the Raja, and consequently supposed to be a favourite, his situation gives him weight in the general estimation.

We were first conducted to the apartment of the Tasse-Zoompoon, whom we met on the day of our introduction to the Raja, in the west angle of the palace. He was a corpulent, unwieldy figure, and not of the most polished manners; but what was wanting in this respect, was amply compensated, by an abundant share of good humour. The Zoondonier was tall and athletic, and gave striking indications of a better understanding than his associate in office: he possessed at the same time an easier and more spirited address. In the beginning of his career in life, he had been employed somewhere on the skirts of the mountains, and had picked up a few words of the Bengalee language, which he was fond of repeating. The ceremony of exchanging a pelong scarf passed between us: tea, of course, we were obliged to partake of, which is never omitted, let visits be made ever so frequently, at any hour of the day. There was nothing worthy recapitulation, in these visits; mere common-place offers of civility on their part, acknowledgments on mine, and mutual wishes to be better acquainted.

The day was far advanced, when we left the Zoompoon and Zoondonier, so that we were obliged to postpone our visit to the Zempi, until the following day. We then found him occupying apartments adjoining to that in which we were introduced to the Daeb, to whom he is nearly related. He was a well-formed young man, neither tall nor corpulent, about twenty-four years of age; remarkably mild in his manners, and of an open and ingenuous deportment. He had less reserve than either of the other ministers, and seemed as yet to have contracted none of the austere habits of high office. He expressed himself earnestly solicitous to cultivate a friendly and familiar intimacy; urging as an inducement, his relative situation, and his age; observing, that in this last respect, there was not much disparity between any of us.

Before we left the Zempi, a messenger from the Daeb invited us to his presence. The Zeenkaubs, who accompanied me from Rungpore had, I found, fallen under the Raja's displeasure. They interceded with me to mediate their peace; and, accordingly, I made a point, on this next visit, of carrying them with me. After the usual ceremonies of introduction, and the common compliments, had passed upon our meeting, I prefaced the business of their mission, by bringing the Zeenkaubs, his servants, to the Raja's notice; and, apprehensive that they had forfeited his favour by some inadvertent error, begged leave to recommend them to his forgiveness; highly commending, at the same time, their zeal and fidelity in his service. The Raja replied, that they had indeed been guilty of a crime of the highest nature, in having returned without receiving his order, or even asking his permission; he added, that it was an immutable law among his subjects, that a person charged by him with the execution of any duty, could never, while he had life and breath, recede from the prosecution of what he had undertaken, or return to his presence, without having completely accomplished the object of his mission, unless by special authority. A striking instance of this implicit deference to the commands of their superior, occurred upon my return to Bengal. The Raja had deputed two of his Zeenkaubs, to accompany me to Calcutta, charged with no particular business, but chiefly out of compliment to me, and to bring him the earliest account of my safe arrival. On coming to Rungpore, I learnt that the Governor General was preparing for a journey to the upper provinces of Hindostan. I soon afterwards received his commands to cross the country, and join him upon the road.

I had the greatest difficulty imaginable, in dissuading the Zeenkaubs from persisting in their intention to go with me. In vain did I state to these hardy mountaineers, the dangers of a burning sun, and the fury of the scorching winds: these conveyed no terror to their minds, equal to the displeasure of the Daeb; and at last I was obliged to leave them, rather in the helpless condition of being unable to follow me, than convinced of the extravagant wildness of their scheme.

Having urged every thing that occurred to me, in extenuation of their crime, apparently without much effect, I was obliged at last to own, that the Zeenkaubs had yielded to the advice of Mr. Goodlad[d] and myself, and not acted of their own accord. I observed, that I had taken upon myself thus much to answer for, being charged with particular dispatches from the Governor General, and entrusted with a confidential communication upon the business of their mission, which respected the ancient boundary, between the Company's provinces and Bootan. Concluding from hence, that their residence at Rungpore was by no means necessary, and thinking that, having been much among the English, and being conversant with our manners, they might render to me and my companions, material service in conducting us through a country, in which we were equally strangers to the customs and the language, I had ventured to determine upon their departure. The Raja then turned to me with much good humour, and said, "Well, since I hear so favourable a report of them, and as they acted by your direction, if they had been guilty of ten thousand crimes, I would pardon them all:" he added, "as being my servants, they were

[d] The Company's Resident at Rungpore.

equally at your command, and did right in obeying you." They were now called into the presence, and made before the Raja, nine prostrations, which is the obeisance paid to him by his subjects, whenever they are permitted to approach; and I had the satisfaction to witness their being re-admitted into favour.

I omit the repetition of all that passed, relative to the business of my commission: an inexhaustible succession of obstacles were urged to oppose the prosecution of it, to obviate which occupied almost all my time, and constituted the principal subject of every conference. To attempt the recital here, would be entering into a tiresome detail, widely deviating from my present design, which is, an endeavour to delineate the appearance of a region, little known, and to mark so much of the manners of the people, as, from an immediate intercourse with them, attracted my observation.

The Raja had invited us to dine in his apartment, which we were assured, was the highest mark of distinction and goodwill, he could possibly confer; since no person in his own dominions, even of the most distinguished rank, ever aspired to the honour of eating in his presence: but we were strangers, from a distant country, and his guests. By particular desire, the table was spread with our own camp equipage, and the dinner was dressed by my servants, much more to our satisfaction, than if furnished from the Raja's kitchen; for we had as yet seen nothing to attach us to Bootan cookery. As soon as the Raja's frugal fare was brought, a plate of roots and boiled rice, we began the meal. He eat with ivory chopsticks, and sometimes used a spoon. I invited him to taste our wine and sweetmeats, which he declined;

giving me to understand, that whoever assumed his robe (meaning the religious dress), is bound to abstain from every sort of inebriating liquor. However, considering that one who had absolution in his hands, might venture at an experiment, which a common subject dared not presume to make, in case a strong impulse of curiosity should occur, I left the means to gratify it—claret and raspberry jam. I cannot say what became of them; but a few days after, I had an application for a fresh supply of the former, with no intention, I believe, that it should be reserved among the relics. We talked much of entertainments, and I attempted the description of an English one.

The Boora Soobah, now Toonso Pilo[e], who some years ago, soon after the conclusion of the war with Bootan, was deputed by the Daeb Raja to the Governor General, the first of his nation who had ever been in Calcutta, had been present at one of Mrs. Hastings's concerts, and, on his return, had given a very lively account of it, accompanied of course with such observations, as resulted from the strong impression, which a scene so novel, must naturally leave on a Booteea's mind. What my interpreter repeated, might serve to revive the recollection; for the Raja listened with attention, looked pleased, and wished himself a spectator in a concert, or a ball room. But to return to our dinner. He was exceedingly astonished at the variety of eatables and liquors that composed an English meal; and could by no means conceive, in his own mind, the advantage of such an heterogeneous mixture: he

[e] That is the Governor of Toonso; Pilo is the general title of provincial governor of the highest order, and Toonso the name of the capital of the province. Soobah is the title given to governors of inferior rank.

was no less surprised to hear that, with us, almost every quarter of the globe, contributed to a very moderate repast. "My food," says he, "consists of the simplest articles; grain, roots of the earth, and fruits. I never eat of any thing that has had breath; for so I should be the indirect cause of putting an end to the existence of animal life, which, by our religion, is strictly forbidden."

After his meal, he drank tea out of a sort of china cup, which only the sovereign Lama has a right to use: it would be little less than sacrilege, were any other person to drink from one of the same form. He favoured us with some dried coagulated milk, fried in butter, but of so stubborn a substance, that I suppose no process could ever tend to mollify it; I did not deem it safe, therefore, to submit it to the powers of digestion. He sent us also a piece of some boiled root: it was small, white, and knotty, of a sweetish taste, and reckoned nutritive. A small quantity of honey, that accompanied this present, gave rise to a conversation on bees. I described to him the mode of hiving them in England, and our profitable management of that industrious race.

He said, that the common people, in his country, were at some pains in the encouragement of bees, and at a proper season collected their honey and wax. We had repeatedly seen large cakes of the comb, pendant from the projecting balconies, to the bottom of which they were attached, hanging always clear of the wall. Their thickness seldom exceeded six inches: every subsequent addition contributed to increase their breadth or length. The form was irregular, but I think I have seen them three or four feet long. Their being allowed to remain long unmolested is, I believe, the only attention paid to bees in Bootan. They appeared to me of the same species with the English, small, short, and yellow. The Raja added, "But these, by my direction, are never disturbed: their labour is employed for the benefit of the community, in laying up a stock, which serves to rear their young, and as a resource when they cease to find food abroad. Were I, availing myself of superior power, to deprive them of this store, accumulated for their future support, how could I expect to enjoy unmolested, that of which I am myself possessed?" His conversation abounded with similar observations, introduced as frequently as the subject will admit, and they breathed sentiments highly honourable to the humane spirit of their religious faith. It grew late; the evening approached; we retired to take our walk, and left the Raja to his customary devotions.

The Gylongs assemble in their chapels three times a day, for the performance of religious service; in the morning, at noon, and at night. We were regularly roused at the earliest dawn of day, by the clamorous noise of numerous instruments, to whose sound they chanted their orisons. At twelve, the Gylongs met again to perform their devotions, and the evening closed with their prayers. The gates of the palace were then shut, as well for the sake of tranquillity and safety, as to prevent a violation of their rigid rules of chastity. Fifteen hundred Gylongs are contained within these walls, and not a female lodges under the same roof. The religious, from their first introduction into the order, are bound by its laws to celibacy, and are interdicted, by the severest penalties, from all connexion with the female sex: the benefit of some friendly offices they are, nevertheless, not denied; and I remarked, that the prettiest women I saw were employed in carrying water into the palace.

Though the life of a Gylong be in an extreme degree, sedentary and recluse, yet, whether it may be ascribed or not to regularity and temperance, they are certainly fairer in their complexions, and more athletic, than the rest of their countrymen. The former advantage, indeed, of which they boast, may be imputed to a very obvious cause; as they are less exposed to the weather, exempt from labour, and more attentive to personal cleanliness, than the rest of their nation.

We used to see them passing in procession, at the base of the eminence on which our habitation stood, in order to cross the bridge, and proceed over a small plain, on the other side, to a little island, at a short distance, where they undressed, and laved their brawny limbs in the waters of the Tehintchieu. This resort of the Gylongs was visible from our windows; and as they went half naked into the water, such a promiscuous assemblage, afforded a fair opportunity of forming a just judgment of their figure: and I know not where in the world, an equal number of men would be met with, so straight, so well proportioned, and so stout. This may be taken as a general character: and I do not remember a single instance of deformity in the space through which I have travelled, unless we reckon as such, the glandular swelling of the throat, of which I shall presently speak more particularly.

The Booteeas have invariably black hair, which it is their fashion to cut, close to the head. The eye is a very remarkable feature of the face: small, black, with long pointed corners, as though stretched and extended by artificial means. Their eyelashes are so thin, as to be scarcely perceptible; and the eyebrow is but slightly shaded. Below the eyes, is the broadest part of the face, which is rather flat, and narrows from the cheekbones to the chin; a character of countenance appearing first to take its rise among the Tartar tribes, but is by far more strongly marked in the Chinese. Their skins are remarkably smooth, and most of them arrive at a very advanced age, before they can boast even the earliest rudiments of a beard: they cultivate whiskers, but the best they produce, are of a scanty straggling growth. In this heroic acquisition I quickly surpassed them; and one of my Mogul attendants, for the luxuriancy of his, was the admiration of them all. Many of these mountaineers are more than six feet high; and, taken altogether, they have a complexion not so dark by several shades as that of the European Portugueze.

Though it be somewhat to their discredit, yet impartiality obliges me to own, that my new friends were far from having any very nice notions of cleanliness. The ablution I have just noticed, is a practice connected with their religion, and not repeated more frequently than it enjoins. The ministers, it may be observed, are totally a distinct class, confined solely to the duties of their faith; and the common people, pretending to no interference in matters of spiritual concern, leave religion, with all its forms and ceremonies, to those who are attached from early habit to its obligations, prejudices, and prescriptions: and hence, no doubt, many find an apology for abjuring the use of water, as nature offers it, either on their persons, or at their meals. During our stay at Tassisudon, the Gylongs marched regularly once in every succeeding week, to the performance of this salutary ceremony. They were conducted by a senior of their order, styled Gooroobah, who led the procession, carrying an iron pot, suspended by a chain to the end of a long wand, and smoking with various sorts of aromatic woods: all the rest followed in his train, forming a long line, which reached from the palace-gate beyond the bridge. They were all uniform in their appearance, with the head, legs, and feet bare. Their dress was extremely simple: it consisted of three pieces; a philibeg hanging nearly as low as the knee, a short vest of woollen cloth, without sleeves, and, over the whole, a large oblong mantle of deep crimson cloth, folded round the body in an artful, but apparently negligent, and easy manner. It was first passed across the breast, then under the left arm behind the back; it was permitted to descend from the shoulders to the feet, and the other end was collected and thrown to rest upon the left shoulder; the right arm was left bare, and unconfined, but might be occasionally drawn under the mantle, which admitted also of being lifted up, to cover the head: the left arm lay across the chest, and in the right they carried their rosaries, scanning their beads as they walked along with dexterous rapidity.

The unsightly tumour to which I alluded, known in Bengal by the name of *Gheig*, and *Aubi*, and which in Bootan is called Bà, or Ke Bá, *the neck swelling*, forms itself immediately below the chin, extending from ear to ear, and grows sometimes to such an enormous size, as to hang from the throat down upon the breast. The same disorder is known to prevail in many parts of Europe; in Italy, near the Alps; Stiria, Carinthia, the Ukraine, and the Tyrol; it is distinguished by the name of Goiter. It is particularly observable among the inhabitants

Lieut.t S. Davis del. James Basire sc.

The valley near Tassisudon, with a procession of the religious to their ablutions.

of the hills of Bootan, immediately bordering upon Bengal; and in the tract of low country watered by the rivers that flow from them to the south, beyond the space of a degree of latitude; but it is not peculiar to these regions. The same malady prevails among the people inhabiting the Morung, Nipal, and Almora hills, which, joined to those of Bootan, run in continuation, and bound to the northward, that extensive tract of low land, embraced by the Ganges and the Berhampooter. Both these rivers, originally flowing from nearly the same source, upon quitting this chain, take their final leave of the mountains, at the wide distance of near a thousand miles from each other, and both afterwards run through a flat country, in copious navigable streams, until they join together, and flow into the sea.

This same disease is also more particularly met with in the low lands, adjacent to these hills. From the frontier of Assam, which I reckon to be in the twenty-seventh degree of north latitude and ninety-first degree of east longitude, it is to be traced through Bijnee, Cooch Bahar, Rungpore, Dinagepore, Purnea, Tirroot, and Betiah, along the northern boundary of Owd, in Gooracpore, Barraitch, Pillibeat, and on the confines of Rohilcund, to Hurdewar, which is situated in thirty degrees north latitude, and seventy-eight degrees twenty-five minutes east longitude. This wen, as I before observed, in Europe is called Goiter, and has the effect, or rather is accompanied with the effect, arising from the same cause, of debilitating both the bodies and the minds of those who are affected with it. The whole extent of this low land, immediately joining to the hills, is skirted by a broad belt, from ten to twenty miles in depth, abounding with the most exuberant vegetation, from that succulent and rank reed, termed in Bengal, augeah-gaus, which grows to the height of thirty feet, and is as thick as the wrist, to the most compact and loftiest timber of the forest. It is hardly necessary to add, that from this exhaustless store, the remotest provinces of India, derive an ample supply of the best materials for constructing boats, and for all the purposes of building. As a proper appendage of so grand a scene, there are here found innumerable herds of that invaluable animal, the elephant, which a beneficent Providence has given, to ease the labour of a slothful and feeble race, and has wisely fitted him for his employment, by a docility equal to his strength.

CHAPTER V.

The Valley of Tassisudon.—Palace of the Chief—its extensive Accommodation containing all the Officers of State, a very numerous Establishment of Gylongs, and a Temple of Worship.—Coldness of the Season—Buildings ill calculated to obviate its Effects.—The Rajah's Stud.—Ancient Site of Tassisudon.—Palace of Lam' Ghassatoo.—Mode of supplying the Valley with Water from the surrounding Hills.—The sacred Sentence enclosed in Temples, inscribed on Tablets, on Flags, and on Rocks.—Brahmennee, or sacred Bull.—Artisans—Paper Manufactory.—Season of the Rains moderate—general Salubrity of our Situation.—Poshtee.—An Excursion.—Wandeechy.—Settlements of the Religious.—A Recluse.—Caution of the Daeb.—Mr. Saunders taken ill—Incantations for his Recovery.

HAVING at length a little time to breathe from the occupations of ceremony, and the no less important concern of domestic arrangements, I shall endeavour to give a general idea of the valley of Tassisudon. A narrow slip of three or four miles in length, and in its widest part not exceeding one mile in breadth, has been made choice of for the situation of the capital. It may rather be termed, I think, a softened glen, which lying betwixt the vast mountains that give a passage to the river

Tehintchieu, ornament its border, by an easy slope of their bases to its sides; thus forming a bank of the richest soil, which the industrious Booteea well knows how to cultivate. It was, upon our arrival, luxuriantly clothed with the most promising crops of rice, which, in defect of rain, all the springs of the surrounding mountains, are artificially conducted to fertilize. There is no town, nor indeed any house, except that which we occupied, within a mile of the palace; but a few clusters of houses, distributed in different parts among the fields, when the eye is weary of contemplating the bold features of near and distant mountains, and scanning their wonderful combinations, serve as points of rest, and call back the wandering mind from a rude incoherent chaos, to repose amidst the fruitful and ingenious efforts of husbandry and population.

The castle, or palace, of Tassisudon[a] stands near the centre of the valley, and is a building of stone, of a quadrangular form. The length of the front, exceeds that of the sides by one-third: the walls are lofty, and as I conjecture upwards of thirty feet high, and they are sloped a little from the foundation to the top: above the middle space, is a row of projecting balconies, to each of which are curtains made of black hair, which are always drawn at night: below, the walls are pierced with very small windows, which I judge to be intended rather for the purpose of admitting air, than light. There are two entrances into the palace: the one facing the south is by a flight of wooden steps, edged with plates of iron, beginning on a level with the ground on the outside, and rising to the more elevated terrace within, the whole being

[a] Plate VI.

Pl. VI.

Lieut.t S. Davis del. James Basire sc.

The Palace of Tassisudon in Bootan.

comprehended within the thickness of the wall. The other, the grand entrance, is on the east front, which is ascended by a flight of stone steps. Even with these we entered a spacious gateway, having two massy doors, fortified with knobs of iron, which stand above the surface of the wood; a large bar of timber, sliding within the masonry, serves to secure them when shut. We passed through this gateway, and came opposite to the central square building, which I must call the citadel; and this is the habitation of the supreme Lama. It contains also the chief of their idols, Mahamoonie, amidst a multitude of others of inferior note. Both to the right and left, the way leads to spacious squares, paved with flat stones, and to the apartments of the Lama. The citadel is connected with the western angle; and there is a communication from the varanda, or covered gallery, which adjoins to it. The citadel is a very lofty building, being no less than seven stories high, each from fifteen to eighteen feet; it is covered over with a roof of a low pitch, composed of fir timbers, sheathed with boards of deal, which project on each side a great way beyond the walls; from the centre, there rises a square piece of masonry, which supports a canopy of copper, richly gilt; and this is supposed to be immediately over the great idol, Mahamoonie. Lam' Rimbochay, the present Daeb Raja, lives upon the fourth floor from the ground; above that, there are two other stories; and the seventh ladder leads to the temple of Mahamoonie, which is covered with the gilded canopy.

We now left the citadel, to take a view of the rest of the building, and found the east, west, and south angles, exactly corresponding with each other, in having apartments on the ground floor appropriated for depositing all kinds of stores. A covered gallery, runs all round them; beneath which are subterraneous places, serving for kitchens. A range of good rooms, with boarded floors, on the first story, accommodates all the officers of state, who are attendant on the Raja; and these again, towards the square, are skirted by a deep varanda, supported by a row of handsome pillars, whose capitals are ornamented with carved work and gilding, and their sides painted with vermilion. The varandas are lofty and broad, and are not, in my opinion, without an air of magnificence.

Over this story, is a sort of terrace of cement, with rooms more roughly finished, which are intended for the inferior officers, styled Zeenkaubs; they are covered only by the roof, which is constructed in the usual manner, of cross beams of fir, resting upon upright posts, and planks of deal placed on them, with large stones to keep them down. These beams are supported high above the walls, and project far beyond them. The north square is, in appearance, a very confused assemblage of apartments; I fear, therefore, that it will scarcely be possible to give an intelligible description of it: let it then suffice to say, that it is composed of a motley mixture of kitchens, cells, and temples.

We had now become tolerably well settled in our quarters; but, notwithstanding a vertical sun, the coldness of the weather, to our feelings, who had been so lately accustomed to the hot region of Bengal, recalled the idea of something beyond the rigour of an Indian winter; and consequently our first care, after taking possession of our mansion, was employed in lining the wainscots of the apartments, with the thickest woollen cloths the country could supply, and in constructing curtains as a defence against the piercing winds, that pervaded the apertures of the balconies. While engaged in thus guarding ourselves against the cold, in order more effectually to obviate its effects, the erection of a fireplace became a matter of serious deliberation; but, before we had finally fixed upon the plan, and procured materials for executing it, milder weather succeeded, and induced us to drop the design; an event, much to be regretted by the present and future race of Booteeas, who, destitute of this most necessary convenience, are obliged to have recourse, to a very offensive way of warming their rooms. The best contrivance in general use, to prevent the fire, when kindled, from communicating to the timbers which compose the chief part of every house, is a large flat stone. This being placed in the middle of the room, the company range themselves round it, prepared to put up with volumes of pine smoke, which, having no exit but by the windows and doors, never fails by its pungency to annoy all who are present, and who at length partake of the same gloomy colour with the ceilings and the walls.

Our habitation, which was within a stone's throw of the palace, was extremely commodious, and well adapted to our use. We entered, by a door on the south side, into a square court-yard; not very large, but it served to confine our cattle, and, indeed, more than we wished to have there. The house was opposite the doorway, and filled one side of the square; the other three sides were enclosed by buildings, which, not being so lofty as the house by one floor, held our baggage, and accommodated all our attendants. We inhabited the upper story, which displayed a good suite of rooms, boarded, and divided by doors that turned on pivots. The eastern front next the river had a commodious balcony, which projected sufficiently to command a view of as much of the valley as was visible from any one point, comprehending all the space from the bridge, far beyond the castle of Lam' Ghassatoo, north: nor, on the south, could any thing pass the palace that was not equally subject to our view, which was at length terminated by a very handsome cluster of pines growing opposite to Wangoka, and narrowing the valley almost to a point.

To the south of the palace, on the road by which we had arrived at it, we thought there was little worthy of our notice; our excursions were therefore commonly directed up the valley; and during our residence at Tassisudon, not an evening elapsed (unless when prevented by rain) in which we omitted to walk.

The Raja's stud of horses, which lay a short mile towards the north, was one of the first objects that claimed our notice. It was well stocked with a choice collection of domestic and foreign cattle; yet the visitor, if he expects to find a breed of Arabs, Persians, or any of the various casts of Toorkees, Tazees, or Magennes, so much esteemed in Hindostan, will be completely disappointed; but, in their stead, he will see the Tangun, a strong and active sort of poney, which I have already described, admirably adapted to the country, and such as a traveller will not hesitate to prefer, in these regions, to the most valuable and beautiful of the species.

The Raja's stud contained also a variety of mules and Tartar geldings, both much esteemed for their docility and strength, which has conferred upon them a higher price, and a decided preference, with the opulent and the aged. There were also three or four fat handsome Toorkey horses, which somehow or other fell into the hands of the Booteeas, during their war with us upon their frontier. They had been brought, I was informed, by the way of Dalimcotta, the safest passage over the mountains to this place, where now it is their fate to remain prisoners in the stable, unless when taken abroad, to be loaded with superb trappings, and to act a part in some grand procession.

Near this spot, I was told, the castle of Tassisudon was formerly situated; but about fifteen years ago, during the inauspicious reign of Daeb Jeeder, being consumed by fire, the royal residence was in consequence removed nearer the centre, being the widest part of the valley.

The low hill on which the palace, or residence, of Lam' Ghassatoo stands, is upon the left, and, as long as they lasted, we were induced to loiter away many an evening, in picking strawberries from its sides, which were clothed with them from its foot to the very foundation of the palace walls. The Gylongs used to look at us from the windows with amazement; they, for their parts, hold this delicious little fruit in contempt, and abandon it to those, who have only to depend on the spontaneous productions of nature, for their support. The species we here found was pointed, conical, of a small size, like the alpine strawberry; rather seedy, and not quite so high flavoured as those that grow in the woods of England.

We sometimes extended our walk, by ascending a path that skirted an adjoining mountain: it was formed by the side of an aqueduct, that communicated with distant springs, and conveyed water, whenever the farmer saw occasion to avail himself of such a resource, to every part of the valley. Three of these aqueducts were ranged one above the other, with a considerable space between them; and, as we looked up to the Raja's villa above them, surrounded with well grown firs, and other choice trees, I thought them highly ornamental to the prospect.

The hollowed trunks of large trees, which were in some parts fixed in the soil which covered the rock, and in others sustained by beams inserted in it, across deep dells, and along the sides of precipices, gave a passage to the waters. The eye could trace these conduits for more than two miles in continuation; they exist as noble though modest monuments of the genius of the people, and lose very little in comparison with the more costly models of antiquity. So plain but ingenious a contrivance certainly merits admiration, especially when we see the inventors of it intrenched, in impervious mountains, among whom, the sciences never yet became a study, and who are totally excluded, as well by natural impediments, as local prejudices, from all communication with more enlightened nations. The most perfect comprehension of the science of hydraulics, could hardly, in the present instance, have suggested to them any improvement.

Our return, when we chose to vary from the road by which we came, was in front of the palace of Lam' Ghassatoo[b], on the south side of which was a long narrow tract of level ground, supporting many tall flagstaffs, that had narrow banners of white cloth reaching nearly from one end to the other, and inscribed with the mystic words,

[b] Plate VII.

Pl. VII

Lieut. S. Davis del. James Basire sc.

The Residence of Lam Ghassa-too.

Oom maunie paimee oom[c]. A small square temple, erected to contain an image, stood in the way. A similar building is seen, placed like a centinel, as it were, by the road side, on each approach towards every consecrated habitation, proportionate in dimensions to the magnitude and importance of the edifice with which it is connected: on each of the three great roads, that lead to Tassisudon, a very spacious one is found. They have one small doorway, which always remains closed, at least I never could succeed in my endeavour to obtain a view of the interior; yet such is the superstitious respect of the inhabitants for its contents, that they constantly uncover their heads, and if travelling on horseback, dismount and walk while they pass by them.

I remember to have seen one of these buildings, which was dedicated to the junction of the Hatchieu with the Tehintchieu, near Kepta. They are often placed at the meeting of two principal roads. I have seen them also at the base of a remarkable mountain, and they are invariably met with, at the entrance of every capital village.

There is another sort of monument occasionally substituted in places of inferior consequence; it is a long wall, commonly about twelve or fifteen feet in length, six feet high, and two deep, with a centre distinguished by being thicker and higher than the sides. On both faces, near the top, are inserted large tablets, with the words *Oom maunie*

[c] Of this form of words, to which ideas of peculiar sanctity are annexed by the inhabitants of Bootan and Tibet, I could never obtain a satisfactory explanation. It is frequently engraven on the rocks in large and deep characters, and sometimes I have seen it on the sides of hills: the letters, which are formed by means of stones fixed in the earth, are of so vast a magnitude, as to be visible at a very considerable distance.

paimee oom, carved in relief. As the inscription, of course, begins at opposite ends on each side, the Booteeas are careful, in passing, that they do not trace the words backwards. This kind of monument very frequently occurs at Chuka, Kepta, Pauga, Noomnoo, Wangoka, the foot of the bridge below Tassisudon, and in many other places.

In front of the palace, a pampered bull sometimes disputed the passage with us. He was the fiercest of his breed, and we were seldom inclined, therefore, to engage in so rude a contest. He appeared to enjoy his existence, upon the same easy terms as the village, or Brahmennee[d], bull in Bengal; and indulgence had rendered him intolerably insolent. Familiarity with the lord of the creation, had subdued his fear, (the great principle of subjection) and taught him to despise a creature vastly his inferior in corporeal strength, and totally at his mercy, whenever he chose to exert his savage powers, and indulge in the mischievous excesses of licentious liberty.

A little further on, nearer to Tassisudon, was a long line of sheds, full of furnaces and anvils, at which some of the sons of Vulcan, found employment in forging brazen gods, and various other ornaments disposed about their religious buildings. Nor must I pass unnoticed, that most excellent orchard, which we so often visited in our way home, stored with delicious fruits. When raspberries and strawberries failed, they were succeeded by apricots and peaches; and hence we constantly obtained a plentiful supply. A small gratuity

[d] Brahmennee, or sacred bull, of the Hindoos, rambles about the neighbourhood without interruption; he is universally caressed and pampered by the people, and to feed him is deemed a meritorious act of religion.

kept the owner always in good humour; and his wife, when he was not at home, would readily attend, and help us to the best fruit. It contained also apples, pears, and walnuts; but the latter were not ripe during our stay, and the former were extremely harsh and coarse.

In our perambulations down the valley, I often rested at the place where the chief manufacture of paper is established, which was made, I found, by a very easy and unexpensive process, of the bark of a tree, here called Deah, which grows in great abundance upon the mountains near Tassisudon, but is not produced on those immediately bordering on Bengal. The method of preparing this material, as well as I could learn, is as follows. When a sufficient quantity of bark is collected to employ the labourer, it is divided into small shreds, and steeped and boiled in a lixivium of wood ashes; it is then taken up, and laid in a heap to drain; after which it is beaten upon a stone, with a wooden mallet, until it is reduced to an impalpable pulp; it is then thrown into a reservoir of water, where, being well stirred about, and cleansed from the coarse and dirty part, which floats upon the surface, it is still further depurated in another large reservoir of clean water. When the preparation is complete, the parts are finely broken, and that which sinks in the water, appears mucilaginous to the touch. All that now remains is to form it into sheets, which is done upon small reeds set in frames. The labourer dips the frame in the water, and raises up a quantity of the pulp, which, by moving the frame in the water, he spreads, until it entirely and equally covers the surface of the reeds; he then raises the frame perpendicularly, the water drains off, and the frame is hung up till the sheet is nearly dry: it is then taken off, and suspended upon lines. The paper thus prepared is of a much stronger texture, than that of any other country with which I am acquainted, as it is capable of being woven, when gilt by way of ornament, into the texture of silk and satins, to which use I have seen it frequently applied in the manufactures of China.

The season of the rains, in these regions, is remarkably moderate; there are frequent showers, but none of those heavy torrents which accompany the monsoon to the southward in Bengal; so that we were seldom interrupted in our exercise both morning and evening; and the weather continued so temperate, that we were occasionally abroad, even at this season, during every hour of the day, without experiencing any inconvenience from the heat of the sun. An equal exposure, in the same parallel of latitude, in the low lands, would, most certainly, not have been hazarded with impunity. Notwithstanding the quantity of stagnant water, confined upon the fields around us, to sustain the advancing crops, and the abundant vegetation, both on the hills and every part of the valley, which philosophers pronounce to be infallible sources of bad air, yet we cannot with justice, question the salubrity of this situation.

During our journey and residence among these mountains, we lost but one man by sickness, and his death could not fairly be imputed to the climate. I thought him a bad subject in the beginning. He was immoderately addicted to the use of opium; and its inebriating quality, had given to his features that heated, wild, and fixed appearance, which commonly distinguishes those who intemperately use it. In the language of Bengal, persons of this description are distinguished by the term Poshtee, that is, eaters of opium, which is considered as a term of the highest reproach.

Our walks about Tassisudon were not very various, but we now ventured on one, longer and more laborious than any we had yet taken. We very early conceived a desire to visit some of the highest mountains by which the valley was bounded; but it appeared to be so tremendous an undertaking, that we long meditated upon the scheme before we executed it. At length, however, the day was fixed; and having taken an early dinner, under favour of intervening clouds, Mr. Saunders and myself set out on the expedition, anxious to explore what new and interesting objects they might yield, as well as to indulge our curiosity, in contemplating these admirable scenes, on which Mr. Davis, the companion of our travels, was at the same time most successfully employing his pencil. His subjects indeed, in themselves, are not more remarkable for their grandeur and beauty, than for the judgment, fidelity, and taste, with which he has seized on and recorded their features. To such as find satisfaction in contemplating nature, in its most gigantic and rudest form, what an inexhaustible fund of delight is here displayed! Gratification waits on every step, and the mind is animated with the sublimest sentiments, while the beholder, fascinated with the ever-varying beauties, pauses to enjoy the rich repast, insensible of fatigue, and turns his eye with reluctance from so magnificent a prospect.

Our route lay by the Raja's villa, Wandeechy, where we rested awhile, and drank of the clear spring, which fills a reservoir behind the mansion, furnishing, even at this high station, in all seasons, an ample supply of water for domestic uses. We continued to ascend along the ridge of the mountain, which runs towards the south west, by many steep windings in the path. The fine stately firs that ornament Wandeechy, give place to less noble plants in these more lofty regions, and vegetation of a dwarfish, hardy species, began to prevail as we approached the summit. Diminutive as Tassisudon, and every object that lay below us, now appeared, the valley, rich with high cultivation, diversified with numerous habitations, and watered by the winding Tehintchieu, presented a beautiful scene, which derived singular grandeur from the towering mountains around it, whose sides sustained many solitary cottages, in strange and fantastical positions, the silent abodes of the recluse. In the mean time, some larger and more populous settlements of the votaries of religion, were visible in various parts. The most luxuriant trees, I observed, clothe the skirts only of the loftiest mountains: these before us, like others which I have seen, carry their heads into an atmosphere, too rare to afford nourishment to the great and flourishing productions of the vegetable kingdom.

Many of the sons of piety plant their dwellings in these pure regions, and in general, judiciously abandon the low hollows, with their putrid and humid exhalations, as best suited to the business of the husbandman. It was with infinite toil that we attained the summit, where we found a spacious stone building, surrounded with a high wall, through which there was one gateway. It was for some time debated, whether or not, we should venture to look within this solitary castle;

for there appeared to us no trace of any living creature either in or near it.

The door was not fastened, and was without difficulty pushed open. We advanced within it, and had scarcely entered the court yard, when a boy approached, and greeted us with his master's invitation. We obeyed, and ascending a flight of wooden steps to the upper floor, were met on the landing-place by a man of decent figure, in the religious habit. He led us to an inner apartment, where cushions and carpets were spread out, and invited us to sit down. A very ample repast of buttered tea, clouted cream, and parched grain, evinced the hospitality of this good humoured recluse. He was extremely talkative, and our dress supplied a copious subject of enquiry and observation. He spoke with evident satisfaction of the good understanding subsisting between the Governor General and the Daeb Raja, as well as the favour and indulgence shewn by the English government to his nation; for which he said we had the prayers of all the Gylongs.

All his attendants, and there were many, assembled to gratify themselves with gazing at us. Amongst them I observed two fine boys, who gave occasion to a loud burst of laughter, when I asked him if they were his sons. He smiled at my want of information, telling me that he was a Gylong, and that Gylongs never marry. The sun had disappeared behind the mountains, and the rapid approach of evening, made it necessary to think of our return. We had now wandered to a great distance from home, and though our progress downwards was, of course, considerably accelerated, yet night surprised us long before we reached our mansion.

The next day I visited the Daeb, and took an opportunity to relate the adventure of the preceding day. He seemed pleased with our account, shewing, as indeed he had frequently done before, much solicitude for our entertainment; but I could plainly perceive that he did not altogether approve of our being abroad after it was dark; he talked of wild beasts and evil genii; and cautioned us against a repetition of walks so long and late. I could not but esteem the advice considerate and prudent; for though no danger immediately presented itself, yet a stranger has always, perhaps, something to apprehend in a foreign country, from the inherent prejudices of the peasantry, amongst whom, a natural contempt and enmity universally prevails against those of a different nation from themselves, and which a long course of time is necessary, completely to remove.

Mr. Saunders, unfortunately, a few days after, was taken extremely ill, and for some time confined by a severe fever. The Raja expressed to me great uneasiness at his sickness, and manifested a sincere concern for his recovery; nor did he omit diffusely to enlarge upon the imminent danger, of too curiously examining unfrequented woods and solitary places, the favourite haunts of evil genii; telling me, at the same time, that the influence of a very powerful Dewta prevailed over the mountain we had ascended, and, of course, concluding that we had been subject to his spells. This opinion gained ground with all our servants; for there is not a Mussulman, or Hindoo, who does not as heartily subscribe to the doctrine of dæmonology, as to the most orthodox tenet of his faith. The Raja ordered solemn incantations to be commenced without delay: a priest accordingly came to our house, performed certain ceremonies about a cauldron of fire, prayed abundantly, and, having received the reward of his labours, departed, well satisfied with the part he had acted. From hence I collected, that there were charms suited to the priests, as well as dæmons of Bootan; and that there is hardly an evil under heaven, for which gold, properly applied, cannot produce an effectual remedy. However, it was not long before Mr. Saunders's fever took a favourable turn, and we had the pleasure shortly after to see him perfectly recover.

CHAPTER VI.

Commotions — excited by Wandipora Zoompoon and a degraded Chief.—Punukka Zoompoon arrives at the Capital to pay the customary Duty of Allegiance.—Popular Administration of the present Daeb Raja.—Ascribed Cause of the Rebellion—prudent Precautions—Subjects called upon for their Allegiance—weak Condition of the Capital—extreme Vigilance—general Alarm — Letter from the Rebel Leader—Insurgents gather Strength—Skirmishes between the contending Parties—some Loyalists badly wounded with Arrows—their Dread of Poison—strong Position of the Rebels. —Invited to visit the Raja—his compassionate Concern for the deluded Mob, and confident Expectation the Tumults would soon be quelled.—Miserable Artillery—humane Motive for desiring to employ it—cautious Conduct of the Combatants—general Trait of these Warriors—the Rebels, after an obstinate Contest, totally defeated.—Military Character of the Booteeas—not deficient in Courage—feeble Attack—want of Discipline—Accoutrements and Arms—Use of Poison.—Raja Mocum Narrain—his Vakeel.—Wandipore invested by Zoon Donier and Punukka Zompoon.—General Thanksgivings.—Reduction of the Castle.—Flight of the Rebels.—Plunder and Spoils.—The Raja meditates a Visit to Wandipore, to settle Affairs in the disturbed Districts—announces his Design—invites me to meet him.

A COMPLETE month had not elapsed after our arrival at Tassisudon, when two turbulent chiefs, the Zoompoon of Wandipore, a keeper of one of the principal castles in Bootan, together with a degraded officer, who had served in an important post under the former government, contrived to raise a commotion, which as it gave the Raja and his subjects much trouble to appease; and which, as it may tend to portray a feature in their character as a warlike people, I intend minutely to detail, from its commencement to its close.

The commandant of the castle of Punukka, the winter residence of the Daeb Raja, arrived at Tassisudon, on the 25th of June, as it is customary at this season of the year for each of the high officers under the government of Bootan, to render an account of his district, and pay his duty of allegiance to the sovereign chief. Immediately on the departure of the Zoompoon from Punukka, it was rumoured that a powerful party of armed people assaulted the castle, and finding it unguarded, (the chief part of the establishment having gone to escort the Zoompoon) obtained possession of it, as it were, by surprise. Though the report was not yet actually confirmed, sufficient was known totally to derange the tranquil order of the state, and suggest the most active military preparations. Armed people were seen to assemble, and resort to be enrolled at the palace all day; whence they were again detached in parties of twelve or twenty, by secret routes across the mountains, for the purpose of throwing reinforcements into Punukka, or to check the progress of the rebels.

Popular and prudent as the administration of the present Raja had been, yet seditious murmurs had long since been known to exist; chiefly because several officers, nominated by the former Raja to the highest posts of public trust, had been displaced on his accession to the government. It is said that the Zoompoon of Tassisudon, and the Zempi, were soon obliged to give way to his particular favourites, while other officers, in various parts of the country, were also superseded. This early use of his authority did not fail to kindle dissatisfaction and disgust, among those who suffered from its exercise; hitherto indeed, they had been kept within decent bounds, till at length a turbulent spirit having broken the peace, an avowed rebellion ensued. The disbanded chiefs were said to have consulted together, and confederated with a resolution to revenge their real or supposed injuries.

During the night of the 26th of June, a large party was posted on the bridge, immediately opposite to the house in which we lived, and a strong guard also took its station at the palace gates. The alarm having gone abroad, and the peasantry far and near being called upon to defend their sovereign, constant additions of force joined the royal standard. The ploughman and mechanic, arranging themselves under the banner of the chief inhabitant of their neighbourhood, repaired martially arrayed to the head quarters, whence they were in different divisions, expeditiously pushed off to relieve the castle of Punukka, concerning which reports were still various: some asserting that it was not yet taken, though all seemed conscious of its danger. In the course of the day, intelligence arrived, of the defeat of a part of the Raja's troops, about six miles south of Tassisudon, the enemy having gained possession of Wangoka, after an obstinate contest, in which some lives were lost.

The same guards still kept their stations on Friday the 27th of June, and others were placed lower down the valley, to prevent the enemy's advance; yet with the same success that attended the beginning of their career, the insurgents that morning became masters of three villages, within two miles of the palace walls, and no material shew of resistance appeared ready to interrupt their progress; for as yet, it would seem, the strength of government was not collected, and its force, weakened by detachments, was inadequate to extend beyond the defence of its immediate seat. Consistently with this plan, every possible exertion was made: strong pickets were advanced in front, and to the right and left occupied the roads across the mountains; double vigilance guarded the gates of Tassisudon, which were shut against the admission of all strangers, except such as had been previously and strictly examined; and no Gylong was, upon any pretence, permitted to go out.

Affairs now seemed to wear a serious aspect, and it was time, we thought, for us to look a little to our defence: accordingly we began to rub up our arms, and muster our stock of ammunition, as a measure preparatory to a siege: not doubting that, if the design of the insurgents was to bring their assault home to the Raja's door, our chateau, as standing in a very important point of view, would have attracted their earliest regard. But whether the rebels were desirous to avoid impelling us to take an hostile part, or whether they wished to secure the assistance of the English to their cause, I cannot pretend to say; we were however saved the trouble of resistance. A few days only before the rupture, I received from the Zoompoon of Wandipore, who was at the head of the rebellion, a present of fruits, with a very handsome congratulatory letter, regretting that urgent business at present prevented his seeing one, who had come from so great a distance, and who belonged to a nation, for which he entertained the highest esteem. His servants, having performed their commission, joined him as he was advancing, and I had certain information, that they were among the numbers, now occupying the conquered villages to the south. A reinforcement to the insurgents, shewed themselves upon the brow of a hill to the south-west, which the pickets in that quarter effectually opposed, and for the present prevented their junction; at the same instant two parties marched from the castle to the attack of the villages; in which the insurgents had taken post; a measure which I considered to be meant merely as a diversion. Both divisions, with some interval between them, advanced at first full in front of the villages, but as they drew near they divided into small parties, and crept slowly along, sheltering themselves behind banks and bushes. The use of the bow and matchlock, on both sides, at first was very slack; but the Raja's people commenced, after a while, a pretty smart fire. The rebels seemed careful of their ammunition, using it sparingly; and not choosing to be drawn out of their post, they remained almost completely concealed, except that now and then a Booteea would start up from behind a wall, which flanked the lower village, and brandishing his sword, shout with an air of defiance. This sort of distant skirmish continued for some time; but the Raja's people gradually advanced till they had arrived within a bow shot of the villages, when they paused, and seemed preparing to make a general assault; but, before they could execute this design, the insurgents suddenly sallied out, and made them precipitately fall back, so that they were inclined, for the rest of the day, to keep a more cautious distance; yet a party of the Raja's made a feint of moving to the right, towards a village on the flank of the other two, which the insurgents seemed not yet to have possessed; but they were sufficiently alert, to defeat the attempt of the loyalists, by a timely and effectual opposition. The Raja's forces, as the evening closed, retreated to their quarters, leaving the enemy, who were reckoned to be three or four hundred strong, masters of the field. But the day did not close without some bloodshed. Three of the wounded were brought to Mr. Saunders; two of them, the Daroga, or master of the horse, and another young man, were shot with arrows, that had pierced through the thigh; and the third received his wound just above the elbow, pointing upwards. He endeavoured to draw out the arrow; but the barbs entangling in the sinews, the shaft alone came away with the effort, when instantly seizing a knife by his side, the courageous youth cut a deep incision, and with his own hand extricated the head.

They were all impressed with a strong dread of poison, with which they apprehended the heads of the arrows to have been charged, and they pretended to be already sensible of its corroding pangs. They submitted however to be dressed, expressing little hope of life, when they heard that there was no certain antidote, against the baneful effects of poison.

The three villages, of which the rebels were now in complete possession, extended across the valley in a line east and west. There was some interval between them; so that the two extremes, I reckon, are rather more than a mile apart. In the morning, it might be observed, that they had very nearly completed a breast-work along the whole of this space, which afforded a safe line of communication from one village to another, the only break being between the westernmost and the centre. This breast-work was a wall of loose stones, over which they could fire when they stood up, but which afforded them a complete cover when they crouched down, the ends of their bows only being visible above it.

About noon, a messenger came to me from the Raja, desiring us to wait upon him, and we immediately obeyed the invitation. He apologized, at the instant of our meeting, for not having seen us during the last three days, his attention, during that time, having been entirely engaged; and exhorted us not to be alarmed at the present disturbances, comparing the insurgents to the Sunneassees and Fakeers, that occasionally traverse, in tumultuous bodies, the borders of Bengal. "They are a disorderly rabble," says he, "led on by a Zempi, whom I dismissed for his misconduct, and suffered to go away unpunished; but he, availing himself of this indulgence, before his disgrace became publicly known, obtained under the sanction of my name, from various officers in my employment, sundry valuable effects, which he embezzled, and then took refuge in the woods. Our searches for him, in every quarter, have been vain; he has lain completely concealed, until this his sudden appearance at the head of a misguided mob."

The Raja then spoke to me of some cannon in his possession, which he wanted to get mounted, and begged me to lend him the assistance of some person who could instruct his people in the management of them; professing a desire to employ them for the preservation of his subjects. He wished to batter down the houses, in which the rabble had lodged themselves; concluding, that when they had lost their shelter, they would disperse to their respective homes. "They are my deluded subjects," said he: "I would reclaim, but not destroy them."

Our conversation chiefly turned upon the commotions abroad, which the Raja repeatedly assured me would soon be quelled. He appeared evidently discomposed, and I determined not to add to his distress by a long visit: so, expressing a wish to take my leave, tea was introduced, and we retired.

It was hinted to us, as we were leaving the palace, that it would be agreeable to the Raja, if we looked at the cannon. We found them lying upon some rising ground, pointed towards the villages. They were two small cast cannon, old and honeycombed; in the calibre of one were hollows, that would receive an egg. They were crammed with powder and shot, almost full. I thought the greatest mischief to be apprehended from this ordnance, was to the person who applied the match. As they were not mounted, we could flatter them with no very essential service from them; but as the best advice we could give, we begged they would be careful how they ventured to discharge them. While we were engaged in viewing this miserable artillery, on a sudden the bells of the palace rang violently, and out rushed a multitude of armed men, equipped for battle: they hurried on, with a wild and savage cry, brandishing their arms with an air of bold and insolent defiance; but the rest of their conduct bore a very different aspect, and the expedition ended rather in a dastardly manner. The rebels came to meet them, and an action commenced with a pretty brisk fire, of which we waited to see the beginning, till the shot ranged past the place where the cannon were, struck the walls, and, as we walked along the other face of the palace, went far beyond it.

From our quarters we could see both parties endeavouring to keep themselves as much as possible under cover, availing themselves of all irregularities in the ground, and now and then making a random shot, though with little effect, whenever they knew there was a collection of people, in consequence of the ends of their bows and matchlocks being visible. This sort of conflict lasted for more than two hours: the assailants were kept constantly at bay, and at length thought proper to draw off.

It is evident that the want of vigour in the Raja's troops was highly calculated to raise the ardour of the insurgents, who all seemed animated in their leader's cause, and steady to his standard; yet, whatever might be the views or motives of this revolt, the rebels had not yet employed their power to its utmost extent, having hitherto made no effort beyond their own intrenchments, except indeed to repel the assaults of their opponents. Had their forces rushed on with the same rapidity with which they at first sprang forth, it would have been to certain conquest. The very first impression of their arms shook the prince upon his throne, made him tremble for the permanency of his power, and instilled a panic through every department of the palace. Bold and daring as the first onset was, the prosecution of their scheme, in this manner, seemed to betray a want of confidence in their strength; for every moment they wasted in inaction, before a defenceless citadel, strengthened the Raja's power; and, whatever might be their object, a very short time placed it for ever beyond their reach. Before sunset a pretty considerable reinforcement joined the insurgents; and it is reported, that early in the day, they received also a large supply of men and ammunition, which seemed by no means improbable, from the frequent firing, and increased numbers of people distinguishable by the telescope, about the houses, and on the skirts of the village.

The following day displayed the same hostile appearance: with busy looks, and in warlike attire, unusual crowds were traversing to and fro the whole of the morning. It was noon, before the consequence of this preparation was fully known; then the warrior, with a stout heart and full stomach, issued forth to battle, having raised his courage and his spirits by an ample meal, and copious draughts of *chong*. Three divisions advanced, in opposition to the extended forces of the foe, who occupied the three villages, situated between rhe river and the foot of the western mountain; an irregular, slow discharge of musquetry took place, and was kept up, with little intermission, upwards of an hour and a half; the Raja's forces gaining ground, and driving back the rebels within their parallels. His troops appeared also more numerous and confident than they had hitherto done, and they exhibited a resolution, which, doubtless, received strength from the slackness of the enemy's fire, and the subsequent discovery of their want of ammunition: for at last the rebels were obliged to resort, as their only means of annoyance, to pelting their adversaries with stones; but these, not being hurled from an eminence, had little effect. It was curious to observe the mixture of defiance and of fear, displayed in the conduct of these combatants. A Booteea, in the moment of his highest exultation, forgets not his personal safety, but is most careful to guard against the danger of missile weapons: he is one instant jumping and twirling himself about, brandishing his sword and shield with an air of defiance, and with a wild and savage shout apparently challenging attack: the next moment, if a gun be pointed, or a bow raised to be discharged, he shrinks into concealment. Nor is the intrepidity of their assaults more exemplary: a party sallying, pursues no longer than the party that advanced, retreats; when it halts, they stand, and then retire again. With frequent fluctuations, sometimes one, sometimes the other side, gaining a momentary advantage, the contest was carried on till about five o'clock, when the loyalists forced the rebels from the centre village, and those on the east and west were pushed very close by the two divisions, that had moved to the attack of each. Soon afterwards a parley took place, in which the rebels seemed to be making terms. The conference lasted more than twenty minutes; when the victorious party came down from the centre village, and hastened the decision. The Eastern village was instantly evacuated; and the insurgents being permitted to withdraw, went off in a confused crowd towards the south. Nearly at the same time the western village was also abandoned; and no magic exhibition could display a more sudden and striking change of scene. In an instant the whole plain, and the rice fields, were covered with an innumerable host; every bank and bush gave up their proportion, which much exceeded even the numbers that rushed from the houses and from behind the walls: yet on the part of the victors there was no pursuit; from whence I concluded, that an unmolested egress was the stipulation made in the parley between the Raja's troops and the enemy. Yet some groups of the latter retreated slowly, making many pauses, that shewed the reluctance with which they submitted to this defeat. Before sunset, each of the villages was evacuated by the enemy, except two houses in the western village, of which a party still held possession, and declared they would never yield themselves prisoners, nor accept of any other terms than a free and uninterrupted retreat.

About an hour after the flight of the rest, we saw these houses surrounded by the Raja's troops, but still occupied by these resolute rebels. We walked through the villages, and saw few marks of disorder. The women, children, and pigs, were enjoying full and quiet possession. The houses were in no respect damaged; except that a great number of impressions had been made by musquetry on their walls. There were not many lives lost in the contest; a few men were made prisoners, some badly wounded, and several horses taken. Thus ended this long conflict, which impressed on us, a very mean idea of their military accomplishments, whatever other qualifications they may boast.

The Booteeas are a strong and hardy race, by no means deficient in manly courage. Their feeble mode of attack and defence is, therefore, imputable only to their want of discipline; to their not fighting in compact files or platoons; and to their consequent distrust of each other; and something also must be attributed to their utter inexperience of war: for indeed, among this crowd of combatants, we find merely husbandmen and villagers, called at once from their peaceful occupations to the field of battle.

Every kind of discipline and order is totally disregarded in their mode of warfare; stratagem is more practised than open assault: they engage in general as marksmen, and wait their opportunity to fire unobserved. Both parties are so careful to conceal themselves, that seldom any thing is visible but the top of a tufted helmet, or the end of a bow: no wonder, therefore, that in their contests very few are killed.

The accoutrements of a fighting man, fully equipped, are extremely cumbrous. A prodigious deal of loose clothing surrounds the body: besides the common mantle, he wears very often a blanket, or thick quilted jacket. This, as well as the helmet, (which is made either of stained cane, coiled conically, or else of cotton rope, quilted between two cloths, with flaps that occasionally turn down over the ears, and a piece to cover the nose,) if not absolutely proof against the stroke of a sword or arrow, must at least considerably weaken its force. He carries upon his arm a large convex shield of painted cane, coiled close, and a long straight sword is worn across the body, thrust through the belt before. To these arms must be added, a bow, and a quiver of arrows, slung by a belt behind the back; the arrows being commodiously drawn from it over the left shoulder. The bow is held in the right hand; it is commonly six feet long, made of bamboo, and, when unstrung, is perfectly straight. The bowstring is a small cord of hemp of appropriate length; its tension, and the consequent curvature of the bow, depending upon the degree of twist given to it before the bow is bent.

The kind of bamboo in use for bows, is peculiar to the hills, and is remarkable for its elasticity and strength; they are made of a split piece, or two pieces united by bands together, the smooth surface being placed without. The string is drawn by the thumb, armed with a ring of bone, or a piece of thick leather, bent round it, and the forefinger, crossed upon the nail, serves to give additional force to the operation.

The arrow is formed of a species of dwarf bamboo, produced also among these mountains: it is headed by a flattened barb of pointed iron, the sides of which are sometimes grooved, or (which appears to answer the same purpose) the barb on either side is a little turned back, to admit the lodgment of poison; with which deadly substance, I was sorry to hear, it is sometimes charged.

The poison made use of, as far as I could collect, is an inspissated vegetable juice; but from what plant it is obtained, I could never distinctly learn: it appeared to my observation black and gummy; in consistence and appearance, much resembling crude opium.

Some Booteeas are armed with matchlock muskets, to the stock of which is attached a fork, which serves as a rest, when the warrior crouches to take his aim. Their fire-arms are very contemptible; evidently of no use, but in the fairest weather, when the match will burn, and the priming, in an open pan, take fire. In the management of the sword and shield they are sufficiently dexterous, and undoubtedly most excellent archers.

They have wall-pieces, to which indeed the calibre of some of their matchlocks is scarcely inferior; but they have no cannon. Other instruments of war were mentioned to me; one in particular, with which they heave huge stones in the attack of strong castles; and a sort of arrow, loaded with combustible matter, for the purpose of setting fire to buildings; but neither of these came under my observation.

The Zempi, it was reported, on Monday the 30th of June, had moved to invest Punukka; but the numerous reinforcements thrown into it, and the natural strength of its position, entirely removed all apprehension for its safety. The conjecture, that Wandipora[a] Zoompoon was with the rebels, was verified to me by a Vakeel[b], who was coming to me from Raja Mocum Narrain[c], and fell in with them on the road. They carried him with them, and detained him in the eastern village. The Zoompoon arrived the day after they had taken these posts; but when they were preparing to abandon them, they left the unfortunate Vakeel, a woeful evidence of their profound respect for property, by stripping him to the skin; yet he was heartily glad to escape with life on any terms.

Various reports were spread of the destination of the rebels; among

[a] The commandant or keeper of the castle of Wandipore.

[b] Agent or ambassador.

[c] The Raja of Bijnee, a district situated at the foot of the mountains to the southward of Bootan.

the most probable was, that the party (disheartened by the check they had met with) were divided, and many of them dispersed. The Zoompoon, with those adherents who were steady to his cause, had retreated to the castle of Wandipore, which he commanded; it lies about twenty-four miles off, in an eastern direction, and is esteemed, according to the nature of fortifications in Bootan, a place of great strength. It is situated on the end of a rock between two rivers, which wash both sides of it, and unite in one stream, at its point.

This is one of the consecrated palaces of Bootan, and a certain number of Gylongs are constantly stationed in it, for the performance of worship in the temple; it has also an establishment of Zeenkaubs, Poës, &c. who act in a civil as well as military capacity, though they properly belong to the latter order. The numbers of the enemy that composed the garrison, were not well known; but detachments were continually marching, during the whole day, to hem them in, and prevent their reassembling in the field. Zoondonier, who is the treasurer and generalissimo, together with the Zoompoon of Punukka, were appointed to conduct the siege of Wandipore: a blockade was understood to be the plan proposed; this castle being considered as not reducible by any other means, than those of intercepting its supplies of water and provisions.

The Raja assembled, as I was informed, all the Gylongs in the temple, on Tuesday the first of July, to offer his thanksgiving for the late victory, to implore an early termination to these unhappy tumults, and the ultimate success of that party, whose chief was best disposed to the performance of the duties of their faith, and the service of the state.

The blockade of Wandipore very expeditiously and completely took place; so that, in a short time, the numbers crowded in it, being reduced to the greatest difficulties, were under the neeessity of taking an opportunity to save themselves by flight.

In the evening, a feu de joye from the palace announced the reduction of Wandipore. The Zoompoon and his party evacuated the castle in the night, but not before they had plundered it of its most valuable furniture, stripped the altars of their portable ornaments, and transported with them, all their golden gods.

Soon after the account of these successes was confirmed, the Raja concerted a design of visiting Wandipore, in order to settle the government of the district, to nominate a new Zoompoon, and to appoint other officers in the room of those who had favoured the late revolt. I took the earliest opportunity, to congratulate the Raja on the success of his arms. I had been admitted to frequent audiences since that which I last noticed; but as nothing occurred material to my purpose, I omit the repetition of ceremonious meetings, as well as the many conferences between us and messengers, who arrived in the height of the troubles, from the Regent of Teshoo Loomboo, since nothing conclusive passed, respecting my commission. I dismissed the messengers on the 29th of June, with replies to the letters they brought; and deeming it a time in which Poorungheer might render me essential service, I ordered him to accompany them, giving him instructions for his conduct, with perfect reliance on his fidelity and attachment.

On the afternoon of Wednesday, the 2d of July, the Raja sent to desire me immediately to wait upon him. He informed me it was his intention to set off the following morning; and, before I took my leave of him, he gave me hopes of being indulged with a sight of Wandipore, as well as of his favourite seat Punukka.

I had not long left the palace, when my Moonshee, or Persian secretary, received a summons to it: he afterwards returned to me, with many instructions from the Raja, particularly enjoining me to come with few attendants, and the greatest secrecy; conditions with which I had no difficulty in complying; but I was much rejoiced to find that his personal regard, could so far overcome the national character of jealousy and distrust.

CHAPTER VII.

The Raja proceeds to Wandipore—sends a Messenger—we prepare to follow—pass Symtoka—dreariness of the Way—meet a Party of the Daeb Raja's.—Improving Appearance of the Country.—A Procession.—Faculty of prolonging the Sound of wind Instruments—instanced also in Bengal.—Matchieu-Patchieu—Tahantchieu Rivers.—Bijnee—Berhampooter—Wandipore.—Liberal Supply of Refreshments from the Raja.—Miserable Quarters.—Lines of the Besiegers—Advantages of Position.—Castle of Wandipore—Tradition regarding it.—Bridge—Lightness and Beauty of its Structure.—Mineral Springs.—General Ignorance of the Contents of these Mountains.—Curious Effect of a strong Current of Wind.—Turbulent Situation of Wandipore.—Process of making Butter.—Departure from Wandipore.—Tame Elephant.—View of the Mountain of Ghassa—Snow—hot Bath.—Palace of Punukka.—Matchieu-Patchieu Valley—Banks of the River—sheltered Situation.—Expensive Decoration of the Palace.—Gardens—Variety of Fruits—advantageous Site for Horticulture.—Laborious Services imposed upon the Female Sex.—Zemrigatche.—Nymphæa Nilotica—its religious Estimation in Bootan as well as in Egypt.—Propitiatory Offerings to the Dewtas.—Narrainee, particular

Account of.—Leave Punukka.—Telagong.—Stupendous Mountains.—Hunnoowunt.—Mutbura.—Madejee Sindia.—Jumma.—Ultimate Defeat of the Rebels.

SOME hours before the break of day, on Thursday the 3d of July, the Raja left his palace to proceed to Wandipore. The following night, while sitting at supper, about ten o'clock, we were most pleasingly surprized by a messenger from the Daeb, who had arrived in safety at Wandipore, and, finding the country sufficiently settled and tranquil, had dispatched his herald to invite us to follow him. We consulted together on the scheme; and so eagerly curious were we, to visit the last station of a rebel, who had raised the people up in arms, from the capital of the country to its most remote extremities, that without hesitation, and with one assent, we determined to lose no time in embracing the opportunity offered.

The next morning was fixed on for our departure; so we hastily packed up the few things that were necessary, and taking each of us a single servant, at sunrise our horses were saddled, and we mounted them to perform the journey; at the same time people attended, by the Raja's order, to transport our baggage.

The beginning of the day was unpromising and dull. A little below the bridge we quitted the road to Bengal, turning to the left; and had not passed far beyond Symtoka, when a small misty rain overtook us, and unceasingly annoyed us through more than half the day, destroying both our pleasure and security, as we ascended by dreary narrow paths, winding about mountains covered with a variety of trees. The beech, birch, maple, pine fir, yew, and cypress, were among the number; we saw also by the road side, with no small satisfaction, bushes loaded with ripe blackberries. Insignificant as this fruit is, yet, recalling domestic partialities to the imagination, and the image of those scenes which youth and health formerly endeared, we plucked and ate them with avidity. A cold philosopher might have contemptuously passed by such trivial trash; but he would not have formed any conception of the luxurious treat which we enjoyed.

About noon, we emerged from these dark woods, and came at once upon a clear level ground, where we found a few of the Raja's servants in low sheds, which they had formed of boughs, sitting about a fire of dried fir leaves. We alighted from our horses, and were admitted of their party. Drenched as our clothes were with rain, the warmth of the fire, and the hot tea which their hospitality prepared for us, enabled us to pursue our way with additional spirit. Their preparation of tea with butter, salt, and flour, the leaf being boiled till it is tender, and all the ingredients intimately blended together, was a regale, from which at first our tastes revolted with disgust; but so early a reconciliation, placed in the strongset point of view, the force of habit, both in creating and effacing prejudices; and, strange as it may appear, convinced me, that this kind of tea-gruel, wants only the recommendation of custom, to be esteemed a luxury.

At a short distance from this place, we passed by a village of considerable extent, situated on the side of a hill, which was almost wholly cultivated. The country now began to open, and improve on our view. Proceeding onwards we forded a stream, not deep, but running with such impetuosity over uneven rocks, that our horses with difficulty kept their legs. On the opposite side, stood a solitary house, where we halted for awhile, and were furnished with fresh horses to continue our journey.

From hence a firm road led us along the sides of the hills, which were covered all over with an equal verdure. A few handsome firs were distributed about, both single and in clusters, at such regular intermediate distances, as to induce a belief, that they owed their disposition rather to the hand of art than chance. The road, as we advanced, evidently improved; it was composed of gravel, perfectly even, not less than eight or ten feet wide, and of an easy ascent.

The weather had now cleared up, and the face of nature had received much embellishment from the late fall of rain. The mountains heaving their swelling ridges, decked with a rich verdant robe, into a bright blue sky, skirted too with luxuriant groves and intersecting streams, which ran winding along their bases, displayed a regularity and softness of feature, that is seldom seen in the wild but sublime scenery of Bootan.

We met on this road, one of the Daeb Raja's brothers, a Gylong, riding on a Tangun horse. He was preceded by many attendants, and among them was a man who played upon a sort of hautboy, or reed instrument, which he blew, from the moment we came in sight, till we had passed beyond the reach of the sound, with a strong and continued blast. Every man of rank, who moves from home upon occasions of ceremony, is attended by a person of this description, who, I am assured, blows his instrument from the time the chief mounts his horse, until he alights at the end of his journey, without any pause, or intermission in the sound. The faculty of prolonging the sound of a wind instrument to any period, is by no means rare among the natives of Bootan; nor does the operation appear to be performed with pain. I have heard them, and endeavoured to mark any variation of countenance, for more than five minutes, without having been able to distinguish the least degree of discomposure.

It has probably occurred to many who have resided in India, and indeed I have myself heard a Brahmen sound his Chaunk,[a] with little variation, but no sensible intermission of sound, for more than a quarter of an hour. This is sufficiently explained, to my satisfaction, by the power of inhaling by the nose, and exhaling by the mouth at the same time; an operation, with a little practice, almost as certain, as though these members were divided by a valve, the quantity of wind which the cheeks are capable of holding between them, being sufficient to keep up the vibration, that produces sound during the act of inspiration.

We were continually approaching a milder climate, and more populous country; and presently, on turning round the sharp projection of a hill, we came at once in sight of the castle of Wandipore; a most respectable object, towering high upon the narrow extremity of a rock, which stands between the Matchieu-Patchieu, and the Tahantchieu rivers, both which streams unite at its sharpened point: they then form together a river of considerable magnitude, that takes

[a] The shell of a species of buccinum, used as a musical instrument in their religious exercises.

the name Chaantchieu, and shapes its course between the frontier mountains, flowing finally along the flat surface of the district of Bijnee into the Berhampooter. A bridge over the Matchieu-Patchieu, conducted us to the hill, on which the fortress of Wandipore stands. I must return to this remarkable structure, to give a particular description of it.

After we had ascended the hill, extremely wearied with eleven hours of toilsome travel, we were conducted to a house near the castle, which we had scarcely entered, when a large pot of tea, accompanied with roasted rice, and many polite inquiries, were brought us from the Daeb. Plenty of poultry, eggs, and vegetables, soon followed; but being destitute of cooking utensils, and without the chance of seeing this night, any of those things which we had dispatched from Tassisudon in the morning, our prospect was extremely dismal, and the profusion rather added to our embarassment, than alleviated our distress. At length, reduced by hunger to the last extremity, we contrived, by the diligence and dexterity of our friends, the Booteeas, to render two fowls subservient to our appetites, and produced a meal, that would have diverted any spectator, whilst the relish with which we enjoyed it, might have excited the envy of an epicure.

Having so successfully surmounted one material difficulty, it had been well, if night had not exposed us to other and more serious evils. We were lodged in a spacious house, of a painted, flattering exterior; but its interior, ill agreed with its outward promise. A short time before, it had been successively occupied by the rabble of the rebel party, and by the loyal forces, who had left behind them, all the evil concomitants of unclean crowds ; vermin, as active in their ravages as the busiest followers of a camp; hosts of fleas, musquitos, and rats ! whose nocturnal freaks were cruelly destructive of the repose, so necessary to wearied travellers. For my own part, after much disturbed and broken sleep, mistaking the light of the moon for the dawn of day, I impatiently arose, and was unspeakably disappointed on discovering the true time. It was scarcely one o'clock, and I was again compelled to associate with my pestiferous companions, till, eager to enjoy the fresh air, and anxious to escape their persecution, I left them on the earliest appearance of morning, not without visible marks of their fury.

In our first walk, on Saturday the 5th of July, we took the beaten path, which conducted us to the intrenched lines, formed by the loyal army when it invested Wandipore: these were about a mile from the castle, and the works remained nearly perfect. They consisted of two thick mud walls, intersecting the hill, and forming a wide street, with sufficient space to admit a double row of huts, and a vacant interval in the centre. A covered channel, near the surface of the ground, conducted water to supply the castle: of this the besiegers took advantage, and opening it, obtained enough for their own camp, turning the superfluous quantity down the sides of the hill. By these means, it was supposed, that they would deprive the besieged of water, which was indeed nearly the case, although the castle commanded the conflux of the rivers and the streams on either side of it; for the point was almost perpendicular, and on both sides a high and steep declivity led down to the water.

The castle of Wandipore, with its gilded canopy, is of equal antiquity with the bridge; and both are said to have been erected by Lam' Sobroo, about one hundred and forty years ago, when he first entered and possessed himself of Bootan. Nor did the conqueror of these regions, shew less judgment than good taste, in selecting Wandipore for the place of his principal residence: as it is a situation, both for strength and beauty, superior to every other that offered to his choice. Perhaps some objection might be made to the violent winds, which are drawn up the deep dells on every quarter, and urged furiously across the surface of the hill; but the strength of Wandipore is not lessened by the more lofty surrounding heights, which carry their high heads far distant, by gradual easy slopes, and contribute greatly to the majesty of the views.

This is considered as one of the consecrated habitations of Bootan; and the Daeb Raja makes it a point to reside here some part of every year. It stands upon the southern extremity of the narrow end of a rocky hill, which is shaped like a wedge: the sides of the hill are washed by the Matchieu-Patchieu on the west, which runs in a swift smooth stream, and by the Taantchieu on the east, which rushes with much noise and agitation over a rocky bed; they both join at the base of the point, below the castle. This is an irregular, lofty building of stone, covering all the breadth of the rock, as far as it extends. The walls are high and solid: there is but one entrance in front, before which, there lies a large space of level ground, joined by an easy slope on the north-west, to the Punukka road. About an hundred yards in front of the castle rises a round tower, on an high eminence, perforated all round with loop holes, and supporting several projecting balconies. It is a very roomy lodgment, has a commanding position, and prevents the castle from being seen even at a small distance.

The bridge of Wandipore is of singular lightness and beauty in its appearance. I am happy to annex a view of this structure[b], taken upon the spot by Mr. Davis, and comprehending also the highly picturesque scenery around, as another proof of the talent, fidelity, and taste, with which my friend seized on every appropriate feature, that marks the character of this peculiar country. The bridge is composed entirely of fir, and has not the smallest piece of iron, or any other metal, to connect its parts. It has three gateways; one on each side the river, and another erected in the stream, upon a pier, which is pointed like a wedge towards the current, but is on the opposite side a little convex; below it, the eddy, produced by the re-union of the divided water, has thrown up a large bed of sand, on which grows a large willow, that flourishes extremely. The gateway on the Tassisudon side, is a lofty square stone building, with projecting balconies near the top, bordered by a breast work, and pierced with a portcullis. The span of the first bridge, which occupies two thirds of the breadth of the river, measures one hundred and twelve feet: it consists of three parts, two sides and a centre, nearly equal to each other; the sides, having a considerable slope, raise the elevation of the centre platform, which is horizontal, some feet above the floor of the gateways. A quadruple row of timbers, their ends being set in the masonry of the bank and pier, supports the sides; the centre part is laid from one side to the other. The beams and planks are both of hewn fir: and they are

[b] Plate VIII.

Pl. VIII.

Lieut.t S. Davis del. James Basire sc.

The Castle of Wandinore

pinned together by large wooden pegs. This is all the fastening I could observe; it is secured by a neat light rail. The bridge from the pier to the hill, is horizontal, and the beams rest on the pier, and on a triple row of timbers let into the bank: it has a penthouse over it, which is covered with shingles. The sound state of this bridge, is a striking instance of the durability of the turpentine fir; for, without the application of any composition in use for the preservation of wood, it has stood exposed to the changes of the seasons for near a century and a half, as tradition goes, without exhibiting any symptoms of decay, or suffering any injury from the weather.

Our baggage arrived early in the morning, and we enjoyed, with much relish, a hearty breakfast. The rest of the morning was passed in a visit to the Raja, who condoled with us on the badness of the weather and toils of our journey: indeed he himself seemed not perfectly to have recovered from his fatigue. He recommended to us, after resting awhile, to amuse ourselves, by rambling wherever we pleased. Our conversation was chiefly ingrossed by observations on the country, and by inquiries respecting what it might contain worthy our curiosity. So little informed as these people are, on subjects of natural history, I was not disappointed in receiving no satisfactory reply.

These extensive ranges of mountains probably contain an exhaustless store of the richest minerals; but while they continue in the possession of a people, ignorant themselves, and unwilling to permit others to explore them, their treasures must for ever remain buried in obscurity. The Raja mentioned to me a medicinal hot spring somewhere in the neighbourhood; but it was too distant, and the road too bad, for us to attempt to visit it. After the usual compliments of tea, trays of fruit were introduced, and among them abundance of ripe peaches.

Taking an early dinner, we proposed a long walk towards the north. The hill of Wandipore is completely covered with a fine even turf: it has a moderate acclivity, as it increases in breadth, for about a mile and a half from the castle, where it joins the side of a very lofty mountain. We struggled some way up it, but found the task too arduous to attempt to reach its summit. It was totally void of large trees, but crowded with clusters of barberry bushes.

We discovered snow, on Sunday the 6th of July, upon the most distant mountains towards the north; but the clouds hung about them, and they were only a short time visible. In the hollow below the castle, on the eastern side, was a large garden; a situation judiciously chosen for its uncommonly fine shelter. We found orange, citron, pomegranate, peach, apple, and even mango[c] trees, thriving extremely well. Of culinary vegetables, it boasted no great variety: there were, however, cucumbers, bangun[d], chili[e]; and it was much overrun with weeds. Though we varied our evenings walk, we saw few objects that were not familiar to us. Having been so long accustomed to the noise of rapid currents, and the view of lofty mountains, diversified with populous villages, groves, and hermitages, the repetition of such scenes could impart to us no pleasure, which we had not already experienced.

On the north-east end of Wandipore hill, grew a cluster of tall fir trees, that had an extremely singular appearance: not a single branch

[c] Mangifera. [d] Solanum. [e] Capsicum annuum; *Linnæi.*

of them pointed towards the east, on which side art could not possibly have rendered them more bare; but on the other side, the branches grew with great vigour, and were full of luxuriant foliage. This curious effect resulted from the peculiar conformation of the hills, which throws a constant current of wind with great fury across that corner. A perpetual hurricane seems to prevail at Wandipore. This character of the situation, would have forced itself upon our notice, had we been less particular in our observations, in consequence of the utter want of shutters, or any other provision made to exclude it from our apartments. To supply this capital defect, we barricaded the windows and balconies of our house, with coarse mats; yet it was with difficuly we could keep a candle burning. The wind still whistled rudely through our matted fence, and, aided by the roaring of the rapid river below, rivalled in noise, the uproar and turbulence of a wind or watermill, when going in full force.

The Raja, perceiving that his business was likely to detain him longer than he had foreseen, and that, in consequence, he should be obliged to drop his design of visiting Punukka, with evident solicitude for our entertainment, proposed to us to go alone. We joyfully closed with the offer. It would have been acceptable, had we considered it as affording an escape from the multiplied evils of our present uncomfortable quarters; but it was particularly so to me, as being, at the same time, the most pleasing testimony of the Raja's having totally thrown aside that jealousy and distrust, which we had been taught invariably to expect. As another instance of his liberal confidence, supposing that I might not have been prepared for so long an absence, he offered me any sum of money I might want, for the discharge of my travelling expences. He ordered a quantity of the roasted grain, (rice) which we used to eat and praise, when we visited him, to be packed up and sent with us; and while we were at Punukka, we received from him daily supplies of most excellent fresh butter, which I thought equal to any I had ever eaten, for consistence, colour, and flavour.

Their process of making butter is as follows. They put the milk destined for the purpose into a narrow upright bucket, with a lid adapted to it, in the centre of which is a hole that admits the passage of a bamboo shaft; round the upper part of this shaft a piece of cord, or thong, is passed, so that two persons, each seizing an end, make it to revolve rapidly, and agitate the contents of the bucket. The upper end of the shaft being pointed, is received in a concave bit of wood, which is occasionally tied to a tree, or any other fixed object which happens to be in the way. The lower end, within the vessel, is split into four parts, to a certain distance; a bandage of twine prevents its splitting higher. The parts are then kept open, to any degree of extension, by a cross piece, which is tied with a thong high or low, in the split part, as it happens to suit the fancy of the operator. Rude as this contrivance is, it contains the principle applicable to the same process throughout all the universe, quick and continued agitation. Whether it be the most expeditious mode is of small importance; it is at least simple, easily applied, and completely answers the purpose.

On the morning of the 8th, horses and a guide being ready to attend us, we left Wandipore; but not till we had visited and taken leave of the Raja, who proposed, when we left Punukka, that we should meet him midway at a place called Telagong, and that we should proceed together to Tassisudon; to which end, he promised to give us notice of the day fixed for his departure.

It was about seven o'clock when we descended the hill of Wandipore, passing by a sort of barn, where a tame elephant was kept, the only one I had met with in Bootan. The steep and narrow roads preclude the use of them here; and though they are so very abundant immediately on the southern frontier, yet is this animal, at but a short distance from his native woods, shut up, and treated as an object merely of curiosity.

We were fortunate in our day: the weather was serene, the atmosphere clear, and the sun shone full upon the distant mountains. In the rear of all, swelling high above the rest, the mountains of Ghassa were distinctly visible, clothed with perpetual snow, whose smooth unsullied surface was nobly contrasted by the deeply shaded rocky eminences in the fore-ground. A few luminous and fleecy clouds hung on the border of the horizon, which, as they verged towards the snow, assumed a darker and thicker appearance, adding much to the effect of this beautiful view.

Ghassa is the capital of a district, and the station of a Zoompoon, or provincial governor. The highest mountain in its neighbourhood, whose head is eternally crowned with snow, sends forth a spring of water at its base, of so great a degree of heat, that few are found capable of bearing, even for a short time, any part of the body immersed in it. Whether the Gylongs have by use surmounted this difficulty, and so far blunted their sensations, as to use the bath established on the spot, without personal inconvenience, I know not; yet it is reported, that none but good and holy men are susceptible of its virtues; the profane who resort hither, being incapable of enjoying its medicinal efficacy, or, in other words, supporting its extreme heat. The desponding invalid, therefore, is usually compelled to have recourse to those, who are in a superior degree endowed with holiness, "to propitiate the genii of the well."

Our road lay near the river, at the foot of the mountains, winding through a verdant valley of unequal width. In general, the mountains terminated with an easy slope; but their sides were divided into small beds, for the growth of corn: and they were not incumbered with trees. The few which were upon them consisted of pine and fir, with some barberry bushes intermixed; and every breeze of wind, diffusing the fragrance of the jessamine, gratefully convinced us of its presence.

The palace of Punukka, in its exterior form and appearance, very much resembles that of Tassisudon, but is rather more spacious and extensive: it has, in the same manner, its citadel and gilded canopy. It is situated on the point of a peninsula, washed on both sides, immediately before their junction, by the Matchieu and the Patchieu. We crossed the Patchieu over a covered wooden bridge, and, turning to the right, passed through a doorway in a wall, that serves to part the court-yard from the Raja's garden. We proceeded on, and took up our residence in a light airy pavilion, belonging to Zempi, erected on the bank of the Matchieu, under a large spreading tree. The valley, to a considerable distance, as far as it extended in a right line between the river and the garden wall, was as even as a bowling green, and with as fresh a verdure. The bank sustained a row of fine old trees, whose venerable branches spread their thick foliage, to the exclusion of the meridian sun, and cast upon the margin of the river, a constant but grateful shade. The pavilion stood supported upon high pillars, and we ascended to it by a wooden ladder: it was commodious, light, and airy; and we were much delighted with the pleasantness and novelty of our situation. Immediately opposite, within the garden wall, was a neat but small summer-house, two stories high, containing three rooms on a floor; and I am informed, that the Raja, when at Punukka, is very fond of retiring hither for his recreation.

Punukka is the winter residence of the Daeb Raja, and, as we were informed, his favourite seat: he has lavished large sums upon it; and I am told its decorations are much more costly, than those of any other of his palaces. I was greatly mortified and disappointed, in not being permitted to see the inside of the palace; a stern porter kept the inner entrance; and, in consequence of an order given during the late tumults, obstinately refused me admittance; nor could I by any means prevail upon him to relent. We had not the same difficulty in gaining access to the gardens which were extensive, and well stocked; containing the orange, sweet and sour; lemon, lime, citron, pomegranate, peach, apple, pear, and walnut trees, loaded with unripe fruit. We gathered many apples; their shape and name were recommendations to us, but we found them coarse, harsh, and extremely ill tasted. A large mango tree stood in the middle of the garden, with its branches bowing down with fruit, which was not expected to ripen till the end of August: in Bengal they are in season in May. Punukka is esteemed the warmest part of Bootan, and, from its soil and situation, is chosen for the culture of exotics. Our English plants suffered by this injudicious care. The gardener brought me a handful of lettuces, weak and bitter, and also a few cabbage leaves, equally degenerate, with a small specimen of potatoes, not bigger than boys' marbles. Mr. Bogle had formed great hopes from the introduction of this vegetable, and they had been taught to call it by his name; but either from ignorance or idleness, they have failed in the cultivation of this valuable root, and the stock is now almost exhausted.

It is much to be regretted that the natives of Bootan possess no knowledge of gardening. What fruits, or what vegetables, might not be here cultivated to the highest perfection! The climate of Bootan affords every degree of variation at this season of the year, from summer heat to the freezing point; for at the same time that the inhabitants of Punukka, are cautious of exposing themselves to a vertical sun, those of Ghassa feel all the rigour of winter, chilled by perpetual snows: yet both these places are within view of each other.

Total strangers to the luxury of the table, the Booteeas cannot think any thing worth their care, which nature has not, in the common order of things, bestowed upon their soil. They have a few fruits indeed in great perfection: their oranges are exquisite, their peaches and apricots very good; so also is the pomegranate; walnuts cannot possibly be better. Yet here nature does every thing ; it remains only for them to extend their hands, and partake of what she offers.

Among their vegetables, the turnips peculiar to this country, deserve a decided preference over all those that I have ever seen. They are large, free from fibres, and remarkably sweet ; and it is with justice, that the inhabitants pride themselves on their great superiority.

Though bad gardeners, they are better husbandmen, and display much industry in the management of their grounds. I have always observed their corn fields very neatly dressed; but in this, the men can claim but little merit, for by far the greatest labour falls upon the fair sex: they plant, they weed, and to them, eventually, the task falls, of applying the sickle and the flail. In a thousand laborious offices, they expose themselves to hardships and inclement weather, while the lords of the creation, wrapt in inglorious ease, enjoy the fruits of their toils.

The heat was rather too powerful to admit our being abroad during all the day, but in the evening of Wednesday, the 9th of July, we took a very long walk up the valley to the Raja's villa, called Zemrigatchee. We found this palace, as well as the adjoining garden, situated upon rising ground, much more elevated than that by which we approached it. We ascended the bank, and turning to the left, came to a small pavilion, erected upon a high perpendicular point, that overlooked the river, and commanded a pleasant prospect down the valley: huge mountains interposed to circumscribe the view above. The palace was not entirely visible from hence, but partially concealed by firs, and clusters of bamboos, growing in the intermediate space. The pavilion, was neat and airy, and we deemed it an inviting situation to rest ourselves awhile. We had not been long seated, when the steward of the villa spread before us a vast profusion of ripe and green apples, oranges, &c. Tea and whisky also made a part of the offering, and fresh curdled milk. Our host (who was very communicative) sat down, and partook with us of the potable part of his treat. When we were a little refreshed, he led us about the garden, and afterwards through every apartment in the palace: nor was he at all scrupulous in exhibiting to our view the fine display of gilded gods, that occupied the recesses in several rooms. Our attendant, who was an active cheerful young man about eighteen years of age, and who just before had been as merry as unclouded spirits and rude health could make him, in a moment became as grave as one of the group of idols, and approached them with devout solemnity to make his nine prostrations.

This palace is similar to all those of the secondary order: its exterior form is a square: in the centre of the front is a quadrangular building, which forms the body of the house, elevated three floors above the three other sides of the square, in which are contained offices for servants, and rooms for all sorts of lumber. The entrance was by the side of the house, through a narrow passage into the area, where a flight of wooden steps conducted us to the first floor of the centre building. The rooms were lofty and spacious; to some, there were projecting balconies, whence might be seen the garden, and a part of the valley; but the prospect was limited on all sides by high mountains, a circumstance which renders Zemrigâtchee rather a gloomy retreat.

The obliging and attentive assiduity of the good man who lived here, and his solicitude to shew us every part of his extensive charge, drew us inadvertently to loiter away more time than in prudence we ought to have done; and, though night was coming on apace, we could not part till he had carried us into a detached garden, abounding with orange and other trees, and on the borders of which was a large pond covered with the lotus (*nymphæa nilotica*) in full bloom; a flower for which the inhabitants have a religious esteem, and which they often place before their idols, deeming it to be peculiarly acceptable to them. It is held in the same religious estimation in India, as it was in Egypt; and serves, among other evidences, to point out a remote connection between the people of Egypt and India, and the religions of both.

It was long dark, before we reached our own habitation; and, though no visible danger obstructed our way, yet it was not unfrequently necessary, to appease the Dewtas (*genii loci*) at several stages, with the occasional offering of a few narrainees; nor was I inattentive to the advice of our guide, notwithstanding that I believed him to have no small interest in these oblations.

The narrainee is a base silver coin, struck in Cooch Bahar, of the value of about ten-pence, or one third of a Sicca rupee. The commodiousness of this small piece, the profits the people of Bootan derive from their commerce with Cooch Bahar, and some local prejudices against the establishment of a mint, have given the narrainee in these regions, as well as in those where it is struck, a common currency, though both countries are perfectly independent of each other, and totally different in their language and manner. The name of the coin is derived from the Hindoo mythology; Narrain being no other than the favourite god Krishna, the Apollo of the Hindoos, the god of dance and music, of pleasure and of sport; who is complimented by his votaries all over India, by that cheerful festival the Hooli: a joyful season, designed to celebrate the arrival of the vernal equinox; as the Dussera, at the end of summer, is appropriate to the autumnal equinox.

The festival of the Hooli takes place the first full moon after the sun has passed the vernal equinox, and is calculated to hail the approach of spring. Its ceremonies consist entirely of the most frolicsome and playful sports; all ranks and ages mix in its celebration; and, among other acts, during its continuance, cast at each other handfuls of a pulverized scarlet flower, the jubba (*ixora Linnæi*), and thin elastic balls, filled with a liquid coloured by the same plant; these burst on the slightest resistance, and cover the whole dress and person of him who is struck by it, with a crimson stain. Nor is it deemed disgraceful, on this occasion, to carry the most obvious traces of the deepest dye; for when once the barrier of the Zennana[f] is broken down, the sovereign himself sets aside his high despotic character, and unbends in frolicsome festivity. Unrestrained liberty of speech and repartee prevails; and the females of every family particularly delight in giving free indulgence to these romping sports, which are equally kept up by the Mahometans and the Hindoos.

I was once at Muttura, in Bindrabund, in Hindostan, at the season in which this festival is held, the vicinity of which place is fabled to have been the scene of the descent of Krishna, whom by this comme-

[f] Zennana, the apartments of the females.

moration they are disposed to honour. Here, as the tradition goes, having discovered the nine Hoolis, diverting themselves with music, songs, and merry frolics, without a single male of their party, he most gallantly multiplied his form into an equal number, and joined hands with them to complete a dance. Thus, to the honour of Krishna, is it not forgotten how mightily he pleased the Hoolis, and how merrily the time passed: as is sufficiently indicated even to this day, to those who understand it, by their songs of joy, the Ragnee, and their chorus of Hooli, Hooli, Hooli[g].

We were lodged much to our satisfaction at Punukka, where we were well disposed to have passed a longer time; but the failure of our resources compelled us to determine upon our return, and we were obliged to set off, without waiting the notice promised us by the Raja.

In the morning of the following day we left Punukka, crossing the opposite bridge to that by which we entered. We travelled over a hill, at first moderately high and steep; and, ascending a second, arrived at Telagong, which is situated a good way up, on a level eminence.

Telagong is one of the places belonging to the reigning Raja, and it serves him to halt at, in passing between his winter and summer residences, Punukka and Tassisudon. This is the station he proposed for our meeting; but his business detained him at Wandipore, and it was impossible to wait his return.

The day was far advanced, the weather fair, and the sun shone in a

[g] A corruption of Holi or Holika.

cloudless sky with most powerful lustre. We were urgently entreated to pass the night here; many arguments were used to dissuade us from proceeding, and we were assured it was utterly impracticable to reach Tassisudon before midnight; but all was in vain; for the recollection of our past sufferings at Wandipore, determined us not to hazard, if we could possibly avoid it, an exposure to similar calamities; a resolution which the wretched appearance of this solitary mansion, and the more comfortable prospect of home, tended strongly to confirm. After partaking therefore of the scanty fare which this miserable place afforded, milk and roasted rice, we mounted our horses, and, in the blaze of day, moved slowly on; for a prodigious high mountain lay before us, clothed with thick woods, and we had to climb it by a steep ascent. We were four hours in arriving at its summit, where we looked, as well as from many openings in the road, upon an assemblage of mountains behind mountains, thrown together, like the fragments of a ruined world, in wild disorder. On the summit, which was crowned with a little level space, was one of those long monuments already mentioned, inscribed with the mystic words, *Oom maunee paimee oom.* We found here two servants belonging to the Daeb, and one of the Tasse Zoompoon's, with whom, having taken a cup of tea, we advanced on our way, greatly refreshed and exhilarated.

The descent was so gradual and short, compared with the preceding ascents of this day's journey, as to strike us very forcibly with an opinion, that the elevation of Punukka was much inferior to that of Tassisudon; and hence we accounted for its superior warmth.

Wild animals are so extremely rare, as far as my experience and information leads me to conclude, in Bootan, that I must not pass, without particular mention, a multitude of monkies which we saw playing their gambols by the road side.

They were of a large and handsome kind; with black faces, surrounded by a streak of white hair, and very long slender tails. They are the Hunnoowunt of India, the largest in these regions, and the gentlest of the monkey tribe: they are held sacred by the Booteeas as well as by the Hindoos, who have given them a distinguished place in their miscellaneous and multifarious mythology.

I once saw a multitude of them at Muttura in Hindostan, which I was informed were daily fed on the produce of a stipend settled for their support, by the Hindoo prince, Madajee Sindia. I ventured amongst them with some diffidence, for they were bold and active; which rendered it difficult to avoid any sort of liberty they might choose to take. Resentment was out of the question; for I was informed they were at all times ready instantly to unite in one common cause. One amongst them was lame from an accidental hurt; and it was surprising, in consequence of this resemblance to his patron, what partial attention, and indulgence he had obtained, of which, indeed, he seemed perfectly sensible. I have also noticed multitudes of the same species, near Amboa in Bengal.

Exemption from annoyance, emboldens all animated nature: I pass therefore from this instance into another element, the water. The scaly inhabitants of the river Jumna, that winds along the borders of Muttura, are found also to be equally protected by the Hindoo faith. The fish, of which that river is full, are frequently seen to rise to the surface of the water, as if expecting to be fed; and there is a merit in giving them a supply. They assemble round the Hindoos when performing their ablutions; and, as they are by the strictest law, guarded from destruction near the city of Muttura, they have been guided, as it were by instinct, to crowd to its vicinity, as to a safe resort.

Not long after we had passed by the herd of monkies, we fell in with the road which led us from Tassisudon, and passing below the castle of Symtoka, arrived at our habitation between six and seven. Upon our return we heard the report of a recent victory, which had been announced in the afternoon, by guns fired from the castle. The next day, visiting Tasse Zoompoon, I learnt that the last remaining remnant of the rebels, had been overtaken by the Raja's forces upon the banks of the Taantchieu, where they had just pitched their tents, and were preparing to regale themselves, when first discovered. They were instantly attacked and gallantly defended themselves, until the appearance of very superior numbers induced them to betake themselves to flight. The chief, with most of his adherents, escaped; but his Zempi lost his life in the affray, being transfixed with two arrows; one entering his temple, the other his throat. His head and right hand were immediately cut off, and carried in triumph to Wandipore.

CHAPTER VIII.

Return of the Raja to Tassisudon—our Visit to him—anxiety to hear our opinion of his favourite Seat—displeased that we were refused admittance—recital of what appeared peculiarly striking.—His marked approbation of Mr. Davis.—Buxa Soobah.—A Buffoon.—Electrical Machine.—Mechanic turn of the Raja—medical Genius.—Ipecacuanha.—Wandeechy.—Fatal accident to our Camp Equipage.—Tibet Dogs.—Entertainment at the Villa.—Marvellous Stories of the Raja—of a Gigantic race of Men—of People with Tails—of Unicorns.—The Raja's Pilgrimage to the sacred Shrine of Pootalah.—Temple of Wandeechy.—Repast—Bull Fight.—Return of the Raja to the Palace.—Messengers from Tibet.—Durga Pooja.—The great Autumnal Festival of the Hindoos.—Dussera.—Dewali.

Some days elapsed before the Raja returned to Tassisudon. He came, attended with little pomp and but few followers, and entered the palace soon after sunrise. His approach was indicated by numerous heaps of fire smoaking by the road side; a token of respect paid, in this region, to every great personage, by the inhabitants bordering on the road, by which he passes, and performed with more attentive care, when they mean to do honour to their chief. In the course of the day I visited the Raja. He asked a thousand questions respecting Punukka, and was extremely curious to hear our opinion of his favourite seat; of course he was equally disappointed, and displeased, that we had been denied admittance. However, I amused him with a recapitulation of our adventures, not forgetting the attentions of the steward of his villa; at which he expressed particular satisfaction: nor did he seem less pleased, that Mr. Davis had improved the opportunity of drawing various views in our route. I never concealed from the Raja, during our stay with him, any of those trivial occurrences which filled up and amused our time. Thus, by an early communication, he was apprised of all that happened to us, and had an opportunity of hearing what I told him, confirmed by his servants who attended us, from whom, no doubt, he obtained a constant account of all our transactions. We eminently experienced the advantages of this conduct: it averted suspicious animadversions and misconstructions, and tended to inspire him with a confidence, which was strongly testified to us, in every possible instance, to the last moment of our stay. We were in no respect abridged in the liberty of ranging where we chose; and the Raja appeared rather to encourage Mr. Davis, in taking views of his different palaces, and of the various scenery exhibited in this wild and picturesque country.

We met our old acquaintance, Buxa Soobah, at the palace. His visit to Tassisudon had been accelerated by the late commotions; in consequence of which, the Raja had summoned him to attend at the head of all the troops which his district furnished; and the Soobah was marching in full force when the news reached him, that the rebels were dislodged from before Tassisudon, and had fled to Wandipore. Upon this intelligence, he halted at Kepta. His men soon after were countermanded; and, upon the Raja's return, he was himself ordered to the capital. It was this morning only he had arrived, and he paid his first visit to the Raja while we were present. He went through the performance of the same humiliations, or mode of obeisance, as was exacted from every subject; and having prostrated himself nine times before the Raja, he then presented him with a white silk scarf, and was directed to sit down upon the floor, on the opposite side of the room. When he had paid his respects, and been some time seated, I took the opportunity of the first pause to address myself to him; and we entered into conversation, at which the Raja seemed not at all displeased; nor did I omit to express my sense of the Soobah's most obliging treatment of us, while we were at Buxadewar. As long as he continued at Tassisudon, we had frequent visits from the Soobah, and we were pleased with his society; for he was a liberal minded man, void of prejudice, modest and unassuming in his manner, and of a more conciliating exterior, than the generality of his countrymen.

The most remarkable among those, who occasionally came to visit us, was a little old man, who wore red robes, the dress of the religious order; some called him the Raja's story-teller, others a jester: he assumed the part of a buffoon; and seemed altogether dependant upon the success of his tricks, for his daily dinner. We were early distinguished by his attention; and he never passed us within hearing, but he hailed us in bad Bengalee; and whoever may follow us while this old man survives, will, if he has not forgotten it, be loudly greeted with the word *khâs*[h]. He was one of those inoffensive, good humoured creatures, sometimes to be met with in the lower rank of people, who enliven their neighbourhood by their careless vivacity, tricks, and drollery; and who, without an irascible particle in their composition, receive composedly the cuffs, and feed upon the caresses, of those whom they entertain. But, not being competent to the comprehension of all his drolleries, we thought his visits, at last, too frequent, and we fairly frightened him from our rooms, by electricity. Never was a creature more astonished than when he received the first shock: we often gave it him afterwards by surprise, till at length he thought himself no where safe; and a single turn of the cylinder would make him run, without stopping, till he was out of sight.

Our electrical apparatus proved a most fertile fund of amusement. The quick and incomprehensible action of the electric fluid, produced frequently a very laughable spectacle, among crowds of Booteeas, who were attracted by curiosity to our apartments. It was extremely entertaining to communicate the shock to a large circle. After the first impression and exclamation of astonishment, there never failed to ensue among them a hearty laugh; each being delighted at the idea of what he supposed the other felt. By the Raja's desire, I carried the apparatus repeatedly to his apartment, and he was much diverted with it. He would never venture to draw even a spark himself, but would occasionally call in parties to be electrified, and

[h] Khâs signifies *good*, *excellent*.

much enjoyed the foolish figure they made on the sensation of a shock. At last we found it difficult to collect volunteers, for they all grew remarkably shy of the machine. The Raja, however, seemed to derive so much amusement from it, that I could not find in my heart to deprive him of such a source of entertainment; so I left the apparatus in his hands, with such directions as I thought necessary: and if its charms do not cease with its novelty, I have no doubt of his being able at any time to use it. The Raja had a mechanic turn, and delighted in exhibiting the works of his artists, which were less remarkable for ingenuity than for strength. He reckoned himself possessed of extraordinary good iron, and indulged a high opinion of the arms fabricated from it. It was a favourite amusement with him, to examine the few mathematical and optical instruments we had with us; and Mr. Saunders afforded him a great treat, by shewing his chirurgical instruments, and explaining their uses.

The versatility of genius, and spirit of inquiry, which he possessed, had qualified him for the practice of physic, equally with any of the profession in his own dominions; and he had a perfect knowledge of every medicinal preparation in use among them: yet he entertained a just opinion of our superior skill; and, desirous of profiting as much as possible by the opportunity, he ordered his chief physician to attend on Mr. Saunders, and avail himself of his instructions. The Raja willingly parted with specimens of all his drugs, and gave an account of their reputed properties: in return, he received from Mr. Saunders whatever he could spare from his chest. The virtues of one medicine he put to the test while we were with him; this was ipecacuanha.

Trusting to his own ideas of its power and effect, for the relief of some disorder that he either felt or fancied himself affected by, he took, according to the directions he had received, a moderate dose; yet, not choosing to run the risk alone, he obliged his doctor at the same time, to try the experiment along with him. Ridiculous as it may seem, I am assured that this is no novel practice; for the Raja never takes any medicine, but his physician is indispensibly obliged to swallow a dose of the same sort.

The ipecacuanha he had taken, being rather tardy in its operation, he repeated the quantity, which soon acted most violently, and for the space of two days, kept him in perpetual agitation. The doctor, being a younger man, and of a stronger habit, was first relieved; but the Raja paid dear for his quackery; and when we saw him next was woefully sick and weak.

The Raja having determined, before the great festival, to retire to his villa, situated upon the ridge of the western mountain, he invited us to come early one morning, and pass the day there, which we agreed to; and soon after he had left the palace, a time was fixed for our visit.

The villa lay within the distance of two miles from our house, yet, notwithstanding this short space, our expedition was marked by a misfortune, the greatest that had yet befallen us. While on the way, we were overtaken by the mournful news, that the Booteea, who was to follow with our dining apparatus, had, previously to his taking up his load, drank a cup too much; nor had he ascended far, before his strength and steadiness forsook him; he reeled, fell down, and precipitated the camp equipage to the foot of the rock, to the total destruction of all its frangible contents.

This was an irreparable loss, aggravated by the prospect before us, of receding still further from the possibility of supplying its place; of necessity we were obliged to submit, and accept the use of such miserable substitutes, as the custom of these regions offered. Not a syllable was said to the Raja of what had happened; for we knew not but death, might have been the reward of the author of this ruin. Having ascended to the gates of the villa, we did not enter it; but, turning to the left, found the Raja seated in a pavilion erected upon the edge of a deep precipice, which it partly overhung, commanding a beautiful prospect of the valley, the castle, and the river, with many populous settlements, distributed over the surrounding mountains. There was a large level space in front, completely covered with a smooth and verdant turf: various sorts of trees grew on the superior eminences; firs, the barberry, rhododendron, vaccinium, and the mountain ash. The mansion stood upon the right; on the left was a row of wooden cages, containing a number of huge dogs, tremendously fierce, strong, and noisy. They were natives of Tibet; and whether savage by nature, or soured by confinement, they were so impetuously furious, that it was unsafe, unless the keepers were near, even to approach their dens.

Below the pavilion, we looked down upon a bed of flowers, consisting of a selection from the most shewy of the hardy species; hollyhocks, sun-flowers, African marigolds, nasturtiums, poppies, and a few weakly larkspurs. The rose appears to be not in its proper climate, giving but a pale and feeble blossom: the pomegranate finds a more congenial soil, and produces the largest and most excellent fruit of its kind.

We were treated, on our arrival, with tea, &c. which was followed by strawberries, and another fruit, growing wild, smaller, but not unlike a ripe sloe. The weather was clear and temperate: there was a delightful, silent serenity in this retreat; and the eye dwelt with satisfaction on the different shades of verdure, in the variegated scene. Two musicians, placed at a distance, played upon reed instruments, in wild and not unharmonious strains, while the Raja held us in conversation, on the customs and produce of foreign countries; subjects on which he sought for information, with insatiable avidity. I selected the most striking peculiarities of all nations for his entertainment; and he, in his turn, told me of wonders, for which I claim no other credit, than that of repeating with fidelity the story of my author.

In the first place, he mentioned a race of people, of uncommon stature, inhabiting a prodigiously high mountain, whose base was many days journey in circumference. The country lay east of Bootan; and being far distant, his subjects had never had any intercourse with it; but two of these people had, some years ago, wandered hither, and they were the admiration of all the inhabitants; being not less, according to his description, than eight feet high. They stayed but a short time, and seemed happy at the thoughts of returning to their gigantic brethren.

In the same range of mountains, north of Assam, he informed me there were a species of human beings, with short straight tails, which, according to report, were extremely inconvenient to them, as they were inflexible; in consequence of which they were obliged to dig holes in the ground, before they could attempt to sit down.

He had a very curious creature, he told me, then in his possession; a sort of horse, with a horn growing from the middle of his forehead. He had once another of the same species; but it died. I could not discover from whence it came, or obtain any other explanation than *burra dûre!* a great way off! I expressed a very earnest desire to see a creature so curious and uncommon, and told him that we had representations of an animal called an unicorn, to which his description answered; but it was generally considered as fabulous. He again assured me of the truth of what he told me, and promised I should see it. It was some distance from Tassisudon, and his people paid it religious respect; but I never had a sight of it.

The last story I shall notice, is an account the Raja gave me of an adventure of his own, designed not less to magnify our opinion of his zeal, than to add respect to his religious character in the estimation of his own disciples: it was introduced in consequence of our conversation turning on Tibet. He painted to me the difficulties of the way, and the wide disparity of country and of climate. " I have seen, I have experienced, and speak from my own knowledge; for," continued he, " some years ago, putting on the appearance of a mendicant or fakeer, I made a pilgrimage to Lassa, and visited the holy temples, sacred as the seats of the superior objects of our worship. My journey was performed all the way on foot, with one companion. I walked over, and saw, every part of the extensive city of Lassa; I paid my devotions at the sacred shrine of Pootalah[1]; and, after a residence of about fourteen days, returned, in the same manner I went, incognito, to Bootan." I could not but express my surprise, that the independent sovereign of an extensive region, who might have commanded every accommodation, attention, and respect from the neighbouring powers, should thus voluntarily relinquish the prerogative of rank, and submit to travel, under every disadvantage, exposed to all sorts of difficulty, hardship, and inconvenience. He answered me, that the humble character he assumed, best accorded with the purpose of his journey, which, to render it meritorious, required some degree of penance; and he hinted at the inconveniences which inevitably arise to the subjects of every state, when a chief moves through the country, with a dignity and pomp suited to his exalted station.

As the hour of dinner now approached, we were desirous awhile to stroll and look about us, which as soon as the Raja understood, he recommended to us to view the inside of his villa, and called a servant to attend and shew it to us. On the lower floor we found a superb temple, in which some of the Gylongs are perpetually employed in reading their sacred writings. The most conspicuous figure in it was an immense idol; it contained also many other gilded images of a smaller size. In recesses, upon either side the doorway, tablets of the expences, and other circumstances, attending the construction of this edifice, were written. Some mythological paintings, and symbols of their system of the creation, decorated the walls; and in a large hall adjoining, were hung up representations of the city of Lassa, and

[1] The chief monastery and residence of Dalai Lama, near Lassa.

the monastery Pootalah, the residence of Dalai Lama; of Lubrong, the residence of Teshoo Lama, in Tibet; and of Cattamandu, the capital of Nipal, and Patan, in the same kingdom, as well as of other places of famed resort. Their representations partook both of plan and perspective; and, without the advantages of light and shade, a pretty good idea of the stile of building peculiar to each country might be collected from them; nor were characteristic figures omitted: for instance, Chinese and Tartars in the views of Lassa; the yellow cap in Teshoo Loomboo; the flowing muslin robe in the pictures of Nipal; and peacocks and prancing Tangun horses made a figure in those of Bootan. The upper apartments had good boarded floors, and were neatly painted. Their favourite colour is vermilion. There were other temples, and many cabinets of diminutive Dewtas, which they had no scruple in conducting us to see.

Some time elapsed, though we hastily ran over the different rooms; and when we descended to the pavilion, we were immediately called to dinner. The Raja's repast consisted of boiled rice, some vegetables, and a kind of bread, resembling pie-crust: a couple of cold fowls, which had been dressed in a cuisinier, with biscuit, cheese, beer, and wine, served us. The Raja supplied a dish of strange heterogeneous composition, for which, not all his rhetoric could give us a relish. It was an olio, consisting of rancid butter, various vegetables, rice, spices, and fat pork: a meat against which, our experience in this country, had inspired us with an invincible prejudice. The fermented infusion, called Chong, was more acceptable, and we drank of it plentifully.

Towards the close of the afternoon we were entertained with the exhibition of a bull fight, between two animals, the strongest and fiercest of the species I ever beheld. They were of a foreign breed, from a more eastern part of the same range of mountains, and in Bengal are termed Gyal. Their heads were small, their necks thick, their chests prodigiously deep, and their fore legs remarkably short. The carcase lessened towards the loins, which made the hind legs appear much longer than the fore. Their colour was a dark brown, almost black. They were led to the ground between many Booteeas, well secured, with strong ropes fastened to them: they struggled violently, as impatient of restraint, and their prominent eyes rolled with fury, as if they were instructed in the fierce purpose, for which they were brought hither. Many men took post round the field of battle, armed with large bludgeons. The bulls were released on opposite sides; and the moment they felt their liberty, they tore up the turf with their horns, elevated the spines of their backs, and appeared animated with the strongest symptoms of rage. They did not at the first instant rush together; but, turning sideways, eyed each other askance, all the while making a slow circular advance, until a very small distance divided them: they then turned, opposing a full front, and ran impetuously, their heads meeting together with an astonishing concussion. The horns, which constitute the guard, as well as weapons of offence, were now entangled, and they maintained the struggle, like wrestlers, for half an hour, with surprising exertions of strength; the ground yielding to their heels as they pressed their brows, and alternately retreated and pushed forwards in the conflict. At length, as their strength diminished, and when victory stood on the point of turning to the most powerful, they were parted. The weakest was driven away by the Booteeas armed with bludgeons; the other, hampered with ropes, was conducted to his stall, highly indignant, and full of wrath. In this manner commonly the battle ends; for, if they can prevent it, they never suffer the strongest bull to pursue his advantage, which would terminate in the certain destruction of his antagonist, who is also exposed to the greatest danger, if he should happen to be thrown down in the conflict. As they are trained for this particular purpose, the Booteeas exert their utmost endeavours to preserve them for future sport.

The bull fight closed the entertainment of the day; after which we prepared to return, while there was a little light; and with an observance of the usual ceremony, parted from the Raja, and descended to our quarters.

Some days elapsed before the Raja returned again to the valley; when a very busy season ensued, in making preparations for the grand festival in the palace. At the commencement of this festival, a second messenger arrived from the Regent of Teshoo Loomboo. A long negociation with him took place; and as he was little accustomed to foreign intercourse, it is extraordinary what absurdities and prejudices I had to combat: at length, however, it ended in his consenting to conduct the same number of persons, as upon a former occasion had visited the Teshoo Lama. He could, on no account, admit a third gentleman of the party; saying, that his life might answer for such a breach of trust.

I understood from Poorungheer that the festival which now occupied the attention of the Booteeas, was the Durga Pooga, the great autumnal festival of the Hindoos.

An effigy of Durga, in combat with the chief of the Raccusses, Soomne Soom, is exhibited during this period amidst a most gaudy group of evil genii, and auxiliary gods, forming a picture, in alto relievo, sufficient to fill the breadth of a large saloon, as shewy as brilliant colours, and tinsel ornaments can make it. This effigy is removed, on the last day at noon, and conveyed in procession to the Ganges, where Durga and her associates are committed all together to the deep. During this latter part of the festival, which is generally known in Calcutta by the appellation of the Nautches, the houses of the most opulent Hindoos, are open to European visitors, and constantly attract a prodigious concourse of company.

This festival, which is one of the most famous among the Hindoos, gives occasion also in Bootan, to a great display of ingenuity. The representation is continued from the commencement to the close of the festival, which lasts, in the whole, ten days. It is here termed Mullaum. I was present only at the commencement of it, during the three first days, and, I am sorry to say, was too ignorant of their mythology, to understand thoroughly the meaning of the masque. The great court yard of the palace, was the scene of representation. The Daeb Raja with all the Gylongs, sat very gravely in the surrounding colonnade looking on. He politely provided us with seats, near himself.

The grotesque figures that exhibited themselves in the combat formed altogether the most fantastic motley group, it is possible to imagine: elephants, horses, apes, and a most frightful figure environed with snakes, were among the representations intended to personate racusses, or evil genii. Virtue appeared in the shape of Durga, with a view to exterminate Vice; and some of the group received pretty hard blows before they would quit the stage; but the force of Durga, as it was intended, never failed to maintain its ground in all the triumph of victory.

The object of this festival was, as I conceived, to celebrate the arrival of the autumnal, as that of the Hooli does the vernal equinox.

Durga poojah is distinguished also as being the well known period, when the armies of the native powers in India, have always been accustomed to take the field; and, till their acquaintance with Europeans taught them the necessity of relinquishing some of their most inveterate prejudices, it was very seldom that any of their troops assembled in the field, till after the celebration of the Dussera, which happens on the first full moon after the equinox. As that has been ever considered as the signal for hostile preparation, so has the Dewali, the following new moon, a festival kept in honour of the dead, when it is usual to make large feasts, to distribute food to the poor, and to make grand illuminations during the night, been commonly the time to set their troops in motion.

PART II.

NARRATIVE OF A JOURNEY

FROM

TASSISUDON TO TESHOO LOOMBOO, *&c.*

NARRATIVE, &c.

CHAPTER I.

Take leave of the Daeb Raja, and the principal Officers of his Durbar.—Depart from Tassisudon.—Ascend the lofty Mountain of Pomæla—pass Phajudee, famed for the Birth of the present Lam' Rimbochay.—Extensive Monastery.—Religious Associations, their obvious Tendency on Population.—Cross the Summit of Pomæla—descend to Paimaitong.—Tibetian Custom of taking Tea—Appendages of Dress—gross Superstitions of these Mountaineers.—Paibesa.—Picturesque View from Dalai-jeung—hospitable Entertainment of its Keeper—Review of the Way.—Paro.—Patchieu.—Paro Pilo, his Extent of Jurisdiction.—Seccum Raja.—Castle of Paro, Parogong, or Rinjipo.—The Valley—its Extent.—Mookhy—temporary Edifices—Exercise of Archery—Market—Manufactures—Mechanics—Thrashing.—Market-place of Paro.—Zeenkaub, Attention of his Friends.—Brood of Tangun Horses.—Fortress of Dukka-jeung.—Snow—Harvest—romantic Scenery.

—Sana—last Post in Bootan—Guard-house—Patchieu Bridge.—The Yak of Tartary, particular Description of.—Gloomy Wilds.—Rude Region of the Frontier.—Of Bridges in Bootan.—Vast Difference between the muscular Form of the Booteea and Tibetian.—Social Groups of Mountaineers.—Ghassa.—Lama of Phari.—Dhy, Kummuz of the Tartars.—Tartar Herdsmen.—Dukba.—Elevation and bleak Site of Soomoonang.

Mr. Saunders and myself now paid our last respects to the Daeb Raja, and to the principal officers of his durbar, and left them all busily engaged, in the fantastic ceremonies of their great festival. On Monday the 8th of September we departed from Tassisudon, accompanied by the Gosein Poorungheer, and a party of Tibetians, in order to pursue our journey to Tibet, after having taken leave of our friend and companion, Mr. Davis, whom the suspicious caution of our conductors compelled us to leave behind, with deep and sincere regret. We passed in front of the palace, immediately beneath the walls, and inclined to the right towards the mountains behind it, till a narrow valley opened to the west, and we at once lost sight of Tassisudon, and turned our backs upon the Tehintchieu. We travelled up this valley, having high hills both to the right and left, and in front, a very lofty mountain.

The ascent of this mountain was at first easy; but the road became extremely steep and toilsome before we attained its summit; so that I have no hesitation in pronouncing it, both from the time and labour it cost, the highest we had yet ascended. I now recollect seeing the remains of snow upon it, even so late as Midsummer-day; and I once intended, as a frolic, to go and make snow-balls there during the dog days. And here I cannot help remarking, that something like a feeling of vexation has constantly occurred to me, on coming to the top of every mountain I had yet ascended. While struggling, and almost exhausted with fatigue, there is a spur which yet animates to the last effort; and the mind anticipates, with some delight, the unbounded view with which it will be presented; but how great is the disappointment, when, after all, you see on every side around you, mountains still higher than that on which you stand; whilst all the space that is visible, is that only which intervenes between them!

> So pleased at first the tow'ring alps we try,
> Mount o'er the vales, and seem to tread the sky;
> Th' eternal snows appear already past,
> And the first clouds and mountains seem the last;
> But, those attained, we tremble to survey
> The growing labours of the lengthen'd way,
> Th' increasing prospect tires our wandering eyes,
> Hills peep o'er hills, and alps on alps arise.

From our present situation, however, we enjoyed a more extensive prospect than any we had yet seen; and it gave me an opportunity of taking the bearings of many objects. There were few that I have not before noticed, except a monastery named Phajudee, situated to the right upon the same range of mountains, belonging to Lam' Rimbochay, and famous for having been the place of his last regeneration, and the scene of his early studies. A small palace, on a similar plan to all the other consecrated habitations in Bootan, has been erected on this memorable spot: it supports a gilded canopy on its centre; and a forest of flag-staves, with inscribed banners, surround it on all sides: there is also a considerable settlement in its vicinity.

On the summit of this mountain, which is named Pomæla, we found an extensive monastery, consisting of many separate buildings: the most commodious of the cluster was occupied by a senior Gylong, who, as president, is stiled Lama; the rest were inhabited by the inferior monks. The religious of this description are numerous in Bootan. Their sole occupation lies in performing the duties of their faith. They are exempt from labour; enjoined sobriety and temperance; and interdicted all intercourse with the other sex. Though many become voluntary members of this establishment, yet its numbers depend most upon the custom, which obliges every family that consists of more than four boys, to contribute one of them to the order: and the same rule, under particular circumstances, extends sometimes to all the males of a village. At the age of ten, they are received into the association, and commence their tutelage. Their first years are passed in learning the rudiments of their profession, and in performing a variety of servile offices to their instructors; in which drudgery, unless elevated by superior talents, they continue beyond the age of twenty. However, though cut off from the enjoyment of some of the most exquisite pleasures of life, there are yet many advantages annexed to this class. They are certain of a liberal education; and, as their minds are more cultivated than the rest of their countrymen, they have the best prospect of being selected for public offices: and, in fact, the greater part of all who are employed in such situations, are chosen from among them. Yet whether the following peculiarity be imputable to early tuition, inability, or disgust, I cannot determine. It very frequently happens, that those who have long enjoyed posts of honour, or emolument, take the sudden resolution of retiring for ever from the business and the cares of life; afterwards, under the sanction of a religious impulse, the inspired devotee chooses some solitary station, perhaps the summit of a mountain, where he builds himself a cottage, and having deposited a hord of grain in it, shuts himself up, determined never again to return into the world, or hold any intercourse with mankind.

Thus secluded from society, if, in consequence of an erroneous calculation, he sees his stock of food about to fail, while life maintains its post in full vigour, and is by no means inclined to quit its hold, the sole reliance of the retired devotee, for future support, must then rest on the adventitious visits of such, as hold converse with the buried living. The benevolence which thus ministers to his necessities, has also its appropriate merit; so that the recluse may yet exist, for months or years, upon the bounty that places his daily food at his door, without the least knowledge of the hand that feeds him; till at length the feeble principle that animates the human frame, and preserves it from dissolution, ceases to perform its functions, and the individual is no more. It is true, he might long have ceased to be of any earthly importance, whatever spiritual esteem is attached to the devotee, the hermit, or the misanthrope, term him which you will: yet this singular bent of character, all circumstances considered, is not very much to be wondered at. Let it be remembered, that, in the first career of life, by a continuance in a state of celibacy, the Booteea is recommended to distinction; as on the contrary, any matrimonial contract proves almost a certain hindrance to his rise in rank, or his advancement to offices of political importance. Having therefore made the first sacrifice to ambition, and remained long single, in the hope of attaining to higher dignities and emoluments; chagrined, at length, by a series of disappointments, if a bare competency has been the fruit of his long service, he withdraws himself from public life: being at the same time somewhat advanced in years, his passion for connubial connection, is weakened, and his natural apathy confirmed. Having been detached by early habit from society, uninfluenced by ties of duty or affection to family or friends, his most prevailing impulse is the love of ease; and indolence and vanity at once direct his choice to religious retirement. The multitude flatter with their admiration the penitential devotee; and motives perhaps merely temporal, falsely obtain the praise of exalted piety.

It will be obvious from hence, since population is opposed by two such powerful bars as ambition and religion, how great a diminution in the number of inhabitants must inevitably be the result. In fact, the higher orders of men, entirely engrossed by political or ecclesiastical duties, leave to the husbandman and labourer, to those who till the fields and live by their industry, the exclusive charge of propagating the species.

Having crossed the summit of Pomæla, we descended between the mountains, passing a lofty precipice of bare rock, from whose base gushed a copious body of water, which poured down rapidly beside the path, and ran through a little village to the right, till it united with another current on its skirts. A bridge just below their junction conducted us to the opposite side; and about two miles beyond, having kept close to their united streams, we arrived at Paimaitong, which is distant twelve miles from Tassisudon, where a spacious mansion lodged us for the night. The Tibetians were already there: they had preceded us, and prepared buttered tea, in due form, for our reception and refreshment.

It is the custom in Bootan to eat whole roasted rice, or parched grain, with tea; in Tibet they take malt meal, reduced to a fine flour, which is stirred about, and mixed in the teacup with an ivory chopstick; this, when not in use, is associated with another, with a knife and toothpick, and sometimes a pair of dice, in a small case which hangs suspended to a girdle, and constitutes one of the constant appendages of the Tartar dress.

This repast, of which we all partook together, afforded our friends a hearty laugh; for, being novices to this new mode of taking tea, we mixed the flour imperfectly, so that when we began to drink, the dry meal flew into our throats, and made us cough violently, to their extreme diversion. This ceremony, with some conversation on our journey, occupied the time till the evening closed: we then parted; and presently after, the tolling of a bell, with its monotonous hum, informed us that the Tibetians had begun their vespers. We sat for some time, brooding over the dull light of a cherâg, or lamp, which, for want of oil and cotton, was made of twisted calico and butter.

Next to a promptitude at expedients, patience is perhaps the most desirable qualification a traveller can possess, to enable him to bear philosophically, the variety of inconveniences that must inevitably chequer a long journey through unfrequented regions. Fortunately for us both, the companion of my travels, as well as myself, enjoyed an eminent portion of this invaluable property, nor were frequent occasions wanting for its exercise.

It was near eight o'clock, and the arrival of our baggage was considered to be extremely doubtful. We held repeated consultations on this subject with our conductor, and the master of the house, who obligingly dispatched emissaries, that found some of the people resting themselves not far off, having set down their burdens for the night. These were brought on, but others who had halted at a greater distance remained, of course, where they were; for it grew late, and a most profound darkness soon put an end to all our doubts. Knowing the gross superstitions which haunt the minds of these mountaineers, who fancy that, on the approach of night, all sorts of hobgoblins are let loose, and that nothing good or honest will be abroad, it was vain to express any further anxiety for our baggage, or hope any longer for its arrival. So of necessity we submitted with composure to our lot: and though our beds were wanting, yet, for my part, as refreshing and sound a sleep visited me on a saddle cloth, with a saddle for my pillow, as any in which a weary traveller ever forgot his fatigue, and lulled his cares to rest.

In the course of the morning of Tuesday, the 9th of September, our baggage by degrees dropped in. We had time to complete our breakfast, and see it dispatched before us; the omission of which, had occasioned us so much inconvenience on the preceding day.

We had to ascend, from the hollow in which Paimaitong lay, up the ridge of a very lofty mountain, and at length, by many zigzag traverses, arrived at a little level ground, about half way up. A fence of young trees surrounding this space, which was paved with flat stones, formed a kind of alcove. We found it a very convenient place to halt at; and while our horses were suffered to recover the tone of their relaxed muscles, our Tibet friends regaled themselves with a pipe of tobacco.

This station was called Paibesa; and hence the view of the mountains around us, was extremely picturesque. They appeared as if fashioned into hanging gardens; their sides were shelved into narrow beds, giving growth to different kinds of grain, in various stages of vegetation; hermitages, villas, and villages, were distributed up and down; their summits were crowned with pines, and their divisions gave passage to the waters of many springs, which, meeting at their bases, rolled in rapid torrents.

Having remounted our horses, they scrambled with us over a firm clayey road, tolerably straight but steep, of a great width, and bordered on both sides with handsome firs. The mountain was covered all the way, with the most perfect verdure. Four hours were employed in reaching its summit, upon the very highest point of which stood a building, square on one side, but semicircular on the other. They called it a castle, and it is known by the name of Dalai-jeung. We were received by its hospitable keeper, who had spread carpets on the ground, and made some preparations for our refreshment. His hospitality was highly acceptable. Our Tibet friends gave a preference to the buttered tea; but we chose the infusion of rice, and drank deeply from a cauldron of it, around which we sat upon the sod. Our grooms, and other humble attendants, imitated the example, forming different groups, in which their cups and pipes very cheerfully circulated.

This halt afforded us an opportunity of reviewing the way we had passed. Though there was an astonishingly deep hollow between, yet we could plainly distinguish the path that led us yesterday over the top of Pomæla; and the large monastery above Symtoka, seen from Tassisudon, was also visible. On the opposite side lay the valley of Paro, exhibiting a most luxuriant verdure, not unfrequently broken by the appearance of populous villages, whilst the river Patchieu glided through it, in a variety of picturesque and beautiful windings.

We put up our cups, and rose to descend towards Paro, our companions the Tibetians having now smoked their pipes, and disposed of the last dregs of their tea, as well as the rich skum that floats upon its surface: this is usually blown aside in drinking, to be mixed with malt meal, and well kneaded with the fingers into a round ball, by way of conclusion of the feast. We proceeded some distance before the castle came in view: it was situated near the foot of the mountain, about nine miles from Paimaitong, overlooking and commanding a bridge stretched across the Patchieu. It is a handsome square building of stone, ornamented in the centre with a gilded canopy, in the manner of all the Raja's palaces. This is considered as one, though I do not understand that the present Raja ever visited it.

The governor of the district, styled Paro Pilo, has his residence here. This post is at present held by a brother of the Daeb's; he was absent from his station, having set out, I was informed, a few days before, to Tassisudon, to celebrate the great festival, as well as for the same purpose which leads all the other chiefs at this season to the capital, to acknowledge their vassalage, and render an account of the revenues of their different districts. His jurisdiction is of the first importance in Bootan: it extends from the frontier of Tibet to the borders of Bengal; to Dalimcotta, adjoining to the territories of Segwim, or Seccum Raja; and it comprehends the low lands at the foot of the Luckidewar mountains. Paro Pilo is always considered as a person of high eminence, and has his establishment of Zempi, Zoompoon, Donier, Cullum[a], Zeenkaubs, Poës, and Gylongs, as well as the Daeb himself.

The castle, or palace of Paro, known also by the appellation of Parogong, and Rinjipo, is constructed, and the surrounding ground laid out, more with a view to strength and defence, than any place I have seen in Bootan. It stands near the base of a very high mountain: its foundation does not decline with the slope of the rock, but the space it occupies, is fashioned to receive it horizontally. Its form is an oblong square; the outer walls of the four angles, near the top of them, sustain a range of projecting balconies, at nearly equal intermediate distances, which are covered by the fir eaves that project, as usual, high above and beyond the walls, and are fenced with parapets

[a] Cullum, a kind of inferior secretary.

of mud. There is but one entrance into the castle, which is on the eastern front, over a wooden bridge, so constructed as to be with great facility removed, leaving a deep and wide space between the gateway and the rock.

Opposite to this front are seen, upon the side of the mountain, three stone buildings, designed as outposts, placed in a triangular position. The centre one is most distant from the palace, and about a double bowshot from those on either side, as you look up to them. The centre building, and that on the left, defend the road from Tassisudon, which runs between them; that on the right, the road from Buxadewar, and the passage across the bridge. On the side next the river, from the foundation of the castle, the rock is perpendicular, and the river running at its base, renders it inaccessible. The bridge over the Patchieu, which is at no great distance, is covered in the same manner as those of Tassisudon and Punukka, and has two spacious gateways.

The valley of Paro exceeds that of Tassisudon, by almost a mile in width; it lies nearly north-west and south-east, and the river intersects it irregularly, as it pursues its winding course.

We were obliged to halt a day at Paro, and make a new arrangement of our baggage: it had hitherto been conveyed by the labour of the people of the country alone; horses were now called in to bear their share in its carriage. The aid we took from hence, both animal and human, was designed to conduct us beyond the boundary of Bootan to Phari, the Tibet frontier.

We had not been long in our quarters at this place, when we were visited by a Mookhy, or agent, whose business it is to conduct that division of the caravan, which goes from hence annually to Rungpore. He brought us a present of fruits, and some other articles, which his own domestic stock supplied; talked much of his journey to Rungpore; and strongly expressed his gratitude for the kind treatment and encouragement he had always experienced from Mr. Goodlad[b] and Mr. Pote[c], as well as the other gentlemen residing there; and he pressed me in return, to employ him in any service he could execute.

It pleased me exceedingly to meet among my new acquaintances, with so strong an instance of a grateful disposition; and it induced me, when he was taking leave, to add something more to the gratuity I made it a point always to give to those who brought me articles of provision; but he declined accepting my present, in a manner that convinced me of his sincerity, and again repeated his offer, to render me any service in his power.

Paro Pilo's absence excused us the trouble of making visits; and though the officers of his household rather expected us to wait upon them, we did not think their importance required such a compliment.

Curiosity, more powerful than the influence of fatigue, tempted us the first evening, to take a walk. We went some way down the river; and though the distance was short, we had a most laborious return, up a long steep slope, paved with smooth stones, which a light shower had rendered extremely slippery. In this excursion, we saw little more than was visible from our own apartments, which were in a very neat small house, built of fir. The floors, roofs, wainscots, and partitions that divided the rooms, were all of the same materials. I did not

[b] Collector of the revenue. [c] Commercial Resident at Rungpore.

observe that they made use of iron, or any other metal, about their edifices. They are good joiners: their wooden divisions are inserted between grooves, and their doors turn on pivots.

This light kind of summer-house stood on higher ground, at only a short distance from the castle, and at the end of a very long grass-plot, where the Booteeas were accustomed to meet every afternoon to practise their martial exercises. They shot with the bow and arrow, at two marks set up in the ground, at the distance of two hundred yards from each other: each archer was furnished with one arrow; and they traversed to and fro, shooting alternately from one mark to the other. There appeared to exist a great degree of emulation among them, and an impartial attention to merit; for I observed, that if the least important, or youngest, of the party, sent his arrow near the mark, he was instantly applauded with a loud shout of triumph.

It was impossible to behold their sport without admiration; for, besides the striking peculiarities in the person and dress of a Booteea, the act of drawing the bow exhibits, in my opinion, one of the most graceful attitudes of muscular exertion: the fencing school has not one that displays an athletic figure to greater advantage.

Paro boasts the only market in Bootan; and it appears to be much frequented. It is also famous for the manufacture of gods, and forging of arms, particularly of swords and daggers, and the barbs of arrows.

The mechanics flocked about us on our departure, on Thursday the 11th of September; and it was impossible to go, without leaving among them some encouragement for the arts.

Not far from our house we saw half a dozen stout women thrashing corn, and their skill well deserved our attention. They confronted each other, three in a row; and the corn was strewed between them; and they thumped it, wielding their flails (two stout staves, joined together by a flexible thong) with such dexterity, that though perhaps not a blade escaped unstruck, yet they never once entangled, nor clashed in the operation.

We were kept by many impediments at Paro till near noon; when, quitting our quarters, we descended the stone slope, and turning to the right, crossed the bridge below the palace, and proceeded up the valley, not far from the banks of the Patchieu. We passed through the market-place, as the peasants were beginning to assemble; none of them left their pursuits to follow us; and the boys that were playing about looked at us only for a moment, with an appearance of surprise, but without any sort of rustic rudeness. Two Booteeas would have passed through few English towns, so peaceably.

The Zeenkaub, whom the Daeb had appointed to attend me to Tibet, invited us to deviate a little from the high road, and we all followed him till we came to some carpets laid upon the ground, beneath a bower, formed with branches of the willow tree, where we were entreated to alight. Benches were immediately placed before us, and almost as instantaneously covered with a variety of fruits, parched rice, &c. and we were plentifully supplied with buttered tea and whisky. Our guide was himself active, in waiting upon us, and considered our acceptance of his invitation to halt, as a peculiar compliment. A village in the vicinity was, I learnt, the place of his birth, as well as the present residence of his family. Some of them came, and took a very affectionate leave of him. Human nature is very much the same, and but little modified in the expression of its fond propensities, amongst the rudest or the most polished nations on the globe. I valued them for their affection, and him for his attachment to his native home. Indeed I felt myself the force of the same sentiment.

> "Where'er I go, whatever realms to see,
> "My heart, untravelled, fondly turns to thee;
> "Still to my Albion turns with ceaseless pain,
> "And drags at each remove a length'ning chain."

After a short delay, we mounted our horses, and advanced through the valley, which contained many villages, and was very completely cultivated. The sides of the mountains to the right and left, were covered with thick groves of pines: they contained also numerous clusters of houses, and some handsome villas, with gardens and orchards. The road was good, and the ascent so easy, as to be scarcely perceptible.

Many of the Tangun horses, peculiar to Bootan, and, I was told, the greatest part of those that constitute the caravan annually sent to Rungpore, are bred in this valley. The number of mares, running at liberty with their foals, were rather troublesome to our party, as they never emasculate the horses in this country, and by nature they are excessively spirited.

About four o'clock we came to the end of our day's journey, a short stage of about nine miles, and entered Dukka-jeung, a fortress built upon the crown of a low rocky hill, which it entirely occupies, conforming itself to the shape of the summit, the slope all round beginning from the foundation of its walls. The approach to the only entrance, is defended by three round towers, placed between the castle and the foot of the hill, and connected together by a double wall; so that a safe communication between them is preserved, even in times of the greatest peril. Around each of these towers, near the top, a broad ledge projects, the edges of which are fortified by a mud wall, with loop holes adapted to the use of the bow and arrow, or of muskets. On the north of the castle are two round towers that command the road from Tibet. On the east side the rock is rough and steep; and close under the walls on the west, is a large bason of water, the only reservoir I had yet seen in Bootan.

The castle of Dukka-jeung is a very substantial stone building, with high walls; but so irregular in its figure, that it is evident, no other design was followed in its construction, than to cover all the level space upon the top of the hill on which it stands. Having ascended to the gateway at the foot of the walls, we had still to mount about a dozen steps through a narrow passage, after which we landed upon a semi-circular platform, edged with a strong wall, pierced with loop holes. Turning to the right, we passed through a second gateway, and went along a wide lane, with stables for horses on each side. The third gateway conducted us to the interior of the fortress, being a large square, the angles of which had three suites of rooms. In the centre of the square, was a temple dedicated to Mahamoonie and his concomitant idols.

During the night, a light sprinkling of snow had fallen below in the valley, and when we rose in the morning, the tops of the mountains were covered with it. The harvest had been gathered in here, and we saw them thrashing out the grain, but not after the active example of the maids of Paro; for the straw was spread upon the ground, and a couple of oxen, driven round in a circle, trod it out.

We travelled up a narrow valley, on Friday the 12th of September, between the mountains, near the river, which poured a perfect torrent, foaming violently among the huge masses of stone that obstructed its course. It was augmented by the way with many currents, flowing from the mountains on the right and left: the road was rocky, with a moderate but perceptible ascent.

In our progress this day, we were presented with many beautiful and highly romantic views. The sides of the mountains thinly cloathed with unthrifty pines, the rapid flow, and hollow roar of the river, partly concealed by clustering trees, enclosed in high verdant banks, which rose, as they receded, into bold bare rocks, with here and there a fir starting from a crevice, while other ridges appeared completely covered with them, served altogether to combine the most striking features of wild nature, in her barren, as well as her most luxuriant dress. It was past noon when we arrived at Sana, eleven miles from Dukkajeung, and the last village in Bootan. It consisted of about ten houses; and we were welcomed to the best of them, by a brisk landlady, with a round fat face and little black eyes, who suffered no want to remain unsatisfied, which her interest and activity could gratify. Our room was hung with military accoutrements, martial caps, and the cane-coiled shield, with quivers, bows and arrows; all of which seemed to have descended, in a pacific train, from one possessor to another, and to have suffered their chief injury, from the impairing influence of time.

There was an industrious appearance in this little village: many people, sitting before their doors, were busied in weaving their narrow woollen cloths, with the hand and shuttle: they are extremely coarse, and bear a very long knap. We saw other villagers mounted upon a large stone, who were thrashing wheat in the following manner. Each person took at a time, as much as could be conveniently grasped in the hand; and, having set fire to the beards, first shook, and afterwards struck the ears against the stone; when what remained of the grain, after the shaking, fell out, and was received upon mats spread beneath; this is the third mode of practice I have observed in Bootan, for disengaging corn from the ear.

At six o'clock in the morning of Saturday, the 13th of September, the thermometer fell, in the open air, to 46°. It was never lower at Tassisudon than 60°.

We set out early, and found, by the river side, a guard-house, where a party of Booteeas were stationed, who permit no one to pass their frontier, without a passport from the Daeb. We crossed the bridge thrown over the Patchieu here, and on the opposite side saw several of the black chowry-tailed cattle; their backs were lightly whitened with hoar frost, which gave them a very remarkable appearance, as their bodies were covered all over with thick long black hair.

This very singular and curious animal deserves a particular description.

The bull is denominated Yak, the cow Dhé.

The Yak of Tartary[d], called Soora Goy in Hindostan, and which I term the bushy-tailed bull of Tibet, is about the height of an English bull, which he resembles in the general figure of the body, head, and legs. I could discover between them no essential difference, except that the Yak is covered all over with a thick coat of long hair. The head is rather short, crowned with two smooth round horns, which, tapering from the root upwards, terminate in sharp points; they are arched inwards, bending towards each other, but near the extremities are a little turned back. The ears are small: the forehead appears prominent, being adorned with much curling hair: the eyes are full and large: the nose small and convex: the nostrils small: the neck short, describing a curvature nearly equal both above and below: the withers are high and arched. The rump is low; over the shoulders rises a thick muscle, which seems to be the same kind of protuberance peculiar to the cattle of Hindostan, covered with a profusion of soft hair, which, in general, is longer and more copious than that along the ridge of the back to the setting on of the tail. The tail is composed of a prodigious quantity of long, flowing, glossy hair; and is so abundantly well furnished, that not a joint of it is perceptible; but it has much the appearance of a large cluster of hair artificially set on: the shoulders, rump, and upper part of the body, are clothed with a sort of thick soft wool; but the inferior parts with straight pendent hair, that descends below the knee; and I have seen it so long in some cattle, which were in high health and condition, as to trail upon the ground. From the chest, between the legs, issues a large pointed tuft of straight

[d] Plate X.

Painted by Stubbs. De la Motte del.

THE YAK OF TARTARY..

From a Picture in the Possession of Warren Hastings Esqr.

hair, growing somewhat longer than the rest: the legs are very short; in every other respect he resembles the ordinary bull. There is a great variety of colours amongst them, but black or white are the most prevalent. It is not uncommon to see the long hair upon the muscle above the shoulders, upon the ridge of the back, the tail, and tuft upon the chest, and also the legs below the knee, white, when all the rest of the animal is jet black.

These cattle, though not large boned, seem, from the profuse quantity of hair with which they are provided, to be of great bulk. They have a downcast heavy look; and appear, what indeed they are, sullen and suspicious, discovering much impatience at the near approach of strangers. They do not low loud, like the cattle of England, any more than those of Hindostan, but make a low grunting noise scarcely audible, and that but seldom, when under some impression of uneasiness.

These cattle are pastured in the coldest parts of Tibet, upon the short herbage peculiar to the tops of mountains and bleak plains. The chain of mountains, situated between the latitudes 27 and 28°, which divides Tibet from Bootan, and whose summits are most commonly clothed with snow, is their favourite haunt. In this vicinity, the southern glens afford them food and shelter during the severity of winter; in milder seasons, the northern aspect is more congenial to their nature, and admits a wider range. They are a very valuable property to the tribes of itinerant Tartars, called Dukba, who live in tents, and tend them from place to place; they at the same time afford their herdsmen an easy mode of conveyance, a good covering, and wholesome subsistence. They are never employed in agriculture, but are extremely useful as beasts of burden; for they are strong, sure footed, and carry a great weight. Tents and ropes are manufactured of their hair, and amongst the humbler ranks of herdsmen, I have seen caps and jackets made of their skins. Their tails are esteemed throughout the East, as far as luxury or parade have any influence on the manners of the people; and on the continent of India they are found, under the denomination of Chowries, in the hands of the meanest grooms, as well as occasionally in those of the first minister of state. They are in universal use for driving away winged insects, flies and musquitoes, and are employed as ornamental furniture upon horses and elephants: yet the best requital, with which the care of their keepers is at length rewarded, for selecting them good pastures, is in the abundant quantity of rich milk which they give, and the butter produced from it, which is most excellent. It is their custom to preserve this in skins, or bladders; and the air being thus excluded from it, it will keep in this cold climate throughout the year; so that, after some time tending their herds, when a sufficient store is accumulated, it remains only to load their cattle, and drive them to a proper market with their own produce, which constitutes, to the utmost verge of Tartary, a most material article of merchandise.

I had the satisfaction to send two of this species to Mr. Hastings after he left India, and to hear that one reached England alive. This, which was a bull, remained for some time after he landed in a torpid languid state, till his constitution had in some degree assimilated with the climate, when he recovered at once both his health and vigour. He afterwards became the father of many calves, which all died without reproducing, except one, a cow, which bore a calf by connection with an Indian bull.

Though naturally not intractable in temper, yet, soured by the impatient and injudicious treatment of his attendants, during a long voyage, it soon became dangerous to suffer this bull to range at liberty abroad. He had at all times been observed to bear a marked hostility towards horses; and, from the accidental circumstance, of a crooked nail's remaining in his horn, after the knob which it had fastened, had been rubbed off, he happened to gore a valuable coach-horse belonging to Mr. Hastings, which had the range of the same pasture with him, and, lacerating the entrails, occasioned his death. After this, to prevent further accidents, he was kept alone within a secure enclosure.

An Engraving of this Bull, from a picture in the possession of Mr. Hastings, painted from the life by Stubbs, is annexed; the landscape was taken from a scene on the frontier of Bootan, by Mr. Davis.

Our road this day lay at no great distance from the river, which rolled all the way, recoiling over its rocky bed a perfect cataract; its spray filling the atmosphere with vapour, and rendering it extremely chill. This region was crowded with vegetation, the offspring of damp and obscurity. Amongst the largest of the trees, hollies made the most conspicuous show, and well accorded with the dark and dismal aspect of the surrounding objects. I never encountered a deeper gloom: the river was seldom visible, but its hoarse roar was every where to be heard. On each side, towered steep and rugged rocks, whose high summits shut out the rays of the sun during every hour of the day, except when it was nearly vertical: many a withered pine impended from their cliffs, and, forsaken by the principle of life, rattled its dry branches together, when agitated by the wind. Here was a solitude! uninterrupted, I believe, by any animated being, brute or human; and the swiftness of the river, I am sure, bade defiance to the efforts of any of the scaly tribes. We were inclosed in these gloomy wilds for the space of about four miles, when we found it necessary to dismount, and clamber up an immensely high and rocky mountain, which frequently obliged us to have recourse to our hands and knees. I was astonished, at the end of our journey, to see the Tanguns and all our baggage up with us, before it was dark, notwithstanding the difficulties of the way.

These rugged and impracticable ways, certainly lessen the importance of those military posts, we so lately passed, Dukka-jeung and Paro. The Booteeas cannot possibly have a better security, than in such a chain of inaccessible mountains, and in the barrenness of their frontier.

We crossed the Patchieu, which was now considerably diminished, for the last time, over a wooden bridge.

Bridges, in a country composed of mountains, and abounding with torrents, must necessarily be very frequent: the traveller has commonly some one to pass in every day's journey. They are of different constructions, generally of timber; and, if the width of the river will admit, laid horizontally from rock to rock. Over broader streams, a triple or quadruple row of timbers, one row projecting over the other, and inserted into the rock, sustain two sloping sides, which are united by an horizontal platform, of nearly equal length: thus the centre is, of course, raised very much above the current, and the whole bridge forms the figure nearly of three sides of an octagon[d]. Piers are almost totally excluded, on account of the unequal heights, and extreme rapidity of the rivers. The widest river in Bootan has an iron bridge[e], consisting of a number of iron chains, which support a matted platform; and two chains are stretched above, parallel with the sides, to allow of a matted border, which is absolutely necessary to the safety of the passenger, who is not quite at his ease, till he has landed from this swinging unsteady footing. Horses are permitted to go over this bridge, one at a time.

There is another bridge, of a more simple construction, for foot passengers, formed with two parallel chains[f], round which creepers are loosely twisted, sinking very much in the middle, where suitable planks are placed, the end of one plank resting upon the end of the other, without being confined, which forms a very good footing. There is also another mode, by which the people of this country contrive to cross deep chasms. Two ropes[g], commonly of rattan, or some stout and flexible osier, are stretched from one mountain to another, and encircled by a hoop of the same. The passenger places himself between them, sitting in the hoop, and, seizing a rope in each hand, slides himself along with facility and speed, over an abyss tremendous to behold. Examples of all these kinds of bridges have occurred in the course of our journey, as I have already related.

[d] Wandipore, p. 132. [e] Chuka, p. 55. [f] Selo, p. 59.
[g] Mountains near Chuka, p. 54.

The variety of scenery we were presented with this day, was highly picturesque and grand. On one spot in particular we viewed, tumbling from its source, in the bosom of a lofty mountain, a copious river, white with foam, and finely contrasted with the dark hued pines, as it rushed over the blackened rock, to meet the Patchieu. We were met by a prodigious number of passengers, carrying burdens, and we overtook others, ascending this lofty mountain. They were really models of athletic strength: it was astonishing to behold the firm, large, and well divided muscles of their limbs, which were powerful indications of the great degree, in which laborious exertion conduces to the increase of strength. Although climate may, in some measure, contribute, yet their very muscular appearance is not wholly to be ascribed to its influence; for it may be observed, that notwithstanding as we advanced, the climate was supposed to improve, and the atmosphere became more pure and rare, there being no stagnant waters, and little vegetation, to charge the air with noxious vapours, yet the people were much less robust. At the same time I must observe, that the Tibetians, always travelling on level ground, carrying a weight of clothing that bids defiance to the most piercing winds, and wearing thick boots, equally proof against the impression of sharp-pointed rocks, or the penetrability of thawing snow, are neither in size, activity, nor ability to endure fatigue, on a level with the Booteeas; who never go abroad but they must climb an ascent; and who go thinly clad, exposing their bare heads to every wind that blows, and trudging with naked feet in the most rugged and the smoothest roads.

In various places near our path, we saw little parties of Booteeas, who, having laid down their loads, were sitting under cavities of the rock, regaling themselves with tobacco, and very sociably puffing, and pushing about the pipe from one to another. They were mixed societies, generally consisting more of women than men; and they chatted together apparently in great good humour, and frequently joined in loud bursts of laughter. The disposition was contagious; nor could we view so much honest mirth without a smile.

We rested near one of these parties: I had carried a compass in my hand, and set it down by me to take bearings. One of the group advanced, and taking it up in his hand, viewed it with attention. I explained to him, as well as I could, the property of the needle; and he passed it to the rest of his comrades, who all considered it with the same expressions of surprise; it was afterwards returned very carefully to the place, from whence it was taken. I never beheld a more florid picture of health than was exhibited in the complexion of the mountaineers we met to-day; the women in particular, with their jet black hair, and clear brisk, black eyes, had a ruddiness, which the most florid English rustic would in vain attempt to rival.

We left on our right, a sort of rude hovel, which they called Gassa. It serves as a resting-place for travellers passing to and fro. Every species of small and larger forest tree, we had now left behind us, and were to look down on the lower grounds for luxuriant vegetation. Nothing but docks and nettles decorate the ground about Gassa. The bleak and lofty summits of this and the adjacent mountains, give growth only to short herbage, with here and there a straggling barberry bush.

A little beyond Gassa we were struck with a very singular appearance. A breach in the opposite mountain discovered a most beautiful valley, which at once surprised me by its sudden burst upon the view, and forcibly excited a desire of closer examination. But the immense chasm between prohibited the attempt; yet I could plainly trace the practicability of climbing to it by a zig-zag narrow path. The mountains rose with steep sides, towering to a prodigious altitude, and branching into many heads. This, in particular, as if compressed, and flattened about a third part of its height, displayed a plain of wide extent, covered with the finest turf, and intersected, as the Booteeas informed me, by a large brook: and here, they said, was the favourite resort of the herdsmen with their droves, at this season of the year. The Patchieu was now seen to shape its contorted course, deep in the division between the mountains, dashing from one side of the rock to the other; sometimes pouring a smooth transparent body over huge stones that lie across its course, and sometimes dashing a perfect cataract. It seemed greatly diminished in size; but the numerous currents that flow down every division of the mountain, and join it in its way, swell it, before it finds the bottom, into an immense torrent.

Travelling on, we inclined towards the right, and came to a sort of break in the ascent; a hollow, formed by the coinciding slopes of many heads of the mountain. We were met here by the Lama of Phari, who had advanced thus far, and pitched some tents for our accommodation, which we entered about four o'clock, after a long and tiresome ascent of ten hours, though the distance we had travelled was little more than twelve miles.

Carpets and cushions were placed ready; and we were no less happy to meet our old acquaintance, the Lama, than to partake of the refreshments he afforded us. We were presented with a profusion of fresh rich milk, and a preparation called, in the language of India, Dhy, which is milk, acidulated by means of buttermilk boiled in it, and kept, till it is slightly coagulated. The Kummuz of the Tartars is mare's milk, prepared by the same process: this is sometimes dried in masses till it resembles chalk; and is used to give a relish to the water which they drink, by solution with it. I have been told, that the operation of drying it, is sometimes performed by tying the Dhy tight in bags of cloth, and suspending it under their horses' bellies. We had also dried fruits, consisting of dates and apricots; buttered tea was not omitted in this repast, nor was it indeed the least acceptable part of it; for habit had not only rendered this composition agreeable to our tastes, but experience most fully proved, that warm liquids, at all times, contribute to alleviate the sensation of fatigue. I was never more disposed to praise the comfortable practice of the country, having constantly observed, that the first object of attention with every man, at the end of a long journey, is to procure himself a dish of hot tea. If you are expected, it is always prepared, and brought to you, the moment you arrive.

While we were assembled in the tents, we debated on our future plan of proceeding: it was at length determined, that the Lama should proceed immediately to Phari, to prepare for our arrival; that Poorugnheer, with some others of the party, should accompany him; and that we ourselves should move, on the following afternoon.

Near our encampment, was a party of Tartar herdsmen, called Dukba, whose sole occupation is tending cattle, and who always live in tents. One of them brought me a large quantity of milk, which was excellent, and some very good butter. The drove of chowry-tailed cattle, at pasture in this neighbourhood, consisted, as I understood, of between two and three hundred, and were the property of three families. At the time of our arrival, they were dispersed, grazing all over the adjacent mountains; but towards the evening, the proprietors collected them together, by a signal and a call; they were then all fastened with ropes, picketed in a double line before their tents, and guarded by two large Tibet dogs. I learned from one of the proprietors, that they had been stationary here about twelve days; that they came from the northward; and that, in the course of nine or ten days more, he intended to conduct them farther south, on account of the approach of winter.

The last was a most bitterly cold night: I was almost frozen in my bed. It might literally have been said that we had lain in the clouds. They hung in the morning exceedingly low; and some of them swept the ground, as they passed in quick succession before a strong wind. Our tent, composed of a single thin canvas, without lining, was as wet as it was possible; and the current of cold air, that pierced through the damp cloth, awoke me, with the same sensation a person feels, on first plunging into cold water. The ground was covered with hoar frost. The mercury in the thermometer stood at 36°.

TIBET.

CHAPTER II.

Small Banners, the Boundaries between Bootan and Tibet.—Plain of Phari—low Mount dedicated to funeral Rites.—Fortress.—Chassa Goombah, Station of the Lama of Phari—his Jurisdiction.—Là, or Musk Deer.—Ghouz—Severity of the Cold—Range of snowy Mountains.—Chumularee.—Hindoo Superstitions—Tongla—Tartar Tents.—Goorkhaw.—Homage to Chumularee.—Superior Elevation of this Part of Tibet—deduced from the Sources of Rivers, the cold Temperature of the Air, and the Mountains clothed perpetually with Snow.—Teuna—feeble Vegetation—numerous Herds—dreary Aspect.—Tempestuous Character of the Frontier.—Mineral Springs—fossil Alkali—Natron.—Dochai.—Lake Ramtchieu—vast Resort of Water-fowl.—Encampment.—Sedjy mutti.—Sublime Scenery—a Tibet Village.—Farther Traits of Superstition.—Dogs of Tibet—their Ferocity.—Comparison between Bootan and Tibet.

After dinner our tents were struck, and we advanced on our way over the summit of Soomoonang. Here a long row of little inscribed flags, fixed in rude heaps of stones, were fluttering in the wind. They mark the boundaries of Tibet and Bootan; and are supposed, at the same time, to operate as a charm over the Dewtas, or *genii loci*, who are paramount here. No mountain is thought to be wholly exempt from their influence; but they are peculiarly given to range in the most elevated regions; where, drenched with dews, and worried by tempestuous weather, they are supposed to deal around them, in ill humour, their most baneful spells, to harass and annoy the traveller.

We descended, by an easy declivity, towards the plain of Phari; and as we proceeded, the first object viewed upon it, from the road, was a low hill, rising abruptly from a dead flat, and crowned with a square stone building, dedicated, as I was told, to funeral ceremonies. According to the custom of Tibet, which, in this respect, is in direct opposition to the practice of almost all other nations, instead of that pious attention which is shewn to the remains of the dead, in the preservation of their bodies from pollution, by depositing them in the ground, they are here exposed, after their decease, like the Persees of India, in the open air, and left to be devoured by ravens, kites, and other carnivorous birds. In the more populous parts, dogs also come in for a share of the prey, and regularly attend the consummation of the last obsequies.

About a mile farther on, the fortress of Phari first came in view, upon the left, standing on high ground. It was a stone building, of very irregular form, but deemed to be of great strength. This must consist in the solidity of its walls; which indeed is all that is necessary, among a people entirely unprovided with artillery. The sun was setting; I saw the last of it about two miles off, when we turned short to the right towards Chassa Goombah; but I had just time to distinguish an extensive suburb, on the north and west sides of Phari: on the south lay a large basin of water; and on the east, a bank of earth projected to a considerable distance, which seemed to fall with an easy slope, from a level with the rampart, into the plain.

The valley of Phari is very extensive, compared with the narrow slips of land we have been used to look at in Bootan. I suppose it to be not less than ten miles in length, and four in breadth; surrounded on all sides with low rocky hills. The little soil on this, as well as on the other, is incapable of cultivation: it was covered with loose stones, and intersected with numberless water channels. Some of them now conveyed shallow streams; but the broadest, which have been worn, as I conjecture, by the torrents produced from the sudden thaw of snow, were dry. At the foot of the rocks, on the western border of the plain, was a large brook, flowing towards the south, which they called Mahatchieu; and added, that it had a passage through the hills of Nipal, into Bengal. Tangun horses climb with ease and safety over the steepest and most rugged roads; but level land is not so familiar to them: mine fell twice upon the plain, between the last descent and Chassa Goombah, where we took up our residence, after a short stage of about eight miles.

This is the station of Phari Lama, a dependant of Teshoo Loomboo, who is here a little potentate, being superintendent of a Goombah, or monastery, and governor of a most extensive range of rocks and deserts, which yield verdure only in the mildest season of the year, when his neighbourhood is frequented by large herds of the long-haired, bushy-tailed cattle: from his character and station, he has great influence among the herdsmen. The musk deer too, which produce a valuable article of revenue, are in great abundance in the vicinity of these mountains. This animal is observed to delight in the most intense cold, and is always found in places bordering on snow. Two long curved tusks, proceeding from the upper jaw, and directed downwards, seem intended principally to serve him for the purpose of digging roots, which are said to be his usual food; yet it is possible they may also be weapons of offence. Mr. Hastings had once in his possession a beautiful deer, of a different species, but armed with teeth of the same construction and position, with which he wounded every other kind of deer in the same inclosure with him; rising on his hind legs, and striking downwards. He was smaller than a common goat, yet had scored deep gashes in the tough skin of a Ghouz, which is the largest species of stag known in India.

I had a great desire to send specimens of these animals into Bengal; but I was discouraged by the reports I heard, that numerous attempts had been already made in Tibet, to convey them alive to Mr. Hastings, one of which only had succeeded. I was moreover assured, that, when separated from its own climate, and its native wilds, the life of the musk deer was always of short duration, and that it was, in fact, incapable of being domesticated; or else its odour, for which it is now persecuted, might probably be obtained, like that of the civet, without the destruction of its life.

They are about the height of a moderately sized hog, which they resemble much, in the figure of the body; but they are still more like the hog deer, so termed in Bengal, from the same similitude.

They have a small head, a thick and round hind quarter, no scut, and extremely delicate limbs. The greatest singularity in this animal, is the sort of hair with which it is covered, which is prodigiously copious, and grows erect all over the body, between two and three inches long, lying smooth only where it is short, on the head, legs, and ears. Upon examination, it partakes in its texture, less of the nature of hair than feathers; or rather, it resembles the porcupine's quill; yet, at the same time, it is thin, flexible, and not straight, but undulated. The colour, at the base, is white, in the middle black, and brown at the points. The musk is a secretion formed in a little bag, or tumor, resembling a wen, situated at the navel; and is found only in the male. The huntsmen, who sell it by weight, have a mode of adulterating it sometimes, before it is brought to market; which, I am informed, is detected by examining the texture of the musk. If it be brown and granulated, there is reason to suppose it sophisticated; but if black and homogeneous, divided in many parts by a thin cuticle, it may be relied upon as pure. They have another more expeditious mode of ascertaining its quality, by running a sharp pointed instrument, or needle, through the musk. I am told that the method of adulterating it is, by injecting blood into it, while the bag is fresh. But as the musk deer[a] is here deemed the property of the state, and hunted only by the permission of government, of course, a great part of the musk passes through the hands of its agents; and all that bears the Regent's seal, may be looked upon as genuine.

[a] The musk deer, in the language of Tibet, is called La; and the vascular covering of the musk, Latcha.

We were lodged in the monastery, in an apartment allotted to the devotions of the Lama. It was a low, square room, with no aperture but the door, which, when shut, made it gloomy enough; and here we reposed, amidst gods and whirligigs. But, not to speak too ludicrously of that, with which their superstition connects very grave and serious ideas, and which is found equally common in the temples of Tibet and in those of Bootan, it is necessary to explain, that this machine is no other than a painted barrel, with gilded letters on it, placed upright in a case, which has an opening to admit the hand. It revolves upon an axis, having a notch in its side, to allow you to give it impulse. In twirling this instrument about, and repeating at the same time the mystic words, *Oom maunee paimee oom,* consists a material exercise of their religion.

Our host, the Lama, was a lusty, venerable, sedate old man: he treated us with great hospitality and kindness, and was very solicitous for our comfortable accommodation. We were indebted to his kitchen for a very good dish at supper: it was a preparation of mutton, minutely incorporated with milk and spices, of which we eat heartily, and thought it excellent cookery. There were also abundance of dates, and dried apricots, with the infusion of rice, by way of liquor for the table. The door of our room not shutting very closely, a keen frosty air found entrance by it, which soon drew from us, wishes for a fire. Our attendants, the Lama's people, flew with eagerness to make one of dried cowdung and slips of fir, which latter, abounding much with turpentine, burn like a torch, and form, therefore, an excellent foundation; but, the instant the blaze subsided, it was succeeded by so pungent and penetrating a smoke, that, almost suffocated, we were as glad to extinguish the fire, as we had been anxious to admit it, and were obliged immediately to throw open the door, and have recourse to the cold air, to get rid of its effects. Time had deprived our friend of half his teeth, and those which remained, kept no good neighbourhood with each other. He had numerous infirmities; shortness of sight, rheumatic pains, and bad digestion: age appeared also to have a share in his afflictions. He endeavoured to trace out the sad catalogue of his complaints to Mr. Saunders, who humanely consoled him with his good counsel and medical advice; and I had the good fortune to alleviate one grievous evil, by presenting him with a pair of spectacles.

In the morning of Monday, the 15th of September, we found ourselves in the vicinity of snow, covering a range of mountains, lying to the north-east, about two miles off. The snow continues on some of them, during all seasons of the year. The most conspicuous of the number is that called Chumularee, which lifts itself above the rest, and terminates in a peak.

Chumularee is highly venerated by the Hindoos, who, as Poorungheer informed me, have been used, from time immemorial, to resort hither in pilgrimage, for the purpose of paying their adorations to its snow-clad summit. I could gain no satisfactory explanation of the superior sanctity attached to this mountain; but it may be observed, that every singular phænomenon in nature, is of the same importance to the superstitious Hindoo: a snowy mountain, a hot well[b], a

[b] As at Setacoon near Monghire, in the province of Bengal.

river head[c], or a volcano[d], is deemed an equally fit object of his adoration.

We were on horseback before seven o'clock, and, having passed through a small village on the extremity of the vale of Phari, travelled along the face of the mountain of Tongla, ascending but little, and nearly in the same degree, as we descended to the next plain, which was more extensive than the former, but not more fertile. On its skirts were large herds of the bushy-tailed cattle, grazing; and we saw some Tartar tents, formed from the hair of these cattle, woven into cloth; the ropes also which fastened them to iron pins driven into the ground, were spun from the same materials.

About eight miles from Chassa Goombah we found tents pitched, which the Lama had sent forwards, with servants to prepare refreshments. We all alighted to partake of them; and after a short halt, parted from our good friend the Lama, who, from motives of civility, had accompanied us thus far. Crossing the rivulet, we advanced over the plain, and at a small distance on the left, saw a great number of animals, which they called wild horses, or Goorkhaw. They were very shy, and kept so far aloof, that we could not well distinguish their marks and make; but with a glass I could discern long ears, like those of an ass, or mule, and a slender tail with little hair upon it, reaching about as low as the hock. The ears, neck, body, and tail, were of one

[c] Hurdewar, the last pass of the mountains, through which the Ganges enters the plains of Hindostan.

[d] Ballacoon, a well near Chittagong, producing inflammable air, and on the surface of whose water, a flame is often seen to play. All these places are deemed peculiarly sacred by the Hindoos.

colour, approaching nearly to what we term a fawn colour; the face, belly, and legs, were lighter, indeed almost white. They are said to be extremely fleet; and are never taken alive to be rendered serviceable, or domesticated: the young indeed are sometimes caught, but they soon pine away and die. I was informed, that the huntsmen in Tibet go in quest of them as game, and, by lying in wait, sometimes shoot them, and esteem their flesh a great delicacy. I have heard, that four of these animals were once in Mr. Hastings's possession: three of them were vicious, stubborn, and untameable; the fourth, a female, was of a different disposition, following a camp, loose, and perfectly familiar with every body, and every thing around it.

By the way, our guide, as well as Poorungheer, deviated a little from the road, to pay their respects to Chumularee. Not choosing to interrupt their devotions, we moved on. The mountain did not appear very lofty from the level of this plain; and I think we passed it, leaving it on our right, at about the distance of three miles: yet the great altitude of this part of Tibet is demonstrated, not only by the many rivers that originate in these frontier mountains, and flow towards the south, with a great descent, through Bootan into Bengal: but because the streams issuing from it a little further to the north, and taking a northerly direction, fall into the Berhampooter, and are finally conveyed with it, to a junction, in the neighbourhood of the sea, with the waters which flow in a contrary course, from the same general store. I conclude, therefore, that spot on which we now stood, constitutes the highest point of land, in what is called Little Tibet.

At the end of the next day's journey, we came to the source of a river, which ran towards the north, near which we travelled all the way to its confluence with the Berhampooter, a little beyond Teshoo Loomboo. The Berhampooter there flows in a very widely extended bed, and passes on, shaping its course to the south of Lassa; it afterwards takes a vast circuit through the mountains on the borders of Tibet, before it enters the kingdom of Assam, and finally joins the Ganges, in Bengal. These great rivers, when united, take together the name of Megna, and flow but a short distance, before they divide into innumerable streams, that intersect the territory, which is called the Sunderbunds, in a most intricate labyrinth, and then finally mix their waters with the sea. The prodigious difference of climate affords, also, strong testimony to the truth of my assertion, respecting the height of this part of Tibet. Perpetual winter may be said to reign at Phari; Chumularee is for ever clothed with snow; and this mountain, from its remarkable form, leaves no room to doubt its being the same, which I have heard described as occasionally visible from Purnea and Rajemahl; and which I once saw, before I set out from Rungpore upon my present journey. I had not the means to ascertain its elevation; but some inference may, perhaps, be drawn from analogy. We hear, that on Mount Lebanon in Syria, snow does not remain through the whole year, except in the highest cavities. Now it is well known that snow, under these circumstances, in that latitude (34° 30′ north), requires an elevation of 1500 or 1600 fathoms above the level of the sea. The loftiest of the Alps, which is Mount Blanc, is estimated at 2400; the Peak of Ossian, in the Pyrenees, is said to be 1900 fathoms above the level of the sea;

Vesuvius, according to M. de Saussure, 3900 feet; Etna, 10,036 feet; Monte Velino, one of the Appennines, 8397 feet. In Owhyhee, (latitude 18° 54′ to 20° north) the summit of the highest mountain, Mouna Kaah, in March was constantly buried in snow. The altitude of the Cordeliers, according to M. de Condamine, or tropical line of snow, is computed at 16,020 feet; the Peak of Teneriffe, or Pico de Teyde, according to Dr. Heberden, 15,396 feet; the mountain Gemmi, in the canton of Berne, 10,110 feet; Chimberazzo, the most elevated point of the Andes, 20,280 feet. The line of congelation of Chimberazzo, or that part of the mountain which is covered perpetually with snow, is no less than 2400 feet from its summit.

Near our encampment at Teuna, which was distant full fourteen miles from Phari, was a small inclosure of green wheat, which had just strength enough to give out its ear, but which I was told would proceed no further; for that the cold is too intense, both here and at Phari, to admit its ripening; and that it is cultivated merely as forage for cattle, when the plains become bare of grass, and they are hindered from going abroad, during the depth of the winter. The periodical rains give birth to a little herbage, whose growth stops immediately as they cease; from the extreme dryness of the air, the grass then begins to wither, and at this time it may be crumbled between the fingers into dust: yet large droves of cattle are fed in this neighbourhood; for though the pasture be short and dry, it is esteemed singularly sweet and nutritive. Animals ranging in a state of nature, are found to prefer it, to the more exuberant herbage of milder climates.

These plains, as well as the adjacent mountains, are frequented by large droves of cattle, shawl goats, deer, musk deer, hares, and other wild animals. I saw also, in this and the last day's journey, many coveys of partridges, and pheasants, some quails, and great multitudes of foxes.

The modes of conveyance here for baggage are altogether different from the usage of the inhabitants of Bootan, where every thing, without exception, is loaded upon the shoulders of the people, and where, to their shame be it spoken, the women bear the heaviest share of so laborious an employment. In Tibet, goods are carried by the chowry cattle, horses, mules, and asses, each animal taking the burdens of two men. We still travelled on horseback; but here a groom is not attached to each horse, as in Bootan, holding the bridle all the time, a precaution very necessary with their headstrong Tanguns, as a guard against the danger of their tremendous precipices, and to keep them within the limits of their narrow roads. Here every rider guides his own horse; and, when he has occasion to dismount, pickets him to the ground with an iron pin, fastened to the end of a spare rein, which you have not the trouble of carrying in your hand, but which is wound round the horse's neck, just behind his head. Their horses are so extremely docile, that you may manage them exactly as you please: they are not natives of Tibet, but are brought from Eastern Tartary, and the borders of Toorkistan, as merchandise; before they are permitted to be transported, care is taken to deprive them of the power of increasing their species: mares are never met with: they are quiet, sure-footed creatures, but slow, and ugly; they have large heads, and the tallest of them are not above fourteen hands high. What adds much to their clumsy appearance, is a coat of long hair, such as nature seems to have denied to bears within the tropics. They are never shod, either here or in Bootan.

The Tibetians are a very humane, kind people; I have, personally, had numberless opportunities of observing this disposition: one instance may be as good as a thousand. Soon after we alighted at our encampment, being much oppressed by a violent head-ach, I went to lie down in my tent, upon a carpet, and had not composed myself more than half an hour, when I perceived my conductor, Paima, creeping softly into the tent; he advanced, and searching about, found a surtout coat and a cloth wrapper, both which he brought and carefully laid over me: I took no notice of what he was about, for I was in pain, and not inclined to speak. He went away, but a short time after, another Tartar came in, who, gently raising my head with his hand, attempted to draw away a small wooden bench, on which I was reclining, the place of which he meant to supply with a pillow he had brought for that purpose. His civility disturbed me much, for I had settled my covering, and accommodated myself to the height of the bench: but, rather than enter into a discussion, for the sake of quiet I was induced to permit the change; this, however, was no disparagement to his good intentions, which, I am sure, were suggested by the genuine impulse of humanity. These circumstances made a lasting and favourable impression on my mind; and, in justice to the national character, I take a pleasure in recording this striking instance of tenderness and attention, so different from the ferocity commonly annexed to our ideas of a Tartar. My friend will be remembered, I have little doubt, by many persons who were at that time resident at Calcutta ; for Paima was the messenger deputed to Bengal, in the year 1773, and was the first native of Tibet who had visited Bengal, at least since it became subject to the British government.

We proceeded early in the morning, on Tuesday, 16th September, over an extensive plain ; a desart, I think, it might be termed, for there was not a vestige of vegetation upon it, except a few thistles, a little moss, and some scanty blades of withered grass. The wind was violently high, and so sharp that we dared not expose our faces to its fury: the want of caution the day before had left our noses, sore mementos of its keen rudeness, and we now rode muffled up in such a manner, that we could but just breathe. To the very great and sudden change of climate I attributed what I had suffered: warmth, and a good night's rest, removed all my ills.

From Phari, to the distance of more than twenty miles north from hence, I was told that the most boisterous winds perpetually prevail; in the dry summer months, raising clouds of dust and sand from the plains, almost intolerable to the traveller; and in other seasons, conveying a degree of cold, unknown even in the severest winters ever felt in Europe. Such, they said, is sometimes the intenseness of the frost here, though in so low a latitude as twenty-eight degrees, that animals exposed in the open fields, are found dead, with their heads absolutely split by its force.

Having travelled about nine miles, we met with three springs issuing out of the plain, near the foot of a hill, to whose waters the Tibetians ascribe medicinal virtues. They send out three separate rivulets, whose streams unite at a short distance from their sources, and run together, to feed a large lake that covers one corner of the plain. All the ground about it, was white with an incrustation, saltish to the taste: it lay thickest upon the tops of little inequalities in the surface; and whether it exudes from the ground, or is the froth blown from the lake, I could not at first pronounce; though on approaching nearer, I was inclined to the former opinion, for I found that the water had no peculiar flavour. This substance, upon inquiry, I understood to be of considerable use: it is collected, and employed for cleansing and washing woollen and cotton cloths, as a substitute for soap, to which they are utter strangers.

We halted a while, at a small village named Dochai, and partook of some refreshments which our conductor had provided. Lubchea Goomba, a large monastery, was seen immediately opposite, seated amidst rocks, which, as well as those which are ranged on the other side, protrude their bases into the lake, and are bordered with a white foam, produced by its agitated waves.

We advanced along the borders of the lake, which was named Ramtchieu, with bare rocky hills on our left, much shattered and torn by severe frost. The stone composing them, was of the colour of rusty iron; and small detached cubical pieces, covered all the ground below, to a considerable distance.

The banks of this lake were perforated with the innumerable burrows of a small animal to which they gave the name of rat: we chanced to see some of them running along, and sitting near the edge of the burrows. They were larger than a musk rat, of a cinereous gray, and I could plainly perceive they had no tails[e]: my attendants all confirmed this observation.

This lake is frequented by great abundance of water-fowl, wild-geese, ducks, teal, and storks, which, on the approach of winter, take their flight to milder regions. Prodigious numbers of saurasses, the largest species of the crane kind, are seen here at certain seasons of the year, and they say, that any quantity of eggs may then be collected; they are found deposited near the banks.

I had several of these given to me while I was at Tassisudon, during the rains; they were as large as a turkey's egg, and I remember being told that they came from this place; but whether or not they were those of the sauras, I cannot venture to pronounce.

The lake gradually narrowed, and from its northern angle, sent off a small brook, which we crossed, over a very rude bridge. It took a western direction, between hills that form a narrow defile, discharging itself at the other extremity, into a much larger lake than that which we had passed.

Our little camp stood midway with respect to the lakes, in a narrow pass between rows of rocks, near the village Chaloo, twenty miles from Teuna, and not far from the brook. The situation was much sheltered; and in this confined valley I saw the first ground in Tibet, which was cultivated with success. It produced a dwarfish wheat, I think, of the Lammas kind; this was now ripe, and falling beneath the sickle.

[e] This animal, I conceive to have been the Daman Israel, of Egypt, or Schafan, of the Hebrews. See Bruce.

Setting out, after an early breakfast, on Wednesday, the 17th of September, we continued for two or three miles, within sight of the stream which I have noticed, till it joined a broad lake, that extended farther than we could trace, being hemmed in by rocks, which obstructed our view.

This lake, I am told, is held in high respect by the inhabitants of Bootan, whose superstitions lead them to consider the increase or decrease of its waters, as portentous of good or evil to their nation. They fancy it to be a favourite haunt of one of their chief deities.

The road, after passing this defile, turned short to the right, round the skirts of a small village, and proceeded over an extensive plain, quite destitute of verdure, of an arid soil, and covered with small stones. On quitting this, we turned round the point of a hill, and came down upon another plain, white with the same sort of incrustation, which we had seen the day before. There was no water, nor did it appear that there ever had been any, on this plain; whence it should seem, that this saline substance is sublimed from the earth, and not a separation from impregnated water. The salt, I believe, is called by the chemists, natron, and by the natives of Hindostan, where it is found in great abundance, *sedgy mutti*: it rises in an efflorescence from the dry plains, resembling a hoar frost. Some deer bounded across our path.

As we proceeded, several narrow prospects opened, of the snowy mountains to the south: not those we had formerly seen, but a continuation, I imagine, of the same range that borders on Bootan, and constitutes its frontier. The brown heath, and russet-coloured rocks, comprehended in the same view, heightened the effect. The snow had assumed ten thousand varying folds, and dissimilar forms, in falling upon the rocks; nor could the finest imagination, directing the pencil of the most skilful painter, possibly express the sublime beauty that characterised the drapery, which this pure light substance had spread over their craggy tops. It was a glorious day; not a vapour obscured the air, or obstructed the view, to the edge of the horizon all around: the sun was not yet so high, as to have totally withdrawn the shadows, thrown by its oblique rays from one mountain on the other, but it imparted to every hill, all the advantage that a prospect could derive, from the happiest combination of light and shade.

We descended from this plain, upon the dry bed of a large lake. The ancient banks, of nearly the same acclivity and height, were clearly to be traced all around. On the eastern side, it gave rise to a brook, whose clearness betrayed numberless shoals of small fish gliding near its bottom, as it hurried over a gravelly bed, to join another stream a little farther off. They formed together no inconsiderable river, which, enlarging as it went along, shaped its course near our road all the way, and fell at length near Teshoo Loomboo, into the Berhampooter.

On the banks that bordered this low ground, which I conclude to have been at some time covered with water, were a vast number of pebbles and loose stones, that bore evident signs of having been rolled and rounded by the action of water. We encamped on its borders, near the village Sumdta, fourteen miles from Chaloo, within a stone inclosure, similar to the walls erected in the hilly parts of England, for the same purpose. Near our tents were a few trees, willows I believe, which were the first we had met with in Tibet; they might easily have been mistaken for tall weeds. A shallow rivulet of clear water, rippled over a pebbly bottom, close by; it harboured multitudes of fish in its deepest parts, which were easily taken, and afforded us a most excellent dish for dinner.

A Tibet village by no means makes a handsome figure. The peasant's house is of a mean construction, and resembles a brick kiln in shape and size, more exactly than any thing to which I can compare it. It is built of rough stones, heaped upon each other without cement, and, on account of the strong winds that perpetually prevail here, it has never more than three or four small apertures to admit light. The roof is a flat terrace, surrounded with a parapet wall two or three feet high; on this, are commonly placed piles of loose stones, intended to support a small flag, or the branch of a tree; or else as a fastening for a long line, with scraps of paper, or white rag, strung upon it like the tail of a kite; this being stretched from one house to another, is a charm against evil genii, as infallible in its efficacy, as horse shoes nailed upon a threshold, or as straws thrown across the path of a reputed witch.

This was a bleak looking place, and there was hardly the appearance of any thing animated about it. Being indolently disposed, and prompted merely by curiosity, I strolled alone among the houses; and, seeing every thing still and quiet, I turned into one of the stone enclosures, which serve as folds for cattle. The instant I entered the gate, to my astonishment, up started a huge dog, big enough, if his courage had been equal to his size, to fight a lion. He kept me at bay with a most clamorous bark, and I was a good deal startled at first; but recollecting their cowardly disposition, I stood still; for having once had one in my possession, I knew that they were fierce only, when they perceived themselves feared. If I had attempted to run, he probably would have flown upon me, and torn me in pieces, before any one could have come to my rescue. Some person came out of the house, and he was soon silenced.

If Bootan, compared with Bengal, exhibits a vast contrast of country and climate, there is no nearer analogy between Tibet and Bootan.

Bootan presents to the view, nothing but the most mishapen irregularities; mountains covered with eternal verdure, and rich with abundant forests of large and lofty trees. Almost every favourable aspect of them, coated with the smallest quantity of soil, is cleared and adapted to cultivation, by being shelved into horizontal beds: not a slope or narrow slip of land between the ridges, lies unimproved. There is scarcely a mountain, whose base is not washed by some rapid torrent, and many of the loftiest, bear populous villages, amidst orchards, and other plantations, on their summits and on their sides. It combines in its extent, the most extravagant traits of rude nature and laborious art.

Tibet, on the other hand, strikes a traveller, at first sight, as one of the least favoured countries under heaven, and appears to be in a great measure incapable of culture. It exhibits only low rocky hills, without any visible vegetation, or extensive arid plains, both of the most stern and stubborn aspect, promising full as little as they produce. Its climate is cold and bleak in the extreme, from the severe effects of which, the inhabitants are obliged to seek refuge in sheltered valleys, and hollows, or amidst the warmest aspects of the rocks. Yet perhaps Providence, in its impartial distribution of blessings, has bestowed on each country a tolerably equal share. The advantages that one possesses in fertility, and in the richness of its forests and its fruits, are amply counterbalanced in the other by its multitudinous flocks, and invaluable mines. As one seems to possess the pabulum of vegetable, in the other we find a superabundance of animal life. The variety and quantity of wild-fowl, game, and beasts of prey, flocks, droves and herds, in Tibet, are astonishing. In Bootan, except domestic creatures, nothing of the sort is to be seen. I recollect meeting with no wild animal except the monkey, in all my travels; and of game, I saw only a few pheasants, once near Chuka.

CHAPTER III.

*Deserted Villages—fatal Effects of the Small-pox—Ignorance of its Treatment—a serious Calamity—Occasion of the Removal of the Seat of Government and Monastery from Teshoo Loomboo to Chamnamning.—Gangamaar—hot Bath—Surface of the Ground adjacent—Labourers in the Fields—rude Expression of Surprise.—Place of Fragments—huge Idol—Mahamoonie—a religious Rite.—Shoohoo.—Nainee—improving Appearance of the Country.—Tehukku.—*Jhansu-jeung.—*Valley of Jhansu.—Woollen Manufactory—Economy in Dress.—Monastery of Jhansu.—Beggars.—Dukque.—Corricle.—Castle of* Painom—*Bridge—Town.—Keesoo.—Tsondue.—Distant View of* Teshoo Loomboo—*Enter the Monastery.*

At sunrise on Thursday, the 18th of September, we advanced, still pursuing the course of the river, through a narrow valley. We passed by much cultivated ground, planted chiefly with wheat and pease: as a vegetable, the latter were acceptable to us, though our friends thought they favoured us, by gathering the oldest they could find.

Near the road were seen the ruins of many villages, deserted, I conjecture, during the prevalence of the small-pox, which is a disorder not less dreaded by the inhabitants of Tibet, than the plague. Indeed, where it rages, it is hardly less fatal, for they neither know, nor use any remedies to obviate its effects; but as soon as the first appearance of it, is publickly known in any village, the healthy hasten to desert it, and leave the infected abandoned to chance, and to the natural course of the distemper. At the same time, every avenue to the place is equally barred against the admission of strangers, and the flight of those who are confined. Under such circumstances, it is no wonder that instances of recovery are rare. The late Teshoo Lama, when the small-pox had broken out among the Gylongs, once moved his court altogether to Chamnamning; and the capital, Teshoo Loomboo, remained for three years without inhabitants, until it was supposed to be completely purged of the pestilential infection. The Lama himself had never had the disorder, and it was the cause of his death, at the early period of forty-six years of age, while on a visit to the Emperor, at the court of China.

We crossed the river at a small village belonging to the government of Teshoo Loomboo, and dismounted upon the opposite bank, to partake of some warm tea, prepared by the principal person in this neighbourhood, who was waiting by the road side, expecting our approach.

After a short halt, we pursued our journey, and came to Gangamaar, situated upon an eminence. Here a complete relay of horses, and cattle for our baggage, was ready for our accommodation.

During the arrangement of this exchange, we joined our friends at Gangamaar, and partook with them, of a very hearty meal, which afforded both them and ourselves, an ample occasion to wonder at the force of prejudice. The table was spread with raw joints of fresh mutton, and some of the same, boiled. We certainly preferred the boiled mutton, which was cold, and exquisitely tender and sweet; but the Tibetians shewed a different taste: and though both of us, were equally pleased, neither envied the opposite propensity of the other; but we were all afterwards equally disposed to join in deep draughts of chong and a social pipe, in the use of which, practice had now rendered me tolerably expert.

A road to Lassa branches off between these hills, east by south from Gangamaar, which village is subject to that government. We continued our journey nearly north, and about a mile and a half farther on, met with a hot well, which was surrounded with a stone wall, and covered with canvas. Within the enclosure, a tent was pitched, which seemed crowded with people. I soon learned, that the virtues attributed to this spring, were various and powerful, not being confined to invalids of any particular description, but extending to all the sick and aged, whether they seek a cure from infirmity or from disease. The mode of treament, is to continue immerged in the water, for some minutes up to the chest, and on coming out to be covered with warm clothing: this is repeated five or six times a day. The mercury of the thermometer stood in the open air at 44°; when plunged into the water it rose to 88°. The vapour arising from the surface had a sulphureous smell; and on all sides, to the extent of two hundred yards, was seen much white incrustation.

The surface of the ground on which we travelled, was a mass of hard matter, like scoria; it sounded hollow, as the horses trod upon it; and some detached pieces that were picked up, were as porous as a honeycomb.

We still followed the course of the river; it was every where harvest time, and numbers of people were busied in the fields. They were not reaping, as we had seen in other places, with the sickle, but they plucked up the corn by the roots, and afterwards placed it, upright, bound in small bundles, to dry. I know not whether the sight of so many horsemen in these solitary ways, or our exotic appearance, principally attracted their notice; but the people were struck with wonder. They desisted from their labour, and looking with amazement, as they grasped the grain, which happened to be in their hands, at the moment of our approach, stood still with wide extended arms, till they had gazed us, out of sight.

Having turned round the point of a rocky hill, we came at length to a road, much encumbered with huge blocks of broken rock. The river had a considerable fall, and hurried with rapid violence over its uneven bed. On either side, rose high rocks, perpendicular and bare, exhibiting an infinite variety of forms, being split by the shivering frost, and shaped into many tall pyramids, and vast impending crags, whose slight support seemed to threaten the beholder with instantaneous ruin, and made their aspect, truly tremendous. On the largest of those that were tumbled in the way, were piled quantities of white flint, to which it is the custom here, for every passenger to make some addition, from a motive of humanity, similar to that of the professors of both religions in India, which induces them to cover the bodies of men, found dead in the fields, with clods of earth, which the rains gradually dissolve and incorporate, forming the loose mass into a compact hillock. This always attracts the same respect, and passengers continue to add to the heap, long after all traces of the body are lost, and its existence forgotten. Thus also the piety of the Tibetians, offers a similar rite, to the bodies of those whom chance may have led to the spot, where the fragment lay at the instant of its fall, though the fatal effects of it may not have been certainly known.

While labouring through this heap of fragments, the traveller is suddenly surprised by a most gigantic figure of the chief idol in their temples, Mahamoonie, carved upon an immense stone in relief, and imaged in the usual attitude, sitting cross-legged. I cannot praise the sculptor for his execution; yet ugly and mishapen as the thing is which he has produced, something at least must be said in praise of his laborious and persevering industry.

Proceeding onwards, we passed a pretty cluster of small houses, situated on a high bank on the other side of the river, which ran below it. A little farther on, we crossed a very rude bridge, composed of large flat stones as a platform, laid upon pieces of workmanship equally rude, which rattled when trod upon, so that the passenger could not help thinking them extremely insecure.

Our quarters were next at Shoohoo, famous for exhibiting a few willow trees, in the midst of which our tents were pitched; and here we were happy to alight, after a toilsome stage of upwards of twenty-six miles.

We advanced early in the morning of Friday, the 19th of September, at first along the same sort of narrow valley through which our journey had lately lain, till turning to the left, it opened at once into a spacious amphitheatre, formed by the receding hills: in the centre of the arch, was seen a very handsome village, situated at the foot of a rock, called Nainee, belonging to Teshoo Loomboo. The buildings were regular and clean, some of them bordered, others striped with red, and being partly hid by branches of willows, had to us a new and extremely neat appearance.

The country now opened and improved, beginning to appear better peopled; and the view of trees and houses, afforded a very grateful change from the dreariness of our late prospects, which I have not seen equalled, in any tract of country through which I ever travelled before.

The greatest part of the space from Phari to this spot, upwards of fifty miles, is certainly very little removed, either in aspect, population, or culture, from a perfect desert. The hills were still bare, of a stiff, dry, unkindly composition: some of them were crowned with high perpendicular steeps like ramparts; whence the mouldering rock, split and detached, had sloped their sides with a loose gravelly soil down to the plain. Observing the manner in which many of them seem shivered by the frost, one would conclude, that not many ages are necessary to reduce them to a level with the ground below.

On passing round a projecting point, the castle of Jhansu-jeung came in view, at the distance of five or six miles, standing upon a rock, which from its perpendicular height, and the irregularity of its cliffs, if not impregnable, must at least be extremely difficult to be subdued by the assaults of any Tartar enemy.

The valley of Jhansu, which is very extensive, has greatly the appearance of having been once the bed of a lake. We descended a high bank, and found the level surface covered with coarse greyish sand and round stones, and intersected by the channels of many water-courses. This conjecture therefore instantly occurred; and the testimony of all whom I afterwards conversed with tended to give weight to it. But they could by no means fix the period of its being drained: the change was too remote to remain impressed upon the minds of those who now inhabit the neighbourhood; and I could obtain no determinate information, whether the discharge of the water was owing to art or nature.

The Tibetians, like their neighbours, possessed of an ardent spirit of devotion, do not hesitate to attribute the merit of every thing great, or singularly beneficial, to the agency of some supernatural being. As no records exist, to immortalize the author of a work eminently ingenious and useful, the lapse of many years is not necessary to involve the memory in complete oblivion; and the credit of it soon helps to aggrandize the importance of some fictitious deity.

It is asserted that Tibet, in remote times, was almost totally inundated; and the removal of the waters that covered its surface, is imputed to the miraculous interposition of some object of their worship, whose chief temple is reported to be at Durgeedin, Gya. He, it is said, in compassion to the few inhabitants which Tibet contained, who in that age were little better than monkeys, drew off the waters through Bengal, and, by sending teachers among them, humanized the wretched race, who were subsequently to people it. In this belief of the Tibetians, which is too general to be totally rejected, it is not difficult to discover strong traces of the universal deluge, though the tradition, as might naturally be expected, is obscured by fable, and disfigured by a mixture of absurdity.

Having forded the river, and ascended the opposite bank, we alighted at Tehukku, a dependency of Teshoo Loomboo, about two miles short of the castle of Jhansu, and twelve from Shoohoo. We were hospitably received by the officer who commanded here, and commodiously lodged in his tents, which were pitched within a small inclosure, formed by a double row of willows. This spot, because it was green, and had trees upon it, they called a garden. Our host was not deficient in providing tea, mattresses and cushions to repose on, as well as liquors, and plenty of provisions, all in the Tartar style. He was very conversable and communicative, and, like most great talkers, was at no loss for subjects of complaint. He brought me a specimen of rock crystal, taken from a solid rock of the same, about a day's journey hence. It was impure, and full of flaws; the largest piece might weigh about ten pounds: one corner of the mass had enveloped within it an infinite number of black hairs, crossing each other in all directions. I do not believe that they knew this to be, what it really was, a crystallization of silver.

The valley of Jhansu I understood to be particularly famous for the manufacture of woollen cloth, for which there is a very great demand. These cloths, which are confined to two colours, garnet and white, seldom exceed half a yard in breadth: they are woven very thick and close, like our frieze: they are very soft to the touch, for the fleece of their sheep appears to be remarkably fine, and supplies an excellent material.

Its superior pliability and warmth induce almost all the priests, both here and in Bootan, to use it for the short vest which they wear next the skin; and those who can afford it, have also their winter mantle of the same. There may perhaps be something of economy in the preference; for I recollect that my Tibet guide rallied my Bootan attendant, with all the pride of nationality, on the superior excellence of his cloth, protesting that it would wear three times as long as the manufacture of Bootan; and telling us how long it had been made, he opened, at the same time, his vest to shew it. I was not disposed to dispute his assertion, for it bore many visible marks of age. But the Tibetians are great economists in their dress, which they always choose to make of the most durable materials: the weight and thickness is never an objection. They are indeed accustomed to wear warm clothing; their summer dress being composed of woollen cloth, and their winter dress of sheep or fox skins, cured with the hair on. I speak of the common people; those who have the means, are dressed in silks and furs. But for this manufacture, the valley of Jhansu, from its central position, is very conveniently situated, both as to receiving the material, and conveying the cloth, when manufactured, to Teshoo Loomboo, Lassa, and Bootan. It has, in consequence, become the principal settlement of manufacturers; and it certainly possesses every natural and essential advantage of space, climate, and fertility.

We proceeded early the following morning, September the 20th, through fields of Lammas wheat, and passed close to the foot of the rock, on which Jhansu-jeung is built. The road, inclining round it, opened suddenly upon a monastery, situated on the concave side of a steep rock: it consisted of about one hundred and fifty houses, which rose in rows, one behind the other. They were square, pretty regular in their form, and the whitened walls had a band about their tops, two or three feet broad, of a deep garnet colour, which, with the addition of temples, gilded ornaments, and the decorated dwellings of their superior priests, made a very handsome and brilliant spectacle. The whole building was surrounded by high walls, which were continued along the ridge of the rock, and crossed by many intermediate gateways or lodgments, so as to command the monastery, which fronted towards the castle, as well as to overlook the other side of the rock, which was extremely rugged, and almost perpendicular.

In this neighbourhood we were pestered by a multitude of beggars, of all ages, and of both sexes: among them were some boys, who put on masks, and played a variety of antic tricks; and we came suddenly upon two old women in rags, at the corner of a street, strumming the cittaur, a rude kind of stringed instrument, and capering clumsily to their own miserable music.

The profession of the mendicant tribe is not unknown, as I perceived, in Tibet, but it is conducted with a better policy than in Europe; as they practise, and perhaps with more success, tricks of merriment, never shocking human nature with the cant of fictitious misery, or with assumed deformity. A few bits of silver, which I threw upon the ground, presently employed them all in a scramble, and gave me time to make my escape.

About a mile farther, crossing the river, we kept by the course of it, through the valley of Jhansu, which was extremely rich with abundant crops of ripe corn, and exceedingly populous. The numerous clustering villages, consisting of from four to ten neat square houses, their whitened walls, interspersed here and there with willows, and the river winding amongst them, were all together happily contrasted with the stiff sterility of the adjacent hills. The weather was clear and serene; and, although the sun shone with its brightest lustre, its warmth, even at noon, was not uncomfortable.

About this time we had arrived at Dongzee, a large village, under the jurisdiction of an officer from Lāssa; and we halted in an extensive grove upon its borders, where we found some tents already pitched. While we waited here to refresh our cattle, we made an ample repast, that gave us fresh spirits to pursue our journey, which we continued, without any remarkable occurrence, until near sunset, when we arrived at Dukque, sixteen miles from Tehukku, and pitched our tents for the night.

Our next day's journey lay within sight of the river all the way, which ran in a smooth stream, sometimes round the foot of the hills, and sometimes through the centre of the valley, but it was now no longer fordable. I saw a boat, placed on its end, in one of the villages, for occasional use, which might easily be carried on the back of the passenger. It was composed chiefly of leather, and consisted of a rude skeleton of wood, with thwarts and ribs, over which a bull's hide was stretched. It appeared to be exactly similar to that kind of boat, which, under the name of coricle[a], still continues in use on the Wye, and perhaps on some other of our English rivers; and it brought forcibly to

[a] See Beloe's Herodotus, Vol. I. p. 195.

my recollection, the important use to which Cæsar[b] once applied this rude and simple invention of our British ancestors.

Having travelled about ten miles, we came in view of Painom castle, with its square and round towers, loftily situated upon a perpendicular rock, washed by the river, which flows at its foot. The Tibetians invariably place their strong buildings upon rocks: these constitute the base of every fortress, and most of the monasteries rest upon the same foundation. I do not remember to have seen a single edifice of strength or importance, that was not situated upon a rock.

At the foot of Painom, over the broadest part of the river, was constructed a long bridge, upon nine piers of very rude structure. The piers were composed of rough stones, without cement, but, to hold them together, large trees, with their roots and branches, had been inserted; and some of them were vegetating. Slight beams of timber were laid from pier to pier; and upon them large flat stones were loosely placed, that tilted and rattled when trod upon: and this, I fear, is a specimen of their best bridges in Tibet. Many of them were extremely dangerous to pass over. The town lay to the south-east of the castle, at the base of the rock, and some of the houses extended even to the foot of the bridge.

As we turned short to the left, travelling due west, upon our right was seen, under a range of rocks, a very considerable monastery, endowed by Dalai Lama; and, about two miles farther on, was just visible, peeping through the midst of some tall trees, a large white

[b] De Bello civili, i. liv.

house, memorable for the birth of the present Teshoo Lama: it was named Keesoo. His father, an uncle of Dalai Lama's, his mother, and also the infant Lama, I was informed, were then residing there.

We halted this evening at Tsondue, three-and-twenty miles from Dukque, and within an easy day's journey of Teshoo Loomboo. The glitter of the gilding betrayed the tops of some of the edifices, as the sun shone obliquely upon them; but we could not, even with our glasses, distinguish much more.

The following morning, however, our guides were determined we should be there early. We were disturbed long before the dawn, though we had to travel only a distance of about ten miles, and by torch-light mounted our horses, so as to arrive at Teeshoo Loomboo just as the sun was rising. If the magnificence of the place was to be increased by any external cause, none could more superbly have adorned its numerous gilded canopies, and turrets, than the sun rising in full splendor directly opposite. It presented a view wonderfully beautiful and brilliant; the effect was little short of magic, and it made an impression, which no time will ever efface from my mind.

We ascended by a narrow street through the middle of the monastery, and were conducted to very splendid apartments, bright with gay colours, and situated in the centre of the palace, amidst a profusion of gorgeous finery. At the instant of our entrance, we heard the deep tone of many sonorous instruments, which were summoning the religious to their morning orisons.

CHAPTER IV.

Messages of Compliment and Congratulation from the Regent and Soopoon Choomboo — Custom of presenting a white Scarf — favourable Tokens of a friendly Disposition.—Preparations for our Reception—Hall of Audience—Lama's Throne— Introduction to the Regent—The Regent's Assurance of the Identity of the Lama —his Friendship for the Governor General in his pre-existent State —Attention and Respect paid him at the Court of China—his Regeneration acknowledged by the Emperor—Satisfaction derived from the Receipt of the Governor General's Dispatches.—Projected Removal of the Lama to Terpaling—the Monastery prepared for his Reception—Tea—Dismission.—Sketch of the Person—Manner—Dress of the Regent.—Bells, a Summons to Devotion.—Visit to Soopoon Choomboo.—Emperor of China—Influence—a Votary of the Tibet Faith.— Umbas—Jasoos—Gesub Rimbochay— Dalai Lama—Soopoon Choomboo, Sadeek—honoured by the distinguished Attention and Favour of the late Lama—promoted by the Emperor —his Character held in high Estimation—important Period in the Annals of Tibet.—First public Tribute of Acknowledgment and Allegiance to the regenerated Lama—Preparations for his Removal from Kylee to Terpaling—Offer to attend the Ceremony.—Party proceeds to escort the Lama—Homage paid by his Votaries on the Way—

Entry into Terpaling—Return of the Regent—Cavalcade—Bonfires —Chinese.—Correspondence with Dalai Lama.—Hostile Disposition of Gesub Rimbochay.—Powerful Influence of the Court of China.

WE had no sooner entered the apartments allotted for our accommodation, than messages of compliment and congratulation were received, both from the Regent, Chanjoo Cooshoo, brother of the late Lama, and Soopoon Choomboo, his cup-bearer, accompanied by a white silk scarf from each. These attentions were quickly followed by a most ample supply of refreshments; large vessels of warm tea, parched grain, dried fruits, and various articles of provision. Such are the forms observed, both here and in Bootan, towards a visitor, upon his first arrival: and perhaps a weary traveller would agree with me, in thinking it a most rational mode of reception, which thus bounteously places at his feet, after the toil of a long journey, every thing that hunger and fatigue render necessary to his relief. Ceremonious visits, on the first day, are always dispensed with; and the stranger is left to seek refreshment and rest, without interruption.

I did not omit to return, by the messenger, who waited upon me, proper acknowledgments for the polite attentions of the Regent, and Soopoon Choomboo; I sent at the same time, a white silk scarf to each; for this is an offering invariably attendant on every intercourse of ceremony, as well in Tibet as in Bootan. A similar piece of silk is always transmitted under cover, with letters, even from the most distant places, whether they be merely complimentary, or relate to public business of importance; and indeed between people of every rank and station in life, the presenting a silk scarf, constantly forms an essential part of the ceremonial of salutation. If persons of equal rank meet, an exchange takes place: if a superior is approached, he holds out his hand to receive the scarf, and a similar one is thrown across the shoulders of the inferior by the hand of an attendant, at the moment of his dismission. The colour that is employed on this occasion, is either white, or crimson; but the latter is least frequently used, white appearing to have an universal preference. This manufacture is of a thin texture, resembling that sort of Chinese stuff called pelong, and is remarkable for the purity of its glossy whiteness. They are commonly damasked, and the sacred words, *Oom maunee paimee oom*, are usually interwoven near both ends, which terminate in a fringe. They differ materially in size and quality, and are commonly proportioned, by him who presents, to his own condition, and the degree of respect he means to pay his guest. Trivial and unmeaning as this custom may appear to Europeans, long and general practice has here attached to it the highest importance. I could obtain no determinate information as to its meaning or origin, but I find that it has indeed a most extensive prevalence. It is observed, as I have before noticed, in all the territory of the Daeb Raja; it obtains throughout Tibet; it extends from Turkistan to the confines of the Great Desert; it is practised in China, and, I doubt not, reaches to the limits of Mantchieux Tartary. I view it merely in the light of an emblem of friendship, and a pledge of amity. In the course of my travels, every person who visited me, observed this mode of salutation; and as we were among a people not very conversant with the various customs of different nations, and who probably would have considered, any obvious deviation from their own, in no very favourable point of view, I never hesitated, when waiting upon the Chief, to salute him in his own way. The letters I received in Tibet and Bootan, were constantly accompanied by a pelong scarf, and, in conformity with the custom, I always sent one in return. Of so much moment indeed, in their estimation, is the observance of this formality, that Mr. Goodlad, the Resident at Rungpore, informed me, that the Raja of Bootan, once returned to him a letter he had forwarded from the Governor General, merely because it came unattended with this bulky incumbrance, to testify its authenticity.

We passed this day with little or no interruption, in a high degree sensible of the superior comfort of a warm and solid habitation, over thin and airy tents. The season was already becoming, to the sensations of a people who had not long quitted the tropics, most keenly cold; and the quiet and retirement we now enjoyed, afforded us a comfortable relief from the fatigue and restlessness of mind, produced by the bustle of a long and rapid journey. Our habitation was found, upon examination, greatly to exceed our expectations. The rooms were commodious, and even elegant; and the arrangement of every thing was as convenient as could possibly be wished. We occupied a part of the palace of the latest structure, which had been built by the late Teshoo Lama, for his private residence.

We had already been abundantly supplied, with all that could satisfy the calls of our immediate wants. Servants belonging to the Regent's household were appointed to attend me, not only in the capacity of messengers, to be sent on any service abroad, but also to assist in domestic business; and these friendly tokens of the good disposition entertained towards us, could not but fill our minds with satisfaction, and intimate the most auspicious presage respecting the event of my mission.

Towards the close of the evening, I received a visit from the person who had been sent to meet me by the Regent, while I resided in Bootan. His appearance and manners were extremely conciliating. The features of the Tibetian, which are in general high and harsh, were in him, softened by a cheerful, intelligent, and placid expression of countenance. I could not but conceive the strongest prepossessions in his favour; nor did any conduct of his, that I ever witnessed, cause me, in the slightest degree, to alter that good opinion. As long as he continued in the monastery, his attentions were unremitted, and few days passed, in which he did not spend some hours with me. He was my instructor in the language of Tibet; and, when tired with the repetition of guttural and nasal sounds, of which I found this language in a great degree to consist, he would, with the utmost cheerfulness, accept my challenge to a trial of skill at chess; in which, though I sometimes came off victorious, I was rather disposed to attribute my success to his urbanity, than to my own superior play. The station and movement of every piece, I found to be the same; and the game was conducted by the same rules, which regulate our play in England. These visits continued regularly, until he was summoned to a distant part of Tibet on the public service. I felt in his departure, the loss of an agreeable companion and an useful instructor, and we really parted,

I believe, with mutual reluctance, which on his part only yielded to a sense of duty.

Early in the morning after our arrival, intimation was brought to me, that the Regent proposed, in the course of the morning, to admit us to an audience. Several messages passed between us, before the appointed time, for the purpose of arranging every thing completely in due form. At length, about noon, Mr. Saunders and myself, accompanied by Poorungheer, as interpreter, proceeded to a part of the palace, with which, though it was at a considerable distance from our rooms, there was a communication, without descending into the street. We were then ushered into the presence chamber, a large and lofty hall, of an oblong shape, surrounded with a colonnade, and enlightened by an opening, over the centre. This central part of the room, contained an area, about twice as wide as the distance at which the pillars stood from the side walls. Light, air, and the grateful warmth of the sun, were occasionally admitted into the hall, by shifting the skreen, or rather moveable roof, which was placed immediately over the opening. The pillars that composed the colonnade were painted with vermilion, and richly ornamented with gold, as were also the edges of the scolloped arches, and the mouldings over them; various symbolical devices were also represented in the gilding above the arches. The walls were painted blue, skirted by two broad fillets of red, and an intermediate one of yellow. The floor was of a mottled composition, apparently of brown and white flint, intermixed with some strong compost, which admitted a high polish. No window, or door, opened into this hall, except that by which we entered, at one end; at the other, immediately opposite, stood the throne of the late Teshoo Lama, placed in a recess, elevated about five feet above the floor, surmounted with cushions of yellow satin, and decorated with hangings on each side, of various coloured silks, and rich brocades. At the foot of the throne were thin tapers, of the composition which they burn as incense in their temples, and vases filled with aromatic woods, which, consuming slowly, with their smoke powerfully perfumed the hall. From this seat, we were informed the Teshoo Lama was accustomed to distribute justice, and confer his solemn benediction upon the people.

Advancing to the upper end of the hall, we found the Regent, and Soopoon Choomboo, each of them habited in the religious dress, and seated under the colonnade, upon the left hand side of the throne, on elevated seats raised with satin cushions. White silk scarfs, according to the established custom of the country, were presented by us, which they received without quitting their seats. I then delivered the Governor General's dispatches into the Regent's hands, with a string of pearl and coral, whilst the rest of the presents were placed before him. Two raised seats of cushions had been prepared, towards which the Regent waving his hand, with a very significant look, directed us to be seated. I then thought it proper to address him nearly to the following effect.

" The few things I have the honour of offering to your acceptance, the Governor General, Mr. Hastings, has sent to you as tokens of his friendship and esteem, and with an earnest solicitude to preserve and cultivate the amicable intercourse, that had so happily commenced between you. This correspondence, in its earliest stages, had been dictated by the purest motives of humanity, and has hitherto pointed with unexampled sincerity and steadiness towards one great object, which constituted the grand business of Maha Gooroo's[a] life, peace and universal good. The Governor General, whose attention is always directed towards the same pursuits, was overwhelmed with anxiety, upon hearing the mournful news of the loss of his respected friend; not only on account of his regret for the departure of so exalted a character, but from an apprehension, lest the friendship established between himself and you, might suffer interruption, and undergo a change. Yet, solicitous for its continuance, as soon as information was brought to him of your return from China, he determined that a person in his confidence should repair to your presence; a measure, which the consoling character of a friend loudly demanded, and which was rendered still more necessary, by his desire to convey his earliest congratulations, upon the joyful tidings of the Lama's re-appearance in the world. In this great event, indeed, all his hopes are now revived; and, persuaded that the present Lama possesses the spirit of his former friend, he has no doubt that, by your good offices, and the will of heaven, every thing that was expected, will at length be effectually accomplished."

The Regent replied, by assuring me that the present and the late Teshoo Lama, were one and the same, and that there was no manner of difference between them; only as he was yet merely an infant, his spirit having but just returned again into the world,

[a] One of the titles of Teshoo Lama. The title is Sanskrit, and signifies the *Great Spiritual Master.*

he was at present incapable of action, and unable to comfort them with his voice. Their thoughts and time, therefore, were solely employed in the care of his person (for this was their duty and delight), in the hope that he might be soon able to confer upon them his blessing. At the same time that he lamented the misfortune of the Lama's decease in Pekin, he assured me of the firm unshaken attachment which Teshoo Lama had entertained for Mr. Hastings, to his latest breath. He added that Maha Gooroo had even begun to open his mind to the Emperor of China upon this subject, confident of his sanction and encouragement of the connection, and trusting that the concord mutually established between them, would extend its beneficial influence over all his votaries, and all the subjects of both empires. He then dwelt upon the great attention and respect paid to Teshoo Lama at the court of China; and told me that the Emperor, immediately on his receiving intelligence of the Lama's regeneration, had sent ambassadors with letters of congratulation, and a rosary of large unblemished pearls, enjoining them in the strongest terms to be careful of the Lama's person, to conduct his education in the strictest privacy, and not to suffer any strangers to be admitted to his presence.

But I must forbear entering into a minute detail of every particular that passed at our different interviews. It would be difficult, or rather perhaps impossible, to preserve the local idiom, and turn of expression, in a translation through two languages; and I am not certain even that my interpreter repeated them correctly in the Hindovi, which was the language that he used to me. Suffice it at present to say, that the Regent was most copious in his professions of attachment to the

Governor General, and loud in his encomiums on the occasion that gave birth to their present friendship, which originated entirely in his granting peace to the Booteeas, who were engaged with us in a very unequal war, in compliance with the intercession of Teshoo Lama. This act he declared to be *bote durm*, or of the greatest virtue.

Soopoon Choomboo also occasionally spoke. Inquiries respecting Mr. Hastings, the satisfaction they derived from the receipt of his dispatches, my journey, the difficulties that had impeded it, and their solicitude to see me, were topics which occupied a considerable share of our time in this conference. Much was also said respecting the sad calamity they had suffered by the Lama's having withdrawn himself from the world, in consequence of their offences; nor did they omit strongly to express their sense of the blessing, that he had been pleased to appear again so early in the flesh.

I was informed, that the infant Lama still continued to reside in the dwelling, where he was first discovered, in the valley of Painom; but that it was proposed to convey him within a few days to Terpaling, a monastery prepared for his reception, near the summit of a mountain at the distance of two days journey from Teshoo Loomboo; and that all the court, were to attend his removal. All the time of the principal officers of state was nearly occupied in preparations for this event, and the Regent gave me to understand, that he had, in consequence, but little leisure, and might possibly, not have it in his power to see me again more than once, before his departure. Near the close of the audience, tea was introduced, and served up in the same manner as in Bootan. We had small benches placed before us, and upon them was set the same kind of cup, which, I remember, the Daeb Raja told me, in his dominions, none but the Raja, or one of the three Lamas, could presume to use. This I notice, not only as being one among their sumptuary laws, but also as an evidence of their disposition to manifest very high respect, as well as civility, in their attentions to us. In shape and size this cup is somewhat similar to a China pint bason; but a round hollow pedestal proceeds from beneath, sufficiently long, to be grasped within the hand, and upon which it will stand upright without support. It is made of the finest porcelain, extremely thin, and purely white, and is stamped on both sides with the impression of the dragon, the imperial emblem, which is visible only, like the water mark in bank paper, on close inspection, at a small distance. Previously to our taking leave, trays of tea, sugar, skins of butter, and dried fruits, consisting of raisins, dates, apricots, and almonds, with some others that I had never before seen, the produce of China and eastern Tartary, were severally presented to us. The Regent gave me many injunctions to communicate all my wants to the person, whom he had directed to attend upon us. We each received a scarf from his own hands, and withdrew, having every reason to be gratified with our reception, which I considered as attentive, and flattering, in the highest degree.

I will now endeavour to give some idea of the Regent's person and manner. In stature he was of the middle size, rather of a broad make, but not inclined to corpulency. He had a short wide face, with the nose a little turned up, small black eyes, and high cheek bones. Though he was by no means handsome, yet there was an agreeable symmetry in his features, and a sweetness of expression in his countenance, which was highly prepossessing. His language was plain and unaffected, neither inflated with the exuberancy of Asiatic diction, nor yet deficient in urbanity; it was delivered with that mild unassuming manner, which strongly characterises Tibetians of good education. His action was void of gesticulation; it consisted in a slight movement of the body forwards, and a bending of the neck, assisted by the variations of an expressive and enlightened countenance; his arms were almost constantly folded beneath his mantle.

His voice appeared to be injured by the loss of his teeth, which occasioned, I thought, rather an indistinct articulation, or perhaps this effect might in some degree be produced by a defect in the roof of the mouth. My interpreter, however, had no difficulty in understanding him, as he spoke slowly, and commanded a ready choice of words; his dress was that of the religious order, which seems to be the regular habit of every attendant on the court. This simply consists of a vest of woollen cloth, without sleeves, of a deep garnet colour, and a large mantle, either of the same, or of a thinner texture, somewhat resembling a shawl. A sort of philibeg, and huge boots of Bulgar hide, lined either with fur or cloth, and designed as well to promote warmth in travelling, as for substantial use within doors, complete the dress. But though it surprised me at first, to see my friends trudging about the house, in their massy boots, yet I soon became sensible of their utility, as a defence against the chill arising in this cold climate, from their marble floors. The great scarcity of timber in Tibet, not admitting them to board the floors of their rooms, hence possibly arise those cramps and rheumatic pains, with which they are so frequently and so severely afflicted.

After taking leave of the Regent, it was my intention to have paid a visit to Soopoon Choomboo; but our audience had been protracted to a great length, and we had no sooner risen, than all the bells of the monastery struck up, as a summons to devotion. The present occasion, the removal of the Lama, called for an extraordinary attendance on the exercises of religion; and all the Gylongs, we were told, applied themselves at this time, with redoubled fervor to the duty of prayer. Not long after we had returned to our apartments, I was disturbed on a sudden, by so confused and tumultuous a noise, that I was utterly at a loss to what cause, to attribute this alarming uproar. At length, I was informed by my attendants, the Goseins, that it was only the Gylongs at their *pooja*, or religious exercises, and I could not possibly refuse, to give them ample credit for their zeal.

The following day I received an invitation from Soopoon Choomboo, and we immediately prepared to wait upon him in his apartments, which, though remote from ours, yet form a part of that large assemblage of rooms, which all together constitute the palace, and accommodate all the officers of the court. In going to them, it was unnecessary to pass along the open street; for, by descending some stairs, ascending others, and traversing several halls and passages, we came at length to the division of the palace, which he occupied. The room in which we found him, was rather narrow, being long and lofty, in comparison of its width; but the advantage of its situation, amply counterbalanced every defect in point of symmetry and proportion. It commanded an extensive view of the valley, and was at once enlightened and warmed by a projecting balcony, which, from its position, admitted the rays of the sun nearly all the day, during the time he has southern declination, which, of course, is their coldest season. When we entered the room, the mohair curtains were partially drawn; but even in this state, we were sensible of a grateful warmth. Soopoon Choomboo was seated close by the balcony. We each of us presented, as usual, a silk scarf, and I delivered to him the letter and presents, with which I had been charged. We took our seats on piles of cushions that had been placed on the opposite side of the room, when Soopoon Choomboo, after a few personal compliments, instantly proposed various inquiries respecting the health and situation of Mr. Hastings. To his numberless questions I gave, as well as I was able, the most satisfactory answers; and I endeavoured to express, in the strongest terms, the great uneasiness to which I had been subject, in the noxious climate (as they esteem it) of the country of Dukba[b]; contrasting my unpleasant situation, while my journey hither stood in suspense, and I dreaded the necessity of returning to Bengal without seeing him, or Maha Raja, with the singular satisfaction I now experienced, in having reached his court in safety. I concluded with assurances, how highly acceptable these tidings would prove to his friend the Governor. He was profuse in his acknowledgments, of the high gratification and honour he derived from the receipt of the Governor General's dispatches, and stated the great anxiety, under which the Regent and himself had laboured, as Poorungheer well knew, in contriving to conduct me to Teshoo Loomboo.

Bootan.

In the recital of their embarrassments, though they are averse to own any immediate dependance upon the Chinese, I could plainly trace the greatest awe of the Emperor of China, of his officers stationed at the court of Lassa, styled Umbas[c], as well as of the Jasoos[d], and the Raja of that place, Gesub Rimbochay, who had usurped even, from the hands of Dalai Lama, the greatest portion of his temporal power.

The rest of our conversation turned chiefly upon my journey, the remote distance, the difficulty of the way, and the difference of climate between Bengal, Bootan, and Tibet: these topics filled up the time till tea was introduced, of which we all partook; this was succeeded by the usual offering of trays of fruit, and we then received from his hands each of us a white silk scarf, and retired. While we were with Soopoon Choomboo, a messenger came in, apparently from a long journey, booted, and carrying a whip in his hand, with some important dispatches. He first pulled off his hat, holding it with his left hand down to his knee, then bowing his body, he drew a crimson scarf from his breast, which he presented, and afterwards delivered his dispatches. Having repeated a few words in a low voice, he bowed again, and was dismissed with a single word and a nod. This is one mode of salutation: another kind of homage, which appeared to be due only to the sovereign Lama, consists in an humble prostration of the body nine times to the earth.

Soopoon Choomboo, who was styled also Sadeek, held the second rank in the court of Teshoo Loomboo. He was by birth a Mantchieux Tartar, and was recommended to Teshoo Lama at an early age, by

[c] Magistrates. [d] Communicators of intelligence.

Chanjea Lama, who is a native of the same region, and who constantly resided near the person of the Emperor of China. Under the immediate care of Teshoo Lama he received his education, and having proved himself a faithful, accomplished, and useful servant, he at length acquired the complete confidence of his master, and became, I was well assured, his particular favourite. As a public acknowledgment of his merit, he was appointed by Teshoo Lama, not long before his death, to the presidency of an important monastery styled Khonjin Shimboi, which had an establishment of three hundred Gylongs, and was endowed with an extensive territory upon the western border of Tibet, near Luddauk. The Emperor of China, during his attendance on the Lama at his court, conferred upon him the title of Mirkin Chassa Lama. As the office he filled at the time of the Lama's death was that of Sadeek, which is synonymous with that of Zempi in Bootan, that is, cupbearer, he became of course invested with the charge of all the Lama's effects, and was to continue in this high trust, until the regenerated Lama should be seated on the musnud[*].

The singular favour he enjoyed, seems to have been no more than was justly due to his integrity and talents; and in the event of the regency becoming vacant, from the general estimation in which he was held, I had no doubt of his advancement to that high honour. His influence indeed at that time, was scarcely less powerful, for he was treated by Chanjoo Cooshoo rather as a colleague, than as a subordinate officer, and his opinion was implicitly attended to on almost every occasion. A more harmonious agreement, or more perfect confidence, could not possibly subsist between them.

[*] Throne.

The age of Soopoon Choomboo, at that time, did not exceed thirty. In stature he was rather low, but well proportioned, and not at all inclined to corpulency. His countenance was open and ingenuous, yet his features were unequivocally impressed with the Tartar character: small eyes, thin eyebrows, high cheek bones, and without even the rudiments of a beard. His complexion was not darker than that of an Arab, or a Spaniard.

Though possessing an acknowledged superiority of talent, information, and influence over his countrymen, he made no parade of these advantages, but conducted himself with singular humility, mildness, and modesty. He was not less communicative in his conversation, than conciliating in his manners, and, as our acquaintance improved, I found him cheerful, and occasionally jocose.

The public office Soopoon Choomboo bore, as I have already observed, was that of Sadeek to the late Teshoo Lama. Were I to seek for a title analogous to Sadeek, in our own language, by which I might render it intelligible to an English reader, I should be at a loss to find one of so comprehensive a signification. Though perhaps I might with some propriety style him, from his situation in the court of the sovereign Pontiff, Prime Minister, or Cardinal, yet who would expect to find the domestic servant, in a person invested with so high a title? Nor yet does, Lord Chamberlain of the Household, Master of the Ceremonies, and Master of the Robes, convey a complete idea of his duties and his station.

The Sadeek receives and communicates the Lama's commands; he is the immediate channel of conveying all information to him; he makes the arrangements necessary for the celebration of the great festivals of religion; he is always personally attendant on the Lama; he is his cup-bearer; he has charge of the wardrobe; and to his immediate care is intrusted all the wealth of the sovereign, whether derived from the religious offerings of his votaries, or from other and less sacred sources. He brings, and places before the Lama, all his food, and in particular, pours out his tea, of which it is the custom first to taste himself, in the presence of his master. In fact, I have been led to understand that Teshoo Lama receives neither food nor raiment from any other hand; yet still he is found to hold a very high rank in the religious order, which is implied by no less a title than that of Lama.

My arrival in Tibet happened at a period of high importance in the annals of the state, as well in a political as a religious point of view; for now they had to acknowledge, in the person of an infant, their future sovereign, to whom also, as to their sacred pontiff, they were about to pay the first public tribute of homage and allegiance, and thereby to give currency and authority to the belief, that he was the regenerated, immortal mediator with the Supreme. On such an occasion, it will easily be conceived, that no mark of respect, no pomp or parade, was omitted, which, in their ideas, could possibly tend, to add dignity and splendour to the solemn ceremony.

The Emperor of China, a votary of the Tibet faith, had commanded a military officer of high rank, with a large detachment of troops, to attend and escort the infant Lama; other Chinese attended, for the purpose of bearing his Tuckt rowân[f], or moving throne; and the

[f] A Persian term, whence probably the use of this stately accommodation is derived.

Regent himself, assisted by Soopoon Choomboo, was to conduct the cavalcade.

A curious desire, I must own, to be personally witness of so singular a ceremony, induced me to make some effort to be admitted of the party. I accordingly ordered Poorungheer to wait upon the Regent, and express my earnest wishes to testify, on all occasions, the respect I entertained for the character of the Lama; and to say, that I should be peculiarly happy to attend his suite, if he thought proper to allow me so great an honour: but however strongly my curiosity had been excited, I had formed no great expectation that my offer would be accepted; and I was therefore but little disappointed when Poorungheer returned to me with excuses from the Regent, declining to accept the offer of my company, on account of the Chinese, whose jealousy of strangers is too well known, and to whom he was particularly anxious of giving no occasion of offence: but at the same time he politely acknowledged my attention, and I had the satisfaction to hear, expressed himself greatly pleased with it.

The party proceeded from the monastery, on Saturday the 27th of September, before the dawn of day, towards Kylee, situated in the valley of Painom, where the infant Lama at this time resided with his parents. The grand ceremony of his removal commenced the next day.

The Lama was attended by a very numerous concourse of people, and followed with every possible display of enthusiastic homage. The place prepared for his reception was not more than sixteen miles from Kylee; yet so great was the retinue, and so frequently were they impeded by successive crowds of votaries, who threw themselves before him in the way, in humble prostration, that it became absolutely necessary to form an intermediate camp, in which they halted for the night.

Moving again early in the following morning, in the course of that day, they made their entry into the monastery of Terpaling. Having then placed the young Lama in the new monastery, together with his father and mother, to whose care he was still very properly committed, after making every necessary arrangement, the Regent and his retinue returned to Teshoo Loomboo.

As the road lay in front of our apartments, I had an opportunity of observing the Regent's approach. He rode attended by two or three hundred horsemen, the greater part of whom preceded him, and he himself followed surrounded by a select party, principally consisting of the officers of state. He was dressed in a garb very different from that, in which I had seen him before. It was a yellow satin robe, lined with sable fur, and fastened with a girdle round the waist. A garnet coloured shawl mantle, partially covering his satin robe, according to their fashion, passed round the body, and its end was gathered up to rest upon the left shoulder, leaving the right arm at liberty. He wore upon his head a round hat, covered with a yellow glossy lacker that glittered in the sun, and he had on red bulgar boots. From his girdle, hung pendant a small knife case, with its implements, and a large purse with a running string, in which he carried a tea cup, and several other small articles, the constant appendages of a Tartar dress. To this also are commonly added, a smaller purse for money, and another filled with tobacco and a pipe, together with a little pouch for tinder, containing a piece of flint, and edged at the bottom with a bar of steel. The horse he rode, was decorated with large crimson tassels, and other splendid trappings, whilst a number of bells, suspended to a collar that hung round his neck, jingled as he moved along with slow and solemn pace. The body of the horse, from the multitude of *Chowrs*, or cow tails, that hung on both sides, could scarcely be seen.

The select attendants were equipped nearly after the same manner. The dress of those of more humble rank differed chiefly in the quality of the materials. They were clad, for the most part, in cloth, either yellow, or red, or striped with these colours, and they wore upon their heads round hats, having large flowing tassels of scarlet silk upon the centre of the crown. Some had narrow braids a little turned up, and others were bordered by broad bands of fur. The most extraordinary in appearance were those worn by the Kilmauks (Calmucs), which were of vast dimensions, I suppose not less than two feet in diameter, with shallow crowns, but monstrous brims; the whole covered with long locks of wool matted together, of a gaudy yellow colour. Some Goseins, wearing turbans and the Indian habit, with Moguls from the borders of Persia, in their national dress, assisted also to compose this motley group. There were none in the whole cavalcade, as far as I could perceive, who bore any kind of arms. Heaps of fire were distinguishable to a very remote distance, burning on either side of the road, and emitting columns of thick smoke. These bonfires, which I have already noticed, are a mark of respect shewn by the inhabitants of Tibet and Bootan to every great personage who travels through their neighbourhood; and when their sovereign passes by, the custom is of course observed with extraordinary zeal and attention.

Many persons on both sides the road prostrated themselves upon the ground, as the Regent with his retinue advanced; and when he drew near to Teshoo Loomboo, banners were hoisted upon the palace walls, and the nowbut[g], trumpets, gongs[h], and cymbals, conspired to announce his entry in their loudest tones.

The Chinese commander, with his detachment of troops, took this route in preference to that by Jhansu-jeung, on his return to Lassa. The ground marked out for their encampment was upon the edge of the plain, just without the limits of the monastery, under the fortress of Shigatzee-jeung, and close upon the banks of the Painom-tchieu. Here the troops halted two days, after which they struck their tents, and marched away.

I sought an early opportunity to congratulate the Regent upon his return, and the safe conveyance of the Lama to Terpaling. This gave occasion to some reflections from the Regent, full of reverence and affection for the late Lama, and tending to establish the identity of the

[g] A sort of kettle drum.

[h] A large circular metallic instrument formed by the hammer, from one and a half to two feet in diameter, with the edge turned up about two inches deep all round. When used, it is suspended by a cord passing through holes made for the purpose near the circumference. In order to excite an equable vibration, it is at first softly struck by the performer upon the external ring, with a ball encased in leather at the end of a long rod; the blows are afterwards repeated with stronger force, and it is then capable of producing a surprising sound.

present, from the unerring signs of wisdom and greatness stamped upon his brow, and the early traits of his sublime character which had been already evidently displayed. Nor did he drop the subject, without enlarging on the partiality which the Lama had entertained for the English in his state of pre-existence, and regretting that his tender age rendered him at present unable to converse with me.

Much conversation afterwards followed, on the subject of my commission, in which he manifested great anxiety to remove any unfavourable idea I might have formed, respecting his friendly disposition, in consequence of the difficulties which had been thrown in the way of my proceeding to his court. He told me that many letters had passed upon the subject between him and Dalai Lama, who was always favourably inclined towards the English; but he principally attributed the discouragement and obstruction I had experienced to Gesub Rimbochay: in his apologies also he glanced strongly at the Chinese.

The Tibetians do not, it is true, bend under the immediate authority of that court; but its influence overawes them in all their proceedings, and produces a timidity and caution in their conduct, more suited to the character of subjects, than allies. The jealousy with which they regard this interference of the Chinese, and their uneasiness under the yoke, though it rests so lightly upon them, was manifest, from the distant reserve with which they treated those officers and troops, who came for no other purpose than to do honour to their high-priest. They were not suffered to lodge within the confines of the monastery; this, I understood, would have been considered as a kind of profanation, for they look upon the Chinese as a gross and impure race of men. They were evidently impatient during their stay, and assumed an unusual air of secrecy, to prevent their obtaining a knowledge of any thing relating to their affairs, until the day of their departure, which was announced to me, by many persons belonging to the monastery with much apparent satisfaction.

CHAPTER V.

Permission from the Regent to view the Interior of the Monastery.—Gorgeous Temples.—Solemn and mysterious Ceremonies.—Numerous Assembly of the Gylongs.—Periods for Devotion.—Loud Vociferation.—Clamorous Noise attending the Performance of their religious Rites.—Serious Attention to the Duties of their Faith.—Profound Respect for their sovereign Lama.—Visit the Mausoleum dedicated to the Memory of the late Teshoo Lama.—Cursory View of this highly venerated Structure.

HAVING previously obtained permission from the Regent, I found a convenient opportunity, before his return from Terpaling, to accomplish an object I had much at heart, and which will consequently claim from me, very minute and particular attention.

From the first day of my arrival at Teshoo Loomboo, I was extremely desirous of viewing the interior of some one of those magnificent edifices, in the midst of which I had taken up my abode, and which continually excited my curiosity by the profuse and costly ornaments bestowed upon their outside.

The frequent recurrence of solemn sounds from a variety of deep toned instruments, after short pauses of profound silence; the low hum of invocation, during both night and day; and occasionally the more vociferous clamour of crowded congregations, joined with a full choral band; left me no room to doubt, that I was close to the scene, of some of the most solemn and mysterious ceremonies of their religion.

I lost little time in endeavouring to ascertain the truth of my conjectures; but I trod upon tender ground. Any indication of extraordinary curiosity, even in the common affairs of life, was sufficient to raise, in an instant, an host of suspicions, against which, I should have been compelled eternally to combat; and religion, especially among a people so bigotted to its forms, was a subject to which I adverted, with still more scrupulous caution.

From various inquiries, however, at length I collected, that the chapel in which the Gylongs met to offer up their daily prayers, was but a short distance from us. Their stated periods of devotion were the rising of the sun, noon, and sunset. Among two thousand five hundred Gylongs, appointed for the service of the monastery, the greater part were expected to be present on each occasion. On every third day, the morning was devoted to proclaiming aloud the attributes and praises of the Supreme Being; a service which was performed with a vehemence of vociferation perfectly astonishing, and, as I thought, altogether inconsistent with the decorum of a well regulated assembly.

The object of this solemn meeting, as far as I could collect, was for every individual present to repeat, and enforce, with all his powers of utterance, the praises of the Deity; and we need not wonder that from such a congregation, who had attained by long practice to a

Stentorian strength of lungs, there should arise the most surprising discord, the very counterpart of that which is produced by the vociferations of an enraged and hostile multitude. But all this was, in fact, nothing more than a pious token of the most ardent zeal, a sort of contest for the palm, a struggle, which should do the highest honour to his supreme and tutelary gods.

To the public exercises of their faith, must be added the private prayers in the apartments of the inferior Lamas, which are always accompanied by music, together with the solemn pageantry of processions moving almost every day around the environs of the monastery. All these, taken together, soon sufficiently convinced me, that I was in the midst of men, who made religion the sole business of their life.

With the errors of their opinions, or their practice, I had no concern. The immediate advantages resulting from them they themselves daily experience. Having voluntarily devoted themselves to the severities and the duties of their religion, they obtain a large portion of grateful respect from their countrymen, whose worldly avocations exempt them from the same particular services. Both, united in one common bond of union, the one part to labour, the other to pray, enjoy in peace and harmony, the fruits of their industry; and find it unnecessary to support a single man in arms, either to defend their territory, or maintain their rights. Placing their sole reliance in the mediation of the sacred Lama, the immaculate vicegerent of the Supreme, they imagine, that he covers them with the broadest shield, from the encroachments of others; and the benign influence of his doctrines teaches them to be benevolent, merciful, and humane, to all around them.

The love, the veneration, the unanimity I saw expressed, effectually convinced me that they were happy. But to return to my narrative: the room in which I wrote, and the suite of apartments allotted to the accommodation of myself, and the companion of my travels, were erected by the late Teshoo Lama for his own private residence, whenever he chose to retire into uninterrupted solitude. In an adjacent building, upon the right hand, are lodged his mortal remains; in another, upon the left, those of a former Lama, whose spirit exchanged its corporeal residence more than a century ago. The Teshoo Lama, I was told, had lavished upon this shrine of his predecessor, immense wealth; yet his own, which was nearly completed before his visit to the Emperor of China, had been since greatly enriched by the tributary offerings made to him on that journey, and was now considered as the most splendid and magnificent of the two.

When I became acquainted with these particulars, situated as I was so near the mausoleum of our departed friend, I wanted not an excellent pretext for desiring to visit it; and having waited for a favourable opportunity, I urged my plea with such success, that the Regent, Chanjoo Cooshoo, immediately signified his most willing acquiescence in my wishes.

Early in the morning my faithful attendant Gooroobah, came to conduct me. Proceeding from my apartment, along the corridor, we descended two flights of stairs, and passing through some passages, without any communication with the street, came to a small gate, which we entered, and found ourselves in the inclosure immediately before the grand mausoleum. Three sides of this court yard, which was paved, were surrounded with a colonnade, for the occasional accommodation of pilgrims, and other devotees. Upon the walls of this colonnade, were rudely painted many emblematical figures, of gigantic proportions, illustrative of various parts of their system of mythology. The two principal figures, of enormous size, depicted with hideous countenances, and coloured with blue and scarlet, represented incarnations of Cali. The pillars were painted with vermilion, and ornamented with gilding; and upon the pediment which they supported, was introduced the imperial figure of the Chinese dragon. In the centre of the colonnade was a large gate, which opened to a principal avenue of the monastery. Immediately opposite to this gate, stood the portico of the mausoleum, on the top of which, within a low railing, was placed the following device, resembling a coat of arms. The centre piece, which was of a spear-like form, resembling the leaf of the pepul tree[a], was placed upon a low pedestal. On each side, was the figure of an animal, not unlike a deer couchant, with the head elevated, the nose pointing upwards, and the throat resting upon the shoulder, or projecting part, of the hastated machine between them, which I conjectured to be about eight feet high. The whole extended from one side of the portico to the other, stood entirely clear of the body of the building, and was very richly gilt. It had all together, the appearance of a coat of arms with supporters, but upon a very large scale. The centre piece, I was informed, contained within it, some of their sacred writings.

Under the portico, sat a priest, who read with a book before him,

[a] Ficus indica.

apparently regardless of our presence. It was his duty, together with others, who occasionally relieved him, to pray eternally upon the same spot, and keep alive the sacred fire, that burns before the shrine. Two ponderous doors, painted with vermilion, and embossed with huge gilded knobs, made the whole fabric ring, as their pivots grated within the sockets, and their massy sides came with strong concussion against the walls. It now appeared, that the building we had hitherto seen, served only as a case, to cover a most beautiful pyramid placed within it. At the base of this pyramid, the body of the late Lama was deposited in a coffin of pure gold, made by command of the Emperor of China, upon the decease of the Lama at his court, and in which the body was conveyed, with the utmost solemnity and state, from Pekin, through the provinces of China and Tibet, to Teshoo Loomboo. His votaries all the way, paid the most profound homage to his manes, and thought themselves peculiarly blessed, if they could but touch the pall, or any part of the bier, as the funeral procession passed slowly along.

It is the custom in Tibet, to preserve entire the mortal remains of their sovereign Lamas only; every other corpse is either consumed by fire, or given to be the promiscuous food of beasts and birds of prey. As soon as life has left the body of a Lama, it is placed upright, sitting in an attitude of devotion, his legs being folded before him, with the instep resting upon each thigh, and the soles of the feet turned upwards. To a person unused to the practice, this must be a posture of extreme constraint; though Lam Rimbochay, of Bootan, has repeatedly placed himself in it before me, with much apparent ease.

The right hand is rested with its back upon the thigh, with the thumb bent across the palm. The left arm is bent and held close to the body, the hand being open, and the thumb, at right angles with the fingers, touching the point of the shoulder.

This is the attitude of abstracted meditation. The eyes, at the same time, being directed downwards, and half closed, indicate that, with the suspended powers of the body, the faculties of the mind also, are completely absorbed in contemplation, effectually guarded against wandering, and shut to every species of external impression.

The late Teshoo Lama is represented in an effigy of gold, which crowns the pyramid, and is placed within the concave of a large shell, radiated alternately, with white and red, the edges being scolloped, and projecting so far as to form a canopy, that incloses within its hollow, the whole body of the figure. The image is represented sitting upon cushions, and has the drapery of a yellow satin mantle, negligently flowing over the lower part, whilst a cap, resembling a mitre, covers the head. As a tribute of respect, which might be gratifying to his votaries, and tend to conciliate their affection, I made an offering of a white pelong scarf, which the attending priest received, and passed over the smoke of the incense burning before the shrine, while the Gosein and others prostrated themselves nine times with devout humility. The priest then ascended a ladder, and put one end of the scarf upon that hand of the image which was a little advanced; the other hung down upon the pyramid. Round the borders of the canopy, were suspended all the various rosaries, of the richest gems, used by the Lama during his life; they consisted of pearls, emeralds, rubies, sapphires, coral, amber, crystal, lapis lazuli, and even beads of humble ser-bu-jya[b]. intermixed together, and hanging in festoons.

The sides of the pyramid were encased with plates of solid silver. On each step that composed the structure, which gradually diminished in breadth and depth, from the base to the vertex, were arranged all sorts of rarities, and articles of curious workmanship, which had been presented at different times as offerings to the late Lama. Among these, were various costly snuff-boxes, and valuable trinkets, the tribute of the Emperor; with choice specimens of China, large jars of old blue japan, and masses of lapis lazuli, variously arranged, and disposed, according to their taste, not without considerable effect.

About breast-high from the base of the pyramid, was one step considerably deeper than the rest, in front of which were represented two lions rampant, carved in relievo, and between them was placed a human figure, with eyes extravagantly large and prominent; his countenance was expressive of the most anxious agitation, and his person thrown into strange contortions: his hands were applied to a stringed instrument, called a cittaur. Other instruments of music, hautboys, trumpets, and cymbals, were placed upon each extremity of the step, immediately before these figures; and the intermediate space was filled with china jars, and vases of silver and blue japan.

On the right side of the pyramid, was placed another image of the Lama, as large as life, and, as Poorungheer assured me, a very faithful resemblance of his person. It was placed in a sort of pulpit, beneath a canopy of silk, in a devout attitude, with a book before it. This

[b] Canna; *Linnæi.*

image, I was given to understand, was not of gold, but solid silver, gilt. In front of the pyramid, on an altar covered with white cloth, were spread about the common objects of daily oblation; such as fruits, and flowers, with various kinds of corn, and oil. Intermixed among the offerings, were seen at the same time, several lamps burning, which, being considered as sacred fire, are never permitted to go out; the smoke arising from these, and from a multitude of odoriferous tapers, filled the surrounding space, and strongly perfumed the air.

On each side of the pyramid, hung suspended from the ceiling by one end, whole pieces of the most beautiful silks and satins. Close to the pyramid were two pieces of black velvet, embroidered all over with pearls, in squares like network, and finished with a border of the same. Some pieces of very handsome English brocades, and Benares gull-budden[c], completed this rich display. On the surrounding walls were painted, from the bottom to the top, many rows of Gylongs, represented in the act of praying.

Upon the floor, and on all sides, were high piles of sacred books, appertaining to the religion of the Lamas, which orthodox professors of that faith, industriously employ themselves to augment with voluminous commentaries.

Having thus endeavoured to give as distinct an account as a cursory view could qualify me to do, of the valuable materials that contribute to enrich and adorn the mausoleum of the Lama, I must here close my description. To attempt to form an estimate of its riches,

[c] A species of silk cloth embroidered with flowers, a manufacture, I believe, peculiar to Benares.

from my own observation, or to repeat the exaggerated reports, which others even relate with diffidence, might equally subject me to the imputation of extravagant fiction.

The shell, or covering of the pyramid, which constitutes the exterior of the mausoleum, is a structure, when viewed at some distance, of considerable magnitude and beauty. It stands upon the side of a rocky hill, and is very conspicuously situated, towering high above the greater part of the monastery. The architecture must not be criticised by scientific rules, for the different orders, as adopted in Europe, appear to be entirely unknown in Tibet, where they seem rather to have chosen the use of a mixed kind. The pillar, scolloped arch, and pediment of Asia, or Hindostan, prevail in the interior apartments; the external decorations are of Chinese, or Tartar origin, similar to those of the watch tower, or temple of the former; the tented canopy and imperial dragon. As far as the mason has been concerned, it is a plain substantial building of stone, with cement. It is longer in front than in depth, and considerably more lofty than either.

The walls are built so much thicker at the base, as to give them a very perceptible slope. The centre of the building has a very large window above the portico, furnished with curtains of black mohair. The walls, in various parts, are ornamented with circular representations either of the sun, or full moon, and with gilded crescents. Above the window runs a headband all round of a deep garnet colour. Higher than this headband, in the centre of the front, within a tablet, the mystic sentence, *Oom maunee paimee oom*, is inscribed, in large golden characters. A blank interval then succeeds, and over that, a space of

Pl.XI

Capt. S. Turner del. — James Basire sc.

The Mausoleum of Teshoo Lama.

Published March 5th 1800, by G & W Nicol Pall Mall.

about ten or twelve feet from the summit of the walls, is occupied by a deep crimson colour. A frieze, and whitened cornice surrounds the top. At the angles, and on different parts along the top of the wall, is placed a sort of ornament, which I term fasces. It is a cylinder of metal strongly gilt, standing upright upon a short supporter fixed in its centre; and is commonly about five feet high, and two or three in circumference. Many of them are covered with black cloth, and these invariably have a broad white fillet, passed round them in opposite directions, horizontally and perpendicularly, so, as to form the figure of a cross. The sides are marked with letters, beaded and fluted; and the top is always crowned with some small ornament. The heads of lions, well executed, projected from the angles of the building; these also were gilt, and had bells depending from their lower lips.

But the most showy part of this structure, which crowns the whole, is a spacious tented canopy, richly gilt, which is supposed to stand immediately over the remains of the Lama, and the centre of the pyramid; it overshadows the summit of the building, from the body of which it is elevated by its own particular support, forming to the whole an elegant and graceful finish. The edges of the canopy swell out in a bold and easy sweep. The ridge is decorated with the Chinese dragon, whose convolutions fill up all that space; and round the canopy are hung a prodigious number of small bells, which, as well as those, which are distributed about all the projections of the building, having thin square pieces of wood fastened to the clapper, make an inconceivable jingle, with every breeze that blows.

CHAPTER VI.

The Regent.—Soopoon Choomboo.—Countries contiguous to Tibet—Bengal endeared to the Tibetians by religious Prejudices.—Gunga Sagur—the Confluence of the Ganges with the Sea.—Jagarnaut.—Performance of Pilgrimage by Proxy.—A Devotee.—Geography—Astronomy.—Pranpooree—his extraordinary Course of Mortifications.—Russia—the reigning Czarina.—Taranaut Lama.—Kharka.—Intercourse between Russia and China.—Pilgrims from Khumbak.—Gallery of Idols—Means by which the Cabinet is occasionally augmented—Teshoo Loomboo famed for the Manufacture of Images.—Lama of Luddauk.—War between England—America and France.—Commerce—of the English Nation.—Spirit of Inquiry and Research.—Siberia—Baikal.—Wandering Tartars.—No Tradition extant of an ancient People inhabiting towards the North.—General Belief of the Origin of Learning.—Inference drawn from the Similarity of the Sanscrit and Tibet Alphabet.—Character in which their sacred Writings are preserved and printed—that of Correspondence and Business.—Regent notifies his Design of leaving the Monastery—commends me to the Care of Soopoon Choomboo in his Absence.—Visits my Apartments, accompanied by Soopoon Choomboo and the Lama of Luddauk.—Science of Palmistry.—Attar, Pawn.

At all times, when I met the Regent, Soopoon Choomboo was in company. The distinguished attention shewn to him, and the part he generally took in conversation, plainly bespoke his consequence. I thought him intelligent, quick of apprehension, and, as well as the Regent, extremely communicative. I was not a little surprised to discover, by their conversation, how accurate an idea they had acquired of the position of different countries, though maps and charts are totally unknown among them. Of China (or Geanna) their own travels had taught them the situation; and they pointed out to me, not only the relative bearings of the countries surrounding them, as China on the east; Siberia on the north; Turkestan, Cashmeer, Almora, on the west; Nipal, Bootan, Assam, to the south, and Bengal beyond these; but also of England, and of Russia, with almost equal truth. Yet, desirous to extend their knowledge, a great variety of questions were proposed to me, relating to the peculiar produce, temperature of climate, and different distances, of remote countries.

Bengal, of which they had from various authorities collected a tolerably distinct idea, they expressed a most eager curiosity to visit. Nor can, perhaps, the inhabitants of a rocky, arid, bleak, and naked region, fancy a scene more enchanting, than is exhibited in a country of wide extent, presenting throughout a smooth and equal surface, clothed with eternal verdure, intersected by numberless deep and copious rivers, abounding with groves of large and shady trees, and yielding an immense variety of fruits and flowers, through every season of the year. But Bengal is rendered peculiarly dear to them, by the powerful influence of religious prejudice. The regeneration of their Lama is said to have taken place, in times of remote antiquity, near the site of the ancient and ruined city of Gowr; and all those places held in veneration by the Hindoos, as Gya, Benares, Mahow, and Allahabad, are equally objects of superstitious zeal, with a votary of the Tibet faith, who thinks himself blessed above his fellow disciples, if he can but perform a pilgrimage to these hallowed spots.

Gunga Sagor, an uninhabited island, situated at the confluence of the Ganges with the sea, and the pagoda of Jagarnaut, upon the coast of Orissa, are also deemed places of equal sanctity, and occasionally visited, from the same motives of zealous but mistaken piety. Nor are the advantages, whatever they may be, resulting from these pilgrimages, confined to those alone, who personally perform them; he who promotes them by his persuasion, and supports the pilgrim by his purse, claims to himself, nearly an equal share of merit. So that agents are often hired, to visit these holy places, from whence they bring to their employers, some sacred pledge, picked up on the sea shore, or a portion of the consecrated stream, possessed of incalculable efficacy in all their subsequent devotions.

The late Teshoo Lama, I was told, had the merit of having thus performed his pilgrimages by proxy, to Cashi, Prag, Gunga Sagor, and Jagarnaut. Indeed, though these pilgrimages cannot be accomplished, but at the imminent hazard, of the pilgrim's falling a martyr to the intemperate heat of Hindostan, or to the enervating atmosphere of the low lands, yet an enthusiastic spirit is not to be repressed, by the melancholy fate of former adventurers.

A poor emaciated meagre devotee came to me, just before I left Calcutta to commence my present journey, who had with infinite labour crossed the mountains of Bootan, encountered the noxious air of Bengal, and, with a perseverance worthy of a better cause, accomplished his purpose of bathing in the sacred stream of the Ganges, in spite of all difficulties, which want and sickness could throw in his way: difficulties pressing with accumulated force, on a solitary stranger, utterly unacquainted with the language of the country. He was then about to return to Tibet, anxious to carry some of the holy water to his employer. I committed him to the care of the Goseins, who live with Poorungheer, in charge of the temple erected at the expence of Teshoo Lama, upon the bank of the river, opposite to Calcutta; and he afterwards travelled with my party to the capital of Bootan, whence I dispatched him with letters to the Regent of Teshoo Loomboo, which he faithfully delivered. While he was in Calcutta, I presented him to the Governor General, a distinction which made him inexpressibly happy; for, being informed of the friendship subsisting between the Governor and Teshoo Lama, he had conceived a reverence for Mr. Hastings, which was only inferior to the veneration he entertained for his sovereign Lama, in his opinion, the greatest of earthly Beings.

In the discussion of geographical topics, the Regent's mind took a very extensive range, and scarcely left any quarter of the globe, untouched. Teshoo Lama had been visited, he told me, not many years before, by an itinerant Gosein, who assured his inquirers, that he had seen a country, in which half the year was day, and the other half night: and he appealed to me, whether this was a false report or not; a circumstance which shews their limited knowledge of the sciences, both of geography and astronomy.

The Gosein alluded to by the Regent, whose name is Prânpooree, exhibited so extraordinary an instance of religious penance, that I cannot resist the temptation of relating some particulars of his life.

Having been adopted by an Hindoo devotee, and educated by him in the rigid tenets of his religion, he was yet young, when he commenced the course of his extraordinary mortifications. The first vow, which the plan of life, he had chosen to himself, induced him to make, was to continue perpetually upon his legs, and neither to sit down upon the ground, nor lie down to rest, for the space of twelve years. All this time, he told me, he had employed in wandering through different countries. When I inquired how he took the indispensable refreshment of sleep, when wearied with fatigue, he said, that at first, to prevent his falling, he used to be tied with ropes, to some tree or post; but that this precaution, after some time, became unnecessary, and he was able to sleep standing, without such support.

The complete term of this first penance being expired, the next he undertook was to hold his hands, locked in each other, over his head, the fingers of one hand, dividing those of the other, for the same space of twelve years. Whether this particular period is chosen in compliment to the twelve signs of the zodiac, or to the Indian cycle of twelve years, I cannot decide. He was still determined, not to dwell in any fixed abode; so that before the term of this last vow could be accomplished, he had travelled over the greater part of the continent of Asia. He first set out, by crossing the Peninsula of India, through

Guzerat; he then passed by Surat to Bussora, and thence to Constantinople; from Turkey he went to Ispahan; and sojourned so long among the different Persian tribes, as to obtain a considerable knowledge of their language, in which he conversed with tolerable ease. In his passage from thence towards Russia, he fell in with the Kussaucs (hordes of Cossacs) upon the borders of the Caspian sea, where he narrowly escaped being condemned to perpetual slavery: at length he was suffered to pass on, and reached Moscow; he then travelled along the northern boundary of the Russian empire, and through Siberia arrived at Pekin in China, from whence he came through Tibet, by the way of Teshoo Loomboo, and Nipal, down to Calcutta.

When I first saw him at this place, in the year 1783, he rode upon a piebald Tangun horse from Bootan, and wore a satin embroidered dress, given to him by Teshoo Lama, of which he was not a little vain. He was robust, and hale; and his complexion, contrasted with a long bushy black beard, appeared really florid. I do not suppose that he was then forty years of age. Two Goseins attended him, and assisted him in mounting and alighting from his horse. Indeed he was indebted to them for the assistance of their hands on every occasion; his own being fixed and immoveable, in the position in which he had placed them, were of course perfectly useless.

The circulation of blood, seemed to have forsaken his arms; they were withered, void of sensation, and inflexible. Yet he spoke to me with confidence, of recovering the use of them, and mentioned his intention to take them down the following year, when the term of his penance would expire.

Other Goseins assured me, though I could not help doubting the fact, that it is practicable to restore withered limbs, thus circumstanced, to perfect use. This is effected, they say, though not without great labour, and some pain, by means of long continued friction, before a large fire, with a certain ointment which they compound. To complete the full measure of his religious penance, I understood that there still remained two other experiments for Prânpooree to perform. In the first of these, the devotee is suspended by the feet to the branch of a tree, over a fire, which is kept in a continual blaze, and swung backwards and forwards, his hair passing through the flame, for one pahr and a quarter, that is, three hours and three quarters. Having passed through this fiery trial, he may then prepare himself for the last act of probation, which is to be buried alive, standing upright, in a pit dug for the purpose; the fresh earth being thrown in upon him, so that he is completely covered. In this situation, he must remain, for one pahr and a quarter, or three hours and three quarters, and if at the expiration of that time, on the removal of the earth, he should be found alive, he will ascend into the highest rank, among the most pure of the Yogee, (Jugi).

The mention of Russia, produced some observations from the Regent and Soopoon Choomboo, upon the government of that Empire. They were no strangers to the reputation of the reigning Czarina, her extent of dominion, and the commerce carried on with China, to the extreme boundaries of their continent. Many overtures, they told me, had been made on the part of Russia, to extend her commerce to the internal parts of Tibet, but their disinclination to enter into any new foreign connections, and the watchful jealousy of the Chinese, had hitherto defeated every attempt of this nature.

Some years ago the Empress of Russia, I learnt, had invited Taranaut Lama to a correspondence, and ambassadors had been sent to him with considerable presents. Among these, I saw a Bible with plates, in the Russian language, which they still preserved. Taranaut, who at that time esteemed Teshoo Lama, as the guardian of the state, and oracle of the Lama hierarchy, forwarded the presents, and the letter to him, for the purpose of receiving his advice upon so important a subject. The Lama gave little encouragement to the Russians, yet consented to a limited intercourse; in consequence of which, the Russian traders have since resorted occasionally to Kharka, the place of Taranaut Lama's residence, where they still carry on by their agents a considerable traffic. This principally consists in the sale of bulgar hides, which are prepared in the adjacent districts, and brought also from Calmuc Tartary to the same mart, where all the rich and valuable furs, that pass in merchandize between the Russians and Chinese, may be procured upon easy terms.

Immediately after this conference, a large party of Tartars from Khumbâk, (a tribe of Calmucs) arrived on a pilgrimage to Teshoo Lama, and engaged the Regent's attention for several days. They brought with them a string of horses, consisting of between two and three hundred, furs, bulgar hides, and skins of butter, as offerings to the Lama, before whom, it is unusual for his votaries to appear, especially when they come from any considerable distance, without presenting something by way of religious tribute.

These Tartars came from a place which they said was situated upon the river Sullum, no less than fifty-two days journey from hence. This place, therefore, according to the common computation of twenty miles to a day's journey, must be one thousand and forty miles distant. The following I understood to be their route, on their return from hence towards home: from Teshoo Loomboo to Lassa, twelve days; from Lassa to Daum, ten days; from Daum to Sullum, thirty days.

My next interview with the Regent, was in a chamber upon the same floor with my own, separated only by a long narrow hall, or rather gallery, into which we were first conducted, and where I found an unexpected amusement, in examining a vast multitude of diminutive images, the representatives of their dewtas and heroes, who had here fixed their abode.

The gallery, as I conjecture, was about forty feet in length; having its aspect towards the south-east. A balcony projecting from the centre, fenced with a slight railing, and sheltered from the weather by curtains of mohair, served for the admission of light; opposite to the balcony, in the most conspicuous part of the gallery, the images were ranged in regular order, upon benches rising one behind the other, from the floor, almost to the roof of the room. They were enclosed by a piece of strong iron net-work stretched before them. Some of these images were composed of that metallic mixture, which in appearance resembles Wedgewood's black ware; but the greater part were of brass, or copper gilt. They were by no means ill fashioned, exhibiting an infinite variety of figures and attitudes, and adorned with such symbolical representations, as are appropriate to the respective dewtas and heroes of the Hindoo mythology. All of these are to be met with in this collection, as I gathered from the communications of the Goseins, with whom I had afterwards frequent opportunities of visiting the gallery at my leisure. The idols, I learnt, were not all of equal sanctity; some of them merely represented devout and pious men, in different acts of religion, or exercises of their faith.

Whilst I resided at Teshoo Loomboo, I accidentally obtained knowledge of one method, by which this cabinet is occasionally recruited. A senior of the Gylongs, or priests, who was styled Lama, which is the highest rank in that order, happened to die in an apartment not far from our own, and the occasion gave rise to a long and noisy ceremony of invocation, prayer, and purification, in the habitation where he had lived. His body, I was informed, was burnt with sandal wood, and its ashes were afterwards carefully collected, and lodged within a small brass image, which was immediately translated to a place, among the other sacred inhabitants of the gallery. This cabinet, therefore, probably contains the earthly remains of a long series of generations of Gylongs, who from their superior sanctity, have in all ages, been deemed worthy to contribute to its decoration, by increasing the quantity of its hallowed furniture. Merit has thus, in Tibet, a brazen monument erected to its memory.

The manufacture of images, is an art for which they are famous in this country. Teshoo Loomboo has an extensive board of works, established under the direction of the monastery, and constantly employed in this manufacture. When images of their fabrication were pointed out to me, by the side of others, which had been brought from China,

Lassa, and Nipal, I could not avoid giving my friends, ample credit for their superior skill.

Besides Soopoon Choomboo, who was his constant companion, I found the Regent attended this day, Monday, the 13th of October, by a young Lama from Luddauk. After the accustomed ceremonies and compliments had passed, we poured out copious libations of warm tea; and a most miscellaneous conversation immediately ensued.

The Regent, who appeared ever anxious to receive and to communicate information, on all points of local, civil, and natural history, first directed his inquiries to the military force, the wealth, and extent of the British empire. He professed himself deeply interested concerning the war, of which he had heard so much, and which, by unhappily interrupting the general intercourse of nations, had augmented the price, and occasioned a scarcity of every article of foreign trade. I gratified him, as well as I was able, by recounting the leading causes of the war between England, and America, which once constituted a part of the English dominions. I endeavoured also to give him a clear idea of the circumstances, which compelled us to engage in a war with France; a war which had involved the Carnatic in confusion, interrupted the communication between India and Europe, and covered the seas with hostile fleets.

They could not avoid expressing their surprise, that a matter of mere local moment, should have thus embroiled the remotest regions, and spread distrust and enmity, over such a wide extent of the habitable world. However, I assured him, that Bengal still enjoyed profound tranquillity; and indeed I felt happy in being able confidently to pronounce, from the information I had lately received, that there appeared the fairest prospect, of a speedy restoration of universal peace.

In discussing the commerce of different countries, and the numerous articles of convenience, as well as of luxury, which one nation derives from its intercourse with another, the bold spirit of enterprise that animates the English nation, claimed the Regent's particular admiration. Yet, at the same time that he allowed due honour to our undaunted perseverance, he could not but attribute the motive, that impelled so numerous a class of Englishmen, to leave their country and their friends, and encounter the danger of inclement climates, and rude inhospitable men, to some great internal defect in their own country. At the same time he was convinced, from what he had heard and seen, that there was not, perhaps, existing, a more ingenious people in the world. In order to account for that restlessness of disposition, which disperses my countrymen, over the whole surface of the globe, I was led to expatiate at some length, on the system of education, prevailing amongst us. This, I told him, was calculated perpetually to awaken genius, and call forth peculiar talents, which might otherwise have rested for ever in a torpid state, unexerted and unknown; but which, when once roused, and improved, would not suffer their possessors to sit down in listless and inglorious inactivity. Hence it was, that numerous branches of respectable families, prompted by curiosity, not less than by a desire of wealth, spread themselves over every region of the universe. I added, that our Sovereign, renowned for his love of science, and encouragement of useful research, had, at various times, commanded ships to be fitted out, at an immense expence, for the purpose of visiting unknown regions, and navigating distant seas. Men of learning and of science embarked on these occasions, to whom the desire of acquiring and diffusing knowledge, were sufficient inducements to attempt the most hazardous and laborious enterprises. In these voyages, lands had been discovered, and nations explored, of which neither history, nor tradition, supplied the slightest information; and navigators, by publishing to the world their observations, and their accounts of these newly-discovered countries, had communicated much curious and important knowledge. Hence followed a succession of queries and remarks, which it would be endless to repeat.

Their own geographical knowledge was very limited. I could not form, with any degree of precision, an idea of the ancient extent of the kingdom of Tibet, or of the age of their religious institutions: for neither of us could recognize places, from the names by which they were known to the other; and dates were equally obscure, since they have no specific æra, from which they begin to reckon the lapse of time. The cycle of twelve years is in use here, as it is in western Tartary. But for my better information on these topics, they promised me an abridged history of Tibet, from their own annals.

This I afterwards received; but my knowledge of the language was not sufficient to enable me to avail myself of the information it contained; and my residence amongst them, though I had the aid of a preceptor, was too short to admit of my making any considerable proficiency in the dialect of Tibet.

The present was an opportunity too favourable to be neglected, and before the conference was concluded, I endeavoured to engage the Regent's attention, with a hope of acquiring some information upon a subject, which I was extremely anxious to investigate.

My inquiries respected an ancient nation, supposed to have once inhabited the borders of the Baikal sea, in the interior of Tartary, and from which some persons conjecture, the learning, arts, and sciences of India, and even of Europe, to have been originally derived. If such a nation ever existed, the remembrance of it seems now to be buried in deepest oblivion.

Siberia and Baikal were names equally unknown to them; however, by setting before them Kiatchta, the point of division, and great scene of traffic between the Chinese and Russian empires, situated at the south-eastern extremity of the latter, I was able to identify the region, to which I wished to draw their attention.

Soopoon Choomboo had travelled from Kharka, the residence of Taranaut Lama, in Kilmauk, to China; he had traversed the borders of the Baikal sea, and lived long, amongst the northern Tartars. The Baikal lake, he informed me, was particularly celebrated for the production of pearls, remarkable for their size, but imperfect in colour and shape, and therefore held in no great estimation. Its neighbourhood, he said, was thinly inhabited, nor to his knowledge, was any monument existing, that bore marks of remote antiquity. The Tartars of that vicinity were found, as was remarkably the case in advancing towards the north, more ignorant, and less civilized, than their southern neighbours. The people beyond the desert, he added, are a wandering race, that inhabit tents, and inherit such powerful prepossessions against dwelling in houses, that they are with difficulty prevailed upon at any time to enter them.

This prejudice is said to have its foundation in a dread of their falling; an apprehension which may perhaps have originated, in remote times, from the calamitous effects of earthquakes. Slight concussions are not unfrequent, as far as I could learn, at this period, though the volcano at the eastern point of Tartary, in the island of Analuska, is situated at so remote a distance.

Another cause may indeed have contributed to instil this dread of a fixed abode, into their minds. I mean, their fearful apprehension of contagious distempers, and more particularly of the small-pox; from the virulence of which disease, they experience the most destructive consequences; since they attempt not to apply any remedy, but leave those who are unhappily visited by it, entirely to chance, and to the common operation of unassisted nature. Hence, they have always been accustomed to seek refuge from its fatal effects by flight, and may perhaps, in consequence, have been led to adopt a mode of life, that might enable them, with greater facility, to change their residence in a moment.

Thus large hordes of Tartars are still found to dwell in tents, tending upon cattle, and placing their chief dependance upon their herds. Different preparations of milk, constitute their principal support. They occasionally find some assistance from the chase, and, in spite of their religious prejudices, I am told, that the flesh of cows and horses, not unfrequently contribute to relieve their wants: to this list too, must be sometimes added the dromedary and the ass, however highly respected amongst them for their hardiness, and patient endurance of labour.

After much inquiry, and long investigation, I could never learn that either their tradition, or written records, mention any ancient people eminent for their knowledge, inhabiting towards the north. The general belief, as I was repeatedly assured by the Regent and Soopoon Choomboo, which prevails amongst them, is, that both the sciences and the arts had their origin in the holy city of Benares, which they have been taught to esteem, as the source and centre both of learning and religion. Hither they refer, as to a common origin, all the knowledge of other nations, as well as the first dawn of light, that beamed upon their own spiritual and civil institutions.

The ancient teachers of the faith which they profess, are said to have first proceeded from this sacred city, and, after having advanced towards the east, over the empire of China, to have directed their course towards the kingdoms of Europe. Their own instruction, in science and religion, they refer to a period, long prior to the appearance of the first gleam of knowledge, which enlightened the European world; though they are just enough to acknowledge their own marvellous deficiency, and confess, that, in these times, the natives of Asia are far surpassed by the inhabitants of Europe. But they attribute the unequal progress which different nations have made in the cultivation of the arts, to the difference of climate, and to the various degrees of application, which local deprivations and defects may have required, to guard against the particular evils resulting from them. As for themselves, they retained so much of the arts as was necessary, or useful, in their peculiar situation and circumstances.

Perfection in philosophy, or mechanics, in an inland region, remote from intercourse with strangers, and shut out from the rest of the world by inaccessible mountains, by Imaus, on the one hand, and by the inhospitable deserts of Cobi, on the other, is not with reason to be expected; and still less is it to be sought for, in more northerly regions, where one half of the year is a season of profound darkness, and the wretched inhabitants are compelled to seek refuge from the severity of the seasons, in deep and gloomy caverns; where, possibly, the powers and faculties of the mind, are in some degree benumbed by the same powerful operation of intense cold, which arrests the progress of vegetable life; and where, certainly, the great mass of the people are doomed to labour perpetually, for the scanty and precarious support of mere animal existence.

In proof of the antiquity of their knowledge of letters, the Regent and his friends urged the similarity of their alphabet to the Sanscrit character, from which they avow it to have been formed; but they profess to have departed a little from the shape and form of the original, when they applied it to express a different language. Still, however, the character in which their sacred writings are preserved and printed, styled *Uchen*, bears a strong resemblance to the Sanscrit; and is quite as distinct from the character of business and correspondence, called *Umin*, as the old Roman text is from the English round hand.

I began now to think it high time to close the interview, which had been protracted to an uncommon length, especially when the Regent himself informed me, that he had fixed upon the morrow for a journey towards the western frontier, and that he designed to visit the hot-wells previous to his return, telling me that his health, no less than public business, called for his presence in that quarter. He said that he should be but a short time absent, and, until his return, he recommended me to the care of Soopoon Choomboo, who would be frequently with me, and attend to all my wishes, which he enjoined me freely to communicate. But the kind and affectionate attention of the Regent would not suffer him to depart, without making, what he deemed, a proper provision for our comfort. Previously to the accustomed ceremonies at parting, he presented Mr. Saunders and myself with complete dresses, made after the fashion of the country; rich satin garments lined with furs, and huge bulgar boots. Indeed, the daily increase of cold most forcibly reminded us, that a change of raiment would soon become indispensably necessary; for so rapidly, had the winter already set in, that water placed in open vessels in our rooms, during the night, became a solid mass of ice; and by the exposure of cream, I obtained every morning a rich repast for my breakfast.

We now rose to take our leave, and were turning to quit the room, when the Regent, Soopoon Choomboo, and the Lama of Luddauk, rose also. The Regent, I was now informed, intended me the honour of a visit, previously to his departure. I cannot doubt, that curiosity had a great share in this compliment, and I was willing to gratify it, by exhibiting to his inspection, all the apparatus I happened to have with me, which, differing in contrivance from what I found here, was likely to attract his notice.

When this compliment was paid us by the Regent, our apartments were thrown open, and upon entering them, one of the first objects that forcibly attracted his notice and that of his attendants, was an iron canopied camp bedstead, with its European furniture.

The commodiousness of bedsteads, in elevating bed furniture from the ground, is totally unknown amongst them; it being their general custom to spread, by way of bed upon the floor, a thick mattress, consisting of two cushions, the upper surface of both being joined by a cloth covering, which, when they rise, admits their being folded upon each other; by day, it serves them for a seat. Travellers usually carry this accommodation with them; it is thrown down upon the ground when they wish to rest; and it may literally be said to be their custom, when they mean to travel, to take up their bed and walk. A variety of mechanical, mathematical, and optical instruments, which I had with me, attracted the attention of my visitors, by their novelty, or their use.

It was matter of great astonishment to them to view, through a good reflecting telescope, remote objects, not visible to the naked eye, and to distinguish even their figure, size, and colour. While a part of my company was engaged in inspecting the new and uncommon objects which had attracted their notice, the young Lama of Luddauk, with a good-natured and arch air, seized me by the hand, and, turning up the palm, attentively surveyed the lines described on it. I submitted to his examination, with no very serious apprehension from his profound knowledge of the occult science of palmistry; and he had too much urbanity to tell me any, but the best of fortunes.

My camp table, and the preparations made for dinner, had a due share of their notice; nor could this excite wonder, since the European manner of serving meals, differs so essentially from their own. It is altogether unusual among them, as far as I can learn, for numbers to assemble together, on any occasion, for the business of gratifying one of the most intrusive demands of our nature. They have, in consequence, no stated times for their meals, but eat when hunger calls for gratification. To contribute to relieve the cravings of thirst is allowed, indeed, to be a meritorious act; and hence tea, according to their miscellaneous mode of preparing it, and *chong*, or *arra*, are served up to visitors, as a repast, at all times of the day; when first they arrive, and commonly before the conclusion of a visit. I soon learnt to consider this as a salutary hint to tedious visitors, like the practice of presenting attar of roses, and pawn, in Hindostan, by way of signal, not to prolong their stay. Pawn[a] is a preparation of an aromatic plant called Beetel, in India, the Piper Betel of Linnæus, two or three green leaves of which are used as an envelope to cover a variety of ingredients, some of a warm, and pungent[b], others of a rough, astringent nature[c]; together with a portion of Kut[d], and shell lime; which latter is added to exalt the flavour, at the same time that it greatly heightens the property which this preparation possesses, of giving a more ruddy colour to the mouth and lips. It is all together called Pawn.

Among the numerous excellencies attributed to this compound, it has the credit of promoting digestion, of relieving flatulency, and being in the highest degree stomachic; it also strongly perfumes the breath, impresses a grateful flavour on the palate, and by its pungency excites thirst, at the same time that it imparts the highest zest to the gratification of it.

[a] Tambuli, Sanscrit. See Wilkins's Hēētōpādēs of Vēēshnōō Sărmā, p. 220.

[b] Cloves, nutmeg, cinnamon.

[c] Sooparee, areca catēchu.

[d] Terra japonica; inspissated juice of the C'hadira, a species of Mimosa.

Innumerable are the advantages attributed to its use; in short, it seems one of those highly esteemed luxuries, which the lovers of cold water are well entitled to appropriate to themselves, and are particularly prone to indulge in. Nor is it surprising, from its reputed good qualities, that it is held in the highest estimation, both amongst the humblest, and the most exalted ranks in society. It is invariably offered on all occasions of ceremony and compliment, in India, by the host to his visitors; it most commonly, as was observed before, is produced immediately before the conclusion of a visit; so that the guest always considers the call for attar and pawn, as the immediate prelude to his dismission, and, of course, prepares to take his leave the moment it is presented.

Such a length of time had been occupied in this, and my first visit, that the evening was rapidly advancing when my company departed.

CHAPTER VII.

Departure of the Regent—his Desire to travel unobserved.—Egypt—Eunani—Singhi.—Use of the Symbol of the Lion in Tibet and Egypt—superstitious Regard for celestial Phænomena—Skill in Science—Bigotry—Court of China—Spectacles for the Entertainment of the Lama—Soomeroo.—Coincidence with the Hindoos in scientific Knowledge.—Benares esteemed the sacred Seat of all human Learning.—Teshoo Loomboo—Geographic Site—particular Description of.—Plain of Teshoo Loomboo—Shigatzee-jeung—Luddauk—Cashmeer—Nipal—China—Russia—Siberia.—Abruptness of the Hills—local Effect.—Vortexes of Wind.—Rock behind Teshoo Loomboo—View from hence.—Berhampooter—Megna—Pudda—Sundrabunds—Pirates—Maunserore—Rise—Course of the Ganges and Berhampooter.—Seasons in Tibet.—Meat preserved by the Action of intense Cold.—Use of undressed Meat.—Sheep, their Value for Food, Raiment, and Use.—Dryness of the Atmosphere in Tibet—Precautions used against it.

THE following morning, long before the dawn of day, the Regent had quitted the gates of the monastery, to commence his march. It is deserving notice, that great men in Tibet, as well as in Bootan, are peculiarly accustomed to travel in the dark, from a desire, as I have heard, that their route may be unobserved, and not productive of trouble to the inhabitants, by withdrawing theirattention from their personal pursuits.

On the day after the departure of the Regent, Soopoon Choomboo sent an invitation to me to meet him in the room, immediately beyond the gallery of idols. He was accompanied by the treasurer: our conversation was extremely miscellaneous. Egypt, in their language, *eunani*, and the lions, *singhi*, were favourite topics of conversation with him. Between this country, indeed, and Tibet, there seemed at some time or other, to have existed a frequent communication; and Egypt appeared even now to merit respectful mention, whenever they named it. From hence perhaps they have derived their veneration for the sovereign of brutes, which they evince by the distinguished place they assign him in their sacred architecture.

There is no religious edifice, but what is adorned with the head of the lion at every angle, having bells pendent from his lower jaw; and the same figure is equally common, at every projection of the palace walls. It is certain, that no contiguous country can supply an example of the animal existing in it, in a state of nature, at this day. The lake Maunserore was mentioned to me, as having lions on its banks, but this assertion I considered as fabulous, originating possibly in a desire to attach greater dignity to the source of the Ganges and Berhampooter, by adding to it one more object of veneration.

Lions are the natives of a warmer region; the burning sands of Nubia, Ethiopia, and Arabia, seem to be their proper habitation. If the lion ever existed in a state of nature here, it must have been at the same time with those vast monsters, whose bones are found in huge heaps in various parts of Tartary and Siberia at this day, and clearly point to some great convulsion, and change, in the order of our globe. But be this as it may, we see the head of the lion held up in Tibet with marks of high distinction and respect, though we can trace no certain clue to discover, by what means he obtained this honour.

My inquisitive hosts led me by their curious inquiries, over a great part of the globe, from the torrid to the frigid zone. It much excited their wonder to hear, that a part of the world was for half the year illumined by the sun, and remained the other half in continual darkness. Much was said to me upon the subject of comets and eclipses, which are phænomena considered by them, as the most certain prognostics of good, or evil.

I told them that both were regarded by us, as mere matters of course, and that the appearance of either was regularly calculated with great precision, many years before it took place. However, it was vain for me to attempt to shake their faith, to efface from their calendar the string of lucky and unlucky days, or to discredit the important omens they draw from a change of weather, either within four or six days after the appearance of an eclipse. I was questioned respecting our mode of reckoning time, and whether the computation we had adopted corresponded like theirs, with the signs of the zodiac, and the cycle of twelve years.

Soopoon Choomboo was desirous of instituting a comparison between the merit of European and Chinese astronomers. Without indulging an unreasonable partiality, I thought I might claim for my countrymen, a decided superiority ; and I ventured to assert that much of the knowledge of the Chinese had been derived from European missionaries, one of whom I was assured at this moment held the highest station amongst the astronomers of China. He promised, as some testimonial of the ancient knowledge of the Chinese, to give me their register of past eclipses, which I afterwards received, though without any satisfactory explanation of its contents.

The burning well of Brahma-koond [a], near Chittagong, gave occasion to some observations and inquiries; I found, by their prejudices, that they esteemed it as holy. I have been informed, that a vivid flame is often seen to play upon the surface of the water in this well, arising probably from the spontaneous combustion of mephitic gas.

Assam and its inhabitants became our next subject of conversation; with this region, it should seem, they hold but an extremely limited intercourse. A large reservoir upon its eastern border, formed, I suppose, by the Berhampooter, on emerging from the mountains, appears to be held by them in some degree of veneration.

Many other topics succeeded in their turn. I was dressed in the warm embroidered vest which the Regent had provided for me. They enjoined me to be extremely cautious in guarding against the approaching cold; and informed me that they had the Regent's command, to contribute by every possible means to my comfort and satisfaction, expressing a hope that they should be happy in frequent opportunities of meeting me.

[a] Brăhmā-koond, fountains of Brăhmā.

In my next interview with Soopoon Choomboo, he entertained me with a description of the gardens, villas, and palaces, of the Emperor of China, and the various entertainments contrived to gratify and amuse the Teshoo Lama, during his residence at that court. One of the first spectacles he noticed, was a most splendid display of fire-works, exhibited in celebration of the commencement of the new year, which greatly engaged his attention and admiration. This entertainment continued for three successive days, during which time the Teshoo Lama, in company with the Emperor, was a frequent spectator of their beauty and effect. The singular magnificence of some of the imperial gardens, had made an equal impression upon his mind. In one of these, according to his description, was a large canal, surrounded with figures of a gigantic size, representing the signs of the zodiac; each figure, as the sun entered its corresponding sign, becoming a fountain of water, which continued to play until his passage to the next.

An extensive menagery, filled with rare and curious animals, among which were tigers, leopards, bears, deer, and the wild boar, was equally successful in attracting their notice. He stated also, that the Emperor had ordered a ship to be constructed on a large lake, and armed with guns, to resemble a first rate man of war. The guns were discharged on board this ship, to give them an idea of a sea engagement.

Feats of horsemanship were not forgotten, with a design to vary their amusements, and fill up the time. In these, he said, the people of China displayed great agility and skill. With such a recapitulation of the various modes, devised to entertain the Lama, during his residence at Jehol, did Soopoon Choomboo with much good humour endeavour to amuse me. I listened with attention to his discourse: he had the reputation of superior talents, and to this, no doubt, he owed his elevation, in the time of the former Lama, with whom he was said to be in high favour; nor was he less distinguished by the present Regent.

A large reflecting telescope, which I had brought with me, afforded an inducement to Soopoon Choomboo, for visiting me in the evening of Sunday, the 19th of October. I shewed him, through it, several stars not visible to the naked eye; but I found, that he was neither ignorant of the satellites of Jupiter, nor of the ring of Saturn; and I learnt from him, that all the distinguished planets, were the seats of some or other of the objects of their veneration. To this circumstance, indeed, the Tibetians attribute their brilliancy and splendour; and point out their revolutions, together with the glorious orb of day, round the imaginary mountain Soomeroo, whose summit is, in their apprehension, the elevated station, of the chief of all the gods.

This may be sufficient to shew the extent, and nature, of their proficiency in the sciences. It intimates also their agreement with their southern neighbours, in an original derivation of their scientific knowledge from one common source. There appears indeed to have been, from the remotest time, a connection and intercourse between Tibet and India. I collected, as I have already hinted, from repeated conferences with the Regent, and with Soopoon Choomboo, as well as from other sources, that the established opinion here is, that they derived their religion and learning from the west. Whether their first Lama, the founder of their faith, had his origin in Gya, (Durgeedin) or Benares,

(Ooroonasse) is not so certain; but Benares, in the present day, seems to have the highest claim to their respect and veneration.

The absence of the Regent, had now restored me to comparatively greater freedom, and left me at leisure to gratify my curiosity, by a more minute examination of the neighbourhood of Teshoo Loomboo.

Here, therefore, I shall throw together, without any strict regard to methodical arrangement, some of the most important observations I was, at this time more particularly, enabled to make, respecting the state of the country around me, and the customs and opinions of its inhabitants.

Teshoo Loomboo, or Lubrong, the seat of Teshoo Lama, and the capital of that part of Tibet immediately subject to his authority, is situated in 29° 4′ 20″ north latitude[b], and 89° 7′ east longitude, from Greenwich. It is a large monastery, consisting of three or four hundred houses, the habitations of the Gylongs, besides temples, mausoleums, and the palace of the sovereign pontiff; in which is comprised also, the residence of the Regent, and of all the subordinate officers, both ecclesiastical and civil, belonging to the court. It is included within the hollow face of a high rock, and has a southern aspect. Its buildings are all of stone, none less than two stories high, flat roofed, and crowned with a parapet, rising considerably above the roof, composed of heath and brush-wood, inserted between frames of timber, which form a

[b] From the medium of six meridian altitudes of the sun, taken with a brass sextant and artificial horizon, both of Ramsden's.

29° 4′ 20″ N. Lat. of Teshoo Loombo.	89° 7′ E. Long. of Teshoo Loomboo.
22 35 ——— Calcutta.	88 35 ——— Calcutta.
6 29 20 North from Calcutta.	32 East from Calcutta.

ledge below, and are fashioned above into a cornice, capped with masonry.

This insertion of brush-wood, is from three to four or five feet in depth. The ends externally, are made even with great care, so that, at a distance, it is not distinguishable from masonry. It is always stained of a deep garnet colour; the same which the custom of these regions has universally adopted, to distinguish places of religious establishment, and which, when contrasted with the white walls, produces, in the appearance of their towns, a very pleasing effect. Of this peculiarity, which is often met with in Tibet, I could never obtain a satisfactory account; and whether it proceeds from an economical use of the materials of masonry; or was designed to lessen the weight of the superstructure; or to admit the snow, upon a sudden thaw, more expeditiously to percolate and pass off, than through small spouts, which might be liable to be clogged, I cannot determine. Had I seen it only in frontier towns, and posts of strength, I should have suspected, that, in a country where fire arms were not in use, it might have been intended as a skreen, to shelter the besieged; or perhaps, to retain the darts and arrows of the assailants, and prevent their being collected again, as they might easily be, if they were suffered to recoil from a solid wall.

If such, indeed, were the original design, it is not now avowed: and since the necessity has ceased, it is as well forgotten, and the contrivance is more esteemed, under the pacific character of an ornamental decoration. All the houses have windows, of which the centre, or principal one, projects beyond the walls, and forms a balcony; they are not closed with shutters, but black mohair curtains. The principal apartment in the upper story has an opening over it, covered with a moveable shed, which serves the purpose of sometimes admitting light and air, and, in the winter season, occasionally, the grateful warmth of the sun.

The tops of the walls are adorned with those cylindrical ornaments I have already described; some of which are plain, covered with black cloth, crossed by a white fillet; whilst others are made of copper, burnished with gold; and as in this article, they have been very profuse, particularly about the palace, and all the mausoleums, the view of the monastery, on approaching it from the plain, is brilliant and splendid.

The plain of Teshoo Loomboo, which is perfectly level, is encompassed by rocky hills, on all sides. Its direction is north and south, and its extreme length about fifteen miles; its southern extremity in breadth from east to west, may be perhaps, five, or six miles. It narrows towards the north, and the rock, upon the southern face of which the monastery is situated, nearly occupies the whole width of the valley. The end of the rock approaches so near to the hills that bound the plain on the east, as to form a narrow defile, which leaves room only for a road, and the bed of the river Painom-tchieu, which runs through it, and at a small distance beyond, joins the Berhampooter.

The fortress of Shigatzee-jeung stands upon a prominent ridge of the rock, and commands the pass. There are many openings in the hills that surround this valley, and the public roads cross none of them, but wind round their basis, over even ground. As I looked from my apartment, I could see, in front, the road that leads to Bootan and Bengal: on my right, the roads to Luddauk and Cashmeer; to the mines of lead, copper, cinnabar, and gold; and also by Tingri Meidân to Nipal: on my left, are the roads to Lassa and China: on the north is situated the territory of Taranaut Lama, bordering upon Russia, and Siberia, and whose influence more especially extends over the Kilmauks, or hordes of Calmuc Tartars.

The abruptness with which the hills rise from this plain is very remarkable; they are all of a rocky texture, of the colour of rusty iron, and are easily shivered by the effects of the weather, into little cubical pieces, small enough to be moved about by strong winds, which consequently spread them abroad, and soon produce a level at their bases. Their summits have the appearance of being scarped, or surrounded by a perpendicular parapet. No vegetation seems at this season, to contribute to clothe them.

Their singular conformation gives rise to an inconvenience, which, during the dry months of the year, from October to May, or the greatest part of that time, must prove an extreme annoyance to the neighbouring inhabitants. These are vortexes of wind, that are incessantly elevating large columns of dust from the surface of the ground, in different parts of the plain, which circling in lofty spires, till they attain the altitude of the hills, then seem to dissipate, and disperse themselves in the air. Nothing else obscures the extreme purity of the atmosphere; from the dawn of light till darkness, not a vapour intercepts the sight, to the most distant edge of the horizon. It is a clearness bordering upon brilliancy, which dazzles and fatigues the eye.

The rock of Teshoo Loomboo is by far the loftiest of all that are in its neighbourhood. In the coldest season of the year, the monastery, which is situated near its base, is skreened by it, from the violence of the north-west winds; though at the same time, as the sun has southern declination, it enjoys all the benefit of its genial warmth. Upon this rock, at least on those parts of it which have the most favourable aspect, I found the scanty remains of some weakly vegetation, and a little low brushwood, sufficient to tempt a few vagrant deer, which I occasionally saw bounding about its summit.

I took an opportunity to ascend the rock, but my expectations were by no means realized by the view I had from it. Bare narrow valleys, naked hills, and a biting frosty air, impressed my senses with a picture inhospitable, bleak, and sterile in the extreme. At another season the impression might probably have been different. At the period which I describe, the whole face of nature in Tibet, had decidedly assumed the character and habit of deep winter: the trees were bare of foliage, and the tops of the loftiest hills, clothed with snow.

From the summit of this rock, the eye commands a very extensive prospect, as it towers high above all the other eminences, in its vicinity. Yet no striking traces of population can be distinguished, though, I am informed that there are considerable settlements, and that the inhabitants crowd into hollow recesses, and place themselves upon the sides of hills, in situations, attractive from the shelter they afford, as well as from their advantageous aspect.

From hence, I had the satisfaction to observe, on the northern side, at the base of the rock on which I stood, that celebrated river, the Berhampooter, in the language of Tibet styled Erechoomboo. It flows in a wide extended bed, and, as though the soil gave it an unwilling passage, it has forced itself through many channels, and formed a multitude of islands in its way. But though its bed appears so wide extended from hence, I was told, that its principal channel is narrow, deep, and never fordable. At this place, it receives the tributary waters of the Painomtchieu, which I traced from it source, soon after my entrance into Tibet, to this termination of its course. Its individuality and its name, are here lost in association with the superior body, like various other streams, which come both from the north and from the south, and contribute to the magnitude of the Berhampooter, before it passes Lassa, and penetrates the frontier mountains, that divide Tibet from Assam. In this latter region, it receives a copious supply, from the sacred fountains of Brahma-koond, before it rushes to the notice of Europeans below Rangamatty, on the borders of Bengal, where it becomes a mighty river, exceeded in size by few that are yet known in the world.

From hence it hastens on to meet its sister stream, the Ganges. These far-famed rivers are nearly related in their birth, as well as united in their termination; after their junction, under the common name of Megna, or Pudda, they run together but a short course, before they mix their waters with the sea, which flows up through a thousand channels to mingle with its expected guests, intersecting a large territory, termed the Sundrabunds, now destitute of inhabitants, but famed for the beauty of its groves.

In infinite meanders, they pervade an extremely intricate labyrinth, the borders of which are sometimes visited by inland navigators, when the long continuance of dry weather obstructs the navigation of other channels of the river. But this passage is never to be attempted without local knowledge, and a sufficient supply of fresh provisions, both of water and food, for neither is to be obtained within these wilds. Infinite dangers are also spread over this inhospitable space, which is beset with the most savage and ferocious both of the human and the brute creation.

It abounds also with pirates, who lie in wait along its channels, in low, long, narrow boats, with from thirty to sixty oars, which glide along with such velocity, that few who traverse these channels in other vessels, can escape from their pursuit. To land here, is totally out of the question, in any case; for the royal tiger is found to reign sole sovereign of these wilds; which, though clothed with the most exuberant vegetation, offer no habitation suited to the purposes of man. They are visited, however, by some inhabitants of the borders, who here follow the profitable, but dangerous, occupation of cutting wood; in which if, by some unlucky accident, they disturb the slumbers of the savage tyrant, who has possession of these wilds, they pay for their temerity, with the forfeit of their lives. But the frequency of such disasters, deters not others from the pursuit of gain; and from hence, the populous city of Calcutta is constantly supplied with fuel, as from an exhaustless mine; no visible impression being made upon its stock. The growth of one season, such is the quickness of vegetation, fully replaces the consumption of the former year; and Bengal is hence assured, of an inexhaustible supply of this grand article in the economy of human life.

Having now conducted the river, on which I looked down, to the termination of its course, I must not take my leave, without paying some further respect to this distant traveller, and marking, at the same time, the veneration attached to these celebrated sister streams, the Berhampooter and the Ganges. The common source of both, is the lake Maunserore; situated, as I was informed, a month's journey north-west from Teshoo Loomboo. Separating at their origin, they flow in nearly opposite directions, one towards the east, the other to the west.

It is the fate of the Berhampooter, to penetrate, in a tortuous course, a rude climate and most stubborn soil, till at length it quits Tartary, and forcing a passage through the frontier mountains of Assam, enters the eastern boundary of Bengal.

The Ganges, by a different course, seeks the milder climate, and more productive plains of Hindostan; no sooner disengaging itself from the embarrassment of mountains, after having passed the Cow's Mouth, and quitted Hurdewar; than it is met by the adoration of suppliant tribes, and receives the homage of the bordering nations, as it flows along; fertilizing the lands it washes, enriching their inhabitants, and bearing the wealth of India in its arms.

In the temperature of the seasons in Tibet, a remarkable uniformity prevails, as well as in their periodical duration and return. The same division of them takes place here, as in the more southern region of Bengal. The spring is marked from March to May, by a variable atmosphere; heat, thunder storms, and, occasionally, with refreshing showers. From June to September is the season of humidity, when heavy and continued rains fill the rivers to their brim, which run off from hence with rapidity, to assist in inundating Bengal. From October to March, a clear and uniform sky succeeds, seldom obscured either by fogs or clouds. For three months of this season, a degree of cold is felt, far greater perhaps than is known to prevail in Europe. Its extreme severity is more particularly confined to the southern boundary of Tibet, near that elevated range of mountains which divides it from Assam, Bootan, and Nipal.

The summits of these are covered all the year with snow, and their vicinity is remarkable, at all seasons, for the dryness of the winds. The range is confined between the twenty-sixth and twenty-seventh degrees of northern latitude. During the winter, a practice is adopted in the neighbourhood of these mountains, similar to that in use in the coldest parts of North America, but in some respects more complete. I mean, that of preparing meat and fish for carriage, by the action of extreme cold; a mode more particularly adopted by the Indians, who convey to their markets, at many hundred miles distance, their poultry, game, and fish, in a frozen state. But in Tibet, the practice is confined, as far as came to my knowledge, to the preservation of mutton alone, and the process is extremely simple. They kill, clean, and strip the animal of his skin; he is then placed upon his legs, in a commodious place, and left exposed to a free access of frosty air, until all the juices in his body are completely dried up, and the whole becomes one uniformly stiffened substance. It is then in a fit state for carriage, to any part of Tibet, and for keeping to any season of the year. No salt is used in the preparation. I had supplies of this prepared meat, during all the time I remained at Teshoo Loomboo, which had been cured in the preceding winter. It was perfectly sweet, though the fat is sometimes liable to become slightly rancid, on exposure to the air; and it is therefore usually kept in close boxes, till it is wanted for use. I was accustomed to eat heartily of the meat thus prepared, without any further dressing, and at length grew fond of it; though I could not possibly surmount the prejudice I felt, against that which was recently killed, and raw.

My Tibet friends, however, gave an uniform and decided preference to the undressed crude meat; and though I listened to their praises of it, in this state, with a desire to become a proselyte to their opinion, yet I was compelled to yield to the force of early prejudice. Their dried meat, though it had not been subjected to the action of heat, or of fire, yet had not to the eye, the appearance of being raw, but resembled in colour, that which has been well boiled. It had been deprived of all ruddiness, by the intense cold. It is not easily cut across, though it admits readily of being broken, or stript in shreds, in the direction of the fibres, which are always distinctly marked, and easily separable: every muscle is completely enveloped in its own sac.

Among the valuable and useful animals of Tibet, their breed of sheep merits a distinguished rank. Their flocks are numerous; and upon them their chief reliance is placed for present support, as well as for their winter food. A peculiar species seems indigenous to this climate, marked almost invariably, by black heads and legs. They are of a small size: their wool is soft, and their flesh, almost the only animal food eaten in Tibet, is, in my opinion, the finest mutton in the world.

They are fed without distinction, wherever sufficient pasture is to be found, but principally upon the short herbage, peculiar to the sides of eminences, and bleak, exposed plains. They are occasionally employed as beasts of burden; and I have seen numerous flocks of them in motion, laden with salt and grain, each carrying from twelve to twenty pounds. They are the bearers of their own coats, to the best market, where it is usually fabricated into a narrow cloth resembling frieze, or a thick coarse blanket. When slaughtered, their skins are most commonly cured with the wool on, and form a most excellent winter garment for the peasant, and the traveller.

The skins of lambs are cured also with the wool on, and constitute a valuable article of traffic. In order to obtain the skin in its highest state of excellency, the dam is sometimes killed before her time of yeaning; a cruel precaution, which secures, however, a silky softness to the fleece, and stamps a very high price upon it, in this region, where the merit of good furs is well ascertained. It serves particularly for lining vests, and is in equal estimation all over Tartary; it bears a very high price also in China. But powerful as the temptation is, I conclude from this circumstance, that the practice is not very frequently adopted.

The dryness of the atmosphere at this season, in Tibet, I thought, very remarkable; it had an effect resembling that of the scorching winds which prevail, and blow over the sandy soil of Hindostan, or along the shores of Coromandel. Vegetation is dried to brittleness, and every plant may be rubbed between the fingers into dust.

Hence, the inhabitants have been compelled to adopt the precaution of covering their columns, the carved decorations of their capitals, and even their doors, with a coat of coarse cotton cloth, which seems, in some degree, to prevent wood-work from being rent in sunder. The few articles of wood, trunks, and boxes, which I had with me, would often startle us, in the dead of night, with a report as loud as that of musquetry. This continued, without intermission, till the glue had intirely quitted its hold, and no longer kept the joints together, which had been previously softened by the humidity of Bengal, so that they were now ready to fall in pieces. As far as I could judge, timber, in this climate, seemed subject to no other injury from time; but was equally exempt from the silent depredations of decay, and the more active violence of any species of destructive vermin.

CHAPTER VIII.

Local Appellation of Tibet—Stricture on the Religion—Use of musical Instruments in their sacred Services—Comparison with the Hindoos —Assemble in Temples for the Performance of religious Duties— Lama, the sacred Superior—Gradations in the sacerdotal Class— Gylong—Tohba—Tuppa—Establishment of the Monastery—Interdictions of the religious Order—Noise and Pomp of their religious Ceremonies—Kugopea—Habit of the Priests—Yellow, the distinguishing Colour, worn by the Sect Gyllookpa—of which the Superiors are Dalai Lama—Teshoo Lama—Tarranaut Lama— Red, by the Shamar.—Lam' Rimbochay—Lam' Sobroo Nawangnamghi—Lam' Ghassatoo—their Contentions—Prevalence of the former.—Humane Trait in the Character of the Tibetian.—Tribute of Respect paid to the Dead—Festival in Honour of the Dead— superstitious Practices—sanctioned and performed by the Class devoted to Religion.—Omens.—Calendar of Time—Cycle of twelve Years.—Art of Printing.

THE country of Tibet is called by the inhabitants Puë, or Puëkoachim; a title, which, as they told me, is derived from PUË, signifying *northern*, and KOACHIM, *snow*; that is, snowy region of the north.

This appellation is said to have been given it, on account of the coldness of the climate, by the teachers who first came from India, and who promulgated the religion which prevails among them.

I shall, for very obvious reasons, decline entering into any formal discussion respecting the nature of this religion. It is evidently a subject, to acquire a competent knowledge of which, necessarily demands a long residence in the country, and an accurate and critical acquaintance with its language. I shall therefore content myself, as I have hitherto done, with communicating faithfully, such superficial information as I was enabled to obtain, respecting the religion of Tibet, and with delineating what occurred to my own immediate observation, respecting its external forms.

It seems, then, to be the schismatical offspring of the religion of the Hindoos, deriving its origin from one of the followers of that faith, a disciple of Budh, who first broached the doctrine which now prevails over the wide extent of Tartary. It is reported to have received its earliest admission, in that part of Tibet bordering upon India, (which from hence became the seat of the sovereign Lamas) to have traversed over Mantchieux Tartary, and to have been ultimately disseminated over China and Japan. Though it differs from the Hindoo in many of its outward forms, yet it still bears a very close affinity with the religion of Brahma, in many important particulars. The principal idol in the temples of Tibet is Mahamoonie[a], the Budha of Bengal, who is worshipped under these and various other epithets, throughout the great extent of Tartary, and among all the nations to the eastward of

[a] This term is Sanscrit, and literally signifies Great Saint.

the Berhampooter. In the wide extended space over which this faith prevails, the same object of veneration is acknowledged under numerous titles; among others, he is styled Godama or Gowtama, in Assam and Ava; Samana, in Siam; Amida Buth, in Japan; Fohi, in China; Budha and Shakamuna, in Bengal and Hindostan; Dherma Raja and Mahamoonie, in Bootan and Tibet. Durga and Kali; Ganeish, the emblem of wisdom; and Cartikeäh, with his numerous heads and arms, as well as many other deities of the Hindoo mythology, have also a place in their assemblage of gods.

The same places of popular esteem or religious resort, as I have already hinted, are equally respected in Tibet and in Bengal; Praag, Cashi, Durgeedin, Saugor, and Jagarnaut, are objects of devout pilgrimage; and I have seen loads of the sacred water taken from the Ganges, travelling over these mountains, (which, by the bye, contribute largely to its increase) upon the shoulders of men, whom enthusiasts have deemed it worth their while, to hire at a considerable expence, for so pious a purpose.

As far as I am able to judge, respecting their ritual, or ceremonial worship, it differs materially from the Hindoo. The Tibetians assemble in chapels, and unite together in prodigious numbers, to perform their religious service, which they chant in alternate recitative and chorus, accompanied by an extensive band of loud and powerful instruments. So that, whenever I heard these congregations, they forcibly recalled to my recollection, both the solemnity, and sound, of the Roman Catholic mass.

The instruments made use of were all of an enormous size. Trumpets above six feet long; drums stretched over a copper cauldron, such as are termed nowbut, in Hindostan; the gong, a circular Chinese instrument of thin hammered bell-metal, capable of producing a surprising sound; cymbals, hautboys; and a double drum, shallow, but of great circumference, mounted upon a tall, slender pedestal; which the performer turns with great facility, striking either side with a long curved iron, as the piece requires a higher, or a lower tone: these, together with the human tibia, and sea conch, a large species of the buccinum, compose, for the most part, their religious band. Harsh as these instruments, individually taken, might sound to a musical ear, yet when joined together in unison, with the voices of two or three hundred boys and men, managed with varying modulation, from the lowest and softest cadence to the loudest swell, they produced to my ear an effect extremely grand.

Other musical instruments are in the hands of the people of Tibet. The mother of Teshoo Lama, on my visit to her (which I shall particularly describe hereafter), sung to me a very pleasing air, which she played at the same time on the guittar, her husband also accompanying her with the flagelet.

From many of the prejudices, essentially interwoven with the religion of the Hindoos, especially such as relate to their various and perplexing distinctions of casts, the Tibetian is almost entirely exempt. I was attended by them, with an assiduity and attention, that left me little room to suspect the existence of such prejudices. I have been served with tea, from the same vessel with the sovereign Lama, for this always constituted a part of the ceremonial, at every interview

Nor, in the great variety of visitors that occasionally came to me, did I ever perceive the slightest scruple to partake either of tea, or of other liquors, as prepared by my own servants. This I notice, as a trait diametrically opposite to the unalterable practice of the Hindoos. A Brahman would deem it a profanation of the deepest dye, even to eat in the presence of one of an inferior cast; much more to partake of the same repast, with a person of a different religion. A rigid Hindoo, though the most needy of his race, would rather suffer death, than submit to such disgrace.

In nothing, however, does there appear so great a difference, as in their religious establishments.

The religion of the Hindoo, without any acknowledged individual superior, and almost without any edifices of magnitude, set apart for its professors (at least in Bengal and Hindostan), mixes all alike in the common business of the world; and a promiscuous multitude is continually passing before the eye, among whom no external distinction of character can be traced, unless by chance you shall discover that sacred and discriminating mark, the Zennâr, which is a small cord, made of the cusa grass, worn next the skin, passing over the shoulder to the hip, by the Brahman only. On such a discovery, I have seen a clean and well dressed man, come up to another, who had been employed as a messenger between two Englishmen, humiliating himself before him with profound respect, touching the ground he trod on, and even kissing his slipper, after he had been passing through wet and dirty roads. Those who are interested in keeping up the illusion, are mixed and blended invariably, with every rank of society; so that the machine, having been once set a going, moves on, in one uniform and incessant round: whilst enthusiasm is sufficiently kept alive by the frequent recurrence of public festivals, in which all are seen to take a share, celebrating them with the most extravagant pageantry and ostentatious parade.

The sober and reflecting character of the Tibetians, exhibits a different picture. Among them, all is system and order. The mind readily obeys the superiority it has been accustomed to acknowledge. A sovereign Lama, immaculate, immortal, omnipresent, and omniscient, is placed at the summit of their fabric. He is esteemed the vicegerent of the only God, the mediator between mortals and the Supreme. They view him only in the most amiable light, as perpetually absorbed in religious duty; and, when called to bestow attention on mortal beings, as employed only in the benign office of distributing comfort and consolation by his blessing, and in exercising the first of all attributes, forgiveness and mercy. He is also the centre of all civil government, which derives from his authority all its influence and power. At the same time that he is the soul which animates their whole system, a regular gradation, from the most venerated Lama, through the whole order of Gylongs to the young noviciate, is observed with rigid severity.

The inferior gradations from the president of a monastery, who is always styled Lama, in addition to the name of the station to which he belongs, are Gylong, Tohba, and Tuppa.

On the establishment of the monastery of Teshoo Loomboo, were reckoned, at that period, no less than three thousand seven hundred

Gylongs, for the performance of daily service in the Goomba, or temple. Four Lamas, chosen from amongst them, superintend and direct their religious ceremonies.

One is annually elected from among the Gylongs, whose duty, for the time being, is that of attending to the due preservation of regularity and order; he inspects the distribution of provisions; has a right at all times to enter the apartments of the priests; is present at all religious assemblies and processions; and is armed, as a badge of office, with a wand in one hand, and a small brazier of burning incense, pendent by three chains from the extremity of a staff, in the other. With these insignia of his office, he is at liberty to mark any visible inattention by slightly burning the party, or by a blow. The terrors of his office and his station, devolve, at the expiration of one year, on another of the Gylongs; during his continuance in authority, he is styled Kegwi.

Youth intended for the service of the monastery, are received into the establishment, at the age of eight or ten years; they are then called *Tuppa;* and are occupied in receiving the instruction suited to their age, and the duties for which they are designed. At fifteen they are usually admitted of the order of *Tohba*, the first step in their religious class; and if, after passing through a careful examination, they are found sufficiently qualified, from that of *Tohba* they are admitted into the order of *Gylong,* between the age of twenty-one and twenty-four. They then become eligible, according to the weight of their interest, or strength of their pretensions, to the superintendence of some endowed monastery, of which there are multitudes spread all over Tibet, with lands assigned to them for their support. In this station, as chief of a flock, the superintendent is styled Lama.

Those who enter the religious order, are enjoined sobriety, forego the society of women, and confine themselves to the austere practices of the cloister. Of nunneries, as well as monasteries, the number is considerable; and the strictest laws exist, to prevent any woman even from accidentally passing a night within the limits of the one, or a man within those of the other. Indeed there appears to be a regulation among them, most completely framed to obviate abuse, and establish respect towards the sacred orders of both sexes.

The nation is divided into two distinct and separate classes, those who carry on the business of the world, and those who hold intercourse with heaven. No interference of the laity, ever interrupts the regulated duties of the clergy. The latter, by mutual compact, take charge of all their spiritual concerns; and the former, by their labours, enrich and populate the state.

I was one day called to the window by a sudden and loud crash of instrumental and vocal music, which struck up at once, at no great distance from my apartments. I soon saw a prodigious crowd advance, and turn into an avenue of the monastery, whether or not for the purpose of acquiring any addition to their party I cannot pronounce; but presently they appeared again, and I observed a most motley group, composed of a very numerous concourse of spectators, as well as a large party of Gylongs, who, as I was told, were engaged in the celebration of some religious festival.

A considerable number of priests advanced by files of two and two, led by a Lama, having a wand in one hand, and in the other a casket or brazier of incense, suspended by three metallic chains from the end of a long staff, which emitted a thick smoke as the procession moved along.

A powerful band of their most noisy instruments immediately followed. First were ten performers with huge trumpets, which they sounded, resting one end upon the ground; next followed twenty men with large tabors, a sort of drum about three feet in diameter, fixed by the side upon a pedestal, and beaten by a long elastic curved iron: then came twenty men with cymbals, and two with the sea shell *(buccinum)*, here termed chaunk.

Having entered the most spacious and open street, they began to arrange themselves in order. The trumpets took their station upon the right; next them the chaunks, and then the tabors; the cymbals were in front. The Lama stood before the whole band, appearing, with his wand, to mark the time, and give them words, which all, except the instrumental performers, chanted to the music. I observed, that the performance of this ceremony, continued for near half an hour, when they formed their line again, and bent their course, passing by the dwelling of Tessaling Lama, a superior of the religious order, towards the extreme limits of the monastery upon the north east.

Here stood a lofty and broad, but shallow edifice, styled Kugopea, filled, as I was informed, with portraits of the sovereign Lamas, and with other sacred subjects appertaining to their mythology; and solemnly dedicated to the festive celebration of some mystic rites of their religion. From this place, after a short pause, the procession moved back again, and returned within the precincts of the monastery, where having reposited their solemn trappings, the priests retired to their respective apartments. A view of the dwelling of Tessaling Lama, with the religious edifice styled Kugopea, on the north eastern boundary of the monastery of Teshoo Loomboo, is given in the annexed plate[b].

The priests were habited in long robes of yellow cloth, with a conical cap of the same colour, having flaps to fall down, and cover the ears. I notice this peculiarity of colour in their dress, as it is a distinction adopted, to mark one of the two religious sects that divide almost the whole of Tartary, from Turkistan to the eastern limits of this continent. The other colour is red; and the tribes are known as belonging to the red, or the yellow cap. The former differ principally, as I understand, from the sectaries of the yellow, in admitting the marriage of their priests. But the latter are considered as the most orthodox, as well as possessed of far the greatest influence. The Emperor of China is decidedly a votary of this sect, and he has sanctified his preference of the yellow colour, by a sumptuary law, which limits it to the service of religion, and the imperial use.

The two sects are distinguished by the appellations of Gyllookpa, and Shammar, but the external appearance, or dress of both, is similar, except the distinction I have mentioned in the colour of the cap, the Gylloopka having adopted yellow, the Shammar red; a circumstance which is strictly attended to, on all occasions of ceremony. Three Lamas are placed at the head of each sect; Dalai Lama, Teshoo Lama, and Taranaut Lama, preside over the Gyllookpa, who have their resi-

[b] Plate XII.

Pl. XII.

Capt. S. Turner del. James Basire f.

The Dwelling of Tessaling Lama, with the religious Edifice stiled Kugopea

Published March 20th 1800, by G. & W. Nicol Pall Mall.

dence at Pootalah, Teshoo Loomboo, and Kharka. This sect prevails over the greatest part of Tibet, and a division of the same, is said to be established in a province of the Decan, called Seurra or Serrora.

In like manner, three Lamas also, Lam' Rimbochay, Lam' Sobroo Nawangnamghi, and Lam' Ghassatoo, preside over the Shammar; these have their residence in Bootan, in separate monasteries, but from the limited extent of that country, at no great distance from each other. The principal of the Shammar sect in Tibet, is styled Gongso Rimbochay, and has his residence at Sakia.

Great contentions formerly prevailed between the sects Gyllookpa and Shammar; and in ancient times the latter is reported to have enjoyed the most extensive power. Khumbauk acknowledged its doctrines, whilst those of the Gyllookpa were settled in Kilmauk: the monasteries of both, were promiscuously scattered over the face of the country, till at length the inhabitants of Kilmauk, the Gyllookpa, assembling together a mighty army, waged war against the sectaries of Khumbauk, the Shammar, and drove them from their possessions in various quarters, more particularly from the neighbourhood of Teshoo Loomboo, where they were then fixed in great numbers, and where they finally established their own authority. The Gyllookpa having thus displaced their opponents from their strongest post, where they had formed a large settlement, now razed it to the ground, and left not an habitation standing: but from the ruins arose the monastery of Teshoo Loomboo. After its establishment, the superiority of Teshoo Lama was firmly fixed, and the power of the Gyllookpa soon attained its highest ascendency, in consequence of the Emperor of China's having

S s

declared in its favour, and adopted for himself the distinction of the yellow hat. This completely turned the balance towards the sectaries of Gyllookpa, while those of the Shammar, no longer capable of maintaining their ground, were under the necessity of retiring where they might be permitted to enjoy a peaceful and uninterrupted station.

The tract of country bordering on Tibet towards the south, marked by a line inhospitable and intemperate in the extreme, which was passed over by the Shammar, was found, on examination, capable of affording them a residence, and shelter from their adversaries. Here then it was, that they established themselves, and fixed their abode, while others, styled Dukba, still live in tents and tend their flocks, rambling from place to place.

I frequently observed many of the ancient and idle inhabitants of this place, loiter away much of their time, in basking in the sun, upon the house tops; from whence I inferred, that the interests and occupations of domestic life were extremely limited. My friend Goorooba, who was a humane, intelligent, good creature as could exist, used to pass many hours in the day, lounging upon the terrace, and having stripped his shoulders of the thick mantle that he wore, turned his back to the sun's rays, as if he derived from it, the most friendly and genial influence. His lips, I could frequently perceive, moved with great rapidity; but for what purpose I cannot pronounce: I gave him credit, however, for his prayers. During this time, he was for the most part employed in rolling up between his fingers little pellets of dough, which he chucked to ravens perched upon the walls; and so familiar were these birds, that they came near enough to catch them before they fell to the ground. They had acquired indeed such an apparent intimacy with man, that they would sometimes take these pellets even from his hand; while kites and eagles kept at a loftier distance, and soared above, watching where they should descend next, and share with dogs and ravens in the funeral obsequies.

The tribute of respect is paid, in this region, to the manes of the dead, in various ways. The sovereign Lamas are deposited entire, in shrines prepared for their remains, which ever after are looked upon as sacred, and visited with religious awe. The bodies of inferior Lamas are usually burnt, and their ashes preserved with great care in little metallic idols, which have places assigned them in their sacred cabinets. Common subjects are treated with less ceremony; some of them are carried to lofty eminences, where, after having been disjointed, and the limbs divided, they are left a prey for ravens, kites, and other carnivorous birds. Others, with less respect, are committed to the usual receptacle of the dead. The last, but less frequent, mode of disposing of the dead, is committing them to the waters of the river. Burial, that is, inhuming the corpse entire in the earth, is altogether unpractised.

On one side of the monastery of Teshoo Loomboo I saw the place, the Golgotha, if I may so call it, to which they convey their dead. It was a spacious area, enclosed on one part by the perpendicular rock, and on the others by lofty walls, raised probably with a view to seclude from public observation, the disgusting objects contained within them. At the top it was totally uncovered, so as to be perfectly open to the birds; and at the bottom a narrow passage was left through the walls, near their foundation, for the sole purpose of admitting dogs, or other beasts of prey. On the rock above, a platform overhung the inclosure, which had been constructed for the conveniency of precipitating the dead bodies with greater ease, over the walls, into the area. And here, I understood, the only rites performed, in honour of the dead, were merely such as tended to facilitate the destruction of the body by dogs, or birds of prey. But though this was the general receptacle, yet there were some who declined the use of it, and conveyed their friends to the summit of some neighbouring hill, where, I was told, they disjointed and mangled the dead body, that it might become a more easy prey to carnivorous birds. I concluded, that there was a strong prejudice in their minds, of some idea of pollution attached to " being given to the dogs," which was sufficient to create a preference of the contrary practice.

In Tibet, as well as in Bengal, an annual festival is kept in honour of the dead. On the 29th of October, as soon as the evening drew on, and it became dark, a general illumination was displayed upon the summits of all the buildings in the monastery; the tops also of the houses upon the plain, as well as in the most distant villages, scattered among the clusters of willows, were in the same manner lighted up with lamps, exhibiting all together, a brilliant and splendid spectacle. The night was dark, the weather calm, and the lights burnt with a clear and steady flame. The Tibetians reckon these circumstances of the first importance, as, on the contrary, they deem it a most evil omen if the weather be stormy, and their lights extinguished by the wind or rain.

It is worthy of notice, how materially an effect depends upon a previously declared design, and how diametrically opposite the emotions may be, although produced by appearances exactly similar. In England, I had been accustomed to esteem general illuminations, as the strongest expression of public joy; I now saw them exhibited as a solemn token of melancholy remembrance, an awful tribute of respect paid to the innumerable generations of the dead. The darkness of the night, the profound tranquillity and silence, interrupted only by the deep and slowly-repeated tones of the nowbut, trumpet, gong, and cymbal, at different intervals; the tolling of bells, and the loud monotonous repetition of sentences of prayer, sometimes heard when the instruments were silent; were all so calculated, by their solemnity, to produce serious reflection, that I really believe no human ceremony could possibly have been contrived, more effectually to impress the mind with sentiments of awe. In addition to this external token of solemn retrospect, acts of beneficence performed during this festival, are supposed to have peculiar merit, and all persons are called upon, according to their ability, to distribute alms, and to feed the poor.

This is a festival of equal celebrity in Bengal and Hindostan, with both Mohammedans and Hindoos; by the former it is called Shubibauraut, by the latter Cheraug-pooja.

Being governed in all the concerns of life, by an awful regard to the dictates of superstition, it is no wonder that we find this people placing implicit confidence in a series of lucky and unlucky days. Devoted to astrology, they yield a willing homage to its professors.

Hence we find no prudent traveller ever attempting to undertake a journey, without previously appealing to this authority, and endeavouring to obtain an auspicious presage. The same signal of favour is deemed indispensably requisite in every important enterprise, and the same wary circumspection enters equally into all the more minute concerns of domestic life. The union of the sexes, and the giving names to infants, are neither of them events to be accomplished without a regular appeal to the same decisive oracle.

Among that order of men, to whom the due performance of every ceremony connected with their religion is committed, some are found who are peculiarly skilled in this obscure science; and the declaration of its decisions belongs, of course, to the discreet, initiated Gylong.

I cannot here enumerate the various modes of seeking out some decisive presage, which they usually practice. The sortes sanctorum is a pious and venerated appeal: in trivial affairs, the mind is often governed by a casual cast of the die; and hence, dice are almost always found to constitute an appendage to a Tartar dress.

The custom of these regions obliged me, sometimes, to have recourse to the oracular denunciations of my attendant Gylong; which indeed I had little difficulty in doing, as I found he had the consideration seldom to suffer his decisions to oppose my wishes. I consequently thought it prudent to travel as he directed, and never commenced a journey without his previous concurrence. I soon learned to confide in his discretion, and he never failed to calculate for me, both every auspicious and inauspicious presage.

The same superstition that influences their view of the affairs of the world, pervades equally their general calculations. On this principle it is, that they frame their common calendar of time. I have one now in my possession; and, as far as I can understand it, from what has been explained to me, a recapitulation of lucky and unlucky times, constitutes the chief merit of the work. Cheeb Lobo was the compiler of this almanack, or *Datow*. The months, *Dowa*, commencing with January, are called *Tumba; Gneba; Sumba; Jheba; Gnabba; Truba; Toomba; Gheiba; Gooba; Chooba; Chucheba; Chuneba.*

The days, *Che*, are reckoned from the appearance of the new moon, in regular succession, till it shews itself again.

New moon; *Che-cheic;* 2, *Che-gnea;* 3, *Che-soom;* 4, *Che-zea,* 5, *Che-gna;* 6, *Che-tru;* 7, *Che-toon;* 8; *Che-ghe;* 9, *Che-goo;* 10, *Che-chutumbha;* 11, *Che-chucheic;* 12, *Che-chugnea;* 13, *Che-chusum;* 14, *Che-chuzea;* 15, *Che-chugna;* 16, *Che-chutru;* 17, *Che-chutoon;* 18, *Che-chughe;* 19, *Che-chugoo;* 20, *Che-gnea chutam-bha;* 21, *Che-gneacheic;* 22, *Che-gneagnea;* 23, *Che-gneasoom;* 24, *Che-gneazea;* 25, *Che-gneagna;* 26, *Che-gneatru;* 27, *Che-gneatoon;* 28, *Che-gneaghe;* 29, *Che-gneagoo.*

Their year, *Lo*, is lunar. The moon is called *Dowa;* the sun, *Neima.* The parts of the day; evening, *pheroo;* night, *noom;* morning, *loobo;* noon, *neimphee.* Their computation of time is, in conformity with the general practice of the East, by a cycle of twelve years. I will subjoin their appellations, as well as in Persia, China, Tartary, and Japan.

IN THE LANGUAGE OF

	Tibet.	*Persia.*	*China.*	*Tartary.*	*Japan.*	
1	Pcheup	Mosh	Chou	Keskou	Ne	Rat
2	Lāng	Nergow	Nieow	Out	Us	Bull
3	Tah	Khirs	Hou	Pars	Tor	Bear
4	Yuh	Shubpurra	Tou	Toushcan	Ow	Bat
5	Bru	Berk	Lang	Lovi	Tats	Lightning
6	Prul	Maur	Che	Ilan	Mi	Snake
7	Ta	Asp	Ma	Junad	Uma	Horse
8	Lù	Nermeish	Yam	Koi	Tsitsuse	Ram
9	Prehu	Boozna	Heou	Pitchin	Sar	Monkey
10	Pchea	Kherosh	Ki	Doukouk	Torri	Cock
11	Kee	Segner	Keou	Eit	In	Dog
12	Pha	Khook	Tchou	Tongouz	Te	Hog

It is asserted that the art of printing has, from a very remote age, been practised in Tibet, though limited in its use, as far as I could learn, by the powerful influence of superstition. It has hitherto remained appropriated principally to sacred works, and to the service of learning and religion. Copies on these recondite subjects are multiplied, when required, not by the aid of moveable types, but by means of set forms, having the subjects of their works carved with appropriate embellishments on blocks of wood, with which they impress their matter upon thin narrow slips of paper, fabricated among themselves from the fibrous root of a small shrub, and the leaf bears the impression of the characters designed for it, on each side. The leaves of a book, when they are completed, are loosely put together, placed upon each other, and enclosed between two equal slips of wood as covers.

The southern Indians, who dwell along the margin of the sea, and never, I believe, possessed the art of printing, engrave their works upon the recent leaf of the palmira tree[c], which, growing at the extremity of a long footstalk, is naturally formed in narrow folds, like a half extended fan, and is easily divided into segments, about two inches in width. In correspondence to the purpose required, the fairest parts of the leaf are selected, and uniformly shaped by means of a sharp knife. On either side of these narrow slips, letters are traced or engraven, by means of a strong steel stylus, which makes an indelible impression; though sometimes, to render the writing more distinctly legible, the traces of the point are lightly powdered, by the dust collected from the fume of their midnight lamps. This simple method of transmitting records to future times, is practised in those countries alone, in which the palm tree thrives. The leaf must be used while fresh; its fibrous substance seems indestructible by vermin.

The printed and written character, appropriate to works of learning and religion, is styled, in the language of Tibet, the *Uchen;* that in which business and correspondence is carried on, is called the *Umin.* As a specimen of the style and manner of writing, a short letter, the fac simile of one in my possession; received from the Daeb Raja, is

[c] Borassus flabelliformis.

given in the annexed Plate XIII, written in the Umin character: underneath follows a literal interpretation of its contents: a few words are also subjoined in the Uchen character. The letters in both run from left to right: the vowels are expressed by marks placed above or beneath the consonant, with which they are sounded.

No. 1.

TRANSLATION.

To Mr. Turner, Saheb

NAMBAR DEO, of the tribe of Paling Dukba, the greatest, most high and mighty Lion of all the quarters of the world—these. With the Deo all is well: and invocations are continually offering for the well-being of him, whose employment is the protection of the humble, and from whose boundless knowledge nothing is concealed. At this time, a letter and presents, bearing my seal, are transmitted, as memorials of regard, to the director and disposer of all public affairs, the Governor General. My wishes are expressed upon an accompanying paper, written in the Bengal language. Let your friendship be perpetually preserved in memory, as heretofore. This is my desire.

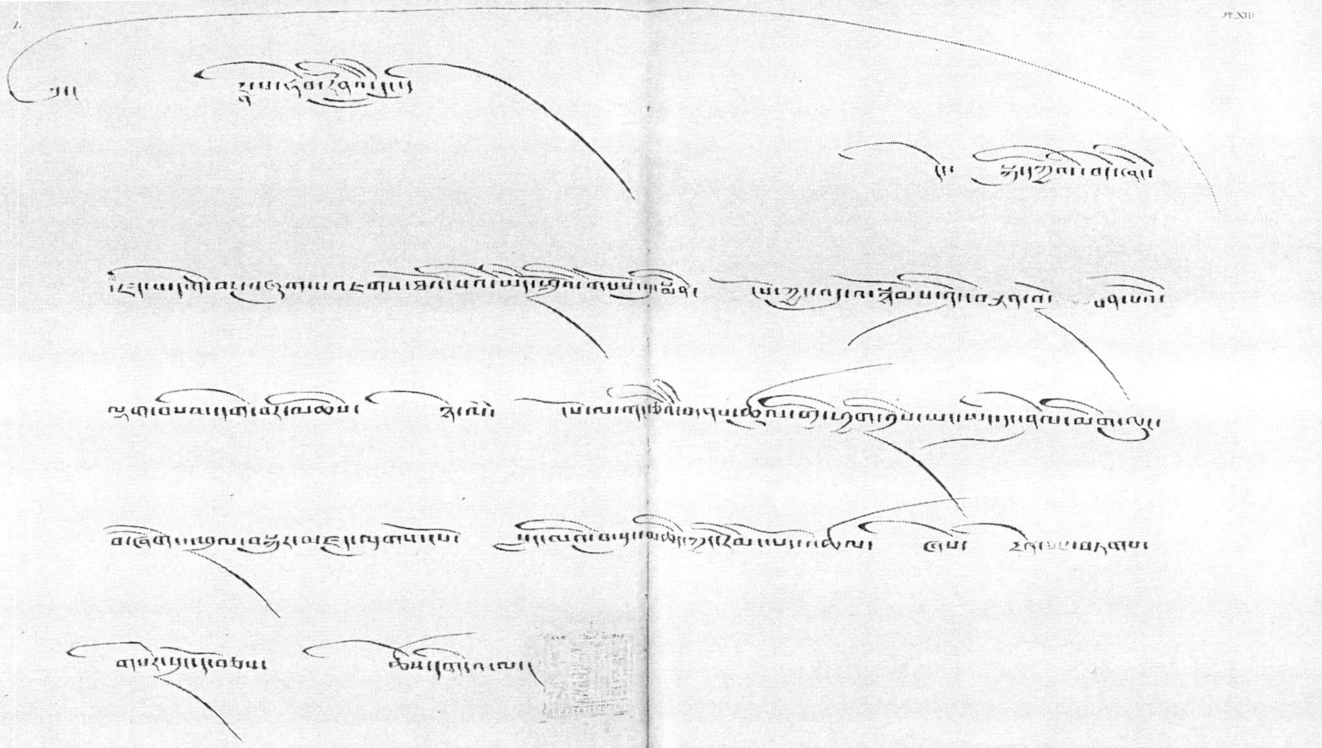

2 ༄༅། །ཨོཾ་མ་ཎི་པདྨེ་ཧཱུྃ།

3 བླ་མ་རིན་པོ་ཆེ

1 པཎ་ཆེན་རིན་པོ་ཆེ

5 དགེ་སློང

6 ཨ་ཏི

Published March [illegible] Pall Mall

SPECIMENS OF THE UCHEN.

No. 2. *Oom maunie paimee oom;* the sacred sentence repeated upon their rosaries; in the same general use, both in Bootan and Tibet.

3. *Lama Rimbochay;* High Pontiff, Chief Priest:

4. *Punjin Rimbochay;* Great Apostolic Master; the mitred professors of religion.

5. *Gylong;* Monks.

6. *Annee;* Nuns.

CHAPTER IX.

Return of the Regent—Time appointed for my Departure—rapid Advance of Winter—Audience of Leave—Soopoon Choomboo—farewell Visits from numerous Friends—prepare to leave Teshoo Loomboo—previous Observance of some superstitious Ceremonies.—Beggars—Mohammedans—Hindoos.—Benevolence displayed at Teshoo Loomboo.—Tsondue.—Skating.—Terpaling.—Interview with Teshoo Lama—Manner and Conduct of the Lama—his Age—Parents—Gyeung—her splendid Dress—Gyap—Invitation to an Entertainment—Officers of the Lama's Household—Impression of profound Respect.—Veneration entertained for the Memory of the late Lama—his humane, intelligent, conciliating Character.—Amiable Manners of Mr. Bogle.—Parents of the Lama—Pavilion—Entertainment.—Gyap—his Delight in manly Sports—his superior Skill—polite Offer to instruct me in the Arts he practised.—Repast—raw Meat—Gyeung, particularly abstemious.—Music—Vocal—Instrumental.—Conclusion of the Entertainment.—Wait upon the Lama—Votaries of the Lama—Calmuc Tartars—liberal Offerings.—Last Visit to the Teshoo Lama, and his Parents.

THE Regent returned to the palace on Wednesday, the 19th of November, after an absence of nearly a month. I had an interview with him the following day, in the chamber adjoining to the gallery of idols. Congratulations on his return, and mutual complimentary inquiries, engaged much of the time allotted to this meeting.

I had suffered a slight indisposition during his absence; and his attentive inquiries, with the affectionate concern he expressed, convinced me, that no event of the smallest importance could occur, during his absence, without his being immediately acquainted with it. He rejoiced that I had so soon recovered; and said much of the severity of the cold in the country, he had visited, which had compelled him to change his habit, and put on warmer clothing. " There," said he, " I became a Dukba, or citizen of the world; now, I am again a Gylong."

The next time I had an opportunity of meeting the Regent, he appeared anxious, from apprehensions of the severity of the approaching season, to fix a time for my return to Bengal, lest an excessive fall of snow, should put a stop to all communication between Tibet and Bootan, and render travelling impracticable. He thought it proper, therefore, not to delay appointing an early period for my dismission. I had afterwards the opportunity of many interviews, but as these chiefly related to the public business on which I came, the result will be better seen in the report of my mission, transmitted to the Governor General.

I waited upon the Regent, on Sunday, the 30th of November, in the hall of audience, where, on the first day after my arrival, I had been originally introduced to him: Soopoon Choomboo was at the same time present. I received from his own hand his dispatches for the Governor General, and the presents designed for him, were spread out before me. He begged me to bear in remembrance his unchanged and steady friendship; to state the misfortune of the Lama's having thought fit to withdraw himself from the world, and their consequent helpless situation; as he was now only an infant, unable to comfort them with his counsel and advice; but, added he, be not cast down; when he shall become of age, and resume the Musnud, all will be well.

On the following day, I again waited upon the Regent, and I had not long been with him, when he accosted me in the following words:

"I had yesterday a vision of our tutelary deity, and to me it was a day replete with much interesting and important matter. This guardian power, who inspires us with his illuminations, on every momentous and great occasion, indulged me with a divination, from which I have collected that every thing will be well. Set your heart at rest, therefore, for though a separation is about to take place between us, our friendship will not cease to exist, but, through the favour of an interposing providence, you may rest assured it will increase, and terminate eventually in that which will be for the best." I now took my leave, after receiving many friendly exhortations, and kind professions of regard.

The arrangements for my departure being completed, I waited upon Soopoon Choomboo, the minister and cup-bearer of the late Lama, to take my final leave; and was charged also with dispatches from him to the Governor General. I now received the visits of many friends, who had shewn me much civility during my residence here, and by their kind attention had relieved the solitary gloom of the monastic life I led, which indeed, except that I was exempt from daily attendance upon the sacred duties, to which the Gylongs were obliged by their vows, was equally dull and uniform. But I could not be insensible of the obliging and attentive assiduity with which all who had access within the monastery, attempted to beguile my time: either by various conversation, by instruction in their language, or by amusing me with the games of which they had any knowledge. Amongst these, chess held a distinguished place, and here I often met with a skilful antagonist.

I commenced my return towards Bengal, on Tuesday, the 2d of December. The last visits of friendship and ceremony detained me at Teshoo Loomboo till the morning was far advanced; and it was past ten o'clock when I quitted the palace. I could not, however, bid adieu to the place, till, in conformity with the custom of these regions, I had bound a white silk scarf round the capitals of each of the four columns, that stood within the apartment I had occupied. I stopped not, to examine nicely, the obligations to this ceremony. If it were meant as a tribute of gratitude, it was certainly due to the comfortable accommodation this dwelling had afforded me. If it were the solemn designation of a long farewell, it equally accorded with my state of mind at the moment.

Having descended to the street, we found our horses saddled at the door, and a multitude of beggars assembled round them. Our conductor would willingly have silenced their importunities, by the active application of a long whip, which he was just upon the point of exercising; when I stopped his hand, and, being not altogether unprovided for the encounter, I opened a passage amidst the crowd, to the right and left, by the most effectual and potent of all instruments, the influence of money. It had the power of magic. The road was cleared in an instant; and while the eager mendicants were busied in scrambling for the different pieces I had thrown to them, we made the best of our time to pursue our way. Though they were less numerous, yet all along our route this day, knots of beggars repeatedly beset us. Many for the love of God, and his prophet, solicited alms of us in Persian. I was told, they came from Turkestan and Cashmeer. Some Mogul fakeers spoke the language of Hindostan; one of them told me he had come even from Surat, and naturally enough inquired of me intelligence respecting his friends, whom he had left, he said, when almost a child.

Thus I unexpectedly discovered, where I had constantly seen the round of life, moving in a tranquil regular routine, a mass of indigence and idleness, of which I had no idea. But yet it by no means surprised me, when I considered that wherever indiscriminating charity exists, it will never want objects on which to exercise its bounty, but will always attract expectants more numerous, than it has the means to gratify. No human being can suffer want at Teshoo Loomboo. It is on this humane disposition that a multitude even of Mussulmen, of a frame probably the largest and most robust in the world, place their reliance for the mere maintenance of a feeble life;

and besides these, I am informed that no less than three hundred Hindoos, Goseins, and Sunniasses, are daily fed at this place, by the Lama's bounty.

We travelled leisurely through the valley, and twice halted to take refreshment, which our conductor had providently secured on the road. Our resting place was the open plain; a carpet spread upon the ground serving us to sit upon, and a bright blue sky being our only canopy. The weather was tranquil, and the genial warmth of the sun most highly grateful.

Our halting place was called Tsondeu, which is reckoned ten miles from Teshoo Loomboo. It was an easy stage, and, as we made an early meal, our afternoon was long. I walked through a grove of willows, where we had pitched our tents, upon the skirts of this village, and found upon its borders a shallow brook, whose waters were completely frozen, and what was my joy, when I found the ice firm enough to bear my weight! My skates were immediately sent for, and I had the satisfaction of skating for two hours upon a piece of ice, which though narrow, was tolerably smooth, and above a mile in length. It was a matter of surprise to most of the spectators, to view the apparent ease and velocity with which we moved; though some who were with me had accompanied the Teshoo Lamá to Pekin, and seen, among the splendid spectacles, exhibited by order of the Emperor, for his amusement, skating in all its forms. They mentioned to me, in particular, one circumstance, which was strongly impressed upon their memories. This was a match between a skater and a horseman, for whom a good road had been made, by the side of a large sheet of ice;

but in which, to their utter astonishment, the skater won the race. But, however the recollection of this feat might lessen the admiration of some, the majority of our party had never seen this mode of moving upon the ice before; and most certainly Mr. Saunders and myself enjoyed the distinction of having been the first of our nation, that ever signalized themselves by skating in Tibet, or, perhaps, in the whole circuit of the globe, in the parallel of twenty-seven and twenty-eight degrees of northern latitude.

We thought it sufficiently early, on Wednesday, the 3d of December, to commence travelling at nine o'clock. The air was still keen, and it had frozen hard during the night. Our road inclined to the west, and here branched off from that, which led immediately to Bengal. We had proceeded but a short distance, when we entered a narrow defile, passing through which, we found bare and lofty hills, without a single tree, or even any vestige of vegetation visible upon them. In some divisions among these hills, were seen falls of water, or torrents, arrested by the frost, and converted into fixed columns of solid ice, of various forms and size, immoveably stationed till the return of spring. A small stream of water had flowed between these hills, immediately by the road side; but that also was fixed, I was informed, until they should experience warmer weather.

We continued to advance through this narrow valley, until we came to the foot of the hill, upon the summit of which was situated Terpaling, ten miles from Tsondeu: we then turned short to our right. The road was of steep ascent, and it was about noon when we entered the gates of the monastery, which not long since had been erected for the reception and accommodation of Teshoo Lama. He resides in a palace in the centre of the monastery, which occupies about a mile of ground in circumference, and the whole is encompassed by a wall. The several buildings serve for the accommodation of three hundred Gylongs, appointed to perform religious service with Teshoo Lama, until he shall be removed to the monastery, and Musnud of Teshoo Loomboo. It is unusual to make visits, either here or in Bootan, on the day of arrival; we therefore rested this day, only receiving and sending messages of compliment.

On the morning of Tuesday, the 4th of December, I was allowed to visit Teshoo Lama, and found him placed, in great form, upon his Musnud; on the left side stood his father and mother; on the other the officer particularly appointed to wait upon his person. The Musnud is a fabric of silk cushions, piled one upon the other, until the seat is elevated to the height of four feet from the floor; a piece of embroidered silk covered the top, and the sides also were decorated with pieces of silk, of various colours, suspended from the upper edge, and hanging down. At the particular request of Teshoo Lama's father, Mr. Saunders and myself wore the English dress.

I advanced, and, as the custom is, presented a white pelong scarf, and delivered also into the Lama's hands, the Governor General's present of a string of pearls, and coral, while the other things were set down before him. Having performed the ceremony of exchanging scarfs with his father and mother, we took our seats on the right hand of Teshoo Lama.

A multitude of persons, all those who had been ordered to escort me, were admitted to his presence, and allowed to make their prostrations. The infant Lama turned towards them, and received them all, with a cheerful look of complacency. His father then addressed me in the Tibet language, in words which were explained to me by the interpreter; he said that " Teshoo Lama had been used to remain at rest until this time of the day, but he had awoke very early this morning, and could not be prevailed upon to remain longer at his repose, for, added he, the English gentlemen were arrived, and he could not sleep." During the time we were in the room, I observed that the Lama's eyes were scarcely ever turned from us, and when our cups were empty of tea, he appeared uneasy, and throwing back his head, and contracting the skin of his brow, continued to make a noise, for he could not speak, until they were filled again. He took some burnt sugar out of a golden cup, containing some confectionary, and, stretching out his arm, made a motion to his attendants to give them to me. He sent some, in like manner, to Mr. Saunders, who was with me. I found myself, though visiting an infant, under the necessity of saying something; for it was hinted to me, that notwithstanding he is unable to reply, it is not to be inferred that he cannot understand. However, his incapacity of answering, excused me many words, and I briefly said, that " the Governor General, on receiving the news of his decease in China, was overwhelmed with grief and sorrow, and continued to lament his absence from the world, until the cloud that had overcast the happiness of this nation, was dispelled by his re-appearance, and then, if possible, a greater degree of joy had taken place, than he had experienced of grief, on receiving the first mournful news. The Governor anxiously wished that he might long continue to illumine the world by his presence, and was hopeful that the friendship, which had formerly subsisted between them, would not be diminished, but rather that it might become still greater than before; and that by his continuing to shew kindness to my countrymen, there might be an extensive communication between his votaries, and the dependents of the British nation."

The little creature turned, looking stedfastly towards me, with the appearance of much attention while I spoke, and nodded with repeated but slow movements of the head, as though he understood and approved every word, but could not utter a reply. His parents, who stood by all the time, eyed their son with a look of affection, and a smile expressive of heartfelt joy, at the propriety of the young Lama's conduct. His whole attention was directed to us; he was silent and sedate, never once looking towards his parents, as if under their influence at the time; and with whatsoever pains, his manners may have been so correctly formed, I must own that his behaviour, on this occasion, appeared perfectly natural and spontaneous, and not directed by any external action, or sign of authority.

The scene, in which I was here brought to act a part, was too new and extraordinary, however trivial, or perhaps preposterous, it may appear to some, not to claim from me great attention, and consequently minute remark.

Teshoo Lama was at this time eighteen months old. Though he was unable to speak a word, he made the most expressive signs; and conducted himself with astonishing dignity and decorum. His complexion was of that hue, which in England we should term rather brown, but not without colour. His features were good; he had small black eyes, and an animated expression of countenance; altogether, I thought him one of the handsomest children I had ever seen.

His mother, who stood by him, appeared to be about twenty-five years of age; she was low in person, but rather handsome, though possessing a true Tartar countenance. Her complexion was somewhat darker than her son's; she had regular features, black eyes, and a character that particularly distinguishes ladies of rank in Tibet; the corner of the eyelids being extended as far as possible, by artificial means, towards the temples. Her hair was black, but scarcely visible, from the vast profusion of ornaments that nearly covered it, consisting of pearls, rubies, emeralds, and coral. Pearls intermixed with beads of gold, and some rubies, constituted the ornaments of her ears. Chaplets of larger gems hung round her neck, among which were balass rubies, lapis lazuli, amber, and coral in numerous wreaths, one chaplet beneath the other, descending to the waist. Her vest was close buttoned round the neck. A girdle embraced it round the waist, which was fastened by a golden buckle, having a large ruby in the centre. A garnet-coloured shawl, wrought with white stars, completed her dress, which descended to the knee; she wore bulgar boots.

Gyap, the father of the Lama, was dressed in a yellow satin garment, wrought with gold, and emblazoned with the imperial dragon. Our conversation was extremely limited; the Lama's father said, that he had instructions from Teshoo Loomboo to entertain me four days, and he pressed me so earnestly to stay one more, on his account, that I could not decline the invitation. The place he named for our meeting on the morrow, was just beyond the borders of the monastery, in a small pavilion, which had been erected for his occasional retirement and recreation; the use of the bow, in which he delighted, being deemed indecorous within the limits of the monastery, as indeed was every kind of idle sport, that seemed inconsistent with the character of the place.

In the course of the afternoon I was visited by two officers of the Lama's household, immediately attendant on his person. They sat and conversed with me some time, inquiring after Mr. Bogle, whom both of them had seen, and then remarking how extremely fortunate it was, that the young Lama had regarded us with so very particular notice: they observed the strong partiality of the former Teshoo Lama for our nation, and said that the present Lama often tried already, to utter the name of the English. I encouraged the thought, hoping that they would teach the prejudice to strengthen with his increasing age; and they assured me that should he, when he began to speak, happen to have forgotten it, they would early teach him to repeat the name of Hastings.

Here let me pause a while, to mark the strong and indelible impression of respect and affection, which the meek deportment and ingratiating manners of the late Lama, seemed to have left upon the minds of all his followers. To these fascinating qualities, more than to the influence even of his sacred character, must be attributed the high veneration with which his memory is still cherished by his grateful countrymen. By the most amiable exercise of extensive power, he won the hearts of all his votaries. His public conduct, on all occasions, bore undistinguished testimony to the benevolent propensities of his nature; and clearly proved that all his actions were uniformly prompted, by a desire of extending happiness to all around him. His humane and considerate temper was eminently displayed in his interposition with the English government, on behalf of the people of Bootan; and, in the opinion of his followers, this successful exercise of his influence, reflected the brightest lustre on his sacred name. But it is not to the partial and interested representations of his own votaries alone, that we are to look for a favourable delineation of the character of the late Lama. His manners are reported by Mr. Bogle to have been in the highest degree engaging. He represents his disposition as open, candid, and generous in the extreme. In familiar conversation he describes him as not merely easy, but even facetious and entertaining. He says, that his thirst of knowledge was unbounded; and that from the numerous travellers, who on religious, or even commercial motives, daily resorted to Teshoo Loomboo, he sought all occasions of extending his information; while at the same time, he was equally free in communicating the knowledge, which he himself possessed. His whole character, indeed, so powerfully excited the admiration of Mr. Bogle, as to have drawn from him this enthusiastic, but sincere expression: "I endeavoured to discover in him some of those defects, which are inseparable from humanity; but he is so universally beloved that I had no success, and not a man could find in his heart to speak ill of him."

That the effect produced on the mind of the Lama, by a disposition and manners perfectly congenial with his own, was great and powerful, cannot excite our surprise. Indeed, towards whatever object it was directed, the patient and laborious exercise of the powers of a strong mind, in my predecessor, Mr. Bogle, was always accompanied by a most engaging mildness and benevolence, which marked every part of his character. I am thoroughly aware of the very favourable impression, which these amiable qualities left behind them in the court of Teshoo Loomboo; and this circumstance, whilst it reflects the highest honour on that judgment, which, free from the bias of partial considerations, could select its agent with such nice discrimination, places, at the same time, in the strongest point of view, the salutary influence of conciliating manners, in men, who are employed as agents, or ministers, to independent states; to those more especially, among whom the British character is imperfectly understood, or entirely unknown.

The following day, about noon, I met the parents of the Lama, Gyap and Gyeung, at the appointed station, where, after the accustomed ceremonies of exchanging scarfs, we took our seats with them. Gyap spoke of the honour, Teshoo Lama had done him, in condescending to enter into his family, and said that it was only in consequence of this high favour, that he had the pleasure of seeing and knowing the English gentlemen. He declared himself propitious to our cause, and was hopeful that our friendship might be lasting, and increase day by day. I could not but join most heartily in the same desire. The usual refreshment of Tartar tea was now introduced; some general conversation then ensued, and after a while Gyeung withdrew. Gyap soon found occasion to commence the history of his fortunes. "Lassa, said he, is my native place, my home; but some years have now elapsed since, vexed by hostile party, I was obliged to relinquish it, and come hastily away. Hence I was compelled, in my haste, to abandon a variety of articles, which I had collected for my amusement, and a fine collection that I possessed of my native arms." He then enumerated to me his particular predilections, that he excelled in drawing the bow, delighted in martial exercises, and was well skilled in the management of the horse; that he was surpassed by no one of his countrymen in mechanical contrivances, and that architecture also had been his study. "Thus attracting their jealousy, continued he, my qualifications soon drew upon me the enmity of the men of Lassa. They strove, by all means, to prejudice the Ambas (Chinese officers) against me, for no other reason, but my superiority to them, in all works of skill and ingenuity. Thus sorely pressed, I applied to Dalai Lama for his advice. He recommended me instantly to retire from Lassa, and seek protection from Teshoo Lama, to whom he would write letters in my favour. I did so, and here I have remained ever since. It was once in contemplation with me, to abandon, altogether, my native home, and seek protection from the Governor General of Bengal; but it happened that my design was changed, partly by the advice of Teshoo Lama, and partly by apprehensions of the intemperate heat of India: yet, driven from my home, I was long dissatisfied with the prospects around me, and the strength of my predilection for the place where I was born, still increased with my absence from it." He then observed upon the dispositions of the chiefs of Lassa. He said they were crafty designing men, of fair exterior, but deep and black at heart; and he concluded this confidential communication by observing, that without mutual confidence, friendship could not subsist. I extolled his patience under the wrongs he had borne, and recommended him to wait the event of time; when Teshoo Lama should be fixed in power, and the unworthiness of the hostile party dismiss them, from the enjoyment of that influence, of which they had made so bad an use; it might then be hoped, that better subjects would be found to succeed to their place. With such consolatory counsels I endeavoured to sooth his anxieties.

I found Gyap to be not only a great lover of manly sports and martial exercises, but also a perfect connoisseur on the subject of arms. His collection was exhibited, and he liberally descanted on the peculiar merits of each weapon. There were arrows famed for their remote and steady flight, which had names inscribed on each of them, and places assigned to them in a quiver, in separate cells. He honoured me with a present of three of these, and a large Chinese bow, near five feet in length, made of the horns of buffaloes, which he had used, he said, for many years. It was then perfect, but I feared, as it has since happened, that the climate of Bengal would destroy its form; though, with the greatest care, I kept it for some time uninjured. His own favourite bows were of bamboo, a species produced in the mountains bordering upon Tibet, of great strength, and almost entirely solid. The bow is framed from two pieces of bamboo, split off next the outside; the inner sides of which, after being well fitted, are united together, by many strong bands. Gyap put one of these bows into my hands, which when bent, was of extreme tension. I was unable to draw the arrow, but taking it himself, he pointed it at a mark upon the opposite hill, at the distance, as I judged, of five or six hundred yards. I could not trace the flight of the arrow, though steadily intent upon it, when he discharged it.

He peculiarly excelled in drawing the bow, and was polite enough to say, that if I would pass some months with him at Terpaling, we might practise together, and daily vary our amusements. I should learn from him the science of archery, and, in return, teach him the use of fire arms. I had an opportunity of exhibiting some skill with a rifle, but as it was a plain piece, I presented him with a fusee I had, which was better ornamented. It seems that the improvement of firelocks is unknown here, all their pieces being fitted with a match. While we were engaged in these sports, Gyap informed me, that there were men in Tibet, who could pass the deepest water courses in an erect posture, so as perfectly to preserve their arms from being touched by the water, and use them if it became necessary, as they sunk not deeper than the waist: this I conceived to be the art, of which I had heard, of treading the water; and it must, if practicable, be a useful military lesson. He mentioned also the dexterity with which an horseman here, would dismount his adversary, particularly when in pursuit, by means of a running noose.

Conversation, and various amusements, occupied our time, until we were called to partake of a repast. It was prepared in the pavilion, where we found Gyeung seated ready to receive us. Our benches, for they use no tables here, were abundantly covered with joints of cold meat, chiefly mutton; some of which had been dried by frost, some boiled, and some raw. Of the two first I could eat most heartily, but I could never conquer my prejudice against meat perfectly raw; and neither the example nor the praises of my friends, could at all prevail upon me to partake of their favourite dish, though Gyap, with much apparent relish, picked many a raw rib, clear to the bone. Our beverage was cold *chong*, a liquor which, in this country, is never taken warm. A desert of dried fruits, when the meat was taken away, concluded the repast. Gyeung fed sparingly, eating only fruit; she was restricted, she said, while suckling the Lama, from all animal food, as well as from the use of spirits, and she complained heavily of the deprivation.

The day was far advanced, when a servant appeared with some musical instruments. Gyap gave into my hand a flagelet, and desired me to use it. I was unable. He then took it, and accompanied Gyeung upon the cittaur, (a stringed instrument, something resembling a guitar) and they played several pleasing airs together. At length, Gyeung accompanied the instruments with her voice, which was by no means inharmonious; and I am not ashamed to own, that the song she sung, was more pleasing to my ear, than an Italian air. I could not but express myself highly gratified. Gyap regretted his inability to entertain me, with a greater variety of instrumental music, saying, that he was obliged to leave behind him his collection, on quitting Lassa. I could not avoid asking, by what means they acquired the variety of tunes I heard; and how the instruments, though so different in their nature, were made to coincide so well together? He told me, that their music was written down in characters, which they learnt. Nor could I doubt it; since how could they otherwise manage, in unison, the powerful bands of instruments, introduced to accompany their religious ceremonies, which I often heard joining together, while at their devotions, from the lowest tones to the loudest swell, with every varied modulation? I regret, that the shortness of my stay in Tibet, prevented my obtaining any accurate knowledge on this subject. The evening was now fast approaching: I took occasion, therefore, once more to express the gratification which their entertainment had afforded me; we then rose, and descended to the monastery. Gyap and Gyeung retired to the apartments of the Lama, and I went to those which were assigned to my accommodation.

I again waited upon Teshoo Lama, on Saturday, the 6th of December, to present some articles of curious workmanship, which I had brought for him from Bengal. He appeared most pleased with the mechanism of a small clock, and had it held up to him, watching for a long time the revolutions of the second hand. He admired it, but with gravity, and without any childish emotion. There was nothing in the ceremony, different from that of the first day's visit. The father and mother were present. After staying about half an hour, I retired, intending to return and take my leave in the afternoon.

The votaries of Teshoo Lama already began to flock, in great numbers, to pay their adorations to him. Few were yet admitted to his presence. Those who came, esteemed it a happiness to have him shewn to them from the window, particularly if they were able to make their prostrations before he was removed. There came this day, a party of Kilmauks, (Calmuc Tartars) for the purposes of devotion, and to make their offerings to the Lama. When I returned from visiting him, I saw them standing at the entrance of the square, in front of the palace, each with his cap off, his hands being placed together, elevated, and held even with his face. They remained upwards of half an hour in this attitude, their eyes being fixed upon the apartment of the Lama, and anxiety very visibly depicted in their countenances. At length, I imagine, he appeared to them, for they began all together by lifting up their hands, which were still closed, above their heads, then bringing them even with their faces, and afterwards lowering them to their breasts; then separating them, to assist them in sinking and rising, they dropped upon their knees, and struck their heads against the ground. This, with the same motions, was repeated nine times. They afterwards advanced to deliver their presents, consisting of tarreema[a], or talents of gold and silver, with the products of their country, to the proper officer; and when he had received them, they retired, apparently with much satisfaction.

Upon inquiry I learnt, that offerings made in this manner, are by no means unfrequent, and, in reality, constitute one of the most copious sources, from which the Lamas of Tibet derive their wealth.

No one thinks himself degraded, by performing these humiliations. The persons I have described, as coming for this devout purpose, were

[a] These are masses of pure bullion, which take the form of the crucible in which they are fused, and allowed to cool. No fixed standard regulates the quantity of metal in each. The value of the mass is estimated by its weight, which is engraved upon it. Those of silver usually vary in worth, from forty to fifty pounds.

attendant on a man of superior rank, who seemed to be more earnest and attentive than the rest, in the performance of the ceremony. He wore a rich satin garment lined with fox skins, and a cap with a tassel of scarlet silk, flowing from the centre of the crown upon the sides all round, and edged with a broad band of Siberian fur.

According to appointment, I went in the afternoon to make my last visit to Teshoo Lama. I received his dispatches for the Governor General, and from his parents two pieces of satin for the Governor, with many compliments.

They presented me with a vest lined with lambs' skins, making me many assurances of a long remembrance, and observing, that at this time Teshoo Lama was an infant, and incapable of conversing, but they hoped to see me again when he should be grown to maturity. I replied, that, by favour of the Lama, I might perhaps again visit this country; that I looked forward with anxiety to the time when he should mount the Musnud, and should then be extremely happy in the opportunity of paying him my respects. After some expressions and protestations of mutual regard, my visit was concluded. I received the scarfs, and took my leave, with a resolution to pursue my journey towards Bengal at the dawn of day.

CHAPTER X.

Quit the Monastery of Terpaling, on my Return towards Bengal—Annee Goomba—Annees, Nuns—Gylongs, Monks.—Cursory View of the interdicted Orders.—Polyandry—Influence on the Manners of the People—Tendency to check the too great Increase of Population—and prevent the inhuman Practice known to prevail in China.—Marriage Ceremonies.—Bleak and dreary Aspect of the Country—Rigour of the Winter—extreme Purity of the Atmosphere.—Precautions to secure the Surface of the Soil, and at the same Time enrich the Lands.—Course of the Seasons.—Dukque.—Lake Ramtchieu.—Skating—Solidity of the Ice—intense Severity of the Frost.—Shawl Goats.—Soomoonang—Punukka—Buxadewar—Rungpore.

As soon as the sun had risen, we quitted the gates of the monastery of Terpaling, and descended to the valley, crossing a narrow water-course, that divided the hill which we had left, from another on the opposite side: having ascended this, we came down soon after upon a wide plain, bounded on all sides by naked eminences; upon the summit of one of which, and on its southern aspect, was a large religious settlement of female devotees. This kind of edifice is styled an Annee Goomba. In this solitary station, like the Gylongs of

Terpaling, the Annees rise to their orisons, chant their mid-day mass, and having concluded their vespers, retire to their solitary cells. This association of nuns had often been mentioned to me, but in the course of my travels I had never yet seen one of them before, though many were said to be existing at that time, in various parts of Tibet. I would gladly have gone to visit these devotees in their secluded station, but it was at some distance from our road, and the loss of time dissuaded me from the attempt. Though nuns, the admission of male visitors among them during the day, is not prohibited; but no male is ever suffered to pass a night within the walls that enclose the Annees, any more than a female is, within those that surround the Gylongs.

That they should be thus drawn, in such multitudes, to these solitary retreats, from the business and the pleasures of the world, will less excite our surprise, when we reflect on the peculiar custom that prevails, with regard to the union of the sexes, in Tibet; a custom, at once different from the modes of Europe, where one female becomes the wife of one male; and opposite to the practice of Asia, at least of very great part of it, where one male assumes an uncontrolled despotism over many females, limiting his connexion with wives and concubines only by the extent of his resources. Here we find a practice equally strange, that of polyandry, if I may so call it, universally prevailing; and see one female, associating her fate and fortune with all the brothers of a family, without any restriction of age, or of numbers. The choice of a wife, is the privilege of the elder brother: and singular as it may seem, I have been assured, that a Tibetian wife is as jealous of her connubial rites, though thus joined to a numerous party of husbands, as the despot of an Indian zennana, is of the favours of his imprisoned fair. Under circumstances so unfavourable, it is no wonder that the business of increasing the species, is but coldly carried on.

Officers of state, as well as those who aspire to such distinctions, deem it, indeed, a business ill suited with their dignity, or duties, to attend to the propagation of their species; and retire from this essential care, abandoning it entirely to mere plebeians. Marriage, in fact, amongst them, seems to be considered rather as an odium, a heavy burden, the weight and obloquy of which, a whole family are disposed to lessen, by sharing it among them.

The number of husbands is not, as far as I could learn, defined or restricted within any limits; it sometimes happens, that, in a small family, there is but one male; and the number may seldom perhaps exceed that, which a native of rank, during my residence at Teshoo Loomboo, pointed out to me in a family resident in the neighbourhood, in which five brothers were then living together very happily, with one female, under the same connubial compact. Nor is this sort of league confined to the lower ranks of people alone; it is found also frequently in the most opulent families.

However this custom, which as a traveller I am obliged to notice, may intrinsically deserve reprobation, yet it must at the same time be allowed, that local laws very frequently result from local causes; and that, in consequence of the peculiar prejudices and opinions of one people, the same practice may be viewed in one country in the blackest light, which another people may not only see fit occasion to tolerate, but even to recommend. Thus we find, that neither the practice of polygamy in India, nor of polyandry in Tibet, is without its advocates.

The influence of this custom on the manners of the people, as far as I could trace, has not been unfavourable. Humanity, and an unartificial gentleness of disposition, are the constant inheritance of a Tibetian.

I never saw these qualities possessed by any people in a more eminent degree. Without being servilely officious, they are always obliging; the higher ranks are unassuming; the inferior, respectful in their behaviour; nor are they at all deficient in attention to the female sex; but, as we find them moderate in all their passions, in this respect, also, their conduct is equally remote from rudeness and adulation. Comparatively with their southern neighbours, the women of Tibet enjoy an elevated station in society. To the privileges of unbounded liberty, the wife here adds the character of mistress of the family, and companion of her husbands. The company of all, indeed, she is not at all times entitled to expect. Different pursuits, either agricultural employments, or mercantile speculations, may occasionally cause the temporary absence of each; yet whatever be the result, the profit of the labourer flows into the common store; and when he returns, whatever may have been his fortune, he is secure of a grateful welcome to a social home.

To descant upon established usages, that have existed far beyond the date of any written records, or the more obscure traces of tradition, with a view to discover their origin, or object, is indeed entering upon a field, which affords ample scope for ingenious and fanciful speculation; but under such circumstances, all the efforts of the speculatist, frequently tend only to raise new doubts, and involve the subject of inquiry in still more mysterious obscurity. Whether or not, at some remote period of time, when population was in its infancy, from the operation of some unknown cause, there existed so great a proportion of males to females in this nation, as rendered the single possession of one woman, a blessing too great for any individual to aspire to, and, in consequence, this compromise may have been adopted by general consent; or whether a too numerous population may have overburdened a meagre soil; I will leave to the determination of others, more able to decide on such a question. It is sufficient for me to mark manners as I find them.

But it certainly appears, that superabundant population, in an unfertile country, must be the greatest of all calamities, and produce eternal warfare, or eternal want. Either the most active, and the most able part of the community, must be compelled to emigrate, and to become soldiers of fortune, or merchants of chance; or else, if they remain at home, be liable to fall a prey to famine, in consequence of some accidental failure in their scanty crops. By thus linking whole families together in the matrimonial yoke, the too rapid increase of population was perhaps checked, and an alarm prevented, capable of pervading the most fertile region upon earth, and of giving birth to the most inhuman and unnatural practice, in the richest, the most productive, and the most populous country in the world. I allude to the empire of China; where a mother, not foreseeing the means of raising, or providing for, a numerous family, exposes her new-born infant to perish in the fields: a crime, however odious, by no means, I am assured, unfrequent. With this, the Tibetians never can be charged. Their custom, as it eventually operates against superabundant population, tends also to prevent domestic discords, arising from a division of family interests, and to concentrate all the spirit, and all the virtues, inherent in illustrious blood.

The ceremonies of marriage are neither tedious nor intricate in Tibet. Their courtships are carried on with little art, and quickly brought to a conclusion. The elder brother of a family, to whom the choice belongs, when enamoured of a damsel, makes his proposal to the parents. If his suit is approved, and the offer accepted, the parents, with their daughter, repair to the suitor's house, where the male and female acquaintance of both parties meet and carouse for the space of three days, with music, dancing, and every kind of festivity. At the expiration of this time, the marriage is complete. The priests of Tibet, who shun the society of women, have no share in these ceremonies, or in ratifying the obligation between the parties. Mutual consent is their only bond of union, and the parties present are witnesses to the contract, which, it seems, is formed indissolubly for life. The husband has it not in his power to rid himself of a troublesome companion, nor the wife to withdraw herself from the husband, unless indeed the same unison of sentiment that joined their hands, should prompt their separation; but in such a case, they are never left at liberty to form a new alliance. Instances of incontinency are rare, but if a married female be found to violate her compact, the crime is expiated by corporal punishment, and the favoured lover effaces the obloquy of his transgression by a pecuniary fine.

If, in general society, the males be sometimes chargeable with coldness towards the female sex, they cannot, therefore, be said with cynical severity, to forbid them all indulgence; since very precise chastity, before they marry, is not expected in the fair sex, though when they have once formed a contract, they are by no means permitted, with impunity, to break it.

We halted for the night, and pitched our tents near a small and solitary village.

The following morning we again proceeded on our route. Tibet does not exhibit, at this season of the year, either a rich or varied prospect; it is all a leafless, dreary scene, not a blade of grass, and scarcely any vestige of verdure is to be seen; one uniform russet brown covers alike the vallies and the hills. On the summits of the latter, in some situations, springs are seen arrested in their fall, and converted into solid monuments of ice, firmly fixed until the genial warmth of summer shall return to make them flow. Some of them, now in view, were of prodigious bulk and altitude, resembling immense columns, and they contributed greatly, together with the universal nakedness of both hills and vallies, to impress the traveller with an idea of the bleakness of the region, and the severity of the season.

The atmosphere, indeed, was now in an extreme degree keen and pure. During three months that I had passed in Tibet, I had not witnessed three cloudy days. The dryness of the soil, and scantiness of vegetation, contributes little towards charging the air with humidity. The atmosphere was clear even to brilliancy, and I had seen no fogs in Tibet since the day I entered it.

The dust, indeed, was for a short time extremely troublesome, but it is the practice of the husbandmen to cover the low lands in the vallies with water, immediately on the approach of winter, which incases their surface, as it were, with a sheet of ice, and prevents their being stripped of the soil, by violent winds. This method is reported to enrich the ground, a material advantage, as they here never use manure, and also to render it, upon the first approach of spring, ready to receive the plough. As soon as the land is prepared, they take the first favourable opportunity to sow it; frequent showers, and a powerful sun, contribute speedily to mature the crops. The autumn afterwards succeeds, which is clear and tranquil; the harvest is cut in a fair and settled season, and left long upon the ground to dry; when the corn is sufficiently hardened, a number of cattle are brought, a circle is cleared, and they are driven in a rank round a centre, to tread the grain from the ear, as fast as it is thrown under their feet; this, in Tibet, is the general mode of thrashing. Their course of cultivation is wheat, pease, and barley. Rice is the production of a more southern soil.

We came early in our march to-day to the post of Dukque, which I noticed in my journey to Teshoo Loomboo. Nothing afterwards occurred, in the course of our journey towards Bengal, which merits particular mention, except the extreme severity of cold, of which we soon became thoroughly sensible, and the extraordinary circumstance of finding large lakes frozen to a great depth, in so low a latitude as twenty-eight degrees. From the report I had heard, I took care that it should be early in the day when I approached the Ramtchieu: we encamped upon its banks, and passed great part of our time, while we remained at this station, upon our skates. This exercise was novel only to the few inhabitants of this solitary neighbourhood; the people who were with me, had already seen us skate at Tsondue; but though I had the superiority in one art, I found that they excelled in another: they were most excellent sliders.

The lake, on which we were, had been frozen over, I was informed, so early as October; but a violent wind soon after arose, which had broken the surface, and thrown the ice, in vast confused masses, upon its borders. A tranquil season then ensued, during which it became uniformly smooth, and it was now a most noble sheet of ice. There were, indeed, some vast cracks, of which I could not, with my cane, measure the depth; these were occasioned by the diminution of the water beneath, and the consequent sinking of the ice to rest upon its surface. When this was ascertained, I had no apprehensions in approaching close to them, and it afforded some variety in our amusement, to leap across them with our skates. A very strong and keen air prevailed while we continued upon the ice. It was great exercise to advance against it, but it required no effort to return; as, by expanding a handkerchief by way of a sail, I glided along upon my skates to a great distance with considerable velocity, without striking a stroke. We were sensible, while we remained abroad, of the benefit of exercise in preserving genial warmth; but when the day closed in, and we were obliged to retire within our tents, we found the cold intense. Though we kept a good fire burning all night, sufficient to line the upper surface of the tent, which was closed on all sides, with a thick cloud of smoke, yet all was insufficient to mitigate the severity of the frost; our breath congealed upon our whiskers, and it cost us some considerable time and pain to clear them of icicles.

It was our first care in the morning, to defend ourselves with our warmest clothing; and indeed our thickest garments were no more than necessary, to guard against the keen severity of the atmosphere. Yet here we saw multitudes of the valuable animal, whose coat affords materials for that exquisitely fine and beautiful manufacture, the shawl. They were feeding in large flocks, upon the thin dry herbage that covers these naked-looking hills. This is, perhaps, the most beautiful species amongst the whole tribe of goats; more so, in my opinion, than the Angola kind. Their colours were various; black, white, of a faint bluish tinge, and of a shade something lighter than a fawn. They have straight horns, and are of a lower stature than the smallest sheep in England. The material used for the manufacture of shawls, is of a light fine texture, and clothes the animal next the skin. A coarse covering of long hair grows above this, and preserves the softness of the inferior coat. This creature seems indebted, for the warmth and softness of its coat, to the nature of the climate it inhabits: upon removing some of them to the hot atmosphere of Bengal, they quickly lost their beautiful clothing, and a cutaneous eruptive humour soon destroyed almost all their coat. I was also unsuccessful in repeated trials, to convey this animal to England. It would neither endure the climate of Bengal, nor bear the sea: though some few of them, indeed, lived to land in England, yet they were in so weak a state, that they very shortly after perished.

We passed the summit of Soomoonang, that lofty range of mountains which forms the boundary of Tibet on the south, and divides it from Bootan, and hastened with our utmost speed to reach a milder region.

This we found at Punukka, the winter residence of the Daeb Raja, who received us with every mark of hospitality and friendship. Compared with the land we had left, we now beheld this garden of Lam' Rimbochay in high beauty, adorned with groves, crowded with rich loads of the finest oranges, citrons, and pomegranates. The mango and the peach tree had parted with their produce, but hoards of apples and of walnuts were opened for our gratification; and this vast profusion of ripe fruit, added to the temperature of the air, most gratefully convinced us of the prodigious disparity of climate, within so short a distance.

My stay with the Daeb Raja, at his favourite palace of Punukka, was not of long duration. I hastened to make all the arrangements that appeared necessary, or expedient, with regard to the object of my mission. The Raja gave me frequent opportunities of meeting him, as well within doors, as by invitation to walk with him in the gardens. Indeed I was treated by him with the greatest freedom and cordiality. He urged me strongly to pass a long time with him, extolling the beauty of the place, and the mild temperature of the weather; but I was obliged to decline the honour.

On the 30th of December I had my audience of leave, and received, at the Lama's hand, the valuable favour of a badge of thin crimson silk, over which various solemn incantations had been performed, and which was in future to secure for ever, my prosperity and success. Valuable as the present was, I fear I have unfortunately lost it. In the evening, I took a long farewell of all the officers of his court, and on the following day, departed for Bengal.

I found the Soobah of Buxadewar absent from that station, having taken up his residence in the valley of Chichacotta, for the winter season, where a temperature of weather prevailed, more mild and congenial even to a Booteea's constitution, than the rude region of his native mountains. I passed a day with him, for I could not resist his pressing solicitations; and on the next, I hastened to join the friends I had left the preceding year, when I departed from Bengal, who had kindly advanced, and formed a camp upon Calamatty plain, to meet me. We proceeded together the next day to Rungpore. I soon after received orders from the Governor General to advance without delay, and join him at Patna, in the province of Bahar. I had the satisfaction there to meet him, and to be honoured with his entire approbation of my conduct in the execution of the commission, which he had been pleased to confide to my charge. My official report of the success of my mission, will be found in the following pages.

PART III.

REPORT

DELIVERED TO

THE HON. WARREN HASTINGS, ESQ.

GOVERNOR GENERAL OF BENGAL,

UPON

THE RESULT OF MY MISSION TO THE COURT OF

TESHOO LOOMBOO.

TIBET.

THE

HON. WARREN HASTINGS, ESQ.

GOVERNOR GENERAL, &c. &c.

HONOURABLE SIR, *Patna, 2d March*, 1784.

BEING now returned from the service on which you were pleased to direct me to proceed, I take the earliest opportunity of communicating to you the progress and result of my mission, in hope that my conduct will be favourably judged, with all the indulgence due to a limited experience, and the novelty of the regions which I was commanded to visit.

I will not presume to occupy your time, by a treatise on the ancient state of Tibet, or an unimportant detail of the peculiar manners and customs of the people; but shall beg leave to follow the example of my predecessor, by enumerating such events as have happened since his return to Bengal, and which seem connected with, or in their nature calculated to affect, your designs in this quarter.

At the time of Mr. Bogle's deputation, Tibet was in a state of perfect tranquillity: Teshoo Lama was then exercising the functions of his office, respected and obeyed through all the region of Tartary; nor was his influence bounded, but by the limits of the extensive empire of China. The Tartars who live in tents, and the natives of Kilmâk and Khumbâk, continually resorted in multitudes, to pay their adorations at his shrine. Even Taranaut and Dalai Lama held him in so great deference and respect, that their votaries looked up to him, as the head and protector of their common faith.

The sanctity of his character, and the wisdom of his administration, had so far diffused his reputation, and exalted his name, that the Emperor of China, anxious to see so renowned a personage, repeatedly solicited him to make a visit to his court. The Lama would willingly have excused himself, but he could not evade the importunity of the Emperor, who had made the most magnificent preparations for his accommodation on the journey, and his reception at Pekin. He accordingly set out, though, from the concurrent testimony of all his people, it was with extreme reluctance; but he arrived in safety in China, where he was received with the highest respect, even the Emperor himself advancing from his capital to meet him. During his residence at the Emperor's court, both his brother, the Regent, and Soopoon Choomboo, his favourite and cup-bearer, who accompanied him, assured me, that the Lama was not unmindful of his connection with the government of Bengal; on the contrary, he took several occasions of representing, in the strongest terms, the particular amity which subsisted between the Governor General and himself. They add, that his conversations had even influenced the Emperor to resolve upon commencing, through the Lama's mediation, an immediate correspondence with his friend. Such indeed was the confidence and esteem which the Emperor manifested for Teshoo Lama, that he promised him a full compliance with whatever he should ask; yet in this instance, the Emperor's liberality, did not exceed the Lama's humility of heart. For he preferred no great demand, and even declined the acceptance of an addition to his territory; requesting only, that the Emperor would cause the administration of the different governments, as had been anciently the custom in Tibet, to be restored to the Lamas; that they might be invested with all the powers which, in their respective stations, they had formerly enjoyed; and particularly, that he himself might be at liberty to grant admission into Tibet, to whatever persons he chose, without control.

To all this, the Emperor readily consented; and that his authority might be complete, he caused his own seal to be delivered to Teshoo Lama, and even took steps for the recal of the Raja, who had been appointed by the court of China, to reside at Lassa. The high honours, and extraordinary distinction, shewn to Teshoo Lama in China, raised the jealousy of some, and the admiration of all ranks of people. But most unfortunately, at this interesting period, it happened, in the plenitude of his influence and power, he was seized suddenly with a violent disorder, which after three days terminated in his death.

I need not enlarge on the vast accession of dignity and consequence to his character, that would have been naturally derived from the honours rendered him in China, and the homage paid him by the inhabitants of the countries through which he passed, had he returned in safety to Tibet. But I must beg leave to observe, that the unfortunate accidents which prevented the proposed deputation of Mr. Bogle, a second time to Teshoo Loomboo, and the untimely death of the Lama himself, were events in themselves, not unlikely to destroy the effect of every former effort; sufficient to revive in the minds of the Tibetians, naturally averse to innovation, all their former distrust, and to interrupt the growing confidence with which they had been so successfully inspired. Yet, in some measure to compensate for these disadvantages, the death of Gesub Rimbochay, offered a new prospect of opening that communication which was the objest of our wishes; for he was remarkable for the turbulence and activity of his disposition, and his violent enmity to all intercourse with the English. Unhappily, however, the expectations formed from this event were defeated by his successor, who succeeded to his place with the same prejudices, and, studying the disposition of the people, has had a view to establish himself in office by a conformity to popular opinions, knowing that the time of his authority was limited and uncertain. His conduct has, moreover, been actuated by a strong spirit of jealousy and animosity, in consequence of Teshoo Lama's negociation in China, through which, he narrowly escaped being deprived of his authority. From the combined influence of all these motives, he is still induced to neglect no occasion that offers, of thwarting the designs of the government of Teshoo Loomboo.

Since the subjection of Tibet to the Chinese yoke, the influence of the Lamas, who were once supreme, has been much weakened by the appointment of an officer to reside at Lassa, the capital of the kingdom, who is invested with the government, and supreme control over the country. The cause which first suggested the expediency of placing such a check over the Lamas, exists no more; and the present Emperor, a votary of their faith, and naturally jealous of their dignity, seems persuaded of this truth, from a conviction of their attachment to his person, and their acknowledgment of the supremacy of the Chinese government. The negociations of Teshoo Lama confirm this opinion, who obtained a promise from the Emperor, to withdraw the officer of his appointment from Lassa, and to commit the government of the country to the management of the Lamas. Orders were consequently issued for the recal of Nimoheïm, who succeeded Gesub Rimbochay, but the decease of Teshoo Lama occasioned their suspension. However, as the time of Raja's Nimoheïm's government is to cease soon after Teshoo Lama shall be seated on the musnud, it is then expected, that the renewal of his application to the Emperor, will be followed by the complete performance of the promises made to him in China; that Dalai Lama and himself will be invested accordingly with the uncontrolled government of the country, and that the temporal authority of these religious pontiffs will, in consequence, rise to its former dignity and splendour.

I will not venture to advance my own surmises, on the probability of the Emperor's consenting to so important a measure as this; but perhaps I shall be excused in repeating the opinion of those, who are more competent to judge of his disposition, from the circumstance of having resided a twelvemonth at his court; I mean, the late Lama's brother, Regent Chanjoo Cooshoo, Punjun Irtinnee Nimoheim, and his confidant Soopoon Choomboo, Cooshoo Shapie, who entertain not the shadow of a doubt of the Emperor's receding from his word, but assure me of their belief, that he will ratify the promises made to the former Teshoo Lama, the moment the present Lama is capable of renewing the application, when the proposed regulations will immediately take place.

The success of your designs is too obviously, and too intimately, connected with this event, to need any comment. If Teshoo Lama shall be made to resume the plans projected by him in his presumed pre-existence, for the recovery of the prerogatives annexed to the office of Lama; the same consistency of conduct will certainly prompt him to look back to the negociations of 1775, to the proposal of a free intercourse of trade between Tibet and Bengal, which then coincided with his desires, and which seems at last to have been one motive, and object, of his solicitude for the extension of his privileges.

I am aware that it may be asked, why the agents of government under Teshoo Lama, were not dismissed with the promised powers? and this omission, I think, may be satisfactorily accounted for, from the consternation, and confusion, in which his sudden death necessarily involved all his attendants, depriving them of the ability to pursue proper measures, for the accomplishment of their designs. I believe the fact is, that they were incompetent to the attempt; for, being merely the agents of Teshoo Lama, they rightly reflected, that their intercessions with the Emperor would have little weight, when their superior was no more. Prudence therefore enjoined their silence.

And probably, their nearest concern was a speedy return to Tibet, fearful, lest so great an event should produce a revolution in the government, injurious to their interests, or subversive of their power.

If they were deterred from a personal application to the Emperor, when present at his court, other considerations have since influenced them to suspend, for a time, all further solicitation, which can only be urged with propriety and effect by Teshoo Lama himself; and, they say, that at the age of three years, he will be perfectly qualified to exert the proper means for accomplishing this design. I have found in the Regent, the best dispositions for encouraging, and assisting, by the authority he possesses, the proposed plans of commercial intercourse; but being neither so able, nor so decided in his character as the former Lama, he is cautious of avowedly and publicly sanctioning a measure, which might possibly raise up some inveterate enemies against him, in the Chinese administration.

Teshoo Lama, from his respectable character, and superior talents, was peculiarly well qualified to obviate popular prejudices against new schemes, to reconcile the Tibetians to an alliance with Europeans, and to remove those jealous apprehensions, which, in a greater or less degree, are cherished by every Asiatic state, in consequence of the vast and accumulating power of the English.

As Tartary, until it became united under the Chinese dominion, was constantly harassed by foreign invasion, by religious feuds, and by intestine broils, its inhabitants are intimidated from entering into new connections, as affording, in their apprehensions, an inlet to war and devastation. Having, by repeated revolutions, been accustomed to submit to a variety of successive usurpers, the powerful principle of independence is now nearly extinguished, and they are fitted for the abject slaves of despotic tyranny; without firmness to assert their rights, and without resolution to resist the pressure of a foreign yoke, however feeble the power by which it is imposed.

Under less authority, therefore, than the sanction of a Lama, your plans cannot be pushed to any great extent. They were first taken up by a man, who dared to deviate from the narrow policy of implicit obedience; who had ability to lead the affections of his own subjects, and command the support of the neighbouring states; and who was urged to extend his connections, as well by an attention to the interests of those over whom he ruled, as by the impulse of ambition. Such was Teshoo Lama. His successor will doubtless assume the office, with strong prepossessions in favour of the same project; and I confidently expect that he will be taught to feel, and to indulge the pride of having first encouraged in his pre-existence, and perfected in his regeneration, a plan evidently designed for universal benefit. The Regent's letter will, I presume, be the best criterion, by which to judge of his dispositions; though it may be observed, that, in receiving me at this time into the country, he has acted rather according to his private sentiments, than in conformity with the wishes of the government of Lassa. Dalai Lama himself, indeed, has not been averse to my admission; but there is a bias on the government, an external force, that turns it from its natural course, and hinders it from pursuing the current of its own interests and inclinations.

Tibet has, from time immemorial, been the resort of merchants.

Necessity has begotten a commerce with foreign countries, which, however, is but languidly conducted, by a people naturally slothful and indolent. The soil and climate of Tibet being favourable to the production of few commodities, render it a proper field for a variety of mercantile projects. But an example of industry is wanting: when men once become acquainted with the pleasures of luxury, and the profits of commerce, they will be roused from their apathy; and new objects of opulence and ease, of which they never dreamt before, being presented to their view, will raise in them a desire of a more splendid way of life than their ancestors enjoyed, and will stimulate them to an investigation and improvement of their natural resources, which at present are, even by themselves, but imperfectly understood. The form of government, which is arbitrary, is inimical to industry and enterprize. Both in Tibet and Bootan, the first member of the state is the chief merchant, and his prerogative, in this capacity, is of great importance to him; for he is invested by it, with advantages above the common adventurer, in the right of commanding the labour of the people, whom the laws compel to bear burdens, and to exert themselves in various ways, when called upon by the mandate of their chief. Hence, emulation is suppressed, and trade monopolized by the sovereign, and by a few other persons in the first offices under government, who are indulged with a limited privilege, and whose traffic is chiefly confined to clothing and provisions, to articles which are in constant demand, and which find at all times a rapid sale. Though the soil of Tibet is, in its greatest extent, unimprovable by cultivation; and though the features of the country are strongly expressive of poverty, yet, whatever is wanting to the people from a defect in fertility, or in the skill of their artists, they possess ample means of obtaining, through the abundant riches of the earth. Their mines and minerals are capable of opening to them such inexhaustible sources of wealth, as to be alone sufficient to purchase every thing of which they stand in need, though their wants are numerous, as they are ignorant of all but the first arts of life, agriculture and clothing.

The advantages resulting from this trade, were once greatly in favour of Bengal. The commotions and disturbances by which the kingdom of Nipal was long distracted, until its ultimate subjugation under one chief, by destroying the security of merchants, interrupted the commerce between Tibet and Bengal; and that country being then the only known channel of communication, Bengal lost ground in trade, which it has been since found difficult to regain. The advantages arising from the present limited commerce, are enjoyed by a few opulent Goseins, and by an agent residing at Teshoo Loomboo, on the joint concern of Cashmeery Mull and Gopal Doss. I beg leave to refer to the annexed paper, for a statement of the articles composing it.

The returns have invariably been made in gold dust, silver, tincal, and musk; the value of which articles always bears proportion to the quantity in the market. The value of gold and silver in Tibet, is very variable, depending on the product of the former from the mines. At this time, a pootree[a] of gold dust sells for twenty-one indermillees[b]. A few years ago, during the prevalence of an excessive drought, the

[a] Bulse. [b] A base coin struck in Nipal, of the value of about one-third of a rupee, and current in Tibet, where local prejudices prevent the establishment of a mint.

earth, by cracking and opening in uncommon chasms, is said to have discovered such an abundance of gold, that the quantity collected, reduced the price of a pootree, to nine indermillees. As these precious metals are merely representatives of labour, and commodities, there will consequently follow great fluctuations in the profits of commerce; the balance, however, will at all times be found on the side of the merchant.

Those articles of trade which are next in importance, amongst the natural productions of Tibet, are, musk, tincal, goats' hair, and rock salt. The first of these articles used to be transported through the country of the Choubeis Rajas, and through Nipal, by the way of Benares, into the upper parts of Hindostan, and the dominions of the Marrattas; but as musk of late has gained much reputation in medicine, and as there is reason to believe, that none but what is greatly adulterated, finds its way to Europe, it, doubtless, must be an important object with the faculty, to receive it in its native purity.

Bootan, Nipal, Bengal, and Hindostan, are supplied with tincal from Tibet. Its value is little more than that of the labour employed in digging it from the bed of a lake, in which it is deposited, at the distance of about fifteen days' journey from Teshoo Loomboo.

The hair of the goats is carried to Cashmeer, and is that superior sort, from which shawls are manufactured.

The demand for salt, is in the consumption of Nipal and Bootan.

Here are also several mines of lead, but, as it is a metal that enters not into their common utensils of life, and is of little use in the country, they are totally neglected. As lead, however, is generally found to contain a greater or less mixture of silver, and as there is but one mine of this metal, known in Europe to be entirely free from it, it is at least not improbable, that the lead ores of Tibet are rich in silver; and that the smelting of them for the silver, the manner of doing which is totally unknown to the natives, might be attended with very great advantage.

Here are also mines of cinnabar, which they use for colouring, in paint, and which contains a great proportion of mercury, that they know not how to extract.

The copper mines furnish materials for the manufactory of idols, and all the ornaments disposed about the monasteries, on which gilding is bestowed.

A very small quantity of specie, and that of a base standard, is current in Tibet. It is the silver coin of Nipal, here termed indermillee; each is in value worth about one-third of a sicca rupee, and they are cut into halves, third parts, and quarters. This, which is the only money, serves to obtain the exigencies of life, but never enters into important contracts in the larger concerns of trade; in all such transactions, the equivalent is made in bullion, that is, talents[c] of gold and silver, which bear a value, in proportion to the purity and specific gravity of the metal.

The commerce between Tibet and China, is carried on principally at a garrison town, on the western frontier of China, named Sinning, or Silling: thither merchants resort from Tibet with their manufacture, viz.

[c] Tarreema, bearing the shape of the crucible in which the metal is fused, and allowed to cool.

a thin cloth resembling frieze, but rather of a more open texture, gold dust, and some other commodities procured from Bengal; which they exchange for tea, silver bullion, brocades, and fruit. In these articles an extensive trade is carried on; and I have been assured that, on the territory of Teshoo Loomboo alone, tea, to the amount of five or six lacs of rupees[d], is annually consumed. From hence too, Bootan is supplied with tea, which is in the same general use there. For further particulars of the commerce with Tibet, I beg leave to refer to the annexed comparative statement.

Studious to ensure, by every possible means, the success of my deputation, I was extremely desirous of proceeding to Lassa, that I might endeavour to conciliate the good will of the chiefs in power, towards our nation, and to obtain their sanction, to a free intercourse between Tibet and Bengal: but I was prevented, by a consideration of the present state of that government, and strongly dissuaded by the Regent Punjun Irtinnee, from making the attempt. He promised to inform himself of the sentiments and wishes of Dalai Lama, in regard to a connection with the English, and afterwards to communicate them to you. Whenever a regular intercourse takes place, between the agents of the government of Bengal and the chiefs of Tibet, I shall consider it as the sure basis of an intercourse with China; and it will probably be, by the medium of the former, that we shall be enabled to arrive at Pekin.

I have not eagerly urged those secondary advantages, that offered themselves to my choice, because I would not, by engaging in any

[d] Sixty or seventy thousand pounds sterling.

imperfect scheme, render abortive the endeavours towards carrying into execution, the more important object of your plan; which I conceived to be an immediate intercourse between the English, and the natives of Tibet. I have obtained the Regent Chanjoo Cooshoo's promise of encouragement to all merchants, natives of India, that may be sent to traffic in Tibet, on behalf of the government of Bengal. No impediment, therefore, now remains in the way of merchants, to prevent their carrying their commercial concerns into Tartary. Your authority alone, is requisite to secure them the protection of the Regent of Teshoo Loomboo, who has promised to grant free admission into Tibet, to all such merchants, natives of India, as shall come recommended by you; to yield them every assistance requisite for the transport of their goods from the frontiers of Bootan; and to assign them a place of residence for vending their commodities, either within the monastery, or, should it be considered as more eligible, in the town itself.

I did not deem it consistent with the spirit of your designs, at the present period, to be importunate for greater privileges than these, to native traders: such as I have obtained will, I trust, be competent to the purpose, of opening the much wished for communication; and as this mode coincided with the Regent's wishes, it appeared to me better to adopt it, than to check the opening trade with a load of taxes, and a variety of embarrassing forms. Let merchants first learn the way, taste the profit, and establish the intercourse; and afterwards the traffic may bear a tax, which if laid upon it in its infancy, might suppress its growth. These concessions, in which the Regent readily acquiesced, will, I presume, be considered as most material, towards reviving the trade, between Bengal and Tibet. For as security and protection are the first essential requisites to the establishment of commerce, so profit will prove its best encouragement; it will most powerfully stimulate the industry of the merchant, who is engaged in so advantageous an undertaking, and impel him to pursue his plans to the greatest possible extent.

To give full force to the license I have obtained, nothing but form is wanting; and, independently of the novelty of written treaties, formalities almost unknown in Tibet, I declined soliciting the Regent to execute such an agreement, because it could be no longer valid, than during the minority of Teshoo Lama; it must have been revocable by him, the moment he should be admitted into his office, and could never be considered as binding, even upon the government which is upheld by his authority, and conducted under the sanction of his name. For the Regent possesses no independent powers, but is the ostensible instrument of administration, under the guidance of his supreme, the Lama: and even supposing the Regent possessed of adequate authority to enforce a treaty of commerce, yet to have pressed him to the conclusion of one, I thought, would have been to abandon the great object in view; for I considered the agency of natives of India, stationed at so remote a distance from control, or any check to restrain their conduct, as a very dubious reliance, and that the benefits resulting from it, would be found, at best, extremely precarious. These reasons suggested to me the expediency, of waving the attempt to secure, by written agreement, those privileges to merchants, for which the Regent pledged his word; especially as the prospect of resuming our negociations is held to be not very distant, and at that period, it is not improbable that a factory may be established, under the guidance of an Englishman. This, I presume, will be deemed the most eligible and certain method, of conducting the commercial interests of the Company, on a respectable footing, and with adequate success.

The regulations for carrying the commerce of the Company through the dominions of Bootan, by means of the agency of native merchants, were settled by the treaty entered into by Mr. Bogle, in the year 1775. The Daeb Raja having acknowledged to me, the validity of that treaty, it became unnecessary to insist on the execution of another; since no new privileges and immunities appear to be requisite, until the commerce can be established on a different footing.

With respect to the views and interests of the Raja of Bootan, by whose concurrence alone, the proposed commercial intercourse with Tibet can be made to flourish, I should be sorry to suggest a doubt, of its ever receiving a check from any conduct in that government, of an hostile tendency. During the long interval I necessarily passed in Bootan, I had an opportunity to judge of the Raja's disposition; and, if an inference may be drawn from the particular civilities and attention he shewed me, while residing with him, I should conclude, that he has a most entire confidence in the good faith and friendly disposition of your government towards him. These favourable sentiments, even if the interests of the Booteeas were not so intimately interwoven with their connection with the English, there is every reason to believe are very far from the probability of a change. The present Daeb Raja, who is related by blood to a very numerous and powerful family, was solicited, it is said, on the decease of Daeb Ruba, to take upon himself the cares of government. He complied with the application; and, by a coalition of offices, became at once the civil and religious ruler. Having now possessed an undivided and uncontrolled influence, as head of affairs, both ecclesiastical and political, for five years, he has had the opportunity of placing many of his relations in the most important offices under that government. He has besides taken care to settle the reversion of the administration in his own family, by having lately nominated his nephew, Lam' Ghassatoo, who is now an infant in arms, for his successor, and by causing him to be publicly invested with the Raaj. However he is yet looked up to as the real ruler, and doubtless will continue to be so, during the minority of the infant Raja; and indeed, as Lama, he will always have a right to inspect and direct the conduct of the reigning Raja.

When hostilities had ceased to distract the Company's possessions; when peace had restored security to commerce, and allowed accumulating revenues, to replenish a weakened treasury; it became with me an object of the highest ambition, at this bright æra of the Company's affairs, to add to their prosperity, by opening a new channel for the extension of their commerce. If I have fallen short of the general expectation, I trust the failure will not be imputed to a want of zeal; no exertion has been neglected which my humble talents qualified me to use. The impediments that existed, it will be observed, were entirely independent of my conduct, and such as it was impossible for me to take any effectual measures to obviate. Affairs being then in such a position, we can only have recourse to fair conjecture, and there is reason to hope that the natural revolution of human affairs, together with the probable course of events, will conspire to remove the obstructions to a free intercourse between the governments of Bengal and Tibet, and to restore the advantages which Bengal has lost. In the expectation of such an event, our best reliance is not merely on the friendly disposition of the present government of Teshoo Loomboo, but also on the superstitious doctrines of the Tibet faith; which, whilst it immortalizes the soul of the Lama upon earth, and admits its transmigration from one corporeal tenement to another, until the end of time, perpetuates also its dispositions and its prejudices. The usual proof of the identity of a regenerated Lama, is an early recognition of the possessions, acquaintances, and transactions of his pre-existence. I am therefore of opinion, that the new Lama will be taught to recur to the connections of the former Teshoo Lama, as one of the strongest marks that can denote his identity, and facilitate his acceptation. And here I ground my hope on presumptions built upon the tenets of their faith, which is the basis on which their government itself is constructed. Were they to adopt a different conduct, they would necessarily abandon the most sacred and immutable positions of their religion, and expose it to every degrading imputation, which is calculated to rob it of its honours, and lay it open to the reproach, or derision, attendant on detected imposition.

During my residence in Tibet it was an object I had much at heart to obtain an interview with the infant Teshoo Lama. But in the Emperor of China's command, requiring his guardians to keep him in the strictest privacy, and prohibiting, indiscriminately, the admission of all persons to his presence, I found an obstacle almost insurmountable; yet the Regent, mindful of the amity subsisting between the Governor and himself, and unwilling, I believe, by any act, to hazard its interruption, at length consented to grant me that extraordinary indulgence.

As the meeting was attended with very singular and striking circumstances, I could not help noting them with most particular attention; and though the repetition of such facts, interwoven and blended as they are with superstition and folly, may expose me to the imputation of extravagant exaggeration, yet I should think myself reprehensible in suppressing them. While, therefore, I divest myself of all prejudice, and assume the character of a faithful narrator, I hope, however tedious the detail, I propose to enter into, may be found, it will be at least received with candour and attention, by those for whose perusal and information it is intended[d]. It is indeed important, were it only to mark that strong feature in the national character, of implicit homage to their great religious sovereign, and to exemplify the very uncommon, I may almost say, unheard of effects, of early tuition. I shall perhaps, be still more fully justified in making this relation, by adverting to that very extraordinary assurance given me by the Regent, but a few days before my departure from his court; which, without further introduction, I shall beg leave literally to recite. At an interview with which he indulged me, after having given me my audience of leave, he said, "I had yesterday a vision of our tutelary deity, and to me, it was a day replete with much interesting and important

[d] Page 333, *et seq.*

matter. This guardian power, who inspires us with his illuminations on every momentous and great occasion, indulged me with a divination, from which I have collected, that every thing will be well. Set your heart at rest; for though a separation is about to take place between us, yet our friendship will not cease to exist; but through the favour of interposing Providence, you may rest assured it will increase, and terminate eventually in that which will be for the best."

I should have paid less regard to so strange an observation, had it not been for this reason, that, however strange their doctrines may be found, yet I judge, they are the best foundation on which we can fix our dependance; since superstition, combining with inclination, to implant such friendly sentiments in their minds, will ever constitute the strongest barrier for their preservation. If opposed to the deep-rooted prejudices of a people, no plan can reasonably be expected to succeed; if it agree with them, success must probably be the result.

I now beg leave to close the present address; and, though the success of my undertaking has not equalled my own wishes, yet I derive to myself some consolation from the assurance, that I shall be acquitted of blame, or negligence, in the execution of your orders; and, permit me to add, I wait with the utmost solicitude, the judgment that shall be passed upon my conduct.

I have the honour to be,

&c. &c. &c.

SAMUEL TURNER.

A LIST OF THE USUAL ARTICLES OF COMMERCE,

BETWEEN

TIBET AND THE SURROUNDING COUNTRIES.

Tibet exports to China,	*China to Tibet.*
Gold dust,	Gold and Silver brocades,
Diamonds,	Plain silks,
Pearls,	Satins,
Coral,	Black teas, of four or five different sorts,
A small quantity of Musk,	Tobacco,
Woollen cloths, the manufacture of Tibet,	Silver bullion,
Lamb skins,	Quicksilver,
Ood, or Otter skins, which are brought from Bengal.	Cinnabar,
	Some China ware,
	Trumpets, Cymbals, and other musical instruments.
	Furs, *viz.*
	Sable,
	Ermine,
	Black fox,
	Dried fruits of various sorts.

This trade of barter is carried on at Silling, a garrison town on the western frontier of China.

Tibet to Nipal.	*Nipal to Tibet.*
Rock salt, Tincal, Gold dust.	Specie, Coarse cotton cloths, Guzzie, Rice, Copper.

Tibet to Bengal.	*Bengal to Tibet.*
Gold dust, Musk, Tincal.	NIPAL is the principal channel, through which English commodities, and the produce of Bengal are conveyed, of which the following is a list. Broad cloth, and especially the inferior sorts, of which the colours in most request are yellow and scarlet; Some few trinkets, such as, Snuff boxes, Smelling bottles, Knives, Scissars, Optic glasses; Of spices, Cloves are most saleable. No sort of spice is used for culinary purposes. Cloves are a principal ingredient in the composition of the perfumed rods, which men of rank keep constantly burning in their presence. Nutmegs, Sandal wood, Pearls,

Bengal to Tibet, continued.

Emeralds,
Sapphires,
Pheirosa, or Lapis lazuli,
Coral,
Jet,
Amber,
Chaunk shells,
Kimkaubs; those of Guzerat are most valued;
Malda cloths,
Guzzie,
Rungpore leather,
Tobacco,
Indigo,
Ood, or Otter skins.

Tibet to Bootan.

Gold-dust,
Tea,
Woollen cloths, the manufacture of Tibet,
Salt.

Bootan to Tibet.

English broad cloth,
Rungpore leather,
Tobacco,
Coarse cotton cloths, Guzzie, &c.
Paper,
Rice,
Sandal wood,
Indigo,
Munjeet.

With Assam, there is no trade or intercourse.

Tibet to Luddauk.	*Luddauk to Tibet.*
The fine Hair of the Goats, of which shawls are manufactured.	LUDDAUK is the mart between Cashmeer and Teeshoo Loomboo. Gamboge, Shawls, Dried Fruits. Apricots, Kishmishes, Raisins, Currants, Dates, Almonds, Saffron.
	Khumbauk to Tibet.
	Horses, Dromedaries, Bulgar hides.

A beneficial traffic is carried on with Lassa, by exchanging Gold dust for Silver bullion.

The rate of carriage from Phari to Teshoo Loomboo, for the hire of one beast of burden, that carries two hundred weight, is three sicca rupees.

PART IV.

SOME ACCOUNT

OF THE

VEGETABLE AND MINERAL PRODUCTIONS

OF

BOOTAN AND TIBET,

BY

MR. ROBERT SAUNDERS, SURGEON.

SOME ACCOUNT[a], &c.

May 11 *and* 12, 1783. *Road to Buxaduar*[b].

THE tract of country from Bahar[c] to the foot of the hills, contains but few plants that are not common to Bengal. Pine-apples, mango tree, jack and saul timber, are frequently to be met with in the forests and jungles. Find many orange trees towards the foot of the hills, of a very good sort, and bearing much fruit. Saw a few lime trees, and found three different species of the sensitive plant. One species is used medicinally by the natives of Bengal, in fevers; it is a powerful astringent, and bitter: another, is the species from which terra japonica is made; a medicine, the history of which we are but lately made acquainted with. The third species is well known as the sensitive plant, and common in Bengal.

The country, from Bahar to the foot of the mountains, to which we

[a] Printed in the Philosophical Transactions, Vol. LXXIX.

N. B. The orthography of the names of places in the following pages differing, in some instances, from what has been adopted in the foregoing work, the mode hitherto made use of, resulting from example, analogy, and attentive observation, when a variation occurs, is always noted at the bottom of the page.

[b] Buxadewar. [c] Cooch Bahar.

approach without any ascent, is rendered one of the most unhealthy parts of India, from a variety of causes.

The whole, a perfect flat, is at all times wet and swampy, with a luxuriant growth of reeds, long grass, and underwood, in the midst of stagnated water, numerous frogs, and insects. The exhalations, from such a surface of vegetable matter and swamps, increased by an additional degree of heat from the reflection of the hills, affect the air to a considerable extent, and render it highly injurious to strangers, and European constitutions.

The thermometer at the foot of the hill, mid-day 86°, fell to 78° at two o'clock, the time we reached Buxaduar, and that hour of the day when it is generally highest.

The soil and appearance of the ground, in ascending the hill, are materially changed. See many loose sparry stones, and rock containing iron: Two springs, conducted from a distant height by spouts, are very pure and good water, without any mineral impregnation. The mountains in view covered with forests of trees, rendered useless from their inaccessibility: those peculiar to the country, are known to the natives by the names of Boumbshi, Toumbshi, and Sindeshi; besides saul timber, bamboo, and plantains.

May 12 *to* 21. *Buxaduar.* Many of the plants peculiar to Bengal, require nursing at Buxaduar. There is one very good banian tree. In the jungles, met with the ginger, and a very good sort of yam; saw some pomegranate trees in good preservation; shallots in great perfection; a species of the Lychnis, Arum, Asclepias, natives of more northern situations, and of little use; a bad sort of raspberry, and a species of the Gloriosa. The plantains in use below, do not thrive here. In the jungles they have a plantain tree, producing a very broad leaf, with which they cover their huts; but the fruit is not eaten. See many weeds and long grass, more common to Bengal than any other parts of Boutan.

From the 15th to the 22d, the rains were almost incessant at Buxaduar. Our people became unhealthy, and were attacked with fevers, which, if neglected in the beginning, proved obstinate quartans. This was the case with several of the natives, whom I had an opportunity of seeing. They scarcely, however, admit that Buxaduar is unhealthy at any season of the year. After allowing for their prejudice, and the possibility of the natives suffering but little from the bad seasons, I cannot help thinking that Buxaduar must be unhealthy, at least to strangers, from the month of May till towards the end of September. It lies high, but is overtopped by the surrounding mountains, covered with forests of trees, and underwood. In all climates, where the influence of the sun is great, this is a never-failing cause of bad air. The exhalation that takes place from so great a surface in the day time, falls, after sunset, in the form of dew, rendering the air raw, damp, and chilly, even in the most sultry climates.

The thermometer at Buxaduar was never, at two o'clock in the afternoon, above 82°, or below 73°.

In the neighbourhood of Buxaduar, there are several excellent springs of water, some of them with less impregnation of any sort than I ever met with; the nicest test, scarcely produced the separation of a sensible quantity of earthy matter. Such waters are generally to be distinguished by the taste, which is insipid and unpleasant. When these springs could be traced to their source, they sunk the thermometer eight or ten degrees below the temperature of the atmosphere.

May 22 and 23. In ascending the hill from Buxaduar, there is to be seen much of an imperfect quartz, of various forms and colour, having in some places the appearance of marble; but from chemical experiments, it was found to possess very different properties. This sort of quartz, when of a pure white, and free from any metallic colouring matter, is used as an ingredient in porcelain. I have not seen any that promises to answer that purpose, better than what is to be met with, in the mountains near Buxaduar. It is known to mineralists in that state, by the name of quartz gritstone. The rock which forms the basis of these mountains, dips in almost every direction, and is covered with a rich and fertile soil, but in no place level enough to be cultivated. Many European plants are to be met with on the road to Murishong; many different sorts of mosses, fern, wild thyme, peaches, willow, chickweed, and grasses common to the more southern parts of Europe; nettles, thistles, dock, strawberry, raspberry, and many destructive creepers, some peculiar to Europe.

Murishong[d] is the first pleasant and healthy spot to be met with on this side of Boutan. It lies high, and much of the ground about it, is cleared and cultivated; the soil, rich and fertile, produces good crops. The only plant now under culture, is a species of the polygonum of Linnæus, producing a triangular seed, nearly the size of barley, and the common food of the inhabitants. It was now the beginning of

[d] Murichom.

their harvest; and the ground yields them, as in other parts of Boutan, a second crop of rice. Here are to be found in the jungles, two species of the laurus of Linnæus; one known by the name of the bastard cinnamon. The bark of the root of this plant, when dried, has very much the taste and flavour of cinnamon; it is used medicinally by the natives. The chenopodium, producing the semen santonicum, or wormseed, a medicine formerly in great character, and used in those diseases from which it is named, is common here.

Found in the neighbourhood of this place, all the European plants we had met with on the road. The ascent from Buxaduar to Murishong is upon the whole great, with a sensible change in the state of the air.

May 25. On the road to Chooka[e] found all the Murishong plants, cinnamon tree, willow, and one or two firs; strawberries every where and very good, and a few bilberry plants.

Much sparry flint, and a sort of granite with which the road is paved. There is a great deal of talc in the stones and soil, but in too small pieces to be useful. Frequent beds of clay and pure sand. Found two mineral wells slightly impregnated with iron, with much appearance of that metal in this part of the country; and they are not unacquainted with the method of extracting it from the stones, but still despise its use in building. Towards Chooka there are many well cultivated fields of wheat and barley.

May 26. ***Road to Punukha***[f]. From Chooka the country opens, and presents to view many well cultivated fields and distant villages; a

[e] Chuka.

[f] Punugga.

rapid change in climate, the vegetable productions, and general appearance of the country. Towards Punukha, pines and firs are the only trees to be met with; but they do not yet seem in their proper climate, being dwarfish and ill shaped; peaches, raspberries, and strawberries, thriving every where; scarce a plant to be seen that is not of European growth. In addition to the many I have already mentioned, saw two species of the cratægus, one not yet described. Saw two ash trees in a very thriving state, the star-thistle, and many other weeds, in general natives of the Alps and Switzerland.

Much of the rock to-day was, I found on examination, pure limestone; a valuable acquisition if they did not either despise its use, or were unacquainted with its properties. It was most advantageously situated for being worked, and the purest perhaps to be met with. There is likewise abundance of fire-wood in this part of the country. In building they would derive great benefit from the use of it. Their houses are lofty, the timbers substantial, and nothing wanting to make them durable, but their being acquainted with the use of lime. As a manure it might probably be used to great advantage. Many fields of barley in this part of the country; now the beginning of their harvest. The thermometer here fell, at four o'clock in the afternoon, to 60°, cold and chilly.

May 27. On the road to Chepta[g], the rock in general dips to the northward and eastward, in about an angle of sixty degrees. Much of limestone, and some veins of quartz, and loose pieces of sparry flint striking fire with steel.

[g] Chupka or Kepta.

Several springs, and one slightly impregnated with iron.

In addition to the plants of yesterday, found the coriandrum testiculatum, inula montana, and rhododendron magnum.

At Chepta met with a few turnips, one maple tree, wormwood, goose-grass (galium aparinæ), and many other European weeds; the first walnut tree we had seen.

Chepta lies high, and not above six miles from the mountain of Lomyla, now covered with snow. The wind from that quarter S. E. made it cold and chilly, and sunk the thermometer at mid-day to 57°. Here are some fields of wheat and barley not yet ripe.

May 29. Road to Pagha[h]. Soon after leaving Chepta found a mineral well, which, on a chemical examination, gave marks of a strong impregnation from iron. I traced it to its source, where the thermometer, on being immersed, fell from 68° to 56°.

A little before we reached Pagha, met with some limestone, and a bed of chalk, which, near the surface, contained a great proportion of sand, but some feet under, was much purer.

The forests of firs of an inferior growth, several ash trees, dog-rose, and bramble

May 30, 31, and June 1. The road from hence to Tassesudon[i], presents us with little that we have not met with; fewer strawberries, and no raspberries; some very good orchards of peaches, apricots, apples, and pears. The fruit formed, and will be ripe in August and September. Met with two sorts of cranberry, one very good. Saw the fragaria sterilis and a few poppies. At Wanakha[k] found a few turnips, shallots,

[h] Pauga. [i] Tassisudon. [k] Wangoka.

cucumbers, and gourds. Near Tassesudon, the road is lined with many different species of the rose, and a few jessamine plants. The soil is light, and the hills in many places barren, rocky, and with very little verdure. The rock in general laminated and rotten, with many small particles of talc in every part of the country, incorporated with the stones and soil. Some limestone, and appearance of good chalk. Several good and pure springs of water.

Tassesudon and its neighbourhood abound with all the plants we have already mentioned. The hills are chiefly wood, with firs and aspen. I have not yet been able to find an oak tree, and the ash is seldom to be met with. The elder, holly, bramble, and dog-rose are common. Found the birch tree, cypress, yew, and delphinium. Many different species of the vaccinium, of which the bilberry is one, and the cranberry another. Towards the top of the adjacent mountains, met with two plants of the arbutus uva ursi, which is a native of the Alps, the most mountainous parts of Scotland, and Canada.

I have likewise seen a species of the rhubarb plant (rheum undulatum) brought from a distance, and only to be met with near the summits of hills covered with snow, and where the soil is rocky. The true rhubarb (rheum palmatum) is likewise the native of a cold climate; and though China supplies us with much of this drug, it is known to be the growth of its more northern provinces, Tartary, and a part of the Russian dominions. The great difficulty is in drying the root. People conversant in that business say, that one hundred pounds of fresh root, should not weigh above six pounds and a half, if properly dried, and it certainly has been reduced to that. I have seen eighty pounds of fresh root produced from one plant; but, after drying it with much care and attention, the weight of the dried root could not be made less than twelve pounds. It was suspended in an oven, with an equal and moderate degree of heat. Little more than the same quantity of this powder, produced a similar effect with the best foreign rhubarb.

The other plants common here, are the service tree, blessed thistle, mock orange, Spiræa filipendula, Arum, Echites, Punica, Ferula communis, Erica, and Viola. Of the rose bush, I have met with the five following species; Rosa alpina, centifolia, canina, indica, spinocissima.

The culture of pot-herbs is every where neglected; turnips, a few onions and shallots, were the best we could procure. Mr. Bogle left potatoes, cabbage, and lettuce plants, all which we found neglected and dispersed. They had very improperly (from an idea, most probably, of their being natives of Bengal) planted them in a situation and climate, which approaches very near to that of Bengal at all seasons, as we shall find afterwards. Melons, gourds, brinjals, and cucumbers, are occasionally to be met with. The country is fitted for the production of every fruit and vegetable, common without the tropics, and in some situations, will bring to perfection many of the tropical fruits.

There are two plants, which I have to regret the not having had as yet an opportunity of seeing; one is the tree, from the bark of which their paper is made; and the other is employed by them in poisoning their arrows. This last is said to come from a very remote part of the country. They describe it, as growing to the height of three or four feet, with a hollow stalk. The juice is inspissated, and laid as a paste on their arrows. Fortunately for them, it has not all the bad effects they dread from it. I had an opportunity of seeing several who were wounded with these arrows, and they all did well, though under the greatest apprehension. The cleaning and enlarging some of the wounds, was the most that I found necessary to be done. The paste is pungent and acrid, will increase inflammation, and may make a bad or neglected wound, mortal; but it certainly does not possess any specific quality as a poison.

The fir, so common in this country, is perhaps the only tree they could convert to a useful and profitable purpose. What I have seen would not, from their situation, be employed as timber. The largest I have yet met with, were near Wandipore; they measured from eight to ten feet in circumference, were tall and straight. Such near the Burrampooter, or any navigable river, might certainly be transported to an advantageous market. I am convinced that any quantity of tar, pitch, turpentine, and resin, might be made in this country, much to the emolument of the natives. Firs, which from their size and situation are unfit for timber, would answer the purpose equally well. The process for procuring tar and turpentine is simple, and does not require the construction of expensive works. This great object has been so little attended to, that they are supplied from Bengal, with what they want of these articles.

The country about Tassesudon contains a great variety of soil, and much rock of many different forms; but still is an unpromising field for a mineralist. I have not found in Boutan, a fossil that had the least appearance of containing any other metal than iron, and a small portion of copper. From information, and the reports of travellers, I believe it is otherwise, to the northward. The banks of the Ticushu[l], admitting of cultivation for several miles above and below Tassesudon, yield them two crops in the year. The first, of wheat and barley, is cut down in June; and the rice, planted immediately after, enjoys the benefit of the rains. This country is not without its hot wells, as well as many numerous springs, some of which I have taken notice of. One hot-well, near Wandepore, is so close to the banks of the river, as to be overflowed in the rains, and we found it impossible to get to it: the heat of this well is great; but I could not learn that the ground about it, was much different from the general aspect of the country. Another, several days' journey from hence, is on the brow of a hill perpetually covered with snow. This hot well is held in great estimation by the people of the country, and resorted to by valetudinarians of every description. I gained but little satisfactory information respecting the degree of heat, or appearance of the ground about it, that could lead me to form a just opinion of either.

September 8 and 9. Left Tassesudon, and arrived next day at Paraghon[m]. Much good rich soil, with more pasture where the ground is not cultivated, than we had yet met with. Many fields of turnips in great perfection; a plant they seem better acquainted with the cultivation of, than any other. Found on the road, many large and well-thriving birch, willows, pines, and firs; some walnut trees, the Arbutus uva ursi, abundance of strawberry, elderberry, bilberry, Chrysanthemum, or greater daisy, and many European grasses. Saw the

[l] Tehintchieu. [m] Paro, Parogong, or Rinjipo.

Datura ferox, or thorn apple, a plant common in China, and some parts of Thibet, where it is used medicinally. They find it a powerful narcotic, and give the seeds, where they wish that effect to be produced. It has been used as a medicine in Europe, and is known to possess these qualities in a high degree. Saw holly, dog rose, and aspin. The present crop, near Paraghon, on the banks of the Pachu[n], is rice, but not so far advanced as at Tassesudon: the same may be said of their fruits. They say it is colder here, at all seasons, than at Tassesudon, which is certainly below the level of this place.

Towards the summit of the mountain we crossed, found some rock of a curious appearance, forming in front, six or seven angular semi-pillars, of a great circumference, and some hundred feet high. This natural curiosity, was detached in part from the mountain, and projected over a considerable fall of water, which added much to the beautiful and picturesque appearance of the whole. Numerous springs, some degrees colder than the surrounding atmosphere, gushing from the rock in the most elevated part of the mountain, furnish a very ample and seasonable supply of excellent water to the traveller. The rock, in many places, laminated, might be formed into very tolerable slate. Near to Paraghon iron stones are found, and one spring highly impregnated with this mineral.

September 11. Our road to Dukaigun[o], nearly due north, was a continued ascent for eight miles, along the banks of the Pachu, falling over numerous rocks, precipices, and huge stones. Here we began to experience a very considerable change in the temperature of the

[n] Patchieu. [o] Dukka-jeung.

atmosphere; the surrounding hills were covered with snow in the morning, which had fallen the preceding night, but disappeared soon after sunrise. The thermometer fell to 54° in the afternoon, and did not rise above 62° at noon.

The face of the mountains, in some places bare, with projecting rock of so many different forms; quartz, flint, and a bad sort of free stone, common. Many very good springs, slightly impregnated with a selenitic earth.

The soil is rich, and near to the river in great cultivation. Many horses, the staple article of their trade, are bred in this part of the country. Found walnut trees, peaches, apples, and pears.

September 12. The road still ascending to Sanha[p], and near to the river for ten miles.

The thermometer falling some degrees, we found it cold and chilly. The bed of the river was full of large stones, probably washed down from the mountains by the rapidity of its stream; they were chiefly quartz and granite. Here was excellent pasture for numerous herds of goats.

Road to Chichakumboo. From Sanha, the ascent is much greater; and after keeping for ten miles along the banks of the Pachu, still a considerable stream, we reached its source (from three distinct rivulets, all in view, ramified and supplied by numerous springs), and soon after arrived at the most elevated part of our road.

Here we quitted the boundary of Boutan, and entered the territory of Thibet, where nature has drawn the line still more strongly, and

[p] Sana.

affords, perhaps, the most extraordinary contrast that takes place on the face of the earth. From this eminence are to be seen the mountains of Boutan, covered with trees, shrubs, and verdure to their tops, and on the south side of this mountain, to within a few feet of the ground on which we tread. On the north side, the eye takes in an extensive range of hills and plains, but not a tree, shrub, or scarce a tuft of grass is to be seen. Thus, in the course of less than a mile, we bad adieu to a most fertile soil, covered with perpetual verdure, and entered a country where the soil and climate seem inimical to the production of every vegetable. The change in the temperature of the air is equally obvious and rapid. The thermometer in the forenoon 34°, with frost and snow in the night time. Our present observations on the cause of this change confirmed us in our former opinion, and incontestably prove; that we are to look for that difference of climate from the situation of the ground, as more or less above the general level of the earth. In attending to this cause of heat or cold, we must not allow ourselves to be deceived by a comparison with that, which is immediately in view. We ought to take in a greater range of country, and where the road is near the banks of a river, we cannot well err, in forming a judgment of the inclination of the ground. Punukha[q] and Wandepore[r], both to the northward of Tassesudon, are quite in a Bengal climate. The thermometer at the first of these places, in the months of July and January, was within two degrees of what it had been at Rungpore for the same periods. They seem in more exposed situations than Tassesudon; and were we to draw a comparison

[q] Punukka. [r] Wandipore.

of their heights, from the surrounding ground, I should say they were above its level. The road, however, proves the reverse. From Punukha to Tassesudon we had a continued and steep ascent for six hours and a half, with a very inconsiderable descent on the Tassesudon side. From the south of the mountain, dividing Boutan from Thibet, the springs and rivulets are tumbling down in cascades and torrents, and have been traced by us near to the foot of the hills, where they empty themselves to the eastward of Buxaduar. On the north side, they glide smoothly along, and by passing to the northward, as far as Tishoolumboo[s], prove a descent on that side, which the eye could not detect. This part of the country, being the most elevated, is at all times the coldest; and the snowy mountains, from their heights and bearings, notwithstanding the distance, are certainly those seen from Purnea.

The soil on the Thibet side of the mountain, is sandy with much gravel and loose stones. On the road we found the aconitum pyreneum, and two species of the saxifraga.

Saw a large flock of chowry-tailed cattle; their extensive range of pasture seemed to make amends for its poverty.

Sept. 15. From Faro[t] to Duina[u] passed over an extensive plain, bounded by many small hills, oddly arranged; some of them detached and single, and all seemed composed of sand, collected in that form, having the plain for their general base.

At Duina found a few plots of barley, which they were cutting down, though green, as despairing of its ripening. The thermometer

[s] Teshoo Loomboo. [t] Phari. [u] Tuena.

at six o'clock in the morning, below the freezing point, and the ground partially covered with snow.

Sept. 16. *Road to Chalu*[w]. Continued on the plain; found three springs forcing their way through the ground with violence, and giving rise to a lake many miles in extent, stored with millions of water-fowl and excellent fish. Of the first, saw the cyrus, solan geese, many kinds of ducks, pintados, cranes, and gulls of different sorts. The springs of this lake are in great reputation for the cure of most diseases. I examined the water, and found it contained a portion of alum with the selenitic earth. On the banks of the lake, I found a crystallization, which proved to be an alkaline salt; it is used by the natives for washing, and answers the purpose as well as pot-ash. The pasture, which is impregnated with this salt, is greedily sought after by sheep and goats, and proves excellent food for them. The hills are chiefly composed of sand, incrusted by the inclemency of the weather and violent winds, seeming, at first view, composed of freestone.

Sept. 17. *Road to Simadar*[x]. Passed a lake still more considerable than the former, with which it communicates by a narrow stream, about three miles long. There never was a more barren or unpromising soil; little turf, grass, or vegetable of any sort, except near the lake. Saw a few huts, mostly in ruins and deserted. The only grain in this part of the country is barley, which they were cutting down every where green.

Passed two springs, one of them slightly impregnated with alum.

[w] Chaloo. [x] Sumdta.

They form the principal source of a river, which empties itself into the Burrampooter, near Tissoolumboo.

The wind from the eastward of south, was now the coldest and most piercing; passing over the snowy mountains, and dry sandy desert before described, it comes divested of all vapour or moisture, and produces the same effect, as the hot dry winds in more southerly situations. Mahogany boxes and furniture, that had withstood the Bengal climate for years, were warped with considerable fissures, and rendered useless. The natives say, a direct exposure to these winds, occasions the loss of their fore teeth; and our faithful guide ascribed that defect in himself, to this cause. We escaped with loss of the skin, from the greatest part of our faces.

September 18. ***Road to Seluh.***[y] Near our road to-day found a hot-well, much frequented by people with venereal complaints, rheumatism, and all cutaneous diseases. They do not drink the water, but use it as a bath. The thermometer, when immersed in the water, rose from 40° to 88°: it has a strong sulphurous smell, and contains a portion of hepar sulphuris. Exposure to air deprives it, like most other mineral wells, of much of its property.

September 19. ***Road to Takui.***[z] Passed some fields of barley and pease, and got into a milder climate. Found, to-day, a great variety of stone and rock, some containing copper, and others, a very pure rock-crystal, regularly crystallized, with six unequal sides. The rock-crystal is of different sizes and degrees of purity, but of one form. Found some flint and granite, several springs of water impregnated

[y] Shoohoo. [z] Tehukku.

with iron, and nearly of the same temperature with the atmosphere Saw a few ill-thriving willows planted near the habitations, which are the only trees to be met with.

September 20, 21, and 22. Road to Tissoolumboo.[a] The remaining part of our journey was over a more fertile soil, enjoying a milder climate. Some very good fields of wheat, barley, and pease; many pleasant villages, and distant houses; less sand, and more rock; part slaty, and much of it a very good sort of flint. The soil in the valley, a light-coloured clay and sand: they were everywhere employed in cutting down their crop. What a happy climate! the sky was serene and clear, without a cloud; and so confident were they of the continuance of this weather, that their crop was thrown together in a convenient part of the field, without any cover, to remain till they could find time to thrash it out.

Before we reached Tissoolumboo, we found some elms and ash trees.

The hills in Thibet have, from their general appearance, strong marks of containing those fossils, that are inimical to vegetation; such are most of the ores of the metal and pyritical matter.

The country properly explored, promises better than any I have seen, to gratify the curiosity of a philosopher, and to reward the labours of a mineralist. Accident, more than a spirit of enterprise and enquiry, has already discovered the presence of many valuable ores and minerals in Thibet. The first in this list is, deservedly, gold: they find it in large quantities, and frequently very pure. In the form

[a] Teshoo Loomboo.

of gold dust, it is found in the beds of rivers, and at their several bendings, generally attached to small pieces of stone, with every appearance of its having been part of a larger mass. They find it sometimes in large masses, lumps, and irregular veins; the adhering stone is generally flint or quartz, and I have sometimes seen a half-formed, impure sort of precious stone in the mass. By a common process for the purification of gold, I extracted 12 *per cent.* of refuse from some gold dust; and, on examination, found it to be sand, and filings of iron, which last was not likely to have been with it in its native state, but probably employed for the purpose of adulteration. Two days journey from Tissoolumboo there is a lead mine; the ore is much the same as that found in Derbyshire, mineralized by sulphur, and the metal obtained by the very simple operation of fusion alone. Most lead contains a portion of silver, and some in such proportion, as to make it an object to work the lead ore, for the sake of the silver. Cinnabar, containing a large portion of quicksilver, is found in Thibet, and might be advantageously employed for the purpose of extracting this metal. The process is simple, by distillation; but to carry it on in the great, would require more fuel than the country can well supply. I have seen ores and loose stones containing copper, and have not a doubt of its being found in great abundance in the country. Iron is more frequently to be met with in Boutan than in Thibet; and, was it more common, the difficulty of procuring proper fuel for smelting the less valuable ores, must prove an insuperable objection to the working them. The dung of animals is the only substitute they have for fire-wood; and with that alone, they will never be able to excite a degree of heat sufficiently intense for such purposes. Thus situated, the most valuable discovery for them, would be that of a coal mine. In some parts of China bordering on Thibet, coal is found, and used as fuel.

Tincal, the nature and production of which, we have only, hitherto, been able to guess at, is now well known, and Thibet, from whence we are supplied, contains it in inexhaustible quantities. It is a fossil, brought to market in the state in which it is dug out of the lake, and afterwards refined into borax by ourselves. Rock-salt is likewise found in great abundance in Thibet.

The lake, from whence tincal and rock-salt are collected, is about fifteen days journey from Tissoolumboo, and to the northward of it. It is encompassed on all sides by rocky hills, without any brooks or rivulets near at hand; but its waters are supplied by springs, which being saltish to the taste, are not used by the natives. The tincal is deposited or formed in the bed of the lake, and those who go to collect it, dig it up in large masses, which they afterwards break into small pieces, for the convenience of carriage, exposing it to the air to dry. Although tincal has been collected from this lake for a great length of time, the quantity is not perceptibly diminished; and as the cavities made by digging it, soon wear out, or fill up, it is an opinion with the people, that the formation of fresh tincal is going on. They have never yet met it in dry ground, or high situations, but it is found in the shallowest depths, and the borders of the lake, which, deepening gradually from the edges towards the centre, contains too much water to admit of their searching for the tincal conveniently; but from the deepest parts they bring rock-salt, which is not to be found in shallows, or near the bank. The waters of the lake rise and fall very little, being supplied by a constant and unvarying source, neither augmented by the influx of any current, or diminished by any stream running from it. The lake, I was assured, is at least twenty miles in circumference, and, standing in a very bleak situation, is frozen for a great part of the year. The people employed in collecting these salts, are obliged to desist from their labour so early as October, on account of the ice. Tincal is used in Thibet for soldering, and to promote the fusion of gold and silver. Rock-salt is universally used for all domestic purposes, in Thibet, Boutan, and Naphaul.

The thermometer at Tissoolumboo, during the month of October, was on an average, at eight o'clock in the morning, 38°; at noon, 46°; and at six o'clock in the evening, 42°: the weather clear, cool, and pleasant, and the prevailing wind was from the southward. During the month of November, we had frosts morning and evening; a serene clear sky, not a cloud to be seen. The rays of the sun, passing through a medium so little obscured, had great influence. The thermometer was often below 30° in the morning, and seldom above 38° at noon, in the shade; wind from the southward.

Of the diseases of this country, the first that attracts our notice, as we approach the foot of the hills, is a glandular swelling in the throat, which is known to prevail in similar situations in some parts of Europe, and generally ascribed to an impregnation of the water from snow. The disease being common at the foot of the Alps, and confined to a tract of country near these mountains, has first given rise to the idea of its being occasioned by snow water. If a general view of the disease and situations, where it is common, had been the subject of inquiry, or awakened the attention of any able practitioner, we should have been long since undeceived in this respect. On the coast of Greenland, the mountainous parts of Wales and Scotland, where melted snow must be continually passing into their rivers and streams, the disease is not known, though it is common in Derbyshire, and some other parts of England. Rungpore is about one hundred miles from the foot of the hills, and much farther from the snow, yet the disease is as frequent there as in Boutan. In Thibet, where snow is never out of view, and is the principal source of all their rivers and streams, the disease is not to be met with; but what puts the matter past a doubt, is the frequency of the disease on the coast of Sumatra, where snow is never to be found. On finding the vegetable productions of Boutan the same as those of the Alps, in almost every instance, it occurred to me, that the disease might arise from an impregnation of the water by these plants, or the soil probably possessing similar qualities, the spontaneous productions of both countries, with very few exceptions, being so nearly alike. It, however, appears more probable, that the disease is endemial, proceeding from a peculiarity in the air of situations in the vicinity of mountains, with such soil and vegetable productions. I am the more inclined to think so, as I have universally found this disease most prevalent amongst the lower class of people, and those who are most exposed to the unguarded influence of the weather, and various changes that take place in the air of such situations. The primary cause in the atmosphere producing this effect, is perhaps not more inexplicable, than what we meet with in the lowlands of Essex, and the fens in Lincolnshire. An accurate analysis of the water used in common by the natives, where this disease is more or less frequent, and where it is not known in similar exposures, might throw some light on this subject.

This very extraordinary disease has been little attended to, from obvious reasons; it is unaccompanied with pain, is seldom fatal, and generally confined to the poorer sort of people. The tumour is unsightly, and grows to a troublesome size, being often as large as a person's head. It is certainly not exaggerating to say, that one in six, of the Rungpore district and country of Boutan, has this disease.

As those who labour most, and are the least protected from the changes of the weather, are most subject to the disease, we universally find it in Boutan, more common with the women than men. It generally appears in Boutan at the age of thirteen or fourteen, and in Bengal at the age of eleven or twelve; so that in both countries the disease shows itself about the age of puberty. I do not believe this disease has ever been removed, though a mercurial course seemed to check its progress, but did not prevent its advance after intermitting the use of mercury. An attention to the primary cause, will first lead to a proper method of treating the disease; a change of situation for a short while, at that particular period when it appears, might be the means of preventing it.

The people of this happy climate are not exempt from the venereal disease, which seems to rage with unremitting fury in all climates, and proves the greatest scourge to the human race. It has been long a matter of doubt, whether this disease has ever been cured by any other specific than mercury, and its different preparations. In defence of the opinion of other specifics being in use, it has always been urged, that the disease is frequent in many parts of the world, where it could not be supposed they were acquainted with quicksilver, and the proper method of preparing it as a medicine. I must own, that I expected to have been able to have added one other specific for this disease, to our list in the Materia Medica, being informed that the disease was common, and their method of treating it successful; nor could I allow myself to think that they were acquainted with the method of preparing quicksilver, so as to render it a safe and efficacious medicine. In this, however, I was mistaken.

The disease seems in this country to make a more rapid progress, and rage with more violence, than in any other. This is to be accounted for from the grossness of their food, and little attention to cleanliness.

There is one preparation of mercury in common use with them, and made after the following manner. A portion of alum, nitre, vermilion, and quicksilver, are placed at the bottom of an earthen pot, with a smaller one inverted, put over the materials, and well luted to the bottom of the larger pot. Over the small one, and within the large one, the fuel is placed, and the fire continued for about forty minutes. A certain quantity of fuel, carefully weighed out, is what regulates them with respect to the degree of heat, as they cannot see the materials during the operation. When the vessel is cool, the small inverted pot is taken off, and the materials are collected for use. I attended the whole of the process, and afterwards examined the materials. The quicksilver had been acted on, by the other ingredients, deprived of its metallic form, and rendered a safe and efficacious remedy.

A knowledge of chemistry has taught us a more certain method of rendering this valuable medicine, active and efficacious: yet we find this preparation answering every good purpose, and, by their guarded manner of exhibiting it, perfectly safe. This powder is the basis of their pill, and often used in external application. The whole, when intimately mixed, formed a reddish powder, and was made into the form of pills, by the addition of a plum or date. Two or three pills, taken twice a day, generally bring on, about the fourth or fifth day, a spitting, which is encouraged, by continuing the use of the pills for a day or two longer. As the salivation advances, they put a stick across the patient's mouth in the form of a gag, and make it fast behind. This, they say, is done to promote the spitting, and prevent the loss of their teeth. They keep up the salivation for ten or twelve days, during which time the patient is nourished with congee, and other liquids. Part of this powder is often used externally, by diffusing it in warm water, and washing sores and buboes. They disperse buboes frequently, by poultices of turnip tops, in which they always put vermilion, and sometimes musk. Nitre, as a cooler, is very much used internally by them, in this disease, and they strictly enjoin warmth and confinement, during the slightest mercurial course. Buboes, advanced to suppuration, are opened by a lancet, with a large incision, which they do not allow to close, before the hardness and tumour are gone. In short, I found very little room for improving their practice in this disease. I introduced the method of killing quicksilver with honey, gave them an opportunity of seeing it done, and had the satisfaction of finding it successfully used by themselves, before we left the country.

This happy climate presents us with but little variety in their diseases. Coughs, colds, and rheumatism, are more frequent here than in Bengal. Fevers generally arise here from a temporary cause, are easily removed, and seldom prove fatal. The liver disease is occasionally to be met with, and complaints in the bowels, are not unfrequent; but the grossness of their food, and uncleanliness of their persons, would, in any other climate, be the source of constant disease and sickness. They are ignorant (as we were not many years ago) of the proper method of treating diseases of the liver, and other viscera; this is, I believe, the cause of the most obstinate and fatal disease to be met with in the country; I mean, the dropsy. As the Rajah had ever been desirous of my aid and advice, and had directed his doctors to attend to my private instructions and practice, I endeavoured to introduce a more judicious method of treating those diseases, by mercurial preparations. I had an opportunity of proving the advantage of this plan, to their conviction, in several instances, and of seeing them initiated in the practice.

The Rajah favoured me with above seventy specimens of the medicines in use with them. They have many sorts of stones and petrifactions, saponaceous to the touch, which are employed as an external application, in swellings and pains of the joints. They often remove such complaints, and violent head-achs, by fumigating the part affected, with aromatic plants and flowers. They do not seek for any other means of information respecting the state of a patient, than that of feeling the pulse; and they confidently say, that the seat of pain and disease, is easily to be discovered, not so much from the frequency of the pulse, as its vibratory motion. They feel the pulse, at the wrist, with their three fore-fingers, first of the right, and then of the left hand; after pressing more or less on the artery, and occasionally removing one or two of the fingers, they determine what the disease is. They do not eat any thing the day on which they take physic, but endeavour to make up the loss afterwards, by eating more freely than before, and using such medicines as they think will occasion costiveness.

The many simples in use with them, are from the vegetable kingdom, collected chiefly in Boutan. They are in general inoffensive, and very mild in their operation. Carminatives and aromatics, are given in coughs, colds, and affections of the breast. The centaury, coriander, carraway, and cinnamon, are of this sort. This last is, with them, the bark of the root of that species of Laurus, formerly mentioned as a native of this country. The bark from the root is, in this plant, the only part which partakes of the cinnamon taste; and I doubt very much if it could be distinguished, by the best judges, from what we call the true cinnamon. The bark, leaves, berries, and stalks of many shrubs and trees, are in use with them, all in decoction. Some have much of the astringent bitter taste of our most valuable medicines, and are generally employed here, with the same view, to strengthen the powers of digestion, and mend the general habit. Their principal purgative medicines are brought by the Chinese to Lassa. They had not any medicine that operated as a vomit, till I gave the Rajah some ipecacuanha, who made the first experiment with it on himself.

In bleeding, they have a great opinion of drawing the blood, from a particular part. For head-achs, they bleed in the neck; for pains in the arm and shoulder, in the cephalic vein; and of the breast, or side, in the median; and if in the belly, they bleed in the basilic vein. They think pains of the lower extremity, are best removed by bleeding in the ankle. They have a great prejudice against bleeding in cold weather; nor is any urgency, or violent symptom, thought a sufficient reason for doing it at that time.

They have their lucky and unlucky days for operating, or taking any medicine; but I have known them get the better of this prejudice.

Cupping is much practised by them; a horn, about the size of a cupping glass, is applied to the part, and by a small aperture at the other end, they extract the air with their mouth. The part is afterwards scarified with a lancet. This is often done on the back; and in pain and swelling of the knee, it is held as a sovereign remedy. I have often admired their dexterity in operating with bad instruments. Mr. Hamilton gave them some lancets, and they have since endeavoured, with some success, to make them of that form. They were very thankful for the few I could spare them. In fevers, they use the Kuthullega nut, well known in Bengal, as an efficacious medicine. They endeavour to cure the dropsy by external applications, and giving a compounded medicine, made up of above thirty different ingredients: they seldom or never succeed in effecting a cure of this disease. I explained to the Rajah the operation of tapping, and shewed him the instrument with which it was done. He very earnestly expressed a desire that I should perform the operation, and wished much for a proper subject; such a one did not occur while I remained; and perhaps it was as well, both for the Rajah's patients and my own credit; for after having seen it once done, he would not have hesitated about a repetition of the operation. Gravelish complaints, and the stone in the bladder are, I believe, diseases unknown here.

The small-pox, when it appears among them, is a disease that strikes them with too much terror and consternation, to admit of their treating it properly. Their attention is not employed in saving the lives of the infected, but in preserving themselves from the disease. All communication with the infected is strictly forbidden, even at the risk of their being starved; and the house, or village, is afterwards erased. A promiscuous and free intercourse, with their neighbours, not being allowed, the disease is very seldom to be met with, and its progress always checked, by the vigilance and terror of the natives. Few in the country have had the disease. Inoculation, if ever introduced, must be very general, to prevent the devastation that would be made by the infection in the natural way; and where there could not be any choice in the subject fit to receive the disease, many must fall a sacrifice to it. The present Rajah of Thibet was inoculated, with some of his followers, when in China with the late Tishoo Lama.

The hot bath is used in many disorders, particularly in complaints of the bowels, and cutaneous eruptions. The hot wells of Thibet are resorted to by thousands. In Boutan, they substitute water warmed by hot stones thrown into it.

In Thibet, the natives are more subject to sore-eyes, and blindness, than in Boutan. The high winds, sandy soil, and glare from the reflection of the sun, both from the snow and sand, account for this.

I have dwelt long on this subject, because I think the knowledge and observations of these people on the diseases of their country, with their medical practice, keep pace with a refinement and state of civilization, which struck me with wonder, and, no doubt, will give rise to much curious speculation, when known to be the manners of a people, holding so little intercourse, with what we term civilized nations.

December 1. Left Tishoolumboo, and found the cold increase every day, as we advanced to the southward, most of the running waters frozen, and the pools covered with ice strong enough to carry. Our thermometer having only the scale as low as 16°, we could not precisely determine the degree of cold, the quicksilver being under that every morning. The frost is certainly never so intense in Great Britain. On our return to the lakes, the 14th, we found them deserted by the water fowl, and were informed, that they had been one solid piece of ice since the 10th of November. Here we resumed our amusement of skating, to the great astonishment of the natives and Bengal servants.

On the 17th, we re-entered Boutan, and in six days more arrived at Punukha by Paraghon. No snow or frost to be met with in Boutan, except towards the tops of their highest mountains; the thermometer rising to 36° in the morning, and 48° at noon.

Took leave of the Debe Rajah, and on the 12th arrived at Buxaduar.

PART V.

LETTER

ADDRESSED TO

THE HON. JOHN MACPHERSON, ESQ.

GOVERNOR GENERAL OF BENGAL,

CONTAINING

SOME PARTICULARS RELATING TO THE JOURNEY OF POORUNGHEER TO TESHOO LOOMBOO;

THE INAUGURATION OF TESHOO LAMA;

AND THE

STATE OF TIBET FROM 1783 TO 1785.

TIBET.

THE

HON. JOHN MACPHERSON, ESQ.

GOVERNOR GENERAL, &c. &c.

HONOURABLE SIR, *Calcutta, February 6th, 1786.*

HAVING, in obedience to the instructions with which you were pleased to honour me, examined Poorungheer, the Gosein, who has at different times been employed in deputations to the late Teshoo Lama, who formerly accompanied him to the court of Pekin, and who is lately again returned from Tibet, and having collected from him an account of the journey he has just performed, and such other information as he could give me, relative to the countries he has left; I beg leave to submit it to you, in the following narrative.

In the beginning of last year, Poorungheer having received from Mr. Hastings, a short time previous to his departure from Bengal, dispatches for Teshoo Lama, and the Regent of Teshoo Loomboo, immediately set about preparing for the distant journey, he had engaged to undertake; the preparations employed him till the beginning of the following month of March, when, I beg leave to recall to your remembrance, I had the honour to present him to you for his dismission. He then commenced his journey from Calcutta, and early in the month of April had passed, as he relates, the limits of the Company's provinces, and entered the mountains that constitute the kingdom of Bootan; where, in the prosecution of his journey, he received, from the subjects of the Daeb Raja, the most ample and voluntary assistance to the frontier of his territory, nor did he meet with any impediment to oppose his progress, until his arrival upon the borders of Tibet. Here he was compelled to halt for near a fortnight, by a heavy fall of snow, that commenced upon his arrival at Phari, and continued for the space of six days, covering the face of the country to so great a depth, as totally to put a stop to all travelling, and rendered it impracticable for him to proceed, until a thaw succeeded to open the communication.

During the time of his confinement at Phari, he says, such was the severity of the cold, and the injurious effect, which so rapid a transition from a temperate climate, produced on the health of himself and his companions, that it left him little room to doubt, if an early change had not fortunately taken place, and permitted his advance, that they must all have fallen victims to the inclemency of the weather. However, as early as it was possible for him to leave Phari, he proceeded, by long stages, on his journey; and, without encountering any further difficulties, on the 8th of May following, reached Teshoo Loomboo, the capital of Tibet.

Immediately upon entering the monastery, he went to the Durbar of the Regent Chanjoo Cooshoo, Punjun Irtinnee Nimoheim, to announce his arrival, and the purpose of his commission.

Quarters were then allotted for his residence, and an hour appointed for him to wait upon the Lama, who, he was informed, the following morning intended to leave the palace, to occupy one of his gardens situated on the plain, within sight of the monastery, where it was visible, a considerable encampment had been formed.

The Lama quitted his apartments at the first dawn of day, and was lodged in the tents, pitched for his accommodation, before the sun had risen. In the course of the morning, at the hour appointed for his admission, Poorungheer went down to the Lama's tents. He heard, on entering the gates of the enclosure, that the young Lama was taking his recreation in the garden, ranging about which, became with him a very favourite amusement. As it was at this time, in Tibet, the warmest season of the year, in order that he might enjoy the benefit of the air, his attendants had chosen a spot, where the trees afforded the completest shade, and had there placed an elevated seat of cushions, for the young Lama to rest upon after his exercise. In this situation Poorungheer found him, when summoned to his presence, attended by the Regent, his parents, Soopoon Choomboo, the cup-bearer, and the principal officers of the court. After making three profound prostrations, at as remote a distance as it was possible, he approached, and presented to the Lama, according to the custom of Tibet, a piece of white pelong, and then delivered the letters and presents with which he had been charged.

The packages were all immediately opened before the Lama, who had every article brought near to him, and viewed them separately one by one. The letter he took into his own hand, himself broke the seal, and taking from under the cover a string of pearls, which it inclosed, run them over between his fingers, as they read their rosaries, and then, with an arch air, placed them by his side, nor would, while the narrator was in his presence, permit any one to take them up.

Poorungheer says, that the young Lama regarded him with a very kind and significant look, spoke to him in the Tibet language, and asked him if he had had a fatiguing journey. The interview lasted more than an hour, during all which time the Lama sat with the utmost composure, not once attempting to quit his seat, nor discovering the least froward uneasiness at his confinement. Tea was twice brought in, and the Lama drank a cup each time. When ordered to receive his dismission, Poorungheer approached the Lama, and bowing before him presented his head, uncovered, to receive his blessing, which the Lama gave, by stretching out his hand, and laying it upon his head. He then ordered him, as long as he continued at Teshoo Loombo, to come to him once every day.

The following morning, Poorungheer waited upon the Regent at his apartments in the palace, to whom, after observing the customary forms of introduction, he delivered his dispatches.

After this, he visited Soopoon Choomboo, the Lama's parents, and others, to whom he was before known; and says, that he experienced, from all quarters, the most cordial and kind reception, for they had all been long accustomed to consider him as an agent of the government of Bengal.

He found no change whatever to have ensued, in the administration, since his attendance upon me in Tibet.

The country enjoyed perfect tranquillity, and the only event that had happened during his absence, of importance in their annals, was the inauguration of the infant Lama; this event took place in the preceding year; and as it is evidently a concern of the highest moment, whether considered in a political, or religious point of view, being no less than the recognizance, in an infant form, of their regenerated immortal sovereign, and ecclesiastical supreme, I was induced to bestow more than common pains, to trace the ceremonies that attended the celebration of so great an event; conceiving, that the novelty of the subject, might render the account curious, even if it should be found to contain no information of real utility. I shall therefore, without further apology, subjoin the result of my inquiries; premising only, that my authority for the description, is derived principally from Poorungheer, and confirmed, with some additional particulars, by the concurring reports of a Gosein, who was at the time, present on the spot.

The Emperor of China appears, on this occasion, to have taken a very conspicuous part, in giving testimony of his respect and zeal, for the great religious father of his faith. Early in the year 1784, he sent ambassadors from the court of Pekin to Teshoo Loomboo, to represent their sovereign, in supporting the dignity of the high priest, and to do honour to the occasion of the assumption of his office. Dalai

Lama, and the viceroy of Lassa, accompanied by all the court; one of the Chinese generals, stationed at Lassa, with a part of the troops under his command; two of the four magistrates of the city; the heads of every monastery throughout Tibet, and the Emperor's ambassadors appeared at Teshoo Loomboo, to celebrate this grand epocha in their political and theological history.

The 28th day of the seventh moon, corresponding nearly, as their year commences with the vernal equinox, to the middle of October, 1784, was chosen as the most auspicious for this solemnity. A few days previous to this, the Lama was conducted from Terpaling, the monastery in which he had passed his infancy, with every mark of pomp and homage, that could be paid by an enthusiastic people. So great a concourse as assembled, either from curiosity or devotion, was never seen before, for not a person of any condition in Tibet was absent, who could possibly attend. Hence the procession was necessarily constrained to move so slow, that though Terpaling is situated at the distance of five and twenty miles only from Teshoo Loomboo, three days expired in the performance of this short march. The first halt was made at Tsondue; the second at Summâr, about six miles off; from whence the most splendid parade was reserved for the Lama's entry on the third day. An account of his entry has been given me by a person who was present in the procession. The road, he says, by which the Lama had to pass, was previously prepared, by being whitened with a wash, and having piles of stones heaped up, with small intervals between, on either side. The procession passed between a double row of priests, who formed a street, extending all the way from Summâr to the gates of the palace. Some of the priests had lighted rods of a perfumed composition, that burn like decayed wood, and emit, as they consume, an aromatic smoke. The rest were furnished with the different musical instruments they use at their devotions, such as the gong, the cymbal, hautboy, trumpet, drums, and sea conch, which were all sounded in unison with the hymn they chanted. The crowd of spectators was kept without the street, and none admitted on the highway, but such as properly belonged to, or had a prescribed place in, the procession, which was arranged in the following order.

The van was led by three military commandants, or governors of districts, at the head of six or seven thousand horsemen, armed with quivers, bows, and matchlocks. In their rear followed the ambassador with his suit, carrying his diploma, as is the custom of China, made up in the shape of a large tube, and fastened on his back. Next, the Chinese general advanced, with the troops under his command, mounted, and accoutred, after their way, with fire-arms and sabres; then came a very numerous group, bearing the various standards and insignia of state; after them a full band of wind, and other sonorous instruments; after which were led two horses richly caparisoned, each carrying two large circular stoves, disposed like panniers across the horses' backs, and filled with burning aromatic woods. These were followed by a senior priest, called a Lama, who bore a box containing books of their form of prayer, and some favourite idols. Next, nine sumptuary horses were led, loaded with the Lama's apparel; after which came the priests immediately attached to the Lama's person, for the performance of daily offices in the temple, amounting to about seven hundred; following them, were two men, each carrying on his shoulder a large cylindrical gold vessel, embossed with emblematical figures, a gift from the Emperor of China. The Duhunniers and Soopoons, who were employed in communicating addresses, and distributing alms, immediately preceded the Lama's chair of state, which was covered with a gaudy canopy, and borne by eight of the sixteen Chinese appointed for this service. On one side of the chair attended the Regent; on the other, the Lama's father. It was followed by the heads of the different monasteries, and, as the procession advanced, the priests, who formed the street, fell in the rear, and brought up the cavalcade, which moved with an extremely slow pace, and about noon was received within the confines of the monastery, amidst an amazing display of colours, the acclamations of the crowd, solemn music, and the chanting of their priests.

The Lama being safely lodged in the palace, the Regent and Soopoon Choomboo went out, as is the customary compliment paid to visitors of high rank on their near approach, to meet and conduct Dalai Lama, and the Viceroy of Lassa, who were on their way to Teshoo Loomboo. Their respective retinues met the following morning at the foot of the castle of Painom, and the next day entered the monastery of Teshoo Loomboo together, where both Dalai Lama and the Viceroy of Lassa were accommodated during their stay.

The following morning, which was the third after Teshoo Lama's arrival, he was carried to the great temple, and about noon seated on the throne of his predecessors. At this time, the Emperor's ambassador delivered his diploma, and placed the presents, with which he had been charged, at the Lama's feet.

The three next ensuing days, Dalai Lama met Teshoo Lama in the temple, where they were assisted by all the priests in the invocation, and public worship of their gods. The rites then performed, completed, as I understood, the business of inauguration. During this interval, all who were at the capital, were entertained at the public expense, and alms were distributed without reserve. In conformity, likewise, to public notice, circulated every where for the same space of time, universal rejoicings prevailed throughout Tibet. Banners were unfurled on all their fortresses. The peasantry filled up the day, with music and festivity, and the night was celebrated by general illuminations. A long period was afterwards employed in making presents, and public entertainments, to the newly inducted Lama, who at the time of his accession to the musnud, or, if I may use the term, pontificate of Teshoo Loomboo, was not more than three years of age. The ceremony was begun by Dalai Lama, whose offerings are said to have amounted to a greater value, and his public entertainment to have been more splendid, than the rest. The second day was devoted to the Viceroy of Lassa. The third to the Chinese general. Then followed the Culloong, or magistrates of Lassa, and the rest of the principal persons, who had accompanied Dalai Lama. After which the Regent of Teshoo Loomboo, and all that were dependent on that government, were severally admitted, according to the pre-eminence of their rank, to pay their tributes of obeisance and respect. As soon as the acknowledgments of all those, were received, who were entitled to the privilege, Teshoo Lama made, in the same manner, suitable returns to each; an occupation which lasted near forty days. Many importunities were used with Dalai Lama, to prolong his stay at Teshoo Loomboo, but he excused himself from incumbering the capital any longer, with so numerous a concourse of people, as attended on his movements; and deeming it expedient to make his absence as short as possible from the seat of his authority, at the expiration of forty days, he withdrew, with all his suite, to Lassa. The Emperor's ambassadors also received their dismission to return to China; and thus terminated this famous festival.

With respect to the lately established commercial intercourse, Poorungheer informs me, that though he returned so early, he found himself not the first person, who had arrived at Teshoo Loomboo from Bengal. Many merchants had already brought their commodities to market, and others followed, before he left the place. He heard from no quarter, complaints of impediment or loss; and concludes, therefore, that all the adventurers met the same easy access, and ready aid, which he himself had experienced. The markets were well stocked with English and Indian articles, yet not in so great a degree, as to lower the value of commodities, below the prices of the two or three last preceding years. Bullion was somewhat reduced in worth, in comparison with the year 1783. A pootree, or bulse of gold dust, the same quantity that then sold for twenty, or twenty-one indermillees, was now procurable, of a purer quality, for nineteen and twenty indermillees.

A tarreema, or talent of silver, which was then five hundred, was now four hundred and fifty indermillees, so that the exchange was much in favour of the trader.

Poorungheer, during his residence at Teshoo Loomboo, had frequent interviews with the Regent and the ministers, and he assures me, that he found the heartiest dispositions in them, to encourage the commercial intercourse, established under the auspices of the late Governor General, whose departure, however, the Regent regretted as the loss of the first friend and ally he became acquainted with, I believe it may be said, in any foreign nation. In him, was acknowledged also, the original cause of opening the communication, and commencing a correspondence between the governments of Bengal and Tibet. But though, in consequence of the Regent's having, from the beginning, been used exclusively to address himself to the agents of Mr. Hastings, his attachment to the English nation, during a long interchange of conciliating offices, had been mixed with a great degree of personality, yet, free from all unworthy capriciousness of temper, he descended not, to take advantage of the opening offered him, to close the new connection. The respect he had learned to entertain for our national integrity of character, was deep and sincere; and apparently from a conviction, that our views tended to no scheme of ambition, but were confined merely to objects of utility and curiosity: Poorungheer assures me, he expressed an anxious desire for continuing, with the succeeding Governor General, the exercise of those offices of friendship, so long supported by his predecessor. And, in the hope that his own would be met with equal good wishes on your part, he determined to invite you to join him, in preserving between Tibet and Bengal, the same intercourse of commerce and correspondence, so essentially calculated for the benefit of both countries. In consequence of these sentiments, the Lama and the Regent of Teshoo Loomboo addressed the letters, which Poorungheer had the honour to deliver to you. Translations of these letters, having applied for them to your Persian translator, in obeisance to your directions, I now subjoin, viz.

From Teshoo Lama.

" God be praised that the situation of these countries is in peace and happiness, and I am always praying at the altar of the Most High for your health and preservation. This is not unknown. You are certainly employed in protecting and assisting the whole world, and you promote the good and happiness of mankind. We have made no deviation from the union and unanimity, which existed during the time of the first of nobles, Mr. Hastings, and the deceased Lama; and may you also grant friendship to these countries, and always make me happy with the news of your health, which will be the cause of ease to my heart, and confirmation to my soul. At this time, as friendly offerings of union, and affection, and unanimity, I send one handkerchief, one kitoo of silver, and one piece of Cochin.

" Let them be accepted."

From the Regent of Teshoo Loomboo.

" God be praised that the situation of these countries is in peace and happiness, and I am always praying at the altar of the Almighty for your health and preservation. This is not unknown. I am constantly employed in promoting the advantage of the subjects, and the service of the newly seated Lama; because the newly seated Lama is not distinct from the deceased Lama, and the light of his forehead is exalted. Grant your friendship to Poorungheer Gosein, and maintain union, and unanimity, and affection, like the first of nobles: and every day make me happy by the news of your health and prosperity; and bestow favours like the first of nobles, and make me happy with letters, which are the cause of consolation.

"At this time, as friendly offerings of union, and affection, and unanimity, I send one handkercheif, three tola of gold, and one piece of Cochin.

"Let them be accepted."

Poorungheer, having received these dispatches, in the beginning of October, after a residence of five months at Teshoo Loomboo, took leave of the Lama, and the Regent, and set out upon his return, by the same route he came, to Bengal.

The weather, at this season of the year, being extremely favourable for travelling, he experienced no delay or interruption, in the course of his journey through Tibet and Bootan, but arrived at Rungpore early in December, whence he proceeded as expeditiously as possible to the presidency. Here, to his great mortification and concern, he finds upon his arrival, that his affairs are involved in great distress.

The little territory his adopted Chela was left in charge of, having during his absence been violently invaded by Raaj Chund, a neighbouring Zemeendar, and to the amount of fifty begas, forcibly taken out of his hands. Prevailed on by his earnest and repeated solicitation, I am induced to say for him, that in your justice and favour are his only hopes of relief from his embarrassments; and he humbly supplicates your protection in restoring, and securing him in the possession of his invaded rights. The liberty of this intercession, I am condent to think, would be forgiven, were it not in favour of one who has rendered various useful services to this government; but though of trivial importance, it affords also an authentic instance, of the encroaching disposition of inferior Zemeendars. Yet another circumstance it may not be improper to point out; that the ground alluded to, is a part of the land situated on the western bank of the river, opposite to Calcutta, which was formerly granted, under a sunnud of this government, to Teshoo Lama, for the foundation of a place of worship, and as a resort for those pilgrims of his nation, who might occasionally make visits to the consecrated Ganges.

Having, in conformity to your commands, done my best endeavours literally to translate all the information Poorungheer could give me, I have now to apologize for the prolixity of the account, in which I have been induced to be particularly minute, as I conceived that every circumstance, however trivial, might in some degree be interesting, which tends to illustrate any trait in the national character of a people with whom we are but recently become acquainted, and with whom, in its extended views, it has been an object of this government to obtain a closer alliance.

I will not now presume to intrude longer on your time, by adding any observations, or conjectures, deducible from the elevated importance your young ally seems rising to, in consequence of the signal respect paid him by the most exalted political characters known to his nation; but I beg leave to repeat, that it is with infinite satisfaction, I learn from the reports of Poorungheer, the flourishing state of the lately projected scheme of trade; to promote which, he assures me, not any thing has been wanting in facility of intercourse; that the adventurers, who had invested their property, had experienced perfect security in conducting their commerce, had carried their articles to an exceeding good market, and found the rate of exchange materially in their favour. These advantages, authorize an expectation, that these first attempts will gradually encourage a spirit of more extensive enterprize; and, permit me to add, I derive a confidence from this infant essay, which inspires me with the strongest hopes, that the commission, which your honourable Board was pleased to commit to my charge, will eventually be productive of essential benefit to the political and commercial interests of the Company.

I have the honour to be,

&c. &c. &c.

SAMUEL TURNER.

PART VI.

SOME ACCOUNT

OF THE

SITUATION OF AFFAIRS IN TIBET,

FROM

1785 TO 1793.

TIBET.

SOME ACCOUNT, &c.

THE affairs of Tibet continued in a flourishing and prosperous state till the year 1792, when intelligence was received, that a race of people who inhabit the mountains of Nipal, which are situated to the south of Tibet, to the west of Bootan, and border on the northern frontier of Bengal, had commenced hostilities against the states of Tibet. A numerous body were reported to be then in motion, and actually engaged in open invasion of the possessions of Teshoo Lama; to whose superior power, a nation without soldiers and without arms, was quickly found to be an easy prey.

The progress of the Nipalese then was rapid in the extreme; and though, roused by the alarm, multitudes assembled in the way, they could oppose no effectual resistance against the rude incursion of an impetuous enemy, naturally daring, and now animated with the hope of plunder. Their advance, therefore, against a panic-struck and unarmed multitude, was but very slightly impeded. No sooner had the alarm been given, than they appeared before Teshoo Loomboo, and, with great difficulty, the Lama, himself, and all the Gylongs of the monastery, found means to escape in time across the Berhampooter. Here, choosing a station remote from the river, the party remained awhile free from annoyance or pursuit; till at length the Lama, when it was perfectly ascertained that his capital had become a prey to the rapacity of plunderers, was conducted by slow marches towards Lassa.

In the mean time the Nipalese, eager to possess the spoils, which the fortune of war had placed within their reach, abandoned themselves entirely to plunder. The valuable booty, which had for ages been accumulating at Teeshoo Loomboo, appears to have been the chief, if not the sole, object of their inroad; for no sooner had they stripped the monastery of its treasures, and robbed the mausolea of the Lamas of all their most valuable ornaments, than they withdrew themselves towards the frontier, in order that they might effectually secure the spoils they had acquired.

In the mean time intelligence was conveyed, with the utmost expedition, to the court of China, of this daring and unprovoked aggression, from a people who had commenced hostilities upon the sacred territory. This information was no sooner received in China, than an edict was issued for the instant formation of an army, to protect and avenge the Lama.

The borders of Tartary, immediately contiguous to China, afforded a force amply sufficient for the occasion; and troops were summoned to assemble, and directed to proceed without delay, to Teshoo Loomboo. The Nipalese, however, had already decamped from thence, with a view immediately to lodge in safety, the treasures of which they had stripped the monastery. This purpose having been completely accomplished, they then reassembled in full force upon Tingri Meidan, an extensive plain, lying about midway between Nipal and Teeshoo Loomboo, where they determined to wait, and try their strength, in case the Tibetians should choose to give them battle.

The Chinese general, with the Tartar troops under his command, advanced without hesitation, and with a fixed determination to attack the enemy, having first directed the Tibetians, whom he came to succour, to keep aloof during the contest, that he might have only, under his command, men who had been disciplined and trained to arms. Thus adopting every necessary and prudent precaution, he marched to attack the enemy, and a severe contest is said to have been obstinately maintained, which at length terminated in the complete defeat of the Nipalese.

The general being determined to pursue his success with all convenient speed, came up with the enemy again immediately, upon the frontier; here he engaged them a second time, with the same good fortune as at first. The Nipalese were now forced to abandon the confines of Tibet, and hastened to enter their own territories. The pass, upon the borders of Nipal, was protected by a military post called Coti, and this they took especial care to strengthen with a powerful detachment, sufficient to keep the Chinese force in check, for a considerable time. From the advantage of position, these troops were enabled at first to maintain themselves against all assaults; but at length worn out by repeated attacks, the Nipalese were ultimately compelled to abandon this place also, and retire within the fastnesses of their mountains: yet this step was not determined on, without the most prudent circumspection. All the roads upon the hills were broken up, the bridges were removed from across the torrents, and every possible obstacle was thrown in the way of the enemy.

Thus closely pressed by a victorious army, and destitute of any immediate resource, the Nipalese were induced to solicit the interference of the British government.

Captain Kirkpatrick, an officer in our service, was at this time appointed ambassador to Nipal, and he was the first of our nation who ever obtained admission into that country. The object of his embassy was considered in different points of view, by the parties that were either directly, or remotely, engaged in the present contest. The Chinese commander is said to have made no very favourable report of the English, at his court, for he viewed our connection with the Nipalese in a most inauspicious light. These representations from him, and our declining to afford effectual assistance to the Lama's cause, had considerable weight at the Chinese court; the similarity of dress and discipline, between the Nipal soldiers and the battalions in the British service, is said, also, to have been most forcibly stated, and not without considerable effect, since the suspicious character of the Chinese, could hardly be persuaded to believe, that we had not given assistance to their enemies.

The Chinese troops, however, pursued their fortune with uniform success; and, daunted by their superior conduct and courage, the Nipalese now began to look upon all further resistance as vain, and immediately had recourse to the most abject and most submissive entreaty.

The Chinese general at length listened to their overtures, and granted them a peace, upon the conditions of an annual tribute to the empire, and the full restitution of all the spoils which they had carried away from the monastery of Teshoo Loomboo. Hostages were delivered for the due execution of these engagements ; the stipulations of the treaty were performed, and the army under the Chinese general withdrew, but not without establishing several military posts along the southern frontier. So careful, indeed, were the Chinese to avail themselves of every possible advantage within their reach, that they occupied an intermediate country between Bootan and Nipal, the territory of a petty chief, denominated Raja of Segwin, or Seccum, who had been sometimes vexed by the hostile interference, and long obnoxious to the caprice and rapacity of the Nipalese, on his offering to become subject to China, and accepting protection from the victorious general. A station was then established, of which a guard was left in charge; and thus the Chinese were put into actual possession of a military post, immediately adjoining to the territory of the East India Company in Bengal.

The Chinese commander attempted to extend his frontier over the country of the Daeb Raja, which bounds the possessions of the Company on the north, by a long continued line ; but he was not permitted to lead his forces over the intermediate mountains of Bootan ; and, in consequence of the opposition made by the Daeb Raja to his design, he was necessarily obliged to become content with establishing a station on their northern boundary, at Phari, which is a post of strength, upon the frontier of Tibet.

This circumstance has unhappily put a stop to all communication between the northern states, and the provinces of Bengál, as the Chinese, with their accustomed jealousy and caution, guard the station they were permitted to occupy. The approach of strangers, even of the natives of Bengal and Hindostan, is utterly prohibited.

A most violent prejudice prevails even against the Hindoo Goseins, who are charged with treachery against their generous patrons, by becoming guides and spies to the enemy, and have in consequence, it is said, been proscribed their accustomed abode at Teshoo Loomboo, where they had been ever patronised in great numbers by the Lama, and enjoyed particular favour and indulgence. From this period, unhappily, is to be dated the interruption which has taken place in the regular intercourse between the Company's possessions, and the territory of the Lama.

APPENDIX.

No. I.

Translation of a Letter from Kienlong, Emperor of China, to Dalai Lama, the Grand Lama of Tibet.

PLACED by heaven at the head of ten thousand kingdoms, my utmost endeavours are employed to govern them well. I neglect no means to procure peace and happiness to all that have life. I endeavour also to make learning and religion flourish. Lama, I am persuaded that you enter into my views, and that your intentions accord with mine. I am not ignorant that you do all, that depends on you, to omit nothing your religion prescribes, and to follow exactly all the laws. You are punctual at prayer, and you bestow the attention that praying well requires. It is principally by this that you become the most firm support of the religion of Fo. I rejoice in it from my heart, and give you, with pleasure, the praises that are your due.

By the favour of heaven I enjoy health. I wish, Lama, that you may enjoy the same blessing, and that you may long continue to offer up your fervent prayers.

The year before last the Punjun Irtinnee set out from Teshoo Loomboo, in order to pray here, upon the occasion of my seventieth birthday, to which I am drawing nigh. He performed his journey in good health. As soon as I was acquainted with his departure, and that he informed me he was to pass the winter at Koumboum, I sent the Lieutenant General Ouan-fou, and another grandee, named Pao-tai, to meet him, and ordered them to convey to him a soutchou[a] of pearls, that I had myself worn; a saddle, and all the accoutrements of a riding horse; some utensils of silver, and other trifles. They found him at Koumboum, treated him in my name with a feast of ceremony, and delivered these presents.

This last year the Punjun Irtinnee having left Koumboum on his route to me, I sent to him, a second time, the grandees of my presence, Our-tou-ksoon and Ta-fou, accompanied by Ra-koo, a Lama of the rank of Hou-touk-too[b]. To these three deputies I committed one of my travelling chairs, one of my camp tents, the small flags, and other tokens of distinction proper to create respect, with which he was to be complimented on my behalf.

They met him at the town of Houhou, and presented to him what they were commissioned with, after having given him, as before, a feast of ceremony.

When I learned that he was no more than a few days journey from the frontiers, I dispatched to meet him the sixth Ague, who is now the eldest of my sons, and caused him to be accompanied by the Hou-touk-tou-tchen-kio. They met him at the Miao, or temple, of Taihan: there they saluted him on my part, gave him a feast of ceremony, and presented to him in my name a soutchou of pearls, more valuable than those first sent; a cap, enriched with pearls; a led horse, with saddle and accoutrements; some utensils of silver, and other trifles.

After his departure from the Miao of Taihan, the Punjun Irtinnee repaired to Tolonor, where he waited some time in order to receive all I designed to send him. I deputed, for the purpose of saluting him, those of the princes of the blood, who have the title Khawn, and guards of my person. They were accompanied by Fenchen and Tchiloun, officers of rank, and by the Lamas Avouang, Patchour, and Ramtchap. They presented to him in my

[a] The soutchou is a string of beads formed of different substances, as of coral, pearl, glass, sweet scented wood, &c. which the Lamas and Mandarines carry as marks of distinction. P. Amiot. And use as rosaries, repeating the sacred sentence, *Oom maunee paimee oom*, as they pass each bead between the finger and the thumb.

[b] Hou-touk-too, are with the Lamas what bishops are with us. P. Amiot.

name a cap of ceremony, ornamented with pearls, and many utensils of gold and silver. On the 21st day of the seventh moon, the Punjun Irtinnee arrived at Ghol, where I then was, and gave me a feast of ceremony, to which the Lamas of his suite, from Loumboo[c] and Poutala[d], were admitted. I gave, in return, a solemn entertainment; but apart, to all the Lamas of Gehol, to the Lamas of the Tchasaks, of the Eleuths, of the Kokonors, of the Tourgouths, and of the Turbeths.

During this festival the Mongoux princes, the Begs, the Taidji, and other principal nobility of the different hordes, as well as the deputies, or ambassadors, from the Coreans, the Mahomedans, and others, who were assembled at Gehol, did homage to him, by performing the ceremonies of respect, used on such occasions.

Delighted with a reception so honourable and so uncommon, the Punjun Irtinnee expressed marks of satisfaction, that charmed all these strangers in their turn. He took this occasion to request that I would permit him to accompany me to Pekin; to which I consented. The second day of the ninth moon was that, on which he made his entry, into this capital of my vast dominions. All the Lamas, many thousands in number, came forth to meet him, prostrated themselves in his presence, and fulfilled, with respect to him, the other duties which their customs prescribe. After all these ceremonies were finished, he was conducted to Yuen-ming-yuen, and I assigned for his habitation that part of my palace, which is named the golden apartment.

I gave directions that every thing worthy of curiosity, in the environs, should be shewn to him: he accordingly went to Hiang-chan, to Ouan-cheou-chan, and other places deserving notice.

He visited the Miaos, or temples, of these different places, and was every where received with distinguished honours. He officiated in person, at the dedication of the imperial Miao, which I had erected at Ouan-cheou-chan, and which was just then completed.

On the third day of the tenth moon, I gave him a grand entertainment in

[c] Teshoo Loomboo, the residence of Teshoo Lama.

[d] Pootala, the residence of Dalai Lama.

the garden of Yueng-ming-yuen; and, during the entertainment, I caused to be brought, in presence of all the court, the various articles I designed for him, and which I added to those already presented.

After the entertainment he repaired, with the principal persons of his suite, to the Miao of the ampliation of charity, and to that of concord. He offered up prayers in the one and in the other, for the prosperity of my reign, and for the benefit and happiness of every living creature.

The Punjun Irtinnee, in undertaking a journey of twenty thousand lys, to contribute to the celebrity of my Ouan-cheou[e], did more than sufficient, to entitle him to all the distinctions, that could evince my sense of his kindness; but the air of satisfaction and pleasure, which diffused itself on all around him, and which he himself manifested, whenever he was admitted to my presence, impressed on my mind, one of the most exquisite gratifications it ever felt. I remarked, with a peculiar sentiment of affection, that he never once spoke to me on the subject of his return. He seemed disposed to fix his abode near my person. But, alas! how uncertain are the events of this life!

On the twentieth of the tenth moon, the Punjun Irtinnee felt himself indisposed. I was informed of it, and instantly sent my physicians to visit him. They reported to me that his complaints were serious, and even dangerous. I did not hesitate to go to him in person, in order to judge myself of his situation. He received me with the same tokens of pleasure, that he had ever shewn when admitted to my presence; and from the words full of satisfaction, with which he addressed me, I might have conceived that he was in the complete enjoyment of health. It was, however, far otherwise; and the venom of the small-pox, had already spread itself through all parts of his body.

The second day of the eleventh moon, his disorder was pronounced to be incurable. The Punjun Irtinnee suddenly changed his corporeal dwelling[f]. The afflicting intelligence was immediately communicated to me. The shock

[e] Seventieth birthday.

[f] This is the consecrated term, to say that he had ceased living, or that he died. P. Amiot.

overcame me. With a heart full of the most poignant grief, and eyes bathed in tears, I repaired to the yellow chapel, where, with my own hands, I burned perfumes to him.

Although I am well aware, that to come and to go, are but as the same thing to the Punjun Irtinnee, yet when I reflect, that he made a most long and painful journey, for the sole purpose of doing honour to the day of my Ouan-cheou; and that after having fulfilled that object, it was not his fate to return in tranquillity, as I had hoped, to the place of his usual abode: this reflection, I say, is distressing to me beyond all expression. To console me in some degree, or, at least, to attempt some alleviation of my griefs, I have resolved to render memorable, the day of his regeneration. I named for the guard of his body Chang-tchaopa, Soui-boun-gue, and some other grandees; and gave them particular orders for the construction of a receptacle for it, worthy of such precious remains, which lie in the interior of the yellow temple. I gave directions also for making a shrine of gold, in which should be deposited the body of the Irtinnee. This was executed by the twenty-first day of the twelfth moon. I then regulated the hundred days of prayer, counting from that day, on which he disappeared. It was only to alleviate, however little, the grief in which my heart was overwhelmed, that I acted so. I also caused several towers to be erected in different places, which I considered as so many palaces that he might have planned himself for varying his abode, or such as I might have assigned to him for his recreation. I bestowed bounties, on his behalf, to the most eminent of his disciples, and to the principal Houtouktous. I gave them soutchous of pearls, with permission to wear them; and I particularly distinguished the brother of Irtinnee, by conferring on him the title of prince of the efficient prayer. I did not neglect the Tchasak Lamas, in the distribution of my gifts. Several amongst them, were decorated with honourable titles, and received from me, soutchous of pearls, pieces of silk, and other things, with which they appeared to be gratified.

My design, in entering with you into this detail, is, to prove to you the estimation in which I hold whatever is connected with you, and the profound regard I have for your person. The number of one hundred days, allotted to prayer, was completed on the thirteenth of the second moon of the present year. I issued my orders for the departure: the body was conveyed with due pomp; and I joined the procession myself, in person, as far as it was proper I should go. I deputed the sixth Ague, now the eldest of my sons, to accompany it to the distance of three days journey from this capital; and I nominated Petchingue, mandarin in the tribunal of foreign affairs, and Iroultou, one of my guards, to accompany it all the way to Teshoo Loomboo. Although the Punjun Irtinnee, has changed his abode, I have full confidence that, with the aid I have rendered to him, he will not long delay to be fixed in another habitation.

Lama, it is my desire that you shew kindness to all the Lamas of Teshoo Loomboo, and respect them on my account: from the conduct they have observed, I judge them worthy of being your disciples. I recommend to you, especially those who accompany the body, and who will perform the number of prayers, that you shall regulate, for the completion of the funeral rites. I hope you will cheerfully execute what you know will be agreeable to me. It only remains for me to add, that I send you Petchingue and his suite, to salute you in my name, and inform themselves of the state of your health. They will deliver to you a soutchou of coral, to be used on grand festivals; a tea-pot of gold, weighing thirty ounces; a bowl of the same metal, and the same weight; a tea-pot and bowl of silver; thirty soutchous of various different coloured beads, and twenty purses, great and small, of various colours.

The fourteenth of the second moon, of the forty-sixth year of the reign of Kienlong.

No. II.

Translation of a Letter from Changoo Cooshoo Punjun Irtinnee Neimoheim, Regent of Teshoo Loomboo, to Warren Hastings, Esq. Governor General, &c. &c. Received the 12th February, 1782.

To the fountain of benefits, abounding in excellencies, ornament of the chief seat of power and of greatness, shedding splendour on the leaders of Europe; repository of valour and magnanimity; exalted in enterprize; high in dignity; the Governor Immaud u' Dowlah. May his fortitude and his existence be perpetuated by the bounty of Almighty God!

Some time before this, the Khawkawn of China called unto him the lord of his votaries, the luminary of the world, Maha Gooroo, with earnest solicitations: and on the 17th of the month Rubbee u' saunie, in the year of the Hejera, 1193[a], the Lama, according to agreement, directed his steps towards the region of China. And when he passed his sacred foot forth from this land, the Khawkawn dispatched forward to receive him leaders of high distinction; and he caused to be prepared, and kept in readiness, cattle to transport his baggage, and conveyances and tents, and necessaries of every denomination. And there is a Soobah, and they call that land Seur Pootaullah, and on the 22nd of the month Rubbee u' saunie, in the year of the Hejera, 1194[b], Maha Gooroo, and the Khawkawn of China met each other in that Soobah, in joy and satisfaction; and they continued there for the space of one month; and they proceeded on from thence to the city of Picheen, that is to say, the royal city, where is the exalted throne of the Emperor: and in that city they remained for six months.

[a] Corresponding to the 17th of June, A. D. 1779.

[b] Corresponding to the 11th June, A. D. 1780.

And in those days the Khawkawn of mighty power, in the abundance of his faith, and his love for the truth, exhibited unbounded proofs of his obedience and submission, and paid the duties of reverence and respect.

And the Maha Gooroo, on whom be the continued blessing of the Almighty! instructed many of the sages of China, and of the sages of Kilmauk, in knowledge; and he caused their heads to be shaven, and received them into the number of the obedient: and he conferred innumerable blessings on the inhabitants of that land, and they received joy and happiness from his presence.

And down to this time the Maha Gooroo was well in health; but the water and the air of China proved adverse, and were as pernicious (to him) as the pestilential and hot blast to a cold and frozen body; and the maladies and the distempers which were produced were many and various. And at this time, such was the will of God, eruptions of the small-pox came forth, and our earnest endeavours, and the application of numerous remedies, availed nothing; for the predominating star of our happiness was reversed and obscured, and the shadow of our protector was withdrawn, and we were excluded from his presence, and the only remedies which remained were resignation and submission. The measure of his existence was filled up, and the lip of the cup of life was overflowed: and he retired from this perishable world, to the everlasting mansions, on the first day of the month of Rujjub, in the year of the Hejera, 1194[*]: and to us it was, as if the heavens had been precipitated on our heads, as if the splendid and glorious orb of day had been converted into utter darkness.

The multitude lifted up, on all sides, the voice of sorrow and lamentation; but what availed it? for fortune, treacherous and deceitful, had determined against us.

And we all bent down on the knee of funeral affliction, and performed the holy obsequies, such as were due. And we now supplicate, with an united voice, the return of the hour of transmigration; that the bodies may be speedily exchanged, and our departed Lama again be restored to our sight.

[*] 5th of July, A. D. 1780.

This is our only object, our sole employment. May the Almighty God, who listeneth to the supplications of his servants, accept our prayers!

And after the death of the Lama, the gracious conduct of the Khawkawn was still the same, or rather his royal favour was still greater than before, insomuch that it might be said Maha Gooroo was still living, such was the excess of his bounty.

And when the funeral solemnities were concluded, we received our dismission. And the Emperor caused supplies of food and raiment, and necessaries of every sort, to be prepared: and he ordered people to be stationed at the different stages, to convey the corpse of the deceased Lama from one to the other.

And when we turned our faces from the land of China, he caused carriages to be given to my followers: and he appointed two Ameer ul Omras to attend the sacred remains of the Lama for its protection; and on the 21st day of the month Shawal, in the year of the Hejera 1195[d], in the morning, I arrived at the place of my abode in safety; and a tomb had been prepared, before our arrival, for the body of the departed Lama; and we deposited his remains therein: and we presented the necessary offerings, and distributed alms to promote the transmigration: and we are unremitting in our supplications, that he may speedily appear again on the face of the earth. May they be accepted!

Poorungheer Gosein arrived here in the year 1193, after the departure of the Lama towards China, and two letters, and nine strings of pearls, without blemish, and perfect in their form; and among them one string of large pearl of great brightness and purity, and two chaplets of coral, which you sent as a gift, arrived safe: and your satisfactory letters, and that which you wrote concerning the village of the Raja, and the remission of all matters relating thereto, to do honour to me; the whole, as there written, was in those days submitted to the inspection of Maha Gooroo; and the joy which he expressed on reading these things was exceeding great: and the friendly letter, and the two rosaries of pearl and coral, one of them intermixed pearl

[d] 23d of October, 1781.

and coral, and the other coral alone, which in the abundance of your kindness and favour you sent as a gift to me, arrived in a happy hour, and was the cause of much satisfaction,

And regarding your refusal to receive the value of the nine strings of pearls, and of the two chaplets of coral, directing, on the contrary, that they should be presented as a gift; as the pearls are of great beauty and of exceeding high price, and forasmuch as your friendship to Maha Gooroo was evident and apparent, in consideration of these things, I could not presume to take them.

I formerly wrote to you, requesting that, with the value of unwrought gold which I sent to you, certain pearls and coral might be purchased, and that the price of the pearls, and the coral, might be balanced by the produce thereof; and if it should be deficient for that purpose, that you would inform me of that deficiency, so that I might write to you, and transmit that which was wanting; and if, on the contrary, there should be a surplus remaining out of the value of the gold, that other pearls, and other coral, of the first quality, might be purchased therewith.

And I have moreover strong hope, and firm expectation, that as you formerly shewed kindness and attention to the application respecting the village of the Raja, so in regard to the certain portion of land, and the mahsool thereon, that favour will be shewn. I presume to repeat the request, that corresponding to the application of Maha Gooroo, you will shew kindness and favour with respect to that portion of land, and in settling the disputes appertaining thereto; and furthermore, that you will grant a lot of land in the noble city of Calcutta, on the bank of the river. Concerning this affair I have spoken fully and particularly to the Gosein, Poorungheer, and he will make known to you the whole thereof, and you will comply with my request.

And I have communicated other matters, and other things, to the faithful Poorungheer, by whom you will be informed of them. In compliance with his wishes, you will permit him to remain under the shadow of your protection, and favour him with such marks of your kindness, as may enable him to pass his days in returning thanks for your goodness.

You must persist in sending to me constant information of your health, that the garden of pleasure and satisfaction may continue to flourish.

To trouble you more would exceed that which is right. May your happiness and prosperity remain firm and unshaken!

Written on the first day of the month Zehijjah, in the year of the Hejera 1195, corresponding to the 16th November, 1781.

No. III.

Translation of a Letter from Soopoon Choomboo, Mirkin Chassa Lama, Minister to the late Teshoo Lama, to Warren Hastings, Esq. Governor General, &c. &c. Received the 12th February, 1782.

To the source of magnanimity; equal in glory to the sun; first of the leaders of Europe; the selected of the mighty and the noble; the exalted in dignity; the Governor Immaud u' Dowlah. May his fortitude and his existence be perpetuated by the beneficence of Almighty God!

Having kissed the earth with the respect of the lowly, the meanest of your devoted (servants), the humblest of your faithful friends, Soopoon Choomboo, represents unto you, that the lord of his disciples, the illuminator of the world, Maha Gooroo, in the year of the Hejera 1193[a], sat in the plenitude of good fortune, on the musnud of authority: and in those days I sent to you an humble writing, by the Gosein, Poorungheer, which you received, and in answer thereto you sent a letter, and choice gifts; and those, and the string of coral, which, in the greatness of your bounty, you conferred upon me, arrived safe, and in happy hour, on the 16th day of the month Rubbee ul Auwul, in the year of the Hejera 1195, at the place which they call Coomboo, in the land of Tibburut, in the region of China; and I was exalted thereby.

And the Khullefah Bugwan, that is to say, Maha Gooroo, on the 17th day of the month Rubbee u' saunee, in the year of the Hejera 1193[b], directed the reins of his intention from Teshoo Loomboo towards the land of China. And the various inhabitants of the environs, and the places round about, of Lhobah, and of Khumbauk, those who sojourn in tents, and those who live in cities, came, and were received according to their degrees, and their stations. And the chief princes of the land, and the pillars of the state,

[a] A. D. 1779.

[b] Corresponding to the 17th June, 1779.

and the great leaders, came forth to meet and to guard him on the high road: and they were waiting his arrival with eager expectation; and they obtained admission to the honours of audience in crowds, crowd after crowd, and they presented their gifts, and their offerings: and he laid his hand, conferring blessings, upon their heads, and made them joyful: and this was the established practice all the way.

Thus he travelled on through the journies and the stages; and in the Soobah of Seur Pootaullah, which is a place exceedingly delightful, the Khawkawn of China met him, and saw him in joy and satisfaction; and he remained there with the King of China for the space of one month; and the king prepared entertainments of various sorts, and made feasts after divers manners.

And during this time the Gosein, Poorungheer, made known those things in which you had repeatedly instructed him; all of them he made known; and all which you had said and directed, was acceptable and pleasing to the Lama; and he took measures, according with the wishes of your noble heart.

And to the dignified sages, who are renowned throughout the earth, both to those of China and to those of Kilmauk, and also to the Khawkawn of China, he explained your sayings; and he instructed them in the things relating to astronomy, and to geography, and in other matters, and in the principles of the religious institutions of which they needed information; and they obtained explanations of these things, and they were favoured thereby; and they heard all which was related to them with the ear of attention.

But at this time, because of our wickedness, the holy Lama accepted to himself severe distempers, and he retired from this perishable world to the eternal mansions; leaving us, his followers, overwhelmed with the sorrows of separation.

For those things which relate to the speedy coming to pass of the transmigration, the Khawkawn of China, and the Lama of Lassa, that is the Dalai Lama, and the holy instructor of the king, Chaungeah Lama, and others, venerable men of those parts, unite their supplications and their prayers, that a new body may be quickly vivified by the spirit of our Lama, so that he may again shine forth among us.

From the relation of Poorungheer, inform yourself of those things which are past, and of those which are present, and of those things which are to come to pass. The hearts of the sacred Bhoots, and the hearts of the Dewtahs, Deovetahs; prophets, founders of their religion, and the heart of the Lama, are one and the same heart. Of this there is no manner of doubt; and according to this, the transmigration of the holy Lama must quickly and speedily come to pass,

With respect to your true friendship, and your firm affection to Maha Gooroo, it is my hope that your kindness will be increased, not that it will be diminished; by the favour of God it shall be still greater than it is; and that you will honour your abject and unworthy friend, Soopoon Choomboo, with your favour, and issue to him your commands, without delay, and without hesitation, on aught which shall appertain to him to do; that from his heart, and from his soul, he may exert himself therein.

May the shadow and the support of the Almighty be on and with you!

On the first day of the month Zehijjah, in the year of the Hejera 1195, corresponding to the 16th of November, 1781.

No. IV.

Narrative of the Particulars of the Journey of Teshòo Làma, and his Suite, from Tibet to China, from the verbal Report of Poorungheer Gosein.

POORUNGHEER Gosein, who attended Teshoo Lama on his journey to visit the Emperor of China, relates, that during the years 1777, 1778, and 1779, Teshoo Lama, or Lama Gooroo, of Bhote, or Tibet, received repeated invitation, by letters, from the Emperor of China, expressed in the most earnest terms, that he would visit him at his capital city of Piechein, or Pekin; but the Lama continued for a long time to avoid complying with the Emperor's requests, by excuses, such as, that the climate, air, and water of China, were very hurtful to the inhabitants of his country; but above all, that he understood the small-pox was a prevalent disorder there, and that his followers, as well as himself, were very apprehensive of that disorder, as few instances, if any, could be given, of an inhabitant of Bhote, or Tibet, recovering from it.

Another letter arrived from the Emperor, still more earnest than any that had yet been received, telling the Lama, "that he looked up to him as the first, and most holy being of those on earth, who devoted their time to the service of the Almighty; and that the only remaining wish, he now felt, was to see him, and to be ranked amongst his disciples. My age," says the Emperor in one of his letters, "is now upwards of seventy years, and the only blessing I can enjoy, before I quit this life, will be to see you, and to join in acts of devotion with the divine Teshoo Lama." On the presumption that the entreaties of age and devotion would be complied with, the Emperor informed him, that houses were erected for the reception of the Lama, and his followers, upon different places of the road by which he would pass, which had cost upwards of twenty lacks of rupees: that all the inhabitants of that part of

China, through which his journey lay, had orders to have tents, &c. in readiness, at all the different stages, and that horses, carriages, mules, money, and provisions, for his whole retinue, should be in constant readiness, at all places, and times, during his journey. The Emperor sent, with his letter, one string of very valuable pearls, and one hundred pieces of curious silks, by the hands of Leamabaw, a trusty person, whom he sent to attend the Lama in his journey.

At the same time, letters were written by the Emperor to the Lama of Lassa, and to several principal inhabitants of Bhote, or Tibet, desiring them to add their entreaties to his, to prevail upon Teshoo Lama to visit him.

They accordingly assembled, and waited upon the Lama, who was, at length, prevailed upon to give his consent to proceed to China; at the same time observing to some of his confidential friends, that he felt some internal repugnance, from an idea that he should not return: however, all things being put in readiness, he began his journey, upon the 2d of Sawun, in the 1836 Sumbutt, or æra of Rajah Bicher Majeet (answering, according to our æra, to the 15th of July, 1779), from his own country, attended by about one thousand five hundred troops, and followers of different kinds, carrying with him presents for the Emperor, made up of all the rarities of his own, and the neighbouring countries.

After forty-six days of his journey, he arrived at the town of Doochoo, on the banks of a river of the same name, where he was met by a messenger, named Woopayumba, from the Emperor, with a letter, and presents of pearls, silks, and many other valuable articles, with a rich palanquin.

A boarded platform, about the height of a man's breast, was always set up where the Lama's tents were pitched, or wherever he halted on the road; this was covered with a rich brocade, and a cushion of the same, upon which he sat, whilst the people were admitted to the honour of touching his foot with their foreheads. The seat was surrounded by a kinnaut, or tent wall, to keep at a distance the crowd, who continually followed him for that purpose.

After journeying for twenty-one days farther, during all which time the Lama, and his attendants, met with every attention from the people on the road, and every kind of entertainment was provided for them, he arrived at a place called Thooktharing, where he was met by eight men of distinction, of the country of Kalmauk, with about two thousand troops, who were to attend him, by the Emperor's orders; but after their presents, which consisted of gold, silver, horses, mules, silks, &c. were received, the Lama dismissed them, not having occasion for their attendance, and he continued his journey nineteen days, at the end of which he came to a place called Coomboo Goombaw, a populous city, where there stands, near a small river, a large and famous Putawlaw, or temple of public worship, to which many thousand Khoseong, or devout men, annually resort. This place is also the residence of great numbers of these poor devout people. In a day or two after his arrival here, the winter commenced, and the snow fell so heavy, and in such quantities, that the whole face of the ground was covered, too deep for the Lama to proceed upon his journey, for the space of four months. During his stay at this place, a messenger from the Emperor arrived with a letter, together with many presents, amongst which were five strings of pearls, a curious watch, snuff box, and knife, all ornamented with jewels, besides many curious brocades and silks.

At this place, as well as during the Lama's journey through Kalmauk, he was continually importuned, by all ranks of people, for *a mark of his hand*, which, being coloured with *saffron*, he extended, and made a full print of it on a piece of clean paper. Many thousand of these were printed off, in the like manner, for the multitude that daily surrounded him, which they carefully preserved as the most sacred relics. At this place, the chief of the province of Lanjoo, named Choondoo, with ten thousand troops, waited upon the Lama, by the Emperor's orders, and presented him with a very rich palanquin, a large tent, twenty horses, several mules, &c. the whole amounting, in value, to upwards of twenty-five thousand illeung: an illeung of silver weighs *3 rs. 4 as.* equivalent to about *7 s.*

During the Lama's stay at this place, he was also visited by a chief, named Choondaw, with five thousand attendants; a man of much consequence, and a religious character, in his country, who tarried with him many days.

Upon receiving his dismission, he made presents of three hundred horses, seventy mules, one hundred camels, one thousand pieces of brocade, and forty thousand illeung in silver. At the end of four months, the weather becoming moderate, and the snow being in great measure dissolved, the Lama proceeded on his journey, and was attended by the chief of Lanjoo, with all his troops, for seven days, when the Lama dismissed him, and continued his journey eight days farther, until he arrived at a considerable city, called Toomdawtoloo, in the province of Allasseah, where he was met by prince Cheewaung, son-in-law to the Emperor, who he received sitting in his tent, and by whom he was presented with one hundred horses, one hundred camels, twenty mules, and twenty thousand illeung in silver. The next day the Lama pursued his journey, accompanied by the prince Cheewaung; and at the end of nine days, arrived at Nissaur, a very large city, where Prince Cheewaung took his leave. The officers of government at this town, made the Lama many presents, and behaved with the most particular attention and respect.

After two days journey from the city of Nessaur, the Lama reached a town called Tawbunkaykaw, in the district of Hurtoosoo, where he was met by nine chiefs of the province of Hurtoosoo; each of these made their respective presents, to the amount of forty-five thousand illeungs of silver, and continued to attend him, in his journey, for sixteen days, to a town called Chawcawnsooburgaw, where, at their joint entreaties, he halted two days, at the end of which they presented him with two hundred horses, twenty camels, five hundred mountain cows, and four hundred illeung in silver, and then received their dismission.

The journey of the Lama was continued for twelve days, until he arrived at the town of Khawramboo, where he was met by a messenger, called Tawmbaw, from the Emperor, with a letter of congratulation, and presents, which consisted of a curious, and rich carriage, on two wheels, drawn by four horses and four mules, one palanquin, two strings of pearls, two hundred pieces of yellow silks, twenty flags, twenty chubdars, and sutaburdars. These compliments, which were received by the Lama, with great humility, were, notwithstanding, offered with the most profound respect; and he continued his journey towards the capital.

After six days he arrived at Taygaw Goombaw, where he was met by the prince, the Emperor's first son, and Cheengeeah Gooroo, a priest, or man of the first religious order, together with ten thousand troops and attendants. The prince was received by the Lama at his tent, who continued upon his seat, until the prince arrived at the door, where the Lama met him, and taking him by the hand, led him to his seat, which was formed of several embroidered cushions, of different sizes, each laid upon a boarded platform; upon the largest of which the Lama placed himself, and seated the prince upon a small one, at his left hand, which he, however, would not occupy, until the Lama had first received from him a string of very valuable pearls, sent by the Emperor. On the next morning the Lama, accompanied by the prince, and his followers, proceeded on his journey for nineteen days, when he arrived at the city of Tolownoor, where, during seven days, Cheengeea Gooroo, entertained the Lama, and the prince, and presented the Lama, at one of these entertainments, with forty thousand illeung of silver, and other customary presents.

After this, continuing their journey for fifteen days, to a considerable town, called Singhding, he was met by another prince, a younger son of the Emperor, who, after being introduced, and his presents received, informed the Lama, that the Emperor was arrived at a country seat, called Jeeawaukho, about the distance of twenty-four miles from Singhding, whither he had come to receive the Lama, and where there were most beautiful and extensive parks and gardens, with four or five magnificent houses.

The Lama proceeded next morning, attended by the princes, &c. to wait upon the Emperor; and being arrived within about three and a half coss, or seven miles, of the Emperor's residence, he found the troops of the Emperor formed in a rank entire, on each side of the road, between which He, and the princes, with his brother, and six of his followers only (the writer of this was one of his attendants at this time, by the Lama's particular desire), passed on all the way to the palaces of Jeeawaukho; and upon the Lama, &c.

entering in the inner garden, where the Emperor's own palace is situated, the Emperor met him, at the distance of at least forty paces from his throne, on which he usually sat; and immediately stretching forth his hand, and taking hold of the Lama's, led him towards the throne, where, after many salutations, and expressions of affection and pleasure, on both sides, the Lama was seated by the Emperor upon the uppermost cushion with himself, and at his right hand. Much conversation ensued; and the Emperor was profuse in his questions and inquiries, respecting the Lama's health, the circumstances of his journey, and the entertainment he had met with upon the road. Having satisfied the Emperor as to these particulars, the Lama presented him with the rarities he had brought for that purpose; all of which the Emperor received in the most gracious manner. After about an hour's conversation, the Lama withdrew, being presented by the Emperor with one hundred thousand taunk, or illeung of silver, and many hundred pieces of curious silks, some strings of pearls, and other curiosities of China. Each of his attendants were, also, presented with one hundred taunk in silver, and some pieces of brocade.

The Lama then withdrew, and was conducted to a magnificent palace, about one mile from the Emperor's, which had been erected for his abode.

On the next day the Emperor, with the princes, and many nobles of the court, attended by five thousand troops, visited the Lama; who advanced half way to the gate to meet them, where he received the first salute from the Emperor. The usual compliments on both sides having passed, the Lama entreated the Emperor to take the seat to the right, which, with some reluctance, he complied with: but, before the Emperor took his seat, he presented the Lama with the following presents: two lockbaws, or cloaks of curious and most valuable furs; one string of rich pearls; four thousand pieces of brocades; fifty thousand taunk of silver; and two curious pictures, ornamented with jewels.

After some indifferent conversation, the Emperor then communicated his wishes more at large, with respect to the desire he felt, of being instructed in some mysteries of the Lama's religion. They accordingly withdrew, attended only by Cheengeea Gooroo, to another part of the palace, where three seats were prepared, the one in the centre, larger than either of the others in extent, and rising considerably higher, upon which the Lama seated himself, placing the Emperor on that lower, which stood to the right, and Cheengea Gooroo on that at his left. The Lama then, bending his head towards the Emperor, whispered in his ear for about a quarter of an hour, and then setting himself upright, began to repeat aloud certain tenets, or religious sentences, distinctly, which the Emperor and Cheengeea Gooroo continued to repeat after him; and in this manner each sentence was repeated, until the Emperor and his Gooroo were perfect in them. This ceremony lasted upwards of three hours, whilst all their attendants were kept at a considerable distance, in the outer apartment, except two or three devout men, whose attendance on the Lama, at certain intervals of the ceremony, was necessary, and were occasionally called in.

The ceremony being concluded for that day, the Lama attended the Emperor half way to the gate, where they separated, and each retired to their respective palaces of residence. After four days the Lama, by an invitation, waited on the Emperor at his palace, where they were entertained for some time with music, and the dancing of boys. After the entertainment, Cheengeea Gooroo, arising from his seat, behind the Emperor, came in front, and addressing him, told him that the Lama wished to mention to him a circumstance, which friendship required him not to neglect. The Emperor then, turning to the Lama, desired he would speak without reserve; when the Lama proceeded to inform him,—" In the country of Hindostan, which " lies on the borders of my country, there resides a great prince, or ruler, " for whom I have the greatest friendship. I wish you should know and " regard him also; and if you will write him a letter of friendship, and " receive his in return, it will afford me great pleasure, as I wish you should " be known to each other, and that a friendly communication should, in " future, subsist between you." The Emperor replied, that his request was a very small one indeed, but that this, or any thing else he desired, should be readily complied with: he continued to inquire of the Lama what that prince or governor's name was, the extent of the country he ruled over, and the number of his forces, &c.? upon which the writer of this narrative was called into the presence by the Lama, and desired, by him, to answer the inquiries of the Emperor, respecting the governor of Hindostan, as he, the writer, had been often in his country. The writer then informed him, that the governor of Hindostan was called Mr. Hastings, that the extent of the country he governed was not near equal to that of China, but superior to any other he knew, and that the troops of that country upwards of three lacks of horsemen. The conversation then took another turn for half an hour, when the Lama withdrew. During twenty-six days, that the Emperor and Lama continued at the palaces of Jeeawaukho, several visits were mutually paid, in the most friendly and intimate manner. The Emperor still continuing to make rich presents to the Lama, whenever he visited him.

Upon their departure from Jeeawaukho towards Piechein, or Pekin, the Emperor, with his retinue, took a road which lay a little to the left, in order to visit the tombs of his ancestors; and the Lama, attended by the princes, and Cheengeea Gooroo, proceeded on the direct road towards Pekin, for seven days, till they arrived at a palace called Seawrah Soommaw, in the neighbourhood of Pekin, about two miles without the exterior wall of the city, where the Lama was lodged in a very magnificent house, said to have been built for his reception. Here, during five days, he was constantly attended by many of the Emperor's relations, from the city, and almost all the nobility of the court.

The ceremony of introduction, and mode of receiving the blessing of the Lama, at the time of being presented to him, may here be best remarked. When any of the princes, or immediate relations of the Emperor's, were presented, they were all received by the Lama, without moving from where he sat, but they were distinguished by his laying his bare hand upon their heads, whilst he repeated a short prayer, or form of blessing. The nobility, or men of the second rank, when introduced, went through the like ceremony, except, that the Lama wrapt a piece of clean silk round his hand, and in that manner rested it on their heads, whilst he repeated the blessing; and for those of inferior note, a piece of consecrated wood, of about half a yard long, was substituted, and held by him in his hand, with the end of which he touched their heads, in like manner as he had the others with his hand.

After five days residence here, during which time he was almost continually employed, in conferring his blessing, as above, information was brought him of the approach of the Emperor towards Sewarah Soommaw, and that he was at the distance of nine or ten coss. The Lama proceeded, next morning, to meet him, and halted at a country house of the Emperor's, about eight miles from Sewarah Soommaw, to refresh. Here he received a message from the Emperor, requesting him not to fatigue himself by coming any farther. The Lama in consequence halted, and sent his brother, with several others, to meet the Emperor, and present his compliments. Upon the Emperor's arrival, the Lama met him at the door, and, taking him by the hand, conducted him to an apartment, where they conversed and drank tea together. After an hour, the Lama was conducted to another house, prepared for him in the garden, by the Emperor himself, who took leave at the door, and returned to his own. He then sent for his eldest son, and gave him orders, that on the next morning, he, with a splendid retinue, should attend the Lama, and conduct him to see all his country palaces, places of worship, &c. in the neighbourhood of Pekin; and also to the great lakes, upon which were two large ships, and many smaller vessels; and that he would be attentive to point out to the Lama every thing that was curious about the city.

The prince immediately waited upon the Lama at his house, and informed him of the orders he had received from the Emperor; and that he, with his attendants, and Cheengeea Gooroo, would be in readiness to attend him accordingly.

Next morning the prince attended the Lama, and conducted him to the famous gardens, and palace of Kheatoon, where only eight of the Lama's attendants were allowed to enter. After examining all the curiosities of the garden, he passed that night in the palace. The two following days were taken up in the like manner; viewing different places, and curiosities, about the city. Reposing himself for the night in the house he had before occupied, he was visited, the next morning, by the prince, the Emperor's eldest son, who informed him, that many of the Emperor's favourite women were in a palace, in a distant part of the gardens, and that they had expressed much anxiety to see the Lama, and receive his blessing; and that it would be agreeable to the Emperor's wishes, that he, the Lama, should visit them, which he accordingly did: and being placed opposite a door of their apartments, upon an exalted seat, a purdow, or skreen, of a yellow kind of gauze, being dropt before the door, the ladies approached it, one by one, and having just looked at the Lama, through the gauze; each, according to her rank, and abilities, sent her offering, or present, by a female servant, who delivered it to one of the Lama's religious companions, that were allowed to continue near him; and upon the present being delivered to him, and the name of the person announced, he repeated a prayer, or form of blessing, for each; all the time bending his head forward, and turning his eyes directly towards the ground, to avoid all possibility of beholding the women. This ceremony, which took up four or five hours, being ended, the Lama returned to the place he had occupied for some nights past, where he continued that night, and the next morning returned, with the prince, and his attendants, to the gardens, where they had left the Emperor.

The next morning the Lama visited his Majesty, and was received with the usual respect and ceremony. After conversing for some time, respecting the curiosities that the Lama had examined for some days past, the Emperor told him, that he had still a greater to shew him, than any that he had yet visited; and, added he, it shall be my own care to carry you to see it; whereupon, rising from their seats, the Emperor took the Lama by the hand, and leading him to a temple, in a different part of the garden, he shewed him a magnificent throne, and informed him, that it was an ancient, and invariable custom, of the emperor's of China, to seat themselves upon it, at certain times, to hear and determine all matters of complaint, that might be brought before them: and that such was the extraordinary virtue of this seat, that according to the justice, or injustice of the Emperor's decrees, his existence, or immediate death depended. This temple, and seat of justice, he said, had been erected by divine command, and had existed for many thousand years.

After having passed an hour, or two, in explanation of this famous temple, the Emperor returned to his palace; and the Lama accompanied Cheengeea Gooroo to the house of the latter, in the same gardens, where he was entertained with great respect; and during the whole night the Lama did not go to sleep, but continued in prayer with Cheengeea Gooroo, and instructing him in certain forms of religion, and prayer. In the morning, on the Lama's departure for his own house, he received rich presents from Cheengeea Gooroo. The Lama reposed there for two days, when he was attended by the prince, and Cheengeea Gooroo, according to the Emperor's commands, to conduct him to the great pond, or lake, on which are two famous vessels of the Emperor's, of a most extraordinary size, and construction; each having five or six stories of apartments, one above the other; all of which are carved, and gilt, in the most curious and superb manner.

There are two islands in the lake; on one of which stands the Emperor's private palace, where his women are kept, and which can only be approached by boats. On the other island stands a very magnificent Chinese Putawlaw, or temple of public worship, which is approached by a handsome stone bridge: here the Lama passed the night; and in the morning proceeded to visit the very famous Putawlaw, or temple of public worship, in the city of Pekin, where hangs a bell, which, the Chinese assured the writer of this narrative, weighs upwards of twenty thousand maunds, and requires an hundred men to ring it. This, however, never is attempted, but to call the people to arms, in case of invasion, insurrection, or on public thanksgivings for any signal blessing, or victory.

Having passed some hours in prayer at this place, the Lama returned to his place of abode, near the city; and after three days, he was visited by the Emperor, on his way to the royal palace, in the fort, which stands in the centre of the city of Pekin. On the following day, the Lama visited him there, and was received with great pomp, and every mark of respect, insomuch, that the Emperor met him at the door, and taking him by the hand conducted him immediately into the private apartments of the Empress, whither no person whatever was suffered to attend them. Their visit to the Empress lasted about half an hour, when they returned into public; where they sat and conversed for an hour longer, and the Lama then returned to his own house.

After some days, the Emperor having informed the Lama, that he wished to perform some acts of devotion at one of the principle temples of worship in the city; they met there at the time appointed, and after having continued in prayer together, for two or three hours, attended and assisted by Cheengeea Gooroo, and a few of the Lama's religious friends. They departed, and returned, the Emperor to his palace, and the Lama to his own house.

Several meetings of this kind occurred at the same place of worship, between the Emperor and the Lama, during a period of some months; and as it was generally the custom to have some refreshments of fruits, &c. at the temple, after their acts of devotion were finished, the Lama, at one of these entertainments, took the opportunity, in hearing of the writer of this, and many others, to remind the Emperor, that he had some time before mentioned to him a Prince, or Governor, of Hindostan, called Mr. Hastings, with whom he, the Lama, held strict friendship; and repeated his wish, that the Emperor should know him, and hold friendly intercourse with him also; by writing to him, and receiving his friendly answers. Much more was said by the Lama on this subject; to all of which the Emperor replied, that he could only assure the Lama he joined most heartily with him, in what he wished, as it would give him much pleasure to know, and correspond, with the Governor of Hindostan, his friend; and to convince him of his sincerity, he would, if the Lama desired it, cause a letter to be immediately written to the Governor, in such terms as the Lama would dictate; or, if the Lama thought it would be more effectual, towards establishing the friendship he wished, that the letter should be in readiness, when the Lama took his departure from China; and that he should take it with him, and have the care of forwarding it, in such manner as he thought best, to the Governor of Hindostan. The latter mode the Lama made choice of, and expressed much satisfaction.

After this, many days were passed by the Lama, at his own house, as well as at the house of Cheengeea Gooroo, in conferring his blessings upon all ranks of people, who continually crowded to him for that purpose, insomuch, that the writer of this believes, that there was not a man, of any denomination whatever, in the extensive city of Pekin, who did not, during the time of the Lama's living there, come to him, and receive his blessing, in the manner already described. At some times the whole day, and greatest part of the night, was occupied in this manner. One evening the cold was so great, and the snow fell so heavy, that the Lama was prevented thereby, from returning to his own house; he slept therefore at Cheengeea Gooroo's, and in the morning they visited the Emperor together, after which they retired to their respective habitations. Within an hour after the Lama's return to his own house, without the city, which he made his place of residence, in preference to the apartments in the Emperor's palace in the fort, that were provided for him, he complained of a violent head-ach, and in less than an hour more, he was seized with a most violent fever, which continued very severe, until about the same hour next day, when his disorder was dicovered to be the small-pox, by many making their appearance all over his skin.

This discovery threw all his friends and attendants into the utmost affliction, as, from their established prejudices and apprehensions of that disorder, they entertained little or no hopes of his recovery. The news of the Lama's illness very soon reached the Emperor, who immediately sent for his own principal physicians, and with them proceeded to the Lama's house, and having seated himself by his bedside, took him by the hand; and, for a considerable time, did not cease to encourage him, with the most soothing and affectionate language, assuring him that his prayers should be constantly sent forth for his speedy recovery. He afterwards turned to the physicians, and holy men, that were, upon the rumour of the Lama's illness, assembled, charging them that they would, in no shape, neglect their respective duties. The former, in administering every remedy that could be devised, and the latter in offering up constant prayers, for the Lama's recovery. The Emperor also ordered several large paintings, representing human figures in almost every stage of the small-pox, to be hung up in the room before the Lama; and having seen all matters thus arranged, he gave strict orders to the prince, his first son, and Cheengeea Gooroo, to remain in constant waiting with the Lama; and that nothing, which could be procured in China, should be wanting, that might tend to mitigate, or ease his pain. After repeating the like orders to all those who were near him, he returned to his palace full of grief and heaviness.

After the Emperor's departure, the physicians paid every possible attention to the Lama, and administered all such remedies as they could think of. On the following morning, the Lama called for his brother, and desired that he would immediately distribute to the Khoseong, poor devout men, and others, whom he might think objects of charity, silver to the amount of three lacks of rupees, that their prayers might be deserved by him. All that day his disorder continued to increase, and on the morning of the fourth day of his illness, he again called for his brother, and six or seven of his own attendants (of whom the writer was one), whom he had occasionally distinguished for their sanctity, and informed them, that he found his disorder so much more than he could support, that he considered their prayers as the only comfort he could now enjoy, and that by joining them to his own, his heart would be entirely eased, whatever effect it might have on his distemper. They accordingly joined in prayer with him; in which they continued until near sunset of that day, when, to their inexpressible grief and affliction, he expired, as he sat at prayer between two large pillows, resting his back against the wall.

The writer describes his death to have been remarkably tranquil, considering his disorder; as he was not moved in the least out of the seat, in which he was performing his devotions.

The news was immediately communicated to the Emperor, who received it with every mark of grief and affliction: and early the next morning he repaired to the house where the Lama died, and where the body still remained, in the same position as when he expired; which, when the Emperor beheld, he shed many tears, and in other respects, manifested the sincerest grief.

The corpse was immediately, by the Emperor's orders, put into a coffin, with great quantities of all kinds of spices, and rich perfumes: and upon his return to his palace, he gave orders, that a small temple, in form of those in which they deposit the objects of their worship, of pure gold, should be immediately prepared, large enough to contain the coffin, when set upright; which, after seven or eight days, was, according to his orders, in readiness. The following morning the Emperor proceeded from his palace to the house in which the remains of the Lama lay, in the same magnificence, and pomp, as when he visited the Lama in his lifetime, with the addition of one thousand Khoseong, or holy men, attending him; and having the golden temple carried with him, fixed on poles, and borne upon men's shoulders. Upon his arrival at the house, where the corpse lay, he caused the temple to be set up, within the temple of worship, belonging to the house of the late Lama, and the corpse to be deposited in it, and joined in prayers with those that attended him, for four hours. He afterwards distributed silver to the amount of four lacks of rupees, to the Khoseong, and then returned to his palace.

The friends and followers of the deceased Lama were overwhelmed with grief, and remained, for upwards of two months, confined to the house, by the heavy snow, and severity of the cold. At length, when three months were nearly expired, and the weather became more favourable, the Emperor, with all his retinue, came to their place of residence, at the house where the Lama's corpse lay; and, after having gone through some forms of prayer, with the Khoseong, in the temple where the corpse was deposited, he ordered silver, to the amount of one lack of rupees, to be left as a kind of offering before the coffin, besides many pieces of rich brocades, and other silks.

The Emperor also ordered presents of silver and silks, to a considerable amount, to be given to the Lama's brother, as well as to all those of his friends, whom the Lama, during his life time, had distinguished by his particular notice, and which they severally received.

The Emperor afterwards sent for the Lama's brother, into another of the apartments of the house, and told him, that every thing was now in readiness for his departure, with the corpse of the Lama, to his own country; that the season of the year was also favourable, and that he hoped he would have a safe and prosperous journey: that he trusted in the Almighty soon to hear of his arrival there; but above all other things he would impatiently long to hear of the Lama's regeneration, which he strictly, and repeatedly charged his brother to inform him of, with the utmost dispatch, after it had happened, first by letters; but that he would expect that the Lama's brother himself would return again to China, with the joyful tidings, as soon as the Lama had completed his third year, taking care to give the Emperor information when he intended to quit his own country, that the necessary preparations might be made upon the road for his journey.

The Emperor also informed him, that a copper temple had been constructed, by his orders, large enough to contain that of gold, in which the Lama's coffin stood, as well as the coffin with the corpse, and that one thousand men, for the carriage of the whole, should be in readiness to proceed with him, to a certain distance, from whence it would remain with himself, in what manner he thought best to convey the corpse to his own country, as he would find every attendance and attention upon the road, the same as when the Lama had passed in his life time; and to obviate any doubts, that might occur to him, on that account, the Emperor ordered two trusty officers, with two hundred horsemen, to attend him until he should reach his own country. The Emperor then gave him his final dismission, conferring upon him, at the same time, a distinguished title: and, on the third day following, the Lama's brother, with all his friends and followers, departed from Pekin; the Lama's coffin being moved, as the Emperor had ordered, within the temples of gold and copper. They proceeded, the first day, about three coss and a half, or seven miles, where the Lama's brother gave orders that the coffin should be taken from within the gold and copper temples; and that they should be taken asunder, and carefully packed up, for the convenience of carriage, which was accordingly done: the coffin being then secured in many wrappers of waxed silk, it was laid on a palanquin, or kind of bier; and in this manner conveyed, upon mens' shoulders, during the journey to their own country; which, on account of the many halts that it was found necessary to make, lasted for seven months and eight days, from the day of their departure from Pekin, until their arrival at Digurchee, or Teshoo Loomboo, the place of the Lama's residence when he lived. Here his remains were deposited in a most superb pagoda, or monument, built for that purpose.

And the two temples of gold and copper, brought from Pekin, were carefully reformed, and set up in the pagoda, or monument, immediately over the spot where the corpse was laid.

Nothing but the great reverence and respect, paid to the Lama in his life time, by the inhabitants of the different countries through which he passed to China, could equal the attention observed by them to his remains, all the way, as he was carried back again: the multitude continually crowding round the coffin, with their prayers, and presents; and those who could only touch it, or even the palanquin, or bier, upon which it was borne, were considered as peculiarly blessed.

FINIS.